Forget Chineseness

SUNY series in Global Modernity

Arif Dirlik, editor

Forget Chineseness

On the Geopolitics of
Cultural Identification

Allen Chun

SUNY
PRESS

Cover image: © Nagee, used with permission

The cartoon, by the artist Nagee, depicts the singer Chou Tzu-yu, who delivered a formal apology in early 2016 for waving the flag of Taiwan while performing on a South Korean television show. The words above the picture say, "Sorry, I've been Chinesed. Today, it's Chou Tzu-yu. Tomorrow, it will be you." It is deliberately written in passive tense (literally: "I was sorried, I was made to be Chinese"), which is not even proper Chinese but corresponds to the forced, hostage-like nature of the illustration.

Published by State University of New York Press, Albany

© 2017 State University of New York

All rights reserved

Printed in the United States of America

For information, contact State University of New York Press, Albany, NY
www.sunypress.edu

Production, Ryan Morris
Marketing, Fran Keneston

Library of Congress Cataloging-in-Publication Data

Names: Chun, Allen John Uck Lun, 1952– author.
Title: Forget Chineseness : on the geopolitics of cultural identification /
by Allen Chun.
Description: Albany, NY : State University of New York Press, [2017] |
Series: SUNY series in global modernity | Includes bibliographical
references and index.
Identifiers: LCCN 2016031420 (print) | LCCN 2016059728 (ebook) | ISBN
9781438464718 (hardcover : alk. paper) | ISBN 9781438464725 (pbk. :
alk. paper) | ISBN 9781438464732 (ebook)
Subjects: LCSH: Chinese diaspora. | Chinese—Foreign countries—Ethnic
identity. | Chinese—Ethnic identity. | National characteristics, Chinese.
Classification: LCC DS732 .C595 2017 (print) | LCC DS732 (ebook) | DDC
305.800951—dc23
LC record available at https://lccn.loc.gov/2016031420

10 9 8 7 6 5 4 3 2 1

Contents

Preface

Ethnicity as Culture as Identity:
Unpacking the Crisis of Culture in Culturalism

This book is in part a follow-up to a paper published in 1996, titled "Fuck Chineseness: On the Ambiguities of Ethnicity as Culture as Identity."[1] At the same time, it is a reply to many queries by scholars over the years who were unsettled by aspects of that argument (including students who offered to write a sequel to it) and my repeated tendency to decline invitations to elaborate on the topic. I suspect that most of the commotion was caused by the obscene title, in which case I would add that it has probably led to many misreadings of the essay. The real subject matter was reflected in the subtitle, which had less to do with Chineseness per se than with muddles in the model involved, when sinologists and social scientists alike transform culture into culturalism. Thus to answer the obvious question, what does Chineseness say about China?, I would say little, at face value. China has been changing, perhaps sui generis, and notions of Chineseness have correspondingly changed as the subtle frame through which actors and institutions ideologically validate their ongoing existence. The same can be said about the various culturalist models that scholars deploy to make sense of China or any other society; they validate in the first instance the disciplinary mindset that inherently governs it.

In the same year, I presented essentially the same argument, albeit directed to a cultural studies or social theory audience, in an essay titled "Discourses of Identity in the Changing Spaces of Public Culture in Taiwan, Hong Kong and Singapore."[2] The ramifications here of Chineseness or culturality as discourse are clearer, especially the politics of subjectivity that invoke it. In both essays, I argue that discourses of Chineseness differ significantly from the concepts of culture that theorists and Asian studies scholars typically utilize in their study of Chinese culture(s) and society(ies). In this regard, the comparison of Taiwan, Hong Kong, and Singapore was deliberately chosen to emphasize that the different ways in which Chinese in diverse societies articulate culturality are largely a product of its embeddedness in different sociopolitical processes, for which we lacked an adequate conceptual language. It was only until later that I spelled out more precisely the nature of this framework, namely geopolitics.[3]

Culturalism, of which Chineseness is a particular discursive representation, is less a social fact sui generis than a crisis invoked not necessarily by the inherent nature of culture but by situations of context. In other words, its imperative resides in essence outside culture. The fact that culture can be codified, systematized, regulated, and even commoditized in ways that are contrary to the spirit of lived experience is in short the source of many crises of modernity, ranging from conflicts pertaining to national identity, inventions of tradition, hegemonies of state, and the domination of culture industries, including mass media. Chineseness has thus been constructed in complex ways in diverse societies, the least of which is from the people themselves. While it is possible and desirable to interrogate Chineseness, one cannot do so without at the same time asking who is speaking for whom and toward what ends? There are also places where Chineseness (and its variants) has been so politicized that one can question whether its discursive manifestation and propagation really has anything to do with culture. Alternatively, one can look at the question in political terms too and ask, is it really necessary to culturalize at all? The content of Chineseness is less seminal than its form and function. On the other hand, it is possible to problematize Chineseness; to demystify, reinscribe, even engender and queer it. But explorations of alternative meanings as cultural critique have not been my primary concern. In the meantime, the ambiguity of ethnicity as culture as identity continues to be a problem endemic to social sciences, which I have elaborated on separately.

In short, this book is no longer about the ambiguities of ethnicity as culture as identity in a Chinese context but rather an effort to transcend such literal discussions of Chineseness and situate them within their respective historical contexts and underlying geopolitical formative processes. To problematize Chineseness as constitutive of an ongoing historical framework, from a comparative perspective and within a transnational or glocal context, serves to problematize the nature of *contexts* that invoke Chineseness as an ethnic or cultural problem, among other things. In the long run, Chineseness is just a superficial reflection of culture's embeddness or ongoing entanglement with more complex social institutional processes, such as modernity, colonialism, nation-state formation and globalization. A deeper probe into such institutions as processes per se should in turn offer a more nuanced articulation of culturality.

Finally, why identify? Identity is, strictly speaking, a subjective relationship that does not by definition necessitate an inherent tie to culture, although many seem to think it does. This marks the transition from geopolitics to pragmatics. As Wang Gungwu rightly pointed out, "the Chinese never had a concept of identity, only a concept of Chineseness, of being Chinese and of becoming un-Chinese."[4] This then begs the question, what is identity, as a concept and strategic process of negotiation? Erik Erikson, who made identity crisis a keyword for our times, argued that it was not just a marker of personal status but relations of "sameness" in a group, if not shared values. If traditional Chinese lacked a concept of identity, then without doubt it became a staple of culture in the era of modern nation-states, where *rentong* literally means assimilation or boundedness to a group. In this sense, the politics of identity should involve by definition strategic choices about relations to groups and their underlying value judgments. Thus, what is the relevance of Chineseness? It involves in sum the construction of meaning and its relevance to the strategies of life choices in relation to groups and values.

The subtitle of the book follows conceptually what I (Chun 2009) first called "the geopolitics of identity." The more explicit focus here on identification underscores the point that identity is more than the fact of being or an attribute of personal status. Identity is the product of a process of becoming (socializing and assimilating). One rarely defines oneself ipso facto or sui generis. On the contrary, the fact that modern identity (national above all) compels one to have one implies that it is hardly a matter of negotiation or personal choice. Identification as strategic negotiation is still rooted in our boundedness to an ongoing social and political context. To term this larger ongoing process *geopolitics* means first of all that it is concretely rooted in what Dirlik (1999) aptly calls "the politics of place." Whether politics is framed by colonialism, nationalism, capitalism, or globalism is a matter of definition that must be carefully distilled from ambiguities and contradictions in the given literature. On the other hand, this process as a regime of practice may resemble more closely what Foucault (1991) characterizes as "spaces of dispersion" in the formation of socializing and culturalizing possibilities that give birth to discursive identities.

Ten of the twelve chapters in this book are either updated revisions or serious rewritings of essays that appeared in diverse academic journals, namely *History and Anthropology; Critique of Anthropology; Social Analysis: The International Journal of Cultural and Social Practice; Cultural Studies; The Journal of the Hong Kong Sociological Association; Contemporary Asian Modernities: Transnationality, Interculturality and Hybridity; Suomen Antropologi; Macalester International; Communal/Plural: Journal of Transnational*

& Crosscultural Studies; *Theory Culture & Society*; *The Australian Journal of Anthropology*; and *positions: east asia critique*. Needless to say, they were not written with area studies specialists as the main intended reader, but motivated by dialogues with a wider multidisciplinary audience. The essays presented herein are re-presented with the hope of making specific points about the ongoing history, culture, and politics of respective societies, but within a systematically consistent framework of analysis that may serve ultimately as a more appropriate discourse of comparison.

Introduction

Beyond Chineseness:
Frames for a Differential Calculus of Historical Process

Textual regimes, documentary forms, and image repertoires *work* as projects to socially organize our lives by decontextualising. This routinised, pleasurable legitimation work all too often goes unremarked—e.g., tax forms, census returns, landownership registries, passport photographs, signatures and the murmuring volume around 'I.D.' (a word we should always speak in full: *Identification*) are part of the taken for granted *mediations of modernity.* They compel us . . . to represent ourselves in certain, often minutely specific, ways; taken as a whole cartography of power, they freeze us through these programs of power into mythic statuses of sedimented language. We become our ID.

—Philip Corrigan and Derek Sayer,
"From 'The Body Politic' to 'The National Interest' "

Framing Cultural Discourses Within Situated, Ongoing Sociopolitical Regimes

To lump together Hong Kong, Taiwan, Singapore, and overseas Chinese communities or to define their shared characteristics and fate as Chinese-speaking societies would invite easy criticism. Yet when looking seriously at any one of them as discrete places and experiences, it is difficult to avoid essentializing them in terms of given disciplinary frames of reference and inherent assumptions. From an Asianist perspective, presumed cultural affinities and shared historical interactions usually form the basis of categorization and comparison, even as the relative importance of other thematic considerations tempers one's interpretation of the above. Social scientific and historical analyses offer their own theoretical grid but always within the framework of specific presumably value-free concepts, definitions, and outcomes. The implicit framing of such societies or their populations as part of a Greater China or East Asia already makes them relevant to each other in particularistic ways vis-à-vis societies in different parts of the world. Needless to say, one cannot deny the overt lineage of historical traditions and institutional systems that characterize textbook accounts and provide a ground for the ongoing present. However, the influence of such traditions as an a priori framework for that history can be questioned. Similarly, East Asian models of culture or society within the scholarly literature are typically coded in analytical terms whose legitimacy is ultimately based on their presumed objectivity or value-free status. If anything, identity is refracted, as though omnipresent and sui generis, from such interpretations of history and civilization.

Identity is not synonymous with culture, history, or society. It is by nature a discourse, a social construct whose emergence and change is grounded in other deep frames of reference that have been evolving and remaking themselves locally in response to mutating conditions at large. I argue that encounters with modernity involve colonialism, nationalism, and global capitalism, among other conditions, which constitute a different point of departure, but the current interpretations prevailing in this literature are themselves problematic, and thus require proper qualification. More importantly, the ways in which these conditions at large impose themselves in any context are also historically sensitive and inextricably intertwined with the specificities of local practice, the engagement between which produces diverse experiences.

Concretely speaking, something must be said about colonialism in Hong Kong, cultural nationalism in postwar Taiwan, the collusion of Party and capitalist oligarchy in the People's Republic of China (PRC), the state's disciplining of race and modernity in Singapore, and the shifting association of Chinese overseas between diasporic and settler ethnicity. These conditions at large are not mutually exclusive processes. Colonialism is present in all the above contexts, albeit more as a state of mind or historical legacy. Nationalism is present everywhere too, though in diverse forms. Above all, it is important or necessary to view each societal context as a conceptual frame of reference that can elucidate an underlying field of interaction and articulate the particularity of experiences, which provide the basis for engendering identifications of all kinds. In the end, direct relevance to shared assumptions of Chineseness or culturality is at best secondary.

The Contradictory Tensions of Colonialism as Inscribed and Practiced

The advent of postcolonial theory in cultural studies and humanities in the 1990s raises pertinent questions as to what exactly is new not only in reference to earlier generations of colonial studies but also to an institution that had effectively declined over a half century ago. Apt criticisms raised by McClintock (1992), Shohat (1992), and Dirlik (1994) regarding the pitfalls of the term *postcolonialism* suggest that one is dealing less with literal definitions of the phenomenon, which has produced its own lineages of political and intellectual discourse in the postcolonies, than a peculiar epistemic mind-set that should be understood in its own terms, despite being flawed by its inherent academic metropolitanism and subtle Eurocentricness (in the sense that it was sparked by a crisis of mind within Western literature rather than issues endemic to fields of colonial studies per se). McClintock criticizes the narrow, distorted usages of the term *postcolonial* to assert that the phenomenon of colonialism is perhaps more rampant than scholars have recognized in order to suggest the wider relevance of postcolonial critique, while Dirlik distances "Euro" postcolonialism from native traditions of postcolonial critique, which on the contrary have always been rooted in ongoing, local political struggles, and thus a different genre of postcolonial theoretical agenda, in order to advocate the priority of thought in praxis. While there are merits in an earlier, more literal and socially rooted postcolonial critique (postcolonialism$_1$), notably in the form of critical Fanonism, subaltern studies, and so on, that gave new impetus to the advent of a more recent postcolonial theory (postcolonialism$_2$), I think the latter postcolonialism$_2$ also offers constructive avenues for theoretical development.

One way to define the advent of postcolonial$_2$ theory is to view it as a sophisticated take on the politics of difference, enhanced with reference to its articulation of a notion of colonial subjectivity. It is not coincidental in this regard that the Fanon of *Black Skin, White Masks* in particular serves as the conceptual template on which a subjectivity of racial difference becomes generalized. Whether one understands this in terms of Bhabha's poststructuralist reading of Fanon's colonized subjectivity in the mirror of self, JanMohamed's rendition of Fanon's Manichean allegory, or Spivak's tendency to view all discourse as colonialist, among other diverse interpretations, the symbolic dynamics of difference that are abstracted from a *presumed* situation of absolute power that is colonial domination become in turn the basis of a global theory (see in particular Gates [1991]). This then magnifies the role of culture.

In other words, culture in difference or the culture of difference becomes the language for a new postcolonial$_2$ speak. To some extent, this is what scholars working in the field of colonial studies regard as the main attribute of postcolonial$_2$ theory. While this constitutes a dominant strain of thought within the broad domain of postcolonialism$_2$, it is hardly the most sophisticated or pathbreaking version of a postcolonialist$_2$ paradigm. The influence here of Edward Said's *Orientalism* (1978) in redefining the field cannot be underestimated. Aspects of culture and difference are salient to his interpretation of Orientalism and its relationship to colonialism, but the collusive relationship between discourse and power or of the role of discourse in obfuscating and sublimating the violence of domination adds a rather different dimension to the *presumed* dialectics of difference between colonizer and colonized.

While Orientalism operates at one level of creating difference through the gazing of the Other in legitimizing the authority of self, it operates at another level of negating difference or domination by colonizer of colonized through the neutrality of discourse. The Orientalist describes and orders reality through systemic observation, coding, and writing. The extent to which he successfully dominates the Other and sublimates the violence of colonial power is a function of the extent to which the Other acquiesces to the system of knowledge within which he is inscribed, not unlike the way people in a modern disciplinary society govern themselves in reference to their conformity to or adoption of institutional norms of thought and behavior. In short, postcolonialism$_2$ can be about the dynamics of cultural difference in the articulation of a critical theory. On the other hand, I suggest also that postcolonialism$_2$ can be about the critical articulation of difference, where difference has already been *discursively* neutralized.

Needless to say, the history of colonialism everywhere has been amply documented; at least, there is no dearth of primary materials and secondary scholarly sources available. Yet one rarely assesses the facts in reference to the authority or presumed objectivity that cloak the writings within which they are embedded. It should be little surprise that even the best scholarly works are written in a way that legitimate the inevitability of prevailing institutions and mind-sets. It should be little surprise also that narratives championing unilineal progress conveniently suppress at the same time exploitative and contradictory aspects of the system. Finally, when the history of colonialism is written as though colonialism does not exist or has been effectively sanitized or purged of its violence, this is a further symptom of Orientalizing. In fact, Orientalism is not peculiar to colonialism and should be a general, abstract process. At issue then is the nature of colonial governmentality and its possible collusive relationship with capitalism, nationalism, and other processes of rule. As ongoing transformative system, it involves not only concrete policies in practice but more importantly interactions at the local level that ultimately engender changing cultural spaces, class dynamics, and public spheres.

From the perspective of institutional history, the evolution of colonialism and empire can, of course, be viewed as a changing lineage of policies and practices, which is a product of its relationship to ideologies and theories of the times that diffused globally in particular ways. Yet at another level, these historical transformations have in the long run produced a complex hegemonic process that is reflected in various regimes of rule. Insofar as they overlap with other institutions, such as nationalism and capitalism, they share a common field of discourse.

The postcolonial$_2$ approach outlined above may be the product of theoretical debates that seem to be most explicitly relevant to the study of colonial societies, *literally* defined, but it is certainly not limited to them. The general import of a cultural politics of difference and the collusive nature of institutional ideologies and practices in the hegemonic construction of its authority are pertinent also to nationalizing regimes and legitimizing processes of the state.

Reading Nationalism as Culturalist Narrative and Political Process

Before its rediscovery in the 1980s within critical circles of cultural studies, historical theory, and literary theory, there had already been several generations of scholarship on nationalism. There has been no shortage of historical ruminations in the 1950s and 1960s on the nature of nationalism, not to its mention ideological roots in nineteenth-century philosophies of history. The birth of the Republic of China in the aftermath of the 1911 Revolution made the nation-state an unambiguous presence both in China and elsewhere in the world. The rise of nationalism has in many ways marked the transition from tradition to "modernity" in standard narratives of world history. To the extent that we attribute this historical rise to the effect of concrete historical forces, such as colonialism and modernization, it has also been easy to associate the form of the nation-state to its Western diffusion, however defined. At the same time, the Chinese rendition of the nationalism as "the principle of peoplehood" (*minzu zhuyi*) has been the end product of intellectualizing by Chinese thinkers leading up to the fact. It intersects in some ways with the nature of the general (abstract) phenomenon, but it is also a peculiarly cultural definition that reflects interpretations of its essential nature. The nation's formation as a concrete sociopolitical institution has been heterogeneous rather than uniform globally, and its intellectualizing at a local level has always been intimately intertwined with, and thus directly reflective of, its concrete particularities. The relationship between the general nature of its diffusion (or modernity in its broadest sense) and its cultural particularities has been the source of ongoing confusion in the literature, insofar as such theorizing has usually been the primary result of one or the other position. Everything is still open to question.

The transformation of China as a modern nation, its prominence in the global arena and the wealth of prevailing scholarship on Chinese history, especially with regard to nationalism, should be obvious reasons, on the other hand, for being wary of alternative interpretations. Influential works by John Fitzgerald, Prasenjit Duara, Peter Zarrow, and Wang Hui, among others, cover in fact a wide diversity of approaches in this regard. Fitzgerald's (1996) work has focused largely on the role of social classes and political actors eventually leading up to the Nationalist Revolution. Its emphasis on concrete processes differs from Duara's (1995) introspection on narratives of history. The "Chinese narrative of History" can be juxtaposed not only against European ones but also against multiple, competing narratives of community. For Zarrow (2012), the same narratives of region, civil society and the state become objects of intellectual rumination. Unlike Duara's system of nation-states, Zarrow's is an abstract reflection on an underlying "political culture" based on notions of citizenship and sovereignty, among others, which legitimated the nation-state. These political principles that gave birth to the Chinese state "after empire" become in Wang Hui's (2014) terms the basis of a deeper conceptual transformation from empire to nation-state. In this regard, intellectual history becomes the terrain for discoursing heavenly principle (*tian li*) as the cosmological nexus of empire. While one cannot deny that such principles have been the source of ongoing debate in successive eras of neo-Confucian thought, Wang's discussion of the emergence of modern identity, as though just the end products of Western concepts of sovereignty and citizenship in a process of political reconsolidation after the demise of empire, leaves much to be desired.

I am less interested in the grand transformation from empire to nation, which is without doubt an undeniable aspect of an important political transformation, than in the evolution of nationalism (ultimately "nationalizing") in the ongoing present and its interactional dynamics with political and cultural processes. Without downplaying the role of concrete institutional and other factors that have contributed to the specific historical emergence of the nation-state globally, Anderson (1983) and Gellner (1983) have pointed to its abstract cultural constitution as the inherent defining characteristic. For Anderson, the modern nation might have been an imagined community, but more importantly it was a genre of empty, homogenous space that transcended whatever ethnic, religious or other attributes (even citizenship and sovereignty) that scholars have typified as concretely essential to nationalism. Community's rootedness to a colloquially based imagination was similar to Gellner's understanding of this culture of the nation, which not only contrasted with its hierarchical, specialized nature in the age of empire but also had to be universally inculcated in the minds of citizens in order for a nation to persist. The embeddedness of Anderson's imagined community in political ideologies and Gellner's emphasis on the primacy of mass education both accented in different ways the function of politics and policies in engendering various underlying cultural imaginations. The nature of such legitimizing regimes should in turn highlight the politicizing constructions of citizenship but also the rationalization of distinctive culturalizing mind-sets that drive them.

Geoffrey Benjamin (1988) aptly characterizes the nation-state as "the unseen presence." Contrary to social scientific definition, he argues that the modern nation-state is an artifactual, imitable, and ideological institution, maintained by processes of ideological mystification, in which both overt politics and scholarship have been responsible for the active *maintenance* of the nation-state's invisibility. Philip Abrams (1988) has made similar claims about the state in arguing that the state is not the reality that stands behind the mask of political practice but rather the mask that prevents us seeing political practice as it is. As he (1988:76) put it, the state is "a third-order project, an ideological project. It is first and foremost an exercise in legitimation—what is being legitimated is, we may assume, an unacceptable domination." Taken together, Benjamin and Abrams's emphasis on the various regimes of mystification that buttress its reified nature as territorially discrete, systemically regulated standard linguistic community, bound by uniform rights and identities, gives a rather different spin on the nature and ideological function of citizenship and sovereignty. Needless to say, prevailing theories of nationalism have, if anything, been obsessed with the superficial presence of nation-states, marked by discrete territoriality, standard cultures or traits, and so on, even as they elude uniform definition in such terms. What Anderson and Gellner do not emphasize explicitly enough is that whatever this imagined community is, it had to be radically new, to transcend the "primordial sentiments," in Geertz's (1963) terms, characteristic of traditional societies. This novelty is at the same time the source of its contested nature, its need for legitimation, and hence the basis of ideological mystification that obscures its unacceptable domination. Culture can in this sense be manifested in diverse discourses and practices. In other words, the cultural aspects of this imagined community define not only the distinctive or historically particular features of nation-state formation but more importantly the nationalizing imperatives underlying it.

Disjunctures of Class and Ethnicity in an Era of "Transnational" Globalization

Arjun Appadurai's (1990) characterization of disjunctures in the global cultural economy and Kenichi Omae's (1990) account of the borderless world have in different ways accented the metamorphosis of global capitalism in the late twentieth century. Multinational corporations, for one thing, do not appear to follow the flag anymore, and subcontracting of the production process globally has made the notion of cultural origins anachronistic. Appadurai's accent on the chaotic flow of ethnoscapes, financescapes, and so on is predicated in large part on Lash and Urry's (1987) proclamation of "the end of organized capitalism" and the breakdown between core and periphery in the modern world system. But as in the case of Omae, the literal focus is on the increasing demise of national barriers and boundaries that has transformed in effect the nature of economies, societies, and cultures. Not only have economies been transformed by labor migration (see, e.g., Basch, Schiller, & Blanc 1994) and societies by changing patterns of settlement and diasporic identity (see especially, Lavie & Swedenberg 1996). Culture itself has moreover become the site of transnational hybridization (Nederveen Pieterse 1995).

The advent of transnationalism as a challenge to nationalizing boundaries and orthodox political regulation has represented the underlying impetus behind Greater China, the notion of cultural China, Sinophone theory, and to a lesser extent the liminal status of Taiwan in the arena of international relations and the global economy. Whether it ultimately represents a destabilizing feature of a prevailing order or an emancipatory alternative remains to be seen. The detotalizing tendencies of transnationalism have always been the consequence of *both* decentralization of direct state control from above as well as localized resistance from below.

The establishment of duty-free trade ports in Hong Kong and Singapore can be viewed, through its denationalization of economic consumption, as a commoditization of culture and society in general. From the perspective of utilitarian economics and libertarian politics, the opening of the market economy is an entity that enables the triumph of individual freedom. In practice, it makes access to resources and power, whether it is in the form of commodities, status, or influence, a consequence of class access or control. In the context of a preexisting colonialism and nationalism, social class competes with political stratification or allocation of resources and power by the state or other political organs. At least in most typical cases of market liberalization, deregulation of the economy has been accompanied by decentralization of political control from above. The exception to this rule is the recent advent of "socialism with Chinese characteristics." The applicability of neoliberalism in specific contexts can also be debated. More importantly in the context of overlapping and competing institutional processes, identity in terms of nation, class, or ethnicity can be politicizing and depoliticizing.

Epistemic Moments Within Transformations of Place:
A Schematic Outline

We live in an era of apps (that resist totalizing). Each of the places discussed in the sections below represent autonomous societies in their own right and have spawned their own histories and scholarly literature. My objective is less to offer systemic interpretations of their history or culture or even to suggest that there are integrated analytical frameworks that one can apply for this purpose. Foucault defined discourses, strictly speaking, as "spaces of dispersion." In this same sense, there are in each venue epistemic moments that depict or exemplify distinctive transitions. They constitute frames, episodes, or junctures for the interaction in the abstract of geopolitical forces. It would not be imprecise to characterize these fields as spaces as well.

The establishment of the Nationalist (KMT) regime in Taiwan after World War II is in a literal sense a continuation of the Republican government on the Chinese mainland. But the construction of its peculiarly cultural nationalist policies and institutions is a complex product of its relationship to many forces. The most obvious one was its Cold War engagement with socialist China. Another was the challenge of recovering and transforming fifty years of Japanese colonial rule. Juxtaposed against both was its underlying relationship to the West, especially the constant shadow of US military protectionism. It is not necessary to ruminate at length here on the nature of geopolitics in the sense of international relations. My focus is more on how geopolitics in these terms provides the ground for engendering a polity defined by peculiar relationships between ethnicity, culture, and nation. In the case of Nationalist Taiwan, Chineseness becomes a master discourse that pits tradition against radical socialism and its culturalness against Japaneseness. As a construction, it is systematically politicized, which has ramifications for how it interprets traditions, such as Confucianism, as a source of its conservatism. Through its dissemination of Sun Yat Sen's Three Principles of the People (filtered further by Chiang Kai-shek's New Life Movement ethics), Nationalist ideology is in strict terms an ambivalent doctrine that weds conservative tradition and scientific modernity, uneasily to say the least. Its rationalization is a product of its institutional inculcation in all aspects of education, society, and politics. In light of all of the above, national identity is not simply a politicized (Nationalist) worldview but more precisely a cultural code of conduct that roots a sense of political community to assumed ties to ethnicity and culture as totalizing entity. The latter is hardly arbitrary; its legitimacy had to be newly imposed, systematically inculcated and reinforced. Most importantly, its intrinsic dualism as cultural mindset exudes a normative, hegemonic presence that has long survived its Cold War origins, even after the emergence of Taiwanese consciousness, and overlaps contradictorily now with the advent of the transnational economy and, most recently, the evolution of an ever greater China

The historical transformation of Hong Kong is more complex than has been portrayed by its superficial change from British colony to Special Administrative Region (SAR) within China. Its nature as colony and its ambiguous aftermath must be problematized in multiple ways. Its meta-morphosis from a "barren island," colonial trading post and cultural satellite of Guangzhou into free trade port and dynamic center of cosmopolitan hybridity, among other things, can viewed in the context of a mutating colonialism at its fulcrum. On the surface of things, its social and economic transformation has transcended the stereotypical analyses that have typi-fied most theoretical discussions of colonialism elsewhere in the literature. Even from the outset, Hong Kong has been an atypical colony. Its colonial caste polity overlapped with its ongoing integration with China in all other respects, marked by open borders and cultural continuity. Contrast with British colonies elsewhere, however, begs critical scrutiny of the apparent fic-tions of "indirect rule" as well as the incommensurable relationship between policy and practices. Contrary to definition, colonialism does not disappear after 1997, and simply mutates with the change of regime, along with the collusive relationship of capitalism to politics. The polity is different from the cultural nationalism engendered in Taiwan, characterized by different relationships between ethnicity, culture, and nation, among other things, which have spawned a different kind of identification, whose politicization has continued to mutate after 1997.

In the PRC, the recent evolution from a Maoist socialist society to one transformed by a free market capitalist economy has become a major focus of debate. Theoretical discussions of an earlier era that explored "the sprouts of capitalism" in grand theories of comparative modernization have largely been replaced by those, on the other hand, emphasizing the policy shift of Deng Xiaoping in kick-starting the free market economy and those advocating a *longue durée* view of global capitalism, between which various other institutional approaches tend to situate themselves. Political policies and economic reforms aside, I argue that it is possible to view the under-lying transformation in broader terms, of changing geopolitical spaces. In the process, the breakdown of socialist humanism as a system of social and political values eventually paved the way for a nationalist identity based on the cultural legitimacy of history and civilization. If anything, nationalist renaissance provided popular support for success of any economic develop-ment, which in turn colluded with postcolonial narratives to reverse centuries of Western imperialist domination. Perhaps unlike the rise of capitalism in Hong Kong, Singapore, and Taiwan, the determination of the state to control economic development by regulating political access to privileged resources made it especially prone to corruption and ties of *guanxi*. The transformation of *guanxi*, which has traditionally been a secondary and nuanced aspect of a cultural complex dominated by notions of face and personal rapport (*renqing*), into a tactical strategy and life routine per se can be seen as a paradigmatic feature of that broader sociopolitical transformation. In institutional terms, the focus of debate has been on a misplaced neoliberal characterization of the new PRC policy. Unlike the state's management of free market policy and economic development in Singapore, the brunt of the PRC's state domination has been on maintaining Party support and political correctness as a compromise to profit maximization and on promoting business collusion in political ventures abroad. Adam Smith in Beijing has in the longer view been the least significant aspect of it.

With regard to the overseas Chinese, the emphasis, in reference to sinological concerns, has mostly been on its marginality or removal from the center, reflected best by the concept of diaspora. Correspondingly, appeals to cultural China and Sinophone theory have in their own ways endeavored to counter the privileging of the center by promoting multivocality and cosmopolitanism. However, I argue that the concept of diaspora, like that of the subaltern, has been maligned as an identity that symbolized ethnic degradation. Its situation of social disenfranchisement can also be viewed as a project of geopolitical positioning, which can by nature change. The increasing unpopularity of diaspora as a term among Nanyang Chinese, once called "Jews of the East," can thus be contrasted with its increasing popularity among Asians in North America. This change in cultural imagination, where authorial subjectivity of speaking, writing, and intellectualizing is only part of broad-based lifestyles and practices, is in the long run the product of its positional situatedness in their respective societal regimes.

In Singapore, the dominant narrative centers on the birth of its modern, disciplinary society and the role of the state in engineering its underlying practices. In many respects, it runs counter to the prevailing model of cultural nationalism. At the same time, the influence of postcolonialism plays a rather different role in contrast to Taiwan and Hong Kong. The ethnic makeup of Singapore's population in a dominant Malay, Muslim milieu and the state's strategy in balancing intrinsic tensions between tradition and modernity in order to embrace a radical path toward national identification represent a rather different terrain of geopolitics. In this regard, disinterested domination by the state grounded in a British rule of law, micromanagement of social organization and practices, a free market economy, and appeal to Asian values of cultural community have been promoted as a uniquely integrative framework. Its unusual geopolitics and the state's role in forging a unique strategy to it thus form a peculiar blueprint for socioeconomic development, ethnic stratification, and its nationalizing mind-set.

In light of the above experiences, a postcolonial subjectivity can ultimately be seen as an epistemic mind-set for Asian studies but only after recognizing the latter's groundedness in the division of labor of international academia and its "ethnicizing" production of knowledge.

Part One

Postwar, Post-Republican Taiwan

Civilizational Mythologies in the Politics of the Unreal

Prisons serve as a clear example (of total institutions), providing we appreciate that *what is prison-like about prisons is found in institutions whose members have broken no laws.*

—Erving Goffman, *Asylums*

One man's imagined community is another man's political prison.

—Arjun Appadurai, "Disjuncture and Difference in the Global Cultural Economy"

Prologue

I argue that the dynamics of ethnicity in the context of Taiwan's nation-statism has been more thoroughly misunderstood than understood by scholars. If anything, the Republic of China in Taiwan is the typical incarnation of a monocultural nationalism, yet Taiwan's experiences have clearly run counter to the norm, especially in ethnic terms. In most other places, such as the former USSR and Yugoslavia, as if to vindicate *The End of History* in Francis Fukuyama's (1992) terms, crumbling socialist regimes have given way everywhere to the real face of ethnonationalism. In places such as South Africa, after blacks were given the vote, they voted quite naturally for majority rule. Only in Taiwan, where everyone knows that native Taiwanese constitute three-fourths of the population, did people (in its first free elections in 1989) vote decisively for a KMT regime by a three-to-one margin that was dominated by alien mainlanders. Any impartial analyst would have concluded that ethnicity per se accounted for little. If anything, Taiwan should have become independent long ago; so what is the real problem here? In actuality, ethnic realities have never been an object of doubt.

They have always, on the other hand, been clouded by political discourses disguised as cultural realities. Yet scholars in and of Taiwan consistently refuse to confront the fictive nature of these discourses for what they are. A politics of ethnicity couched in such terms is driven at a deeper level by an impoverished, even vulgar, definition of politics.

If normal politics is unreal, how unreal can it get? During the first PRC missile crisis, while trying to explain the incomprehensible calm that enveloped most of Taiwan in the face of PRC saber-waving and the Western media's depiction of an Iraqi-Kuwaiti–like crisis in the making, I wrote (mostly to the horror of PRC colleagues) that China would not invade. This would be like cutting off one's arm, just because it began to shake uncontrollably. Yet in the midst of all this commotion about reunification and independence, few of us bothered to ask, what kind of "unification" were people really talking about? I think for many Chinese (on both sides), 500 years is not a long time to wait for reunification. One of the popular myths about the fall of the Manchu Qing dynasty noted that someone discovered a dusty placard in the imperial rubble, proclaiming "Restore the Ming," as if to suggest that it was worth waiting 268 years for this. In this postmodern, globalized era, the very thought of it is totally unreal. What are people fighting and dying for *in actuality*, if not an anachronistic fiction? What deserves detailed scrutiny is the extent to which such fictions are institutionally inscribed.

Chapter 1

Chineseness, Literarily Speaking

The Burden of Tradition in the Making of Modernity

In his passage about Paul Klee's painting *Angelus Novus*, Walter Benjamin wrote that the appalled Angel of History, who seems to be contemplating in dismay modernity's piles of wreckage upon wreckage, "would like to stay, awaken the dead, and make whole what has been smashed." But through nationalism the dead are awakened, this is the point—seriously awakened for the first time. All cultures have been obsessed by the dead and placed them in another world. Nationalism rehouses them in this world. Through its agency the past ceases being "immemorial": it gets memorialised into time present, and so acquires a future.

—Tom Nairn, *Faces of Nationalism: Janus Revisited*

What is a nationalist ideology? By addressing this question, I seek to show how the writing of political discourse reflects on the role of the state as a thinking and practicing subject. In postwar Taiwan, the Kuomintang (KMT) or Nationalist Party government took a heavy-handed role in invoking icons of traditional authority, myths of civilizational unity, and the legitimacy of shared values but primarily through the mediation of culture. Within a process of cultural construction, the metamorphosis of Sun Yat-sen's Three Principles of the People typified the KMT's attempt to impose its utopian ideals not just in accordance with changing times but by reference to the authority of texts that could not change. The KMT's peculiar Orientalism in a literal sense reflected an ambivalent project of tradition-qua-modernity. More important than the content of its ideology, this imagined community

---

This is a major revision of "An Oriental Orientalism: The Paradox of Tradition and Modernity in Nationalist Taiwan," *History and Anthropology* 9(1):27–56, originally published in 1995.

so engendered established the basis of a nationalizing mind-set rooted inherently in ethnicity that transcended changes of political regime and has continued to frame the contemporary course of Taiwan's culture and society.

The Objectification of Others in the Writing of a National Self

The publication of Edward Said's *Orientalism* has in past decades sparked sharp debate within academic circles. Area specialists engaged in the study of Oriental history or society were among those most directly affected by Said's attack on Western scholarship on the non-Western world. Said's contention that Western scholars exoticized the Orient as an object of gazing, then with the full force of their "authority" constructed a worldview out of it that had little to do with the "real" Orient incited extreme reaction.[1] Objectification in this sense had a double entendre. By identifying the Orient as a bounded object of discourse where none had existed, Orientalism was in the first instance an imaginative, if not exaggerated, fiction of those societies. Second, by virtue of its distancing, Orientalism was hardly an "objective" account, despite its best intentions, and at worst a solipsistic projection of its Occidentalism.[2] Said's explicit critique of Orientalism therefore resided in his questioning of the subjective interpretation of the *author* and ultimately the institutional legitimacy of his authority (not only as writer but also as political actor and agent of those underlying interests).[3]

At the same time, it also became clear that Said's criticism had serious ramifications for humanistic and social scientific writing.[4] Anthropologists were implicated insofar as much of their work dealt explicitly with other peoples or other cultures. While Said offered little to resolve the "authorial dilemma" of the anthropologist's attempt to decode, interpret, and analyze the culture and society of other peoples as they "really" exist, except through critical reflection of his own modes of interpretation or writing, he located the problematic source of such study above all in the *writing* of such scholarship and in its inherent Eurocentrism.

By making Orientalism, at least in the first instance, a problem of the West (rather than of its other), Said appeared to suggest that the Orient was immune to the charges of exoticism and objectification that were intrinsic to Western scholarship. According to Said (1978:2–3), Orientalism is "a style of thought based upon an ontological and epistemological distinction made between 'the Orient' and 'the Occident.' " As "a corporate institution for dealing with the Orient—dealing with it by making statements about it, authorizing views of it, describing it, by teaching it, settling it, ruling over it, Orientalism can be seen ultimately as tied into a larger political and economic project of colonizing 'the East' " (Said 1978:10).[5] The focus on othering made the idea of an Oriental Orientalism inconceivable. Said never questioned native discourse, which he assumed to be the Orient as itself, unadulterated by Orientalism.[6]

The issue of concern here then is namely those indigenous discourses that are silenced by the citationary authority of Orientalism and referred to by Said (1978:2) as the absent other.[7] In the case of China, there is no lack of native discourses on Chinese culture or civilization. Before the advent of the nation-state, China was a cultural state of mind.[8] The middle kingdom, China's traditional depiction of itself, should be distinguished from its modern incarnation as territorially bounded nation-state characterized by rights of citizenship, a standardized national language and uniform educational system. At best, it invoked a set of core values that linked persons in time and place to an all-embracing cosmic hierarchy.[9] The terms *zhongguo* (middle kingdom) and *huaxia* (civilization as rooted in the mythical Xia dynasty) are most widely used to characterize China or Chineseness; they actually have their origins in a feudal past symbolized by a confederation of states claiming to share a common culture or civilization.[10] The sense of unity engendered by this kind of cultural order easily explains the Chinese perception of an unbroken historical continuity despite the rise and fall of dynasties—indigenous and barbarian, the myth of a common ethnicity born in the Yellow River valley, and an attachment to the languages and values of an ongoing literary tradition.

This does not exhaust the range of possible native discourses on Chinese culture and Chineseness. It suffices to say here that there are many native discourses of the self that can be distinguished from Orientalist constructions of the Chinese other. These discourses have their own historicity, but these images of timelessness or unbroken continuity with the past should be distinguished from Eurocentric discourses of an unchanging Orient prevalent in the Enlightenment-era humanistic and social scientific literature (culminating in the Asiatic mode of production, Oriental despotism, etc.). The assumption of harmony with a primordial past, despite the real history of dynastic upheaval, barbarian conquest, and alien religions, represents a *myth* of or imagined communion with a sacred origin. This myth of shared sacredness is a definition of Chineseness that also transcends ethnic identities and political realities.[11] By transcending ethnic identity, Chineseness can be viewed as a set of values that is distinct from considerations of material customs. By transcending political realities, Chineseness in this sense does not depend on the physical autonomy of a state or nation in order to be effective. Such indigenous conceptions of (a cultural/civilizational) China contrast sharply, on the other hand, with the way Europeans have attributed the sociopolitical unity of China to its dynastic lineage. Ethnically rooted national definitions of Chineseness are modern conceptions, which have a different kind of historicity.

The points made above about native constructions of Chinese culture and Chineseness have a seminal bearing on contemporary reality. Postwar Taiwan—that is to say, the Republic of China as transplanted to Taiwan at the conclusion of World War II, following Taiwan's retrocession by Japan back to China after a fifty-year interregnum—is an interesting example of the crisis of culture in a Chinese context. As part of the KMT's effort to continue the legacy of the Republic in their retreat from the mainland and in the process to nationalize Taiwan, the government embarked on a program to resuscitate "traditional Chinese culture." "Tradition" in this sense represented a defense of political ideology (as opposed to "socialism") but more importantly by virtue of its defense of culture. The crisis of culture involved first of all the KMT's attempt to *nationalize* Chinese culture (by making the latter a metaphor or allegory of that imagined community called the nation-state) where no such culture (of the nation) really existed. By invoking "tradition," they appeared to resuscitate elements of the past, but they were clearly inventing tradition (by virtue of their selectivity) in ways that did not differ from "the invention of tradition" found elsewhere.[12] The ways in which culture was framed (as ideology), then strategically deployed (in practice), reflected the distinctiveness of the Taiwan experience. The crisis of traditional Chinese culture in contemporary Taiwan, not unlike the phenomenon of Orientalism and the invention of tradition, was really a crisis of *modernity*. In the case of Taiwan, I argue that this crisis of modernity was precipitated by the need for the state to establish *new* foundations of spiritual consciousness, ideological rationality, and moral behavior that could conform to the dictates of the modern polity or *nation-state*, in ways that primordial notions of Chineseness, strictly speaking, could not. This need to forge a new *hegemony* ultimately prompted these (mystifying, hence unnatural) discourses on culture.

The institution of nationhood necessitated novel forms of Chineseness in many respects. Before the 1911 Nationalist Revolution, which resulted in the overthrow of the Qing dynasty and the founding of the Republic, the notion of society as a territorially distinct, politically bounded and ethnically solidary community did not exist. Many terms were borrowed from Japanese (Han & Li 1984). Up until the mid-nineteenth century, it was unnatural for Chinese to call other ethnic groups "ethnic groups," just barbarians. Only during the early Republican era did intellectuals associate *zhonghua minzu* (Chinese as ethnic group) with *zhongguo ren* (citizens of China), which tied people of China territorially to a common polity.[13] Moreover, Chineseness in terms of material culture, ethnicity, or residence was never clearly defined (Wu 1991:162). The Chinese rendition of nationalism (*minzu zhuyi*) as the "principle of a common people" underscored the notion of a bounded citizenry as the distinctive feature of nationhood (in contrast, for example, to the purely institutional characteristics of the nation-state).[14] This was pointed out by Sun Yat-sen, the founding father of the Republic, who in a famous phrase criticized the traditional Chinese polity for being "a dish of loose sand" (*yipan sansha*). This can explain why the promotion of "societal consciousness" (*minzu yishi*) and spiritual values has been repeatedly highlighted in the aftermath of nationalism as the primary obstacle to national solidarity, in the face of both Communism and the modern world system.

If discontinuity brought about by the advent of nationalism was a basis for reinvoking culture and tradition, one can also argue that the renaissance of traditional Chinese culture in postwar Taiwan had to be a modern phenomenon as well. In this sense, by creating notions of collective identity and societal consciousness that mirrored the boundedness of the nation in ways that primordial notions of Chineseness could not, recourse to tradition relied less on authenticity of content than on novelty of form. As an Orientalism in Said's terms, Chinese culture became an object of discourse not only in political terms (vis-à-vis Chinese socialist doctrine), but also as objects of scholarly investigation (through the chronicling of history, philological archiving, archaeological preservation, social scientific knowledge), and habits of everyday practice (through family training, educational cultivation, peer group socialization, workplace supervision).[15] Tradition was reinvented, and its mystification coincided with the hegemonic process of state formation.[16] More importantly, this mystification of Chinese culture, in its capacity as imagined community, represented an orchestrated effort to create a productive ideology of *truth* (about the Chinese self) in a way that simultaneously distanced itself from an implicit other, opposed not only to a Communist China but also the world.[17]

Post Hoc Discourses on Sun Yat-sen's Three Principles and the Changing Utopianism of Nationalist Ideology

Aside from the substance of its political thought, the source of appeal of any Nationalist ideology should entail to some extent the commensurability of its cultural ethos. In postwar Taiwan, national culture as rhetorically invoked and politically deployed by the state involved not only a multiplicity of *things* (markers of national identity, icons of patriotic fervor, and national treasures) but also the authority of different kinds of rhetorical *statements* (shared myths, beliefs, and values; common language, ethnicity, and custom as well as the codification of discursive knowledge) whose systematicity reflected the utopianism of a Nationalist polity.

The writing of culture as national self should not be seen as peculiar to Taiwan, but rather general to the modern nation-state. As Cohn (1988) has argued, the state produced its own forms of knowledge, necessitating documentation in the genre of statistics, investigations, commissions, and reports pertaining to the accountability of its citizens in domains such as finance, industry, trade, health, demography, crime, education, transportation, and agriculture. The need of the state to know and document laid the basis of its capacity to govern. Thus, the will of knowledge to power provided the state a mode with which to define and classify spaces, separate public from private spheres, demarcate frontiers, standardize language, and personal identity, as well as to license the legitimacy of certain activities over others. Or as Corrigan and Sayer (1985:3) preferred to put it, "the state never stops talking."

The self-production of documentary knowledge, political discourse, rituals of state, and routines of rule is then part and parcel of the state's project to define itself, and in the process rationalize its continued existence. The multiplicity of representations and statements at its disposal extended beyond the need to fabricate a sense of national identity and boundedness. Although grounded in the empty, homogenous space of a standard linguistic community and the synthetic commonality of a public culture in senses already well described in the work of Anderson (1983) and Gellner (1983), this imagined community of shared symbols and values also begged legitimacy that an imagined ethos of political ideology endeavored to appeal to.

In many respects, the Three Principles of the People by Sun Yat-sen made sacred by the KMT as the founding doctrine of the Republic represented an important frame for conveying the imagination of a Nationalist society. It was widely known that the doctrine of the Three Principles was not a formal treatise but rather a series of lectures compiled in large part after the death of its author. In his preface, Sun stated that rebel insurgents who attacked his Canton headquarters in 1922 destroyed his original manuscript. He resorted to giving lectures on topics, which became regrouped under the rubrics of the Three Principles (nationalism, democracy, and livelihood). However, Sun died before finishing all of the projected lectures.

Yet in spite of his death, these lectures became a point of departure for continued writing and formulation of the Three Principles, and it was really these post hoc discourses and their ongoing mutations that characterized the changing utopian vision of a Nationalist ideology and national culture. Of the continued changes in substance, the most important being the appendage of two supplementary chapters by Chiang Kai-shek on the principle of livelihood, which nearly equaled the length of Sun's entire manuscript, the Three Principles eventually became an important object of educational dissemination as textbook knowledge taught at all levels of the curriculum from elementary to university. This expanded discourse, rather than the original text of the Three Principles, represented a continual process of writing, to say the least, but one should really spell out in detail how these permutations of substance and form were engendered as a function of *ideological investment* and *institutional normalization.*

In essence, the *malleability* of Nationalist ideology, which suited different sociopolitical conditions, rather than its textual *authenticity*, was what enabled the Three Principles to transform itself from political doctrine, strictly speaking, into a broadly conceived cultural ideology consistent with all other representations of the imagined community. For much of the early history of the Republican era following the Revolution of 1911, Nationalist ideology served mainly as revolutionary agent of sociopolitical change.[18] Party organization during this early era was influenced by the Soviet Leninist model, which explains the propagandistic role of ideology. Shen Zongrui (1991:5) has noted seven features of KMT Party–controlled government organization during this early period: (1) use of ideology by the Party as a tool of articulation; (2) focus on the spirit of revolutionary nationalism; (3) adoption of a centralized policy decision-making apparatus; (4) establishment of a central standing committee (*zhong chang hui*), which functioned as an administrative arm of centralized control to coordinate all activities in the spheres of political culture, media dissemination, and intelligence surveillance; (5) appropriation of the military as a subordinate agency within the government; (6) creation and maintenance of a youth corps to promote activities and recruit future party members from the youth; and (7) relegation of autocratic control over the state apparatus to a single leader.[19]

Many aspects of the KMT's revolutionary state apparatus in the sense of its ideologically based, Party-dominated mode of governmental operation carried over into later times, despite the KMT's break with the Communist Party (CCP). They included its continued centralized control over culture, media, and security; increased institutional linkages between the party, government, military, and education; and a heightened emphasis on maintaining a collective ethos based on the perceived synonymity of one people, one race, one family, one language, one ideology, one culture, and one history. On the other hand, some important differences in the KMT's interpretation of the Three Principles enabled Nationalist policy to deviate from socialist practice on the mainland. The first concerned the establishment of constitutional government as a means by which popular representation was accorded to the people, and the second was a belief in the principle of equity in private property. The latter prompted the large-scale implementation of the Land Reform Act in 1950, which reapportioned land among small landholders and tenant cultivators. Constitutional government and private property no doubt paved the way for some degree of democratic representation and a market economy, albeit still controlled by a centralized bureaucratic system.

The shift in Nationalist ideology away from revolutionary pragmatism had much to do with Chiang Kai-shek's modern, scientific interpretation of the Three Principles, and his particular emphasis on ethics, democracy, and science.[20] As the CCP continued to regard the Three Principles as a revolutionary doctrine written mainly from a precommunist petty bourgeois perspective, the ideological split between the two Parties intensified. Moreover, it was not until the KMT's takeover of Taiwan that the systematic transformation of the Three Principles into a doctrine of conservative traditionalism began to take place. Much had to do naturally with the continued state of war, but more importantly it involved the changing uses of ideology in this "war of maneuver," using Gramsci's (1971) terms.

In the early phase of Taiwan's occupation from 1945–67, officially called "The Glorious Restoration" (*guangfu*) by the KMT, the basis for a different kind of nationalist imagination was beginning to take shape. During the previous half-century from 1845–1945, Taiwan had been ceded to Japan. Despite the Han ethnic origins of its local Taiwanese inhabitants, the radical nature of this new "imagined community" cannot be underestimated. According to Anderson (1983), the establishment (in this case, forced imposition) of a standard linguistic community was an important precondition for the formation of a new national consciousness. In the case of Taiwan, this new collective consciousness had to be by definition a *cultural* nationalism insofar as it involved re-anchoring a local Taiwanese population to the mythic origin of Chinese civilization, as implied by an essentialist notion of *huaxia*. The shift back to a Chinese cultural holism was accompanied by the rejection of Japanese culture, including a ban on all Japanese language materials, such as films, literature, media, and so on, and reinforced by the forward-looking spirit of ethics, democracy, and science that Chiang Kai-shek wished to promote through the Three Principles. In a phase of cultural unification, standardization of a new linguistic community based on Mandarin Chinese (to the exclusion of Taiwanese and native dialects) became the vehicle for legitimizing the continuity of Chinese history, habits of ethnic custom, artifactual treasures of civilization, and traditional social values as standard bearers for a new Chinese national identity. The kind of culture being promoted during this initial phase of Taiwan's reunification into the Republic of China had to be qualified, however. Although the imposition of culture was meant to invoke the highly literate civilization of an imperial past and the legitimacy of the new regime as guardians of that past, there was no serious effort to systematically reconstruct the nature of that culture or tradition. Culture's primary function in this regard was to provide a myth of shared civilizational origin that could further serve as the groundwork for instilling patriotic sentiment and a community of shared values.

During 1967–77, primarily in reaction to the Cultural Revolution in the PRC, the KMT embarked on a second phase of cultural discourse, explicitly titled "cultural renaissance" (*wenhua fuxing*). Cultural renaissance was directed at the highest levels of government policy as a deliberately heavy-handed mode of ideological warfare and carried out as a large-scale social movement involving active coordination between the Party, media, local level government, schools, and various grassroots organizations.[21] It was really during this phase that the activist revolutionary character of Nationalist ideology began to be supplanted by a conservative rhetoric tied fundamentally to the survival of Chinese tradition-at-large.

The cultural renaissance movement was promoted to coincide roughly with the one-hundredth anniversary of the birth of Sun Yat-sen and formally inaugurated by a four-page essay by Chiang Kai-shek, titled *Zhongshanlou zhonghua wenhuatang luocheng jinian wen* (in short, *Zhongshanlou* Commemorative Essay). In the following year, a committee was established at a provincial level to promote the Chinese cultural renaissance movement. The provincial committee then set up regional committees at the city district and rural township levels to carry out cultural renaissance activities, primarily through the agency of the elementary and middle school. The fact that schools were called on to serve as active centers for the promotion of cultural learning and awareness in the daily curriculum and in extracurricular activities was a central tenet of government policy to extend the level of public consciousness to the local level. The government's design of cultural renaissance was far reaching and meant to combine administrative planning, media dissemination, and scholarly research, as well as to engage the coordinated efforts of the Party, newspaper and broadcasting industry, and various state-sponsored "people's interest groups" (grassroots organizations). The work of tradition in these domains was driven by four explicit guidelines: (1) allow the media to sow the seeds of public dissemination and incite education to take the initiative, (2) exemplify and actively lead through the expression of social movement, (3) use the schools as activity centers for the extension of the culture renaissance movement to the family

and society-at-large, and (4) use the full network of administration to step
up coordination and supervision.[22]

The promotion of the cultural renaissance movement beginning in the
mid-1960s was not a spontaneous discovery of traditional culture and values.
It was a systematic effort to redefine the content of these ideas and values,
to cultivate a large-scale societal consciousness through existing institutional
means and to use the vehicle of social expression as the motor for national
development in other domains, economic as well as political. In other words,
not only was there an organized effort to cultivate a spirit of national unity
through recourse to tradition, but there was also an effort to lead people to
believe that this spirit of cultural consciousness was the key to the fate of
the nation in all other respects. Thus, achievements as diverse as economic
progress and athletic success were all seen as consequences of this spirit of
national unity. That the cultivation of a spirit of cultural consciousness was
explicitly linked with the policy of cultural development in other aspects,
such as the extension of ties with overseas Chinese and foreign cultural
agencies, financing of grassroots cultural groups, development of the tourist
industry, increased publication of the classics, preservation of historical artifacts, large-scale promotion of activities in science, ethics or social welfare,
development of sports, and use of mass media to step up cultural coverage
and intensify anticommunist propaganda, was not accidental.[23] This was the
first step in a program to objectify (commoditize) culture.

At the local level, cultural renaissance was in effect a three-step process
involving public dissemination, moral education, and active demonstration.
In the schools, courses on society and ethics as well as citizenship and morality were taught at elementary and middle-school levels, respectively. In high
school, introduction to Chinese culture, military education, and thought
and personality became a staple part of the curriculum in addition to regular
courses in natural and social science. Outside the classroom, essay and ora-
tory contests on topics pertaining to Chinese culture were regularly held as
well as peer-group study sessions to discuss current speeches and writings.
These were supplemented by occasional activities in all aspects of traditional
culture, such as music, dance, folk art, painting, calligraphy, and theater.
Moral education was not limited to schools and children and extended also
to the family and local community in the form of family training groups,
social work teams, and women's and neighborhood associations. Local organizations regularly awarded prizes to model youth, model mothers, model
teachers and model farmers on occasions like Martyr's Day and birthdays
of national heroes such as General Yuefei, the Qing dynasty naval warrior
Koxinga, and the penultimate teacher Confucius. Even teachers underwent

similar moral supervision and training by participating in occasional study groups and various grassroots activities and attending talks given by scholars on topics pertaining to Chinese culture.

In the cultural renaissance movement, there was clearly an attempt by the government to (re)write "traditional Chinese culture" in postwar Taiwan. Obviously, it was not the only attempt; it was only the most obvious attempt. Yet in order to assess its significance vis-à-vis other forms of ideological writing, one should emphasize that the movement itself was predicated on the need first of all to construct what Fox (1990:3) has called "ideologies of peoplehood," a common consciousness which persons could identify with as being part of the same nation. This consciousness was not just an esoteric, abstract sense of common identity; it had to be provoked by feelings of social solidarity, which had roots in established symbols, myths and narratives. Moreover, spiritual unity was not something provoked for its own sake; it was presumably the key to defeating communism as well as the cure for all problems of national development, economic, social, or other. The way in which cultural renaissance was promoted in Taiwan, that is to say, backed by the full force of institutional power, also had ramifications for the nature of cultural authority. It is not enough to say that the writing of culture in Taiwan was political in origin and motivation. That the cultural renaissance movement could not be spontaneously initiated and defined from bottom up but had to be carefully orchestrated instead from above meant, of course, that the state was the sole arbiter of culture. In essence, the state defined culture by making culture (in terms of tradition) conform to the exigencies of the new polity and the "rational" ethos of a KMT worldview. Yet while the cultural renaissance movement was not the sole definition of culture in postwar Taiwan, it was surely the basic framework around which all other levels of public discourse revolved, especially in relation to the construction of a national political culture.

Insofar as culture in Taiwan invoked tradition, it also invoked to some degree a call to Confucianism as the rational basis of Chinese tradition. Not unlike other discourses of tradition, Confucianism was invoked here not as a system in itself but as a set of stripped-down ethical values that had a particular role in the service of the state. As a generalized moral philosophy or a kind of social ethics that could be easily translated into secular action, Confucianism here meant for the most part devotion to filial piety, respect for social authority, and etiquette in everyday behavior.[24] This was a far cry from the permutations of Confucian ideology that emerged in different schools of Confucian learning and that came to influence the practice of imperial government in past dynasties. Thus, recourse to Confucian tradition, especially in its emphasis on filial piety, was actually an attempt to extend feelings of family solidarity to the level of the nation thus could not be viewed just as neutral cultural values.

The defense of Chinese traditional culture sparked by the cultural renaissance movement later spawned the politicization of Confucian ideology, the archivalization of historical and archaeological knowledge, a heightened emphasis on standardization of traditional thought, the sinicization of Western science and modern life, custom and behavior, and other attempts to "invent" tradition. This conservative turn of events sparked a basic reformulation of the Three Principles from a doctrine of pragmatic revolutionary nationalism to an ethical worldview steeped essentially in traditional, even Confucian, values.

In this regard, it was well known that the original Three Principles lacked a consistent philosophical framework, thus much attention was devoted to developing its foundations in traditional Chinese thought.[25] The development of such a philosophical framework was an important step in the ideological warfare being waged at the time. Underlying the rhetoric of anticommunism was a perceived necessity to legitimize Nationalist political ideology in terms of accepted social values. In other words, the fate of traditional Chinese culture and Nationalist ideology was intertwined insofar as it could be seen as grounded in a set of social values within which appeal to Confucianism played a part. In reality, the Three Principles was always an uneasy mix of Western scientific pragmatism and Chinese ethical philosophy, which made it open to interpretation from many angles.[26] Sun's spirit of Western scientific positivism was pertinent to his anti-Manchu revolutionary nationalism, yet, on the other hand, he also cast his faith in scientific positivism within a Confucian humanist (*ren*) framework in a way that was not unlike the practitioners of the *tiyong* school. There were many attempts in the early Republican era to synthesize a consistent philosophical framework from Sun's scattered writings and thoughts. In the politically edged atmosphere of cultural renaissance, the influential voice that emerged was a collection of essays on the philosophy of the Three Principles edited by Dai Jitao (1978), prefaced in 1925 by Dai but became resurrected then reproduced widely in KMT government publications. In a larger work, Dai (1954:34) cast Sun's thought squarely within a tradition of philosophy traceable from mythic times through the era of Confucius and centered essentially on a morality of livelihood. Others reiterated Sun's explicit references to (primarily Sung) Confucian concepts and placed them alongside his vision of a Chinese nation linked to the continuity of history and civilization.

Throughout the 1950s and '60s, there were many efforts to systematically cast the Three Principles as a coherent, consistent body of thought.

In many cases, works making explicit reference to the Three Principles tended to be sweeping generalizations based on the entire corpus of Sun's work.[27] Other attempts at synthesis focused on the perceived importance of specific functional aspects of his work, such as his philosophy of livelihood, scientific world view, political ideology, and economic theories.[28] The production of knowledge in relation to Sun's thought also brought about endless anthologies of his writings, most of which were used in conjunction with courses.[29] Yet despite the massive quantity of writing produced, very few of these "scholarly" studies constituted serious or even original research, choosing instead to standardize well-known material into an easily digestible, politically correct form. Insofar as tradition was invoked, its reference to the past (as might be the case of nostalgia) was clearly less important than its selectivity and rhetorical use in the present.

In the 1970s, the government established graduate departments in major universities and research centers like Academia Sinica to explicitly promote the study of the Three Principles. Yet despite institutional promotion of the Three Principles in the academy, scholarly writing within these institutes has always displayed two divergent trends, which Zhang Zhiming (1990:3) has referred to as "the Three Principalization of Scholarship" (*xueshu sanmin zhuyi hua*) and "the scholarly transformation of The Three Principles" (*sanmin zhuyi xueshu hua*). Much of the previous efforts to systematically reconstruct a Nationalist political ideology on the basis of Sun's scattered texts had been part of the former trend to rationalize and sanctify the ideological purity of Sun's thought. Without a doubt, work along these lines continued in the academy and was consistent with the conservative climate of ideological politicization and anticommunist sentiment. Yet at the same time, these institutes became a venue for the scientific rationalization of the Three Principles by adapting technical expertise from cognate disciplines like political science, economics, and sociology then transforming Sun's thematic concerns with nationalism, democracy, and livelihood into blueprints for modern practice.

The applied scientific nature of academic research conducted in these institutes of the Three Principles became increasingly apparent with the advent of reformist policies adopted at the end of the 1970s and into the '80s by Chiang Ching-kuo, Chiang Kai-shek's son and successor. The younger Chiang gradually moved away from the heavy-handed politics that had characterized the Cold War tensions of a previous era of cultural renaissance, choosing instead to promote full-scale economic growth, often at the expense of ideological purity. It was generally during this phase of economic liberalization and reformism that the face of the Three Principles shifted from being standard bearer of Chinese traditional culture to a modern, scientific blueprint for progressive society, with relevant functional applications for the future.

The gradual changes in research program at the Three Principles Institute at Academia Sinica clearly reflected the changing ethos of the Three Principles and its practical role in the construction of the nation-state. Created in 1974 as a preinstitute with thirteen research fellows, it was established as a formal institute in 1981. By 1984, it expanded swiftly to encompass a full-time research staff of thirty-four, eleven of whom were economists, nine historians, six sociologists, five political scientists, one philosopher, and only two specializing in the Three Principles. Despite the professional composition of the research staff, the internal research sections within the institute were still divided according to the Three Principles, namely nationalism (composed of sociologists and historians), democracy (composed of political scientists), and livelihood (composed of economists). According to the institute's research prospectus, its primary aims of development were, first, to construct a theoretical framework based on the Three Principles and, second, to conduct empirical studies with broad relevance for national policy. Serving the nation-building principles of Sun's Nationalist ideology, it also aimed to serve the needs of international scholarly research and national reconstruction.[30] In 1988, the disciplinary makeup of the research staff changed negligibly, but research programs within the institute were radically reorganized into five sections, named (1) the Three Principles and historical research, (2) the Three Principles and sociological research, (3) the Three Principles and political scientific research, (4) the Three Principles and economic research, and (5) the Three Principles and legal research. Its statement of purpose in the institute's prospectus was now revised to state that, in addition to research on the Three Principles proper, focus was also placed on interdisciplinary research with adjoining functional specializations, ultimately with a view toward expanding its theoretical horizons and practical applications more in line with international research.[31] By 1990, all five research sections dropped reference to the Three Principles altogether, and the institute's name was officially changed to Sun Yat-sen Institute of Humanities and Social Sciences. The scientific rationalization of the Three Principles thus became complete. By upgrading the Three Principles, the rest of humanities and the social sciences now provided a direct service in the making of a (progressive) national ideology.

The winds of change reverberated over to other departments and institutes involved in the teaching or promotion of the Three Principles to the point of overhauling the content of courses and their required status at all levels of education. Ironically, yet consistent with its orientation in an age of reform, many of these institutes became a hotbed for developments in postmodern and critical theory, regularly citing the likes of Giddens, Habermas, and Gramsci. While calls for reform (including the abolition of the Three Principles from the curriculum) increasingly came from the teaching establishment, this was met surprisingly with counterappeals from the Ministry of Education to intensify propagation of the Three Principles.[32] Thus depending on one's point of view, the Three Principles (in its conservative form) had either become obsolete or (in its modern incarnation) a vehicle for renewed Nationalism.

Political Thought as Cultural Pedagogy and Disciplinary Practice

In *The Political Unconscious*, Frederic Jameson (1981:30–31) described the ideological investment that enabled Biblical narrative to be rewritten at many different levels of textual transformation. Beginning with the collective history of the people of Israel, the plight of the people became allegorically represented in the form of biographical narrative through the life and suffering of Christ. This allegorical interpretation was then the apparatus for the writing of moral narrative through which historical events (e.g., the deliverance of the people from Egypt) and heroic biography (resurrection of Christ) became imbued with psychological meaning. Finally, the moral narrative generated the analogical dimension of text, where the narrative was transformed again into a genre of collective myth or universal history. This mythical, universal form of narrative established the political legitimacy of the people.

The rewriting of narrative and ideological investment enabling people, events, concepts, and things to become imbued with different levels of meaning was certainly not limited to Biblical myth. The writing and rewriting of culture in the process of nation-state formation in Taiwan was a similarly complex process of ideological investment. It involved more than just the manipulation of master symbols such as the flag, national anthem, and other icons of patriotic fervor. Nor was there any single allegorical basis that provided in Jameson's terms the interpretive code or blueprint for all subsequent transformations of text. To be effective, the political construction of culture as representation of state and new societal consciousness had to be sublimated and inscribed at many levels of writing. The fact that the government was able to invoke many sources of tradition in this regard not only established its legitimacy according to a set of accepted sociocultural values, but more importantly made possible the construction of different kinds of narrative outside the realm of politics per se, for example, popular public discourse, scholarly treatises on history, and the culture industry, that provided in turn a framework of writing from which cultural production reinforced societal consciousness.

The teaching of Nationalist ideology was an example not only of how national culture was rewritten at all levels of interpretation but also of how its writing had to be viewed as the collective labor of various agents in the system insofar as it involved the regulation of public behavior at all levels of everyday practice. It was decided early on that public education would be devoted primarily to political training and that the Party would be an active agent in the writing of the curriculum. In 1919, the Ministry of Education formally implemented a course on "Party ideology" (*dangyi*) as the nucleus on which the government aimed to base its vision of Nationalist education. In 1932, the course was renamed "citizenship" (*gongmin*) then broadened to include topics on ethics, morality, politics, law, and economics. This was taught as a required course in high school. At the same time, other courses on "common sense," "health training," and "civic training" were created at elementary and middle-school levels. The guideline underlying the mapping of the curriculum was clearly spelled out in Ministerial directives: the focus at the elementary-school level would be on the application of concrete life practices, in middle school on the correct learning of concepts, and in high school on the study of underlying principles. Even after courses shed the title of "party ideology," it continued to be disseminated at all levels of education and expanded in content to include other aspects of social life, ethico-moral values, and personal conduct, in other words ultimately all aspects of public behavior. By the time the course on "citizenship" was renamed "The Three Principles (of Sun Yat-sen)" in 1944 and again in 1950, following the restoration of Taiwan, the KMT government had already begun to systematically program the focus of education toward the long-term cultivation of a Nationalist worldview.

This systematic program was initiated by an essay in 1953 written by Chiang Kai-shek, titled "Two Amendments to the Cultivation of the Principle of Livelihood" (*minsheng zhuyi yule liang pian bushu*). The next fifteen years saw experiments with courses at the elementary and middle- to high-school level. Foundational courses on common sense and society at the elementary-school level designed in the 1930s were renamed "knowledge of citizenship" and "morality of citizenship," and then amalgamated into a single course on "citizenship and morality." Upper-level courses at middle- to high-school levels shifted between "rules of disciplinary practice" (*xunyu guitiao*) and "rules of life routine" (*shenghuo guitiao*). In 1968, the nature of the curriculum was revamped, this time for the next thirty years. "Citizenship and morality" at the elementary school level was renamed "life and ethics," while its corresponding middle- to high-school course became "citizenship and morality."[33]

While the systematic reconstruction of the Three Principles at all levels of education was in historical terms the direct consequence of an explicit program to politicize education from the point of view of the Party, the addition of courses on personal conduct, moral behavior, and civic values made clear that successful acquisition of correct political ideology was founded on the prior cultivation of an ethico-moral lifestyle in all other respects. Thus, piety, etiquette, and deference were not just limited to family virtues, as might be the case of a Confucian notion of filial piety, in strict terms. They were meant to be the moral foundation of all societal relationships. The cultivation of these values in the practice of everyday life was the precondition for successfully inculcating the broader vision of Nationalist society as well as orthodox political views. In other words, in order to achieve this goal of politicizing education, it was important to see how political ideology as theoretically conceived was the "natural" culmination of moral education and the normal practice of everyday social life.[34]

Like the four-tiered transformation in Jameson's interpretation of Biblical narrative, the writing of nationalist ideology in Taiwan also manifested a multi-level transformation. At the lowest level of elementary training, one can see a focus on the practices of the individual body, personal hygiene, and individual welfare as well as the acquisition of common sense.[35] At the intermediate level, with courses focusing more on civics and society, there was further ideological investment of values previously at the individual-experiential level to one where knowledge of interpersonal relationships in society as things in themselves became the focus of education. The displacement of learning from a collective-experiential domain to the level of collective-theoretical knowledge became complete at the high-school level with the teaching of Sun Yat-sen's political thought (*guofu sixiang*).

The writing of national ideology in the context of education has been from the outset a crucial dimension of the KMT's attempt to define culture and use the symbols of a common culture as the basis by which to cultivate a unitary societal consciousness, thus legitimize or reproduce the nation-state. Needless to say, the government's political authority to construct and define culture was one that was backed by the power of the totalitarian state, but the construction of a culture of the nation (in all its flavors) through the writing (and practice) of political ideology (as ethics and moral behavior), promotion of master symbols of the body politic, and various rites of national celebration and rituals of state as the basis on which to maintain solidarity of the nation (in the process guarantee continued domination by the state) was predicated by a different kind of politics altogether, namely hegemony. Underlying the overt politicization of cultural renaissance in the public arena of national ideology was the internal transformation of political values in the context of education into sublimated form by invoking tradition or appealing to ethical virtue and moral conduct. The transformation of political ideology at various levels of ethics/morality, followed by the active promotion of the latter as "culture," thus constituted the framework on which hegemony was created.

The writing of culture/ideology in this hegemonic process can be viewed as part of an even larger project of socialization in institutional terms. For it was really within this larger framework of socialization that the active promotion of culture represented in reality a crucial part of the government's effort to impose routines of disciplinary lifestyle in various domains of social interaction, such as the family, school, military, and workplace. In this regard, filial piety, moral codes of disciplinary conduct, national ideology, work ethics, and contractual obligations were manifestations of a larger set of life principles that had as its ultimate goal "the making of the moral person" (*zuoren*). Literally speaking, the concept of *zuoren* simply meant displaying the proper conduct, and in the context of specific institutions *zuoren* became in practice a code word for conformity to the routines and norms of the respective institution, whatever they were. Moral education through display of correct attitudes and moral training (*shouxun*) through emulation of proper conduct were thus inalienable aspects of socialization.

In practice, such moral regulation depended on the collusion of many institutional agents at a local level, the most important being the Party and the military. Given the single Party politics of the state, the line separating Party from government was always ambiguous to begin with. Civil servants were obliged to be active members of the Party. Party units were set up in each institution, and members were not only actively engaged in recruiting more members but were constantly on the outlook, supervising the actions and thoughts of colleagues.[36] The use of military personnel as *jiaoguan* ("school officers") or enforcers of correct moral behavior in the middle school and university was an extension of the state into the disciplinary apparatus of the school. One responsibility of the *jiaoguan* was to oversee the activities of the China Youth Corps (literally Anti-Communist China Youth for National Restoration Corps, a Party-sponsored youth activity group to which many students belonged). The presence of the military, while seen as a direct imposition of the Party in the operation of the school, was also portrayed as part of the overall socializing environment of the school.

The reinforcement of everyday etiquette was not just limited to institutional socialization within the school. This same normalizing behavior was a core feature of other institutions, where this socializing notion of "training" was applicable, notably during military service and in the workplace. The creation of disciplinary spaces with the advent of institutions like the hospital, school, military, and factory are well-known to readers of Foucault (1977:135–94). Military training, KMT style, however, had as much to do with training the soul as the body. Much of basic training was spent in the classroom, and a large proportion of that time was devoted to teaching political ideology and moral values, after which students were instructed to write reports to "express heartfelt thoughts" (*baogao xinde*). Similarly, organizational meetings were a regular activity within military camp, during which everyone was expected to "speak out" (*biaotai*) much in the way that students were expected to do so in public rallies during the cultural renaissance movement. The purpose of such "confessional" rites was to express outwardly one's inner feelings, and performance of proper moral behavior was one of the things usually taken into consideration by supervisors when making periodic assessments (*kaoji*). In the workplace, the importance of maintaining proper moral behavior or etiquette in face-to-face interactions (*renji guanxi*) was equally pertinent, although not necessarily to such a ritualistic extent. Bonuses were usually also based on results of one's *kaoji*.

In retrospect, there were three phases in the promotion of the Three Principles, which corresponded to changing political-intellectual discourse in the Nationalist era, namely that of revolutionary pragmatism, conservative traditionalism, and scientific reformism. Its ongoing discourses were as much a function of changing strategies of political survival as changing utopian visions of the modern nation-state. In the formation of the state, political ideology was part of a larger discourse of culture, whose existence epitomized Party unity but in a way that relied on mutual support of other coexisting discourses. In this sense, culture was not unlike what Foucault (1991:55) aptly called a space of dispersion, an open and indefinitely describable field of relationships. The formation of cultural discourses was in these terms a play of specific remanences involving a multiplicity of different kinds of rhetorical statements. As discursive formation, cultural renaissance showed the relative influence of extradiscursive dependencies involving a panoply of economic, political, and social practices. In the writing of the Three Principles as Nationalist ideology, the transformation from cultural pedagogy to disciplinary practice introduced intradiscursive dependencies that enabled common elements to disperse across discursive fields, linking different levels of ideological investment.

The Nationalist Ethic
and the Spirit of Chinese Rationalism

In his analysis of what he called "the paradox of rationalization" in Max Weber's account of the Protestant Ethic and the spirit of capitalism, Wolfgang Schluchter (1979:42) singled out three elements of the Calvinist worldview that provided the basis for the inherent dissolution of a religious ethos of radical world rejection and its transformation into a totally secularized ethos of radical world domination. They were, namely, (1) the interpretation of the secular "world" as a religiously worthless cosmos of things and events to which the heterogeneity of natural and ethical causality applied; (2) the idea of this "world" as an object of fulfillment of duty through rational control; and (3) the compulsion to develop an ethically integrated personality, which demanded one's total commitment. The Calvinist worldview attempted to fuse all three elements into a unified attitude, so that, in the name of God, one had to exert rational, methodical control over one's total conduct and dominate the world through the incessant accumulation of good works in one's vocation. At this point, however, this ethos confronted in practice a paradox, which led to the devaluation of the religious ethic and its subordination to secular values of its modern vocational calling. This religiously devalued "world" forced one to recognize its own laws; the more this happened, the more independent the world became. In their mutual confrontation, alienation between the religious ethos and the impersonal ethic of capitalism became obvious. That is to say, by attempting to master the world in its own terms, the overt religious meaning of inner-worldly asceticism became displaced by the secular values of a routinized code of rational conduct. It was in this sense that the accumulation of good works as an ethical code of conduct became a self-motivated act or an ongoing thing in itself even after it lost its intrinsic religious meaning.

I do not mean to suggest that Sun Yat-sen's Three Principles was an Asian version of Weber's Protestant ethic, despite close resemblance of what Schluchter has called practical rationalism, metaphysical-ethical rationalism, and scientific-technological rationalism to what I characterized as the revolutionary pragmatism, moral conservatism, and scientific reformism of Sun's thought. Yet there is clearly a paradox of traditionalism at the level of discourse that must be spelled out in order to explain the nature of this underlying Nationalist ideology.

First, one must stress again that Nationalist political ideology in postwar Taiwan referred less to the Three Principles, as Sun Yat-sen had actually conceived of it, which still remains a contested reality, than to the utopian vision of it filtered through Chiang Kai-shek's emphasis on ethics, democracy, and science. This utopian worldview provided an epistemic blueprint for subsequent polemic debate over the systematicity of Sun's thought, engendered a space of dispersion on which other discourses of culture (unified language, Confucian ethics, shared history) operated and were seen to be correlated, finally provided an allegorical code for permutations at the level of institutional practice (through pedagogical dissemination and disciplinary routinization). In historical terms, the state of war between Taiwan and the PRC, and the Cultural Revolution in particular, had much to do with the conservative turn in political ideology, the invention of traditional Chinese culture, the promotion of movements to raise spiritual consciousness, the archivalization of historical knowledge, and the defense of national treasures. At an interdiscursive level, these events cultivated in effect an imagined community and a shared destiny predicated by the equivalence of one language, one custom, one history, one civilization, one ethos, one family, and one nation. The multiplicity of icons and rhetorical statements that colluded to form complex representations of "national identity" was certainly a crucial component of the state's explicit project to define a *national culture* where none existed in the (traditional) past. The paradox of traditional Chinese culture in the Taiwan present, however, resided less in the internal inconsistencies of that traditional vision than in the inconsistencies that emerged out of the KMT's attempt to use a unified set of values (rooted in political ideology and moral philosophy) to merge divergent interests in an idealized tradition and scientific progress. Perhaps not unlike the confrontation between religious and secular values engendered by a Calvinist ethos driven by the methodical accumulation of good works, the waning of Cold War tensions reduced considerably the need to use ideology as a weapon based on a spirit of national unity (*liguo jingshen*) to counter mainland China and other competing nations in the modern world system.

Chiang Ching-kuo's scientific reformism during the 1970s and '80s preempted the rise of a resistance that increasingly viewed traditionalism as something antithetical to the spirit of scientific positivism. The younger Chiang's reformism promoted economic modernization, indigenization of the KMT, defusing longstanding ethnic tension, and the depoliticization of culture by creating a Committee for Cultural Reconstruction (*wenhua jianshe weiyanhui*) to advance cultural/aesthetic activities in line with a rising economic standard of living. All of these developments were to some extent predicated by the achievements of a previous era of cultural renaissance, which inculcated in one's minds a totality of representations associated with Chinese culture. Yet it was this new push to promote technoscientific rationalism and redefine the role of existing ideology in relation to it as a subordinate or dependent element within the whole that led scholars to question the continuing validity of a worldview bound, as though frozen in time, to the orthodoxy of Sun's thought. Although much of the current debate over the future fate of the Three Principles focused essentially on a conflict of interpretation (as spirit of national unity), it would inevitably be decided, on the other hand, by a conflict of interest, that is, between those who did not find it necessary to make reference to the Three Principles in order to embrace the virtues of modern progress and those within the KMT who still found it necessary to continually upgrade the Three Principles in line with the changing times in order to reiterate the continued coherence and relevance of Nationalist ideology, and by implication, therefore the legitimacy of the existing regime. It is clear then that the issue of textual authenticity in Nationalist ideology has always been secondary to the function of ideology in making meaningful the cultural authority of texts to a community constituted on the fiction of equal, autonomous individuals.

The secondary nature of the Three Principles as political thought inevitably raised the question of to what extent credibility of this doctrine would be affected by ongoing criticism of its substantive content and relevance for the present. Despite its required status in the school curriculum, one could question the degree to which students have been successfully influenced by orthodox preaching in this regard. Clearly, the rumblings of discontent that emerged from the practitioners of such knowledge within academia itself suggested strongly that the effectiveness of political brainwashing per se had been limited, except in its most general reading as an anticommunist ideology. Yet, on the other hand, it would be difficult to underestimate its embeddedness within a wider field of cultural ideology as well as in the pattern of everyday social behavior that has been characteristic of society in Taiwan vis-à-vis its Chinese counterparts in Hong Kong and the mainland. In this regard, effective criticism of the status of the Three Principles as Nationalist ideology would seem more likely to come from the realm of public culture and underlying notions of national identity as a whole.

To say the least, the contagion of democracy that has afflicted many parts of the globe in recent years has also brought about significant changes in Taiwan's political climate. The surge in ethnic nationalism has accelerated the dismantling of communist regimes in Eastern Europe despite decades of totalitarian rule. In Taiwan, these trends have been deflected by a policy of political reform and economic liberalization. Thus in 1986, Chiang Ching-kuo legalized the existence of opposition parties as a prelude to free legislative elections. This was followed by the lifting of strict censorship over the press in 1987, and the lifting of martial law in 1988. Political liberation not only allowed for the emergence of Taiwanese independence, formerly a taboo topic of discussion; it allowed for the emergence of all other forms of counterculture as well, namely the youth culture, intellectual dissidence, artistic freedom, even the flourishing of tabloids and sexual liberation.

By far, the most explicit challenge to the KMT's monopoly of political power has come from the Democratic Progressive Party (DPP), running on a platform of indigenous rule by ethnic Taiwanese, who constitute three-fourths of the island's population, and Taiwanese independence, in its more extreme factions. Yet despite the DPP's appeals for ethnic nationalism, the KMT continued to do well against the opposition, garnering three-fourths of the popular vote in the first free legislative elections of 1989, and two-thirds support in the legislative elections of 1992. Despite appearances to the contrary, this was clearly not an ethnically dormant Yugoslavia or USSR.

While the KMT's apparent success was in no way synonymous with popular support for its Party ideology, it nonetheless underscored broad based acceptance of the cultural-national identity that had been inculcated over decades of explicit cultural policy and institutional practice in ways, which have subverted to a large extent indigenous ethnic sentiments that had been suppressed throughout the postwar era. On the other hand, despite the explicit challenge by the DPP to the KMT's political agenda in at least one respect, there was little indication that the opposition had been able to put forth an alternative cultural vision, which could successfully unmask the hegemonic fictions of the prevailing regime, choosing instead to advocate a different homogenous ethnic nation-state to counter that of the KMT. This reflected the tacit importance already built into a generation of KMT cultural indoctrination, which had presupposed the imagination of a shared cultural (both ethnic and historical) consciousness as the seminal condition of national survival and societal progress in all other respects. Subsequent changes of regime and political ideology later led to the decline of the explicit legacy of Sun's Three Principles and the rise of Taiwanese indigenous consciousness, but the cultural nationalist mind-set has remained deeply embedded in the politics of identity in Taiwan. Its inability to transcend the prison house of identity makes it hopelessly tied to it.

Chapter 2

The Moral Cultivation of Citizenship as Acculturating and Socializing Regime

The very existence of obligatory schools divides any society into two realms: sometime spas and processes and treatments and professions are "academic" or pedagogic" . . . The power of school thus to divide social reality has no boundaries: education becomes unworldly and the world becomes non-educational.

—Ivan Illich, *De-Schooling Society*

The Norm and the Normal, or Education as Social and Societalizing

In East Asia, education was not just the evolution of a modern regime made compatible with all other socializing institutions, such as the family, military, and workplace. Above all, it was a systematic construction of the state, with historical lineages in an imperial system that reproduced a meritocracy. The omnipresence of the Ministry of Education epitomizes ultimately the hegemonic role of education, especially in the making of the nation-state. More than socializing, it manufactures a normality of belonging where culture, citizenship, and structured modes of routinized behavior perform overlapping disciplinary functions.

There is an abundance of critical literature on education in sociology and pedagogy. The work of Pierre Bourdieu as well as that of Michael Apple, Henri Giroux, and Peter McLaren, following the footsteps of Paolo Freire, to name a few, have underscored not only the role of education

---

This is an adaptation of a paper published in 2013, titled "De-Societalizing the School: On the Hegemonic Making of Moral Persons (Citizenship) and Its Disciplinary Regimes," *Critique of Anthropology* 33(2):146–67.

in reproducing the structure of class domination but also the function of cultural production in this regard.[1] However in this critical literature, there is more attention to efforts to produce *oppositional* educational values and practices that challenge hegemonic authority and less consideration of the *multiplicity* of cultural practices that engender these institutions. In Taiwan, mass education was part of a process of Westernization that brought about the dissemination of the modern nation-state. Perhaps even more so than in Europe, mass education was a top-down construction, regulated by the Ministry of Education, which promoted a meritocratic government and bureaucratic elites. Disciplinary institutions in this sense were not really autonomously evolving modern processes but more precisely regimes that were intimately tied to the maintenance of state power and the cultivation of a particular ethos and culture (societal mind-set) compatible ultimately with its nationalist worldview. Of the many "socializing" regimes, education played a relatively important role. The norm did not simply mark the legitimacy of social institutions and social values but more importantly cultivated routinized cultural behaviors and thoughts in the conduct of its everyday practice.

Education is "normal" in multiple senses. Modernity gave birth to a notion of society as the social structural framework on which various institutions, behaviors, rites, and practices were seen as functionally integrative. The idea that society in practice was normal rather than imaginative or inherently violent was maintained by social scientific theories that made the norm sacred (as a mode of thought).[2] Objective description and statistical analysis of various kinds reified societal institutions, as the product of a sui generis evolution, when they were also impositions of political policy or social order. Within the social "system" and in conjunction with the politics of the state, some institutions are more "normal" than others.

In many modern societies, education epitomizes the realm of the normal. In Taiwan, the Normal University is perhaps patterned after *les écoles normales* of France (otherwise called Teachers' Colleges). Education not only inscribes the normal; the normal itself becomes in turn the very essence of pedagogy. Normal then is to pedagogy what the norm is to social scientific theory. As methodology, it puts into practice the rites and routines of normal life in ways that complement the ideology of the norm as it is epistemologically constructed. By reinforcing in practice normative rules, education is tied ultimately to socialization, which as a process embodies society into persons, as citizens. Thus, citizenship inscribes socialization, by inculcating in ontological terms the morality and ethics of being a citizen. In the final analysis, education not only performs a seminal role. The normal epitomizes the soci(et)al.

Yet in the realm of the state, normal becomes a political construction par excellence. Its institutional existence and vitality are intertwined with the exercise of political power. It relies not only on discipline as a mode of administrative and social regulation, backed by sanction. Education is itself a kind of policing that evokes various technologies of power that buttress the state.[3] The salience of education in the ideology of the state (and citizenship) differs from place to place, but it can also be seen as a function of changing principles and policies. At an ideological level, educational principles and policies are products of specific cultural and intellectual influences. Their moral and ethical substance is an integral part of the modern form that gives it social shape as well as the process that maintains it in practice.

In this regard, cultural identity and political citizenship are not just national in Taiwan but also Nationalist, insofar as they are in substance products of changing political ideologies and perceptions of society.[4] Within the cultural geography of Nationalist identity, citizenship, culture, and ethos occupy different niches yet are mutually intertwined at the same time. As spaces within a social imaginary, they invoke distinct notions of person and personhood that contribute somehow to a social commonality. But as spaces within a political praxis, they entail an adherence to shared values and beliefs that crosscut the hierarchy of social rank and political privilege. In other words, identity aims to be communal within a real world marked by distinctions of class and status. Its nature as *discursive* fiction should be viewed in terms of its *ideological* substance as well as its *politicizing* functions in maintaining social order.

Identity and citizenship tend to be the language of shared values and mass society, and their relationship to the educational regime has a complex history. In postwar Taiwan, which is in basic respects the continuation of the Nationalist polity in early Republican-era China, nationalism and nationalist identity have always played an explicitly significant role in defining the nature of the state, even as the state in institutional terms evolved from moments of feudal warlordism to centralized bureaucracy. The evolution of a Nationalist state reached a degree of institutional maturity in postwar Taiwan, and this maturation in institutional terms corresponded to its increasingly explicit articulation of cultural policy in other respects. The adoption of the calendrical system, capitalistic disciplinary routines and new ontologies of the body were unconscious features of everyday life that inculcated a modern social regime, and they corresponded with overt militarization of society and the development of new rules of social etiquette, as embodied, for example, in Chiang Kai-shek's New Life Movement, in the political realm. All of these things were *encoded* into what eventually became known as "Three Principles Education" (*sanmin zhuyi jiaoyu*), following the writings of Sun Yat-sen. Three Principles Education was not just the teaching of Sun's political ideology; its being synonymous with mandatory education at all levels transformed the *space* of education into the *regime* within which citizenship was taught and practiced, then reproduced in other domains.[5]

Instead of being the pure product of ongoing cultural influences, as though reflective of a pan-Chinese experience, the discursive-institutional relationship that ties notions of identity and citizenship to the educational system and other regimes of socialization, such as military service, the workplace, and bureaus of immigration and customs control, is in large part the historical interplay of events and developments that are peculiar to early Republican China, which carried over into postwar Taiwan. The Cold War served to polarize such developments and politics. Thus if education has epitomized the normal in Taiwan, it is primarily because it is the complex nexus through which both socializing forces and conscious political ideologies collude to shape bodily ontologies and socializing routines of institutional and cultural life.

Early works on the function of ritual in the socializing regime of the school have pointed to the nature of culturalizing practices. Judith Kapferer's (1981) study of schools in Australia maintained that the institution of ceremonial practices and ritual routines in private schools contrasted with the secular policies of state schools by developing collective solidarity that underscored family, class, religion, and social values in relation to support communities. McLaren (1999) aptly labeled school ritual performance in social reproduction hegemony. In Taiwan, where the role of the state in standardizing the educational process is different, the same kinds of rituals have had similar socializing functions in relation to the polity. In effect, the state has articulated its modernity by actively cultivating *personhood* through rituals.

Rituals of Belonging in the Making of Moral Persons

The educational system in contemporary Taiwan is the product of traditional and modern institutions. The examination-based systems that form the pedagogical framework in other Asian countries, like Japan and Korea, are without doubt a product of its Confucian heritage and Mandarin meritocracy.[6] As a competitive, achievement-based regime, this examination system can be seen as the epitome of a standardized knowledge-based educational system that has served as the framework for modernization and of the social dissemination of skills in the postwar era. Pure reliance on standardized examinations as an evaluative criterion of this system has tended to give the impression that education in such a regime puts a high premium on utilitarian aspects of knowledge acquisition. While one cannot doubt the purely utilitarian aspects that seem to characterize the institutional backbone of this educational system, one cannot ignore as well the evolution of modern Asian education as part of the process of nation building, generally speaking, and the socializing functions of the latter.[7] In this regard, the functions of the central state in defining the content and form of education, as epitomized by the dominant role of the Ministry of Education and the hegemonic nature of the standardized curriculum, all point to the existence of a direct relationship between nation-building interests and education in general. The practice of education as an institutional regime shows that its scope is not limited only to the utilitarian dissemination of knowledge and skills within society. The broadly disciplinary functions of the school in the regulation of everyday thought and behavior also underscore its seminal role as an agent of socialization.[8]

In the context of Taiwan, this disciplinary regime, which is a general feature of everyday life in schools everywhere, mimics not only the spread of modernity as the basic pattern of routine life but is intertwined also with militarization and politicization *of all kinds*. The wearing of uniforms, the application of uniform codes of social conduct, and expected obeisance to political authority all make school life a microcosm of a militarized and politicized polity that is already being played out in society-at-large.[9] Richard Wilson's (1970, 1974) work on political socialization of children in Taiwan, in the specific context of the school, has tended to overemphasize the priority of politicization in the socializing process as a whole, with its stress on allegiance and patriotism. It is clear that there is socialization of all kinds, through inculcation of social values, assimilation to culture, appropriation of a certain kind of moral conduct, active involvement in sanctioned institutional activities, in addition to filial respect for authority, from family to teachers other forms of political authority.[10] The very fact that socialization is part of a totalizing and systemic process that invokes all kinds of cultural rules and moral behavior makes it important for one to analyze this in its systemic totality.

Thus, if education in Taiwan is understood less as an autonomous process of knowledge dissemination and instead as an integral part of the state project of nation building, it will be easier to understand how the curriculum is an important framework for the dissemination of social values, cultural identity, and political ethos of citizenship. The structure of its content within the framework of *mandatory* education, otherwise titled "Three Principles Education," can be read as a *process* of national identity, or what it takes to be a moral person in Nationalist society. More importantly, these values, identities and concepts are inculcated in the process of routine life and throughout the socializing regime of the school. The school, with direct ties to the state in the form of regulation by the Ministry of Education, is in turn a microcosm for Nationalist society-at-large, with its embodiment of Nationalist principles.

So, what is Three Principles Education? Initial formulations can be found in policy discussions of the early Republican era beginning in the late 1910s and early 1920s. The extent to which Three Principles Education derives from the Three Principles ideology of Dr Sun Yat-sen, the founder of the Chinese Republic, is questionable. Its incompleteness and ambiguity became a point of departure for its divergent interpretations on mainland China as a bourgeois revolutionary ideology and in Nationalist Taiwan as blueprint for scientific modernization. It then became part of the implementation of Chiang Kai-shek's New Life Movement, which was initially formulated in the 1930s, then became the vehicle for a revised Nationalist ideology.

In its initial policy formulation as Three Principles Education, ideas such as citizenship (*gongmin*), morality (*daode*), military training (*junxun*), and health (*weisheng*) were touted as basic requisites of this moral education, and early policy debates witnessed different attempts to implement the teaching of such concepts. The emphasis on bodily health in terms of personal hygiene, civilized etiquette, and physical training was part of Chiang Kai-shek's New Life ethos, which was inculcated at the primary level of education. Military discipline became the focus in courses at middle- and high-school levels, while courses on morality and citizenship were rooted in Confucian ethics and modern political values and disseminated through the middle- and high-school curriculum, which overlapped with more explicit courses on Sun Yat-sen's thought and political theory. *Moral education* in the above senses was a seminal aspect of *nation building* that transcended the pure dissemination of knowledge.

In this regard, the substance of citizenship and morality as concepts in themselves was less important than their function in the process of socialization or the state's project of moral regulation.[11] What kind of person (or citizen) is being cultivated here ontologically in the process of education and morally in terms of ethical behavior? Such notions of citizenship went beyond the overt pressures of political allegiance and respect for authority that accented Wilson's notion of political socialization. A citizen is a particular kind of thinking, acting, and feeling being. Political correctness is only one aspect of being a citizen. He or she must act in a particular way and in the right context of public expression. Identifying with a collectivity also involves appropriate sentiments of a kind that are often invoked in moments of patriotic fervor and national pride. Such thoughts, actions, and feelings are not simply taught in the substance of courses but also routinely played out in the performance of everyday practice.

The transformation of moral education from its embodiment of Nationalist ethics to its politicization of Chinese culture underscored in the final analysis the key role of the school per se as a constant locus in the construction of *identity*, the cultivation of moral persons, and the socialization of citizens in the making. Its functional operation as a "total institution," in Goffman's (1961) terms, made it an ideal site for using disciplinary control of time (through regulation of curricular and activity schedules) and space (through maintenance of social and spatial hierarchies) to reproduce the existing sociopolitical order. Its direct relationship to state *control* tied the school into the larger political space of the nation. In the latter context, the school may be a privileged institution of socialization by virtue of its omnipresence in the public domain, but it was at the same time one of *many* institutional nodes of socialization regulated by similar disciplinary regimes that could reinforce notions of cultural identity and moral citizenship. More than just inculcating norms, practices made perfect.

In an early essay, Ruey Yih-fu (1972) argued that the Chinese notion of culture (*wenhua*) was actually an abbreviation of a Confucian phrase *wenzhi jiaohua*, meaning "to govern by literacy and transform by teaching." The heavy emphasis in Confucian thought on morality and ritual propriety explains why Confucian traditions of education have always privileged moral cultivation, in its diverse senses, over pure knowledge. *Jiao*, which serves as the suffix *ism* in religion (or ideologies classified as such), also makes Chinese notions of learning more rooted in notions of personal transformation than assumptions of logos in Western notions of knowledge. While the focus on morality and ritual propriety in modern Chinese educational regimes can be seen as an extension of cultural traditions in this regard, I would argue that it is important to show how they overlap with and become transformed by other forms of moral regulation that emerge with modern nationalism and are institutionalized by the state through imposition of political ideology and implementation of socializing practices. In the end, such new constructions of identity as citizen serve as seminal core features in this education. The transformative role of education thus engenders acculturation in many senses.

Spatial, Temporal and Informational Distributions

The school is a moment in time and space. As social institution, it is characterized by its neutrality. At the same time, it is a product of its times, a creation of modern discipline as well as an agent of state hegemonic control. The middle school in the northern Taiwan city of Hsinchu that I observed during the academic year of 1991–92 had been known locally as a generally high achiever in national school exams, but otherwise it seemed to be a typical state school of its type, whose students represented a broad cross-section of city residents. Peiying Middle School was established in 1959. Built on the site of an old primary school with seven classrooms, it went through minor name changes after its transformation from an all girls' school to a mixed-gender school and as its administration shifted from the county to the city government. The number of students expanded from 300, occupying six classrooms initially, to about 2,640 thirty years later, totaling fifty-eight classrooms. In 1990, the faculty and administrative staff members numbered 139. Overall, it was an average-sized urban school.

Peiying is one of ten state schools in Hsinchu, and the principal of the school there then, Mr. Xu, had served three years there, having been appointed directly by the provincial Board of Education (*jiaoyu ting*), where he served prior to being principal. Despite its appearance on the surface, the school was anything but an island unto itself. Academic development and school activities were tightly coordinated at three levels of bureaucracy from the Ministry of Education (*jiaoyu bu*) down to provincial Board of Education (*jiaoyu ting*) and local Bureaus of Education (*jiaoyu ju*). Even education was not the exclusive domain of the school but one of many various supporting institutions, which included county or municipal cultural centers (*shili wenhua zhongxin*), Anti-Communist Youth Corps (*jiuguo tuan*), Committee for Cultural Renaissance (*wenhua fuxing weiyanhui*), and PTA family associations (*jiazhang weiyanhui*). The internal administrative structure of the school mirrored the fact that the school was only one node in a tightly knit network. To facilitate vertical integration, each administrative unit in the school answered directly to higher levels of office within the Education bureaucracy. The provincial level Board of Education was composed of twelve divisions (*ke*), which included a secretarial division, military training division, general administration division, personnel division, financial division, and academic supervision division that had local offices down to the lowest levels. Educational policy at the county or municipal level was subdivided into five sections: general academic affairs, national education, social education, physical education, and academic personnel affairs. Within this hierarchy, municipal-level bureaus of education coordinated the activities of a broad spectrum of institutions, such as schools, libraries, social education agencies, youth corps groups, extracurricular activity committees, and cultural renaissance movement committees. The head of the local Bureau of Education was the administrator in charge of putting into practice educational policy originating from above.

Vertical integration of all administrative divisions from the highest levels of educational bureaucracy to its lowest-level agencies enabled official notices to be distributed seamlessly throughout the system and *uniform* policy to be implemented at all schools. Not surprisingly then, one would also expect the physical and social organization of the school to conform to the same overall patterns and principles. Within such a system, innovation and individuality were unwelcome elements that actually disrupted the effective flow of things and activities.

Perhaps the most significant aspect of spatial and temporal organization of the school is its compactness and an environment that is formed to maximize productivity of movement and work. Its linearity and functionality are obvious; peoples' work lives are also organized in a way that deliberately leaves little space for idle time. The main campus is a rectangular enclosure that occupies 39,755 square meters total. Its fifty-eight classrooms and various administrative offices as well as science laboratories and library are largely spread across four rows of two- to three-story concrete buildings. Two long rows of buildings run parallel to each other across the long rectangular flat campus. Two other short rows of buildings are situated perpendicular to each other along the front and side ends of the campus in a way that envelops the rectangular public space in the center of campus. The main entrance, which faces a major road and is at the base of a small incline on which the campus rests, actually faces north (unlike Chinese ritual artifices, there is no particular directionality for schools). It is situated to one side of the center and opens into a short row of classroom buildings to the right, a large rectangular grass court directly in front, and the auditorium and large meeting hall complex to the left. The rectangular grass court, which is the only large public space on campus, is marked by the placement of three statues. The first one to be encountered, which is situated in the middle of the walkway that leads up from the main entrance, is a statue of Confucius. Further up the concrete walkway in the direction of administrative offices that occupy one end of the first row of long buildings, is a bronze statue of Sun Yat-sen. In the center of the rectangular grass court is a statue of Chiang Kai-shek. Classrooms are clustered according to year. Year-one (grade 7) student classrooms occupy the front row of buildings closest to the main entrance; year-two and year-three students' classrooms run sequentially along a line within the campus. The administrative wing of offices is somewhat centrally located, in that it is the first set of offices one encounters when walking directly from the main entrance up the concrete walkway. It is composed of the principal's office and the school archival office on the first floor, which is surrounded on the ground floor directly below by a general administration office, academic affairs office, extracurricular activities office, student counseling office and teachers' offices, joined by the personnel office and financial affairs office in an adjacent wing. Science labs and special function rooms such as the computer lab, music conservatory and art room are located on various parts of the campus. The track field and sports ground, which is used for schoolwide assemblies, is located on the plateau above the main campus and is enclosed by surrounding hills. By the school's own assessment, there is a shortage of classrooms and special function rooms for students, not to mention specialized sports facilities and technical classrooms. In short, the spatial organization of the school exudes a sense of hierarchy, much of which is expected or obvious. The clearest separation is that between students and school staff. There is no sense of private space but instead different kinds of public or collective spaces. Its architectural design is functional by maximizing *use* value; its public spaces are *politicized*. Teachers have desks in large, shared offices that are arranged in rows. Students sit in numbered seats allocated by the teacher according to rank.

Staff members also occupy particular niches within this spatial organization, and they can be differentiated according to rank and in terms of the respective trajectories that define the course of the work. Of the 139 full-time staff, 132 are considered permanent employees, including the principal, 118 teaching faculty, within which 58 concurrently serve as tutorial supervisors, 13 serve as administrators in the school bureaucracy, and 47 are engaged only in full-time teaching. There are also 13 full-time nonacademic clerical staff members, and the remaining 7 nonpermanent full-time employees are custodians, who may perform a number of miscellaneous duties. Of those involved in administration, in addition to the principal, five hold positions as division heads (*zhuren*), twelve are section chiefs (*zhuzhang*), five are clerks (*ganshi*), and three are classed as assistants (*zhuliyuan*). Finally, there is at least one military supervisor (*jiaoguan*), a uniformed officer who is usually appointed directly by the armed forces. Although the role of military supervisors has declined over the years, they have been a permanent fixture in most schools beginning from the intermediate level, where courses in military training begin to be taught, up to the university level, where they serve in secular capacity as masters of student dormitories and assist in security. In the middle school, they are often called on to serve as school policemen and to act as disciplinary (in Chinese called *xundao*, "training and guidance") advisors, whose role is more often one of putting juvenile delinquents in place instead of offering psychological help. The existence of such military supervisors and the principal, who is appointed by the Board or Bureau of Education and not the school, clearly illustrates the direct involvement of government bureaucracy and military in the operation of the school. While many school principals are themselves former teachers, they are in fact a class of bureaucrats who rarely return to teaching. Their periodic training (*shouxun*) consists more of insuring that they are politically correct (being active members of the Party) and are in tune with various policies handed down from the Ministry of Education.

Of the thirteen nonacademic clerical staff, the four involved in the personnel and financial accounting divisions were considered specialist jobs, but this is a misnomer that reflects the different routes of specialization that actually mark the work of different kinds of personnel. There is, on the one hand, a distinct barrier between academic and nonacademic staff in terms of their formal training. Academic faculty usually have academic degrees that qualify them in specific fields of learning, and most gain promotion on the basis of work performance instead of advanced degree learning. Nonacademic clerical staff have their own formal merit criteria that may suffice as certificate qualification, which they can attain by passing clerical civil service examinations (*gaokao*), but the majority of the non-academic clerical staff rarely pass such exams and move up the system on the basis of work experience (or apprenticeship). Especially among those in the older generation, many could have worked up to positions of high administrative responsibility as a result of long years of apprenticeship, starting from low entry-level jobs. There is a gray area within the administrative bureaucracy that marks the boundary between administrators who have become division or section heads as a result of full-time clerical work and academics who also serve as head of administrative units such as library or academic management on the basis of their overall leadership quality.

While the spatial organization of the school exudes an atmosphere of total containment and internal separation between different strata of people, the mobility of people within the social system, based on general distinctions between academic staff, administrative clerks, and political appointees, is in reality more fluid. Curricular and extracurricular activities usually entail coordination and intense cooperation between all categories of people. Work tends to be based on principles of functional *integration* instead of functional specialization. Teachers do not merely teach. They actively take part in organizing extracurricular activities, most of which are initiated directly from the Board of Education, and spend much time supervising students and liaising with parents. Military supervisors do not just teach military training courses. They also serve as campus police and are present at all school activities, especially when called on to exert "authority." The school principal

also straddles many roles, not only as a role model of the ultimate educator but also in internal administrative functions and as interlocutor within
various outside educational and government agencies. In school activities
and sports contests, government agencies routinely send representatives to
"attend" these events to underscore their role as omnipresent sponsors and
promotional cheerleaders. Active participation by all walks of people in
school activities makes education by nature an act of socialization. Education is not just about knowledge. This knowledge is officially sanctioned to
conform to standards and political correctness. Most extracurricular activities are similarly *mandated* from above and organized to promote spiritual
education (*jingshen jiaoyu*) and cultural enlightenment of all kinds, rather
than strict competition and professional sports achievement per se. There is
no school activity that does not entail active involvement by people inside
and outside. The practice of education makes it socializing.

The temporal organization of the daily schedule is also tightly regulated
and leaves little space for personal activity. From 7:00 a.m. to 7:20 a.m. students are expected to come to school, and other "on-duty" students are seen
sweeping the school ground and picking up trash. Homeroom is from 7:20
a.m. to 7:50 a.m., during which time students are supposed to be reading. The
flag-raising ceremony is from 7:50 a.m. to 8:10 a.m., during which all students
report to the sports field, standing in class formation to observe the raising
of the flag. At this time, the principal usually makes a daily speech. He is
then followed by the disciplinary adviser (*xundao zhuren*), who makes assorted
announcements, after which the academic adviser speaks (*jiaowu zhuren*), if
necessary. While this goes on, the military supervisor monitors students' dress
and hairstyle to pick out students who do not conform. From 8:10 a.m. to
12:00 a.m., there are four successive class periods, each of which is separated
by ten-minutes intersession. After lunch (12:00 p.m. to 1:00 p.m.), there are
three successive class periods from 1:10 p.m. to 4:00 p.m. (with an additional
hour for tutorial supervision or makeup examinations). On Saturday, there
is another half-day of classes, mostly devoted to extracurricular and tutorial
activities. There are generally no free or elective class periods.

Spatial containment, social hierarchy, and temporal regulation characterize the essential framework by which to understand the ritualized behaviors and etiquettes that represent the nature of social relations between
teachers and students, as well as between staff members and the system.
While the educational system makes students the object of socializing discipline, with teachers and staff being agents of that system, the system also
disciplines staff members as well, in the process of work, through similar
regimes of supervision and evaluation. These disciplinary regimes operate in
parallel, but they are largely predicated by similar principles.

The kind of behavior that epitomizes the relationship of students to teachers and staff in the school can be properly called etiquette. *Etiquette* is not just another term for manners (*limao*) or ritual demeanor (*liyi*), but invokes instead Elias's (1978) conception of it—an expressive behavior whose ritualized restraint is largely the end product of social control of sentiment, as both phylogenetic and ontogenetic processes. Student-teacher relationships are symbolized by a face-to-face decorum and attitude of veneration, which reflect mutual hierarchical difference. Decorum dictates that students greet teachers (*laoshi*), when meeting each other face to face. This applies not just to teachers they know personally but also to all teachers in general. Etiquette also extends to behavioral norms that are the product of disciplinary routines of the system. Etiquette means in this regard knowing when to be silent (*sujing*) and when to speak (*biaotai*). It means conforming militarily to authority in some contexts and being religiously supportive in other contexts. A more accurate way of explaining the kind of etiquette that is cultivated is to say that the ultimate goal of such socialization (ultimately acculturation, through the inculcation of core cultural values) is one of learning how to "act as a person" (*zuoren*). "Acting as a person" is not just a cliché for behaving properly, but more precisely acting appropriately in ways that are consistent with norms and situations. In essence, citizenship and morality (*gongmin yu daode*) form the content of moral education, but the practice of moral behavior as everyday etiquette is the goal of this sino-socialization.

The role of and pressures on teachers and staff in the system must also be understood in light of the same morally regulative regime of discipline, through its enforcement of spatial orders and temporal schedules. The way in which people survive, adapt, and move through the system is also a function of the way they perform or are expected to perform. In essence, the same system of domination and vertical integration that puts students in their place can be seen to put other people in their place as well. Their everyday behavior and ritual demeanor must be seen in the context and as a direct product of a total institutional discipline.

In both processes of socialization, the emphasis is less on work performance in the sense of productive efficiency than moral reward or spiritual gain (*xinde*). Constant self-evaluation through writing of reports places a premium on making conscious one's personal reflections on work and study. The focus from within on moral cultivation is consistent with Confucian values, as invoked in Three Principles Education. However, the focus from above on total regulation is a product of a modern regime of discipline, enhanced by inherent militarization and Cold War politicization. Seen together, they constitute the crux of nationalizing impulses that are characteristic of Taiwan's cultural imagination of a Republic of China and its values.

Learning to Culturalize: Identity as Assimilation

The recent advent of Taiwanese cultural indigenization that, for many, was epitomized by the election of the first president from the (Taiwanese independence leaning) Democratic Progressive Party (DPP) has had considerable impact on the nature and continuing destiny of Three Principles Education, at least in government policy-making circles. Three Principles Education had always been linked with rule of the Nationalist (KMT) Party, not only for its efforts to memorialize the legacy of Sun Yat-sen and his ideology but also for the KMT's staunch defense of the Republic of China as against an independent Taiwan (i.e., "The Three Principles is what unifies China" [*sanminzhuyi tongyi zhongguo*]). The rise of Taiwanese consciousness is a complex historical phenomenon that was promoted not only by Taiwanese independence activists but also by the dominant Taiwanese faction within the KMT. Three Principles Education had already been the subject of criticism in the last decade but became officially reviewed and revised after the election of Chen Shui-bian, the first opposition party president. The major result of it was the introduction of a set of courses titled Knowing Taiwan (*renshi taiwan*).[12] Yet the corpus of existing courses on body and health, citizenship and ethics, military training, and Sun Yat-sen's thought ironically did not change substantially.

Recent changes in the nature of Three Principles Education indicate that the discourse of mandatory education has centered mostly on the primacy of defining national identity (either as part of China or a culturally, historically distinct Taiwan) and focused less on the nation's abstract understanding of citizenship and ethics. Not surprisingly, the unchanged substance of existing courses indicates that the new regime's relationship to the nation and the practice of nation building has remained unchanged for most part as well. The role of the school as an agent of socialization has remained active as ever, the normalizing routines that constituted everyday etiquette go on as usual, and the relationships of power that bound the school to the state and its subsidiary units continue to reinforce each other. Its politicization in substance has not affected its routinization of form. What does this then say about forms and practices?

Moral education, as inculcated above all in Three Principles Education, goes beyond the explicit content of course teachings and everyday etiquette. It is also replicated in various extracurricular activities organized by the Disciplinary Office (*xundao chu*), whose overlap in content has to do with the fact that such activities are labeled a part of "honesty education" (*chengshi jiaoyu*).[13] The Bureau of Education holds activities relating to honesty education at least once a month. During academic year 1991–92, this started with an announcement, on September 26, from the Bureau of Education citing "Ministry of Education Special Action Plans to implement the strengthening of honesty education at all school levels." This was followed, on October 8, by the Disciplinary Office's installation of an "Honesty Opinion Box" (*chengshi yijianxiang*) and the establishment of "Public Statutes on Honesty" (*chengshi gongyue*). The Bureau of Education, on October 17, then issued a register of names of heads for committees "to strengthen the promotion of honesty education" and a notice from the Board of Education "detailing matters for the supervision of honesty education activities by Bureau of Education officers." Saturday discussion groups (*banhui*), on October 26, organized forums on honesty education. Officials from both the Ministry and Board of Education, on October 29, visited the school to view results of the promotion of honesty education activities. The Office on Social Education (*shejiao guan*) sent a letter on the same day to organize an "honest spirit, happy spirit" (*chengshi xin, kuaile xin*) activity in relation with Ministry of Education directives. The Disciplinary Office's Bulletin of November 2 then asked tutors to use three to five minutes in class to announce honesty education activities. The Disciplinary Office, on November 3, set up a column on the corridor bulletin board to display news of honesty education activities. The Social Education Office sent a letter, on November 4, planning a forum discussion on honesty education. The Bureau of Education sent a letter, on November 7, announcing that "honesty education" should be included in the promotional activities of family education (*jiating jiaoyu*). The Bureau of Education sent a letter, on November 16, to explain assessment guidelines regarding special action plans to strengthen honesty education in primary and secondary schools. The Disciplinary Office, on November 17, held an art competition in relation to honesty education. The Bureau of Education sent a letter, on November 21, to hold "honest spirit, happy spirit" writing competitions. It also sent, on November 29, a letter to announce the fifth theme of Hsinchu's literary education (leisure education and honesty education). It then sent, on December 4, a timetable and report form to monitor honesty education activities in all schools. It circulated to students, on December 4, bookmarks printed by the Ministry of Education bearing the word "honesty" (*chengshi*). The Office of Social Education sent, on December 24, a further notice on "honest spirit, happy spirit" writing competitions. The Bureau of Education then sent the Ministry of Education guidelines for promoting honesty education. In this set of guidelines to implement honesty education, on December 26, the Bureau of Education exhorts the school to be vigilant of cheating, observe traffic rules and uphold respect for teachers. Jianguo Middle School sent a letter, on December 30, to propose an open forum to exchange ideas and experiences on honesty education.

The frequency, intensity, and coordination of activities pertaining to "honesty education" ultimately illustrate how moral education in a broad sense is used to encompass all manner of actions and behavior that are nonetheless linked with school life. Its implementation also transcends the work of each institution. Institutions interact not only in regard to activities but also abstract processes. More than defining conditions of modernity, the nation-state has welded the function of the school as a disciplinary regime to other parallel institutions.[14] The same kinds of socialization can be seen to take place generally in other countries, but culture plays an important part here by specifying the framework of power in which various social institutions interact and overlap. It is too much of a cliché, following Rohlen's (1976) study of Japan's high schools, to characterize Asian educational systems simply as collectivist, in the way it fosters both conformity to group consciousness, through deference to authority and peer group pressure, and uniform standards of education, reinforced by an all-determining monolithic exam system.[15] The Confucian notion of filial piety (*xiao*) encompasses various kinds of social hierarchies between ruler and subject, teacher and student, father and son, and employer and employee, as a function of the same essential ethical bonds that mirror or work in conjunction with each other. It is not surprising thus that the state, school, family, and the workplace function in the same way (as socializing regimes) by reinforcing each other as a process through long-term cultivation of the same kind of ethos, norms, and etiquette.

As has already been described in the case of Japanese schools, harmonious relationships between teacher and student rely heavily on teachers forming good working relationships with parents, who are viewed as an extension of classroom teaching as well as the first line of communication in matters of student behavior and performance. Parents are expected to be an active participant in assisting with a child's education, thus are seen as morally responsible to some extent for his or her successes and failures. Perhaps like Japan, in Taiwan the brunt of this responsibility usually falls on the mother, especially if she is a housewife who is in charge of domestic affairs. Her role in actively supervising homework is, on the other hand, largely a function of the excessive amount of schoolwork that is usually assigned to students, beginning from primary school and accelerating up to the years preceding "examination hell." However, the symbiotic relationship between family and the state is in this regard a function of the fact that these institutions view themselves as being based on the same ethical principles thus should play supporting roles in the larger social order of things. Peer pressure or allegiance to political authority is less relevant than their ethical form and social practice.

Insofar as activities of the school and the Bureau of Social Education overlap (through coordination and direct supervision by the Ministry of Education or its local bureaus), one might say that there is already a strong institutional working relationship between the school and various government institutions regarding education in general. The school has explicit functions to promote "social education" by taking leadership roles in community education or social service in much the same way that families are mobilized as an extension of classroom learning. This includes (1) the advancement of citizenship training and lectures on improving various aspects of national life while making available school facilities to residential groups for certain sports and leisure activities; and (2) the offering of guidance on matters pertaining to public health, emergency training, air defense, prevention of epidemics, and dissemination of public information on events and activities. According to policies of the Executive Yuan, on April 8, 1965, themes included within the domain of community services performed by the school include social insurance, employment, social assistance, public housing, welfare services, social education, and community development. The school is an *activist* in local life.

In ontogenetic terms, military service is in many ways a continuation of the socialization process patterned in school. In addition to military and physical training, conscripts spend time in the classroom. *Shouxun* (literally "undergo training") here means more precisely undergoing the same kinds of spiritual indoctrination and political correctness that is part of learning as a whole. The exact proportion of classroom training tends to be much higher for officers undertaking military service (graduates of military academies as well as postgraduate degree holders in general) than for regular recruits. The term *shouxun* is also used to refer to periodic training that people in the workplace undergo, especially after gaining promotion or transfer to new positions. Classroom work includes not only learning of required skills but also doing reports, written and oral, where one is typically forced to express one's feelings of accomplishment (*baogao xinde*). In a military context, allegiance is based just as much on political correctness as moral substance. Both become intricately intertwined in the end.

Ultimately, the kind of socialization (with its emphasis on moral cultivation in a Taiwan context) seen in the routinization of school life and military service forms the rudiments of a disciplinary regime that is in many ways replicated and expanded on in various kinds of workplaces. It is impossible to generalize on the nature of the latter, given the diversity of institutions that characterize any enterprise (civil service, private corporate, family firm, not to mention its urban-rural setting and cultural (Chinese, Western, and Japanese) influences), but in the case of the school it is clear that teachers, clerks, and administrators are disciplined and socialized in a work setting in ways that are similar to the way students are "subjected" (if not objectified as well). Not only does the work regime reflect the moral regulation of a school as a particular kind of workplace but also the influences of other institutions (the state and various bureaucratic appendages) that constantly control, nurture, and interact with it.

In sum, the ethnography of everyday practice and the role of cultural values and norms in sustaining them are not just objective descriptions of life, as though taken for granted matters of fact. The school is in the long run a microcosm of routines that form the pattern of ritual behavior and normative worldview that in turn shape cultural identity in relation to the polity. Their politicization, explicit and implicit, makes them anything *but* neutral. Their hegemonic omnipresence makes their fact-ive existence problematic, if anything. It might be easier to argue, from a different perspective, that what we see in ethnographic fact is the end result of the complex interplay of socially abstract forces, which through elaborate processes of imagination and systematic regulation in practice produce fictions (that one *mistakenly* calls cultural reality). Through identification with these values and behaviors, one ultimately identifies with the underlying imagined community and one's role in it. In this regard, ethnographic description can be used not just to represent society, as though objective, but rather as a first step that ultimately informs the reflexive, critical project of cultural studies.

In Taiwan, nation-state as imagined community has invoked more specifically complex ethical visions of a polity, ideologically driven or discursively framed in policy and practice, that in turn precipitated disciplinary, socializing regimes of life thought and routine.

Chapter 3

The Coming Crisis of Multiculturalism

When the Imagined Community Hits the Fan

> A multiculturalism for which the unity of a given culture counts as an
> established fact is still a disguised monoculturalism . . . Multicultural-
> ism must not be a culturalism. It must be concerned neither with the
> mere conservation of the purported integrity of cultures, nor with their
> mere perpetuation. A culture that does this, that is not active—even if
> inexplicably and in a mediated fashion—as a protest against social and
> political injustice and which does not stand for a social and political
> praxis of justice is nothing but an amusement park, a technique of
> entertainment, "garbage," as Adorno writes.
>
> —Werner Hamacher, "One 2 Many Multiculturalisms"

Contrary to official, internationally recognized definitions, I argue that Taiwan may very well be the first "transnational nation." Few noticed its presence internationally, until it became a major exporter to the world economy,
which was a change of policy prompted largely by its expulsion from the
United Nations (and diplomatic recognition of the PRC). Its subsequent
attempts to jockey for admission into the United Nations can largely be
seen as a strategy to build on its newly established role as a world economic
player. One significant feature of transnational capitalism is reflected in
Taiwan's success, which demonstrates that the official status of nation was
not important or relevant to its success in economic and other terms. Thus,
in an era of transnational flows, one might say, national identity, cultural
consciousness, and territorial boundedness are clearly secondary. In some

This is an updated version of "The Coming Crisis of Multiculturalism in 'Transnational'
Taiwan," *Social Analysis: The International Journal of Cultural and Social Practice* 46(2):102–22,
initially published in 2002.

senses, this seems to be true, but this is overly simplistic. The end of organized capitalism, as advocated by Lash and Urry (1987), has led many to
believe that the free flow of capital has broken down national barriers in
respect to all other kinds of flows, but in fact transnational flows of people
have been regulated by and subject to other kinds of forces, political as well
as cultural in nature, that have disrupted emerging forms of cosmopolitanism and threatened to expose conservative, if not reactionary, biases in the
constitution of traditional society.[1] In Taiwan, the growing emergence of
transnational cosmopolitanism has run parallel with the increasing rhetorical
importance of multiculturalism. But the latter is the product more precisely of a wave of "indigenization." At a deeper level, both (cosmopolitan)
"transnationalism" and (indigenous) "multiculturalism" are in my opinion
incompatible and mask an imminent future crisis.

The Illusion of "Multiculturalism" in a Newly "Indigenized" Taiwan

Multiculturalism is "in." As an official policy, the advent of multiculturalism (*duoyuan wenhua zhuyi*) seems to have been a phenomenon that culminated with, among other things, the election of the first president from
the opposition Democratic Progressive Party (DPP). Its advent marked a
formal recognition of multicultural or multiethnic equality. Only a mere
decade ago, Hou Hsiao-hsien's acclaimed film *City of Sadness* dared to invoke
memories of the holocaust of February 28, 1947 (called 2-28), in which
soldiers acting under orders of a newly installed Chinese Nationalist (KMT)
regime massacred thousands of Taiwanese under the pretense of suppressing
political rebellion. What is astonishing in retrospect is that, even though
local viewers knew that the events depicted were of 2-28, nowhere in the
film is 2-28 explicitly mentioned. Even in the early years of postmartial law
Taiwan, such a topic was still largely regarded as taboo. Much has changed
since then, of course. Not long afterward, demonstrations lambasting the
era of "white terror" (*baishe kongbu*) took place. President Lee Teng-hui
later publicly apologized for the tragedy of 2-28, prompting the declassifica-
tion of highly secret police archives on the subject, then open support for
multiculturalism rapidly spread in further light of the KMT government's
official (post-1988) tolerance of dissent. Not only did it become politically
correct to promote Taiwanese culture and consciousness; support of other
ethnic minorities, in particular Hakka Chinese and Austronesian aborigines,
benefited as well. The election of President Chen Shui-bian, whose Party
platform was based on a policy of ethnic equality, was thus the culmination
of a process already in the making.[2]

In actuality, support for multiple ethnic identities had always been on the rise, and such long-term events could be seen as a culmination of an even longer-term process of political transformation and discursive mutation within the KMT Party, beginning in the late 1970s. The trend toward recognition of local Taiwanese identity and ethnic rights was a switch in position from the staunch monocultural nationalist policies of the KMT, which was not just predicated on a Republic of China that tried to subordinate regional ethnic differences within a larger civilizational fold but more importantly subjected native Taiwanese to the rule of "outsider" ethnic Chinese. At the same time, such multiculturalism was a facet of Taiwan's broader *political* indigenization that directly followed from its expulsion from the United Nations and a policy to promote market liberalization in the global economy. In this sense, multiculturalism represented the recognition of diverse cultural or ethnic identities as basic political right, but this embrace of multicultural principles was more precisely a product of *indigenization* (Taiwan for native Taiwanese) as a principle of ethnic equality. The growing influence of a Taiwanese faction in the KMT led by Lee Teng-hui, following in the footsteps of President Chiang Ching-kuo, simply accelerated eventual adoption of multiculturalism.[3] In the process, the Ministry of Education took a major first step by establishing departments in teachers' colleges devoted specifically to the study and teaching of multiculturalism.[4]

One must qualify the notion of multiculturalism used here by saying that it probably did not refer to some inherently universal embrace of worldly values, which is usually invoked by such a term, but rather something whose meaning was largely a function of the speaker's local frame of reference. Due to its association with indigenization in Taiwan, the meaning of multiculturalism could be rendered simply as a principle of equality for ethnic minorities, but it did not by definition embrace all of humanity. In a postcolonial setting such as Great Britain or the melting pot of the United States, multiculturalism was juxtaposed semantically against the tradition of essentialist cultural regimes but pragmatically in a domestic context that now endeavored to recognize or incorporate the existence of nonnative cultures (or ethnicities). In Taiwan, multiculturalism was semantically juxtaposed against a monoculturalist national regime but pragmatically in a context that only attempted to recognize or incorporate internal others. Multiculturalism became in other words a closed, *inward*-looking concept.

Similarly, one illusion created by the advent of postmodern theory was the misleading assumption that it had liberated the multiple identities in us all. However, multiculturalism is hardly a new *phenomenon*. Most societies from time immemorial have been multicultural or multiethnic. The reason why we view multiculturalism and multiple identities as inherently new is the fact that, in a short history of nationalism, we have come to believe that persons ipso facto have a notion of identity built on the assumption of *shared* values, a *collective* conscience and *common* traditions. The intensity of postmodernity's search for hybridity and multiple identities is in the first instance less a function of the apparent proliferation of (latent) multiculturalism as a phenomenon everywhere than of *problematic* notions endemic to the nation-state's standard definition of culture and the state's need to discursively erase de facto ethnic or cultural differences, which has in turn prompted a need to transcend them.

The resurgence (of a *discourse*) of multiculturalism within a context of transnationalism has given the advent of borderless economies, glocal identities, and free flows of ideas and technologies (following global capital) everywhere the added impression that amorphous transnational flows of people will eventually dissolve territorial rootedness and place-based identities altogether.[5] New waves of migration to the United States and (to a lesser extent) Europe have witnessed inflows of Mexican, Caribbean, or Turkish laborers; Asian engineers; Filipino domestics; and astronaut expatriate businesspeople.[6] These movements have intensified with the general demise of centrally planned economies, relaxation of customs tariffs, and lifting of travel restrictions throughout the world. In this recently evolved "mode" of transnational capitalism, core-periphery relations, and implicit cultural imperialism that have characterized the modern world system in a previous era have clearly been replaced by the blurring of once-pristine cultural origins and discrete identities. Given Taiwan's active integration within the global capitalist order, there was every reason to think that these same transnational flows of people seen elsewhere should bring about the advent of a similar multiculturalism.

The process of globalization that has been invoked by transnationalism in the sense of chaotic flows of capital, ideas, and people (or scapes in Appadurai's terms[7]) can be attributed in large part specifically to the mutations of this changing global capitalism, but contrary to assumptions of inherent disorganization the flows of various commodities were unequal and tended to be regulated by different processes and powers. Thus, the process of glocalization has heretofore been seen as an attribute of the inherent disorganization and hybridity brought about by the global "system" instead of the selective process of cultural synthesis itself.

What Is a "Foreigner," or the Politics of Ongoing Nationality Debates

Recent social scientific work (especially in anthropology) has followed the "discovery" of globalization by shifting the primary frame of analytical ref-

erence away from the totality of self-contained societies to a more explicitly transnational, comparative perspective (and its functional disjunctures),
without really giving explanatory force to the selectivity of culture as an
actively appropriating and synthesizing factor in glocal interaction. The
sociopolitical ground (of which geopolitical forces and market demand are
seminal factors) constitutes, of course, a primary basis for the functioning
of ongoing institutional processes. However at the same time, this ground
can in different cultural contexts be perceived (and has in fact always been
mediated or accommodated) in different ways.[8]

Discursive constructions of social reality can run counter to how the
latter appears to be functionally constituted, and Taiwan's experience is a
good case in point. Taiwan has made a quick transition to a free market
economy largely by successfully integrating itself into the transnational capitalist order, which in the process thus dismantled a preexisting centralized
economy based on protectionist barriers and strict border controls. Yet in
local discourse, its success seemed to be attributed less to Taiwan's increasing
integration to the global system than to the inherent values of Confucian
discipline, democratization, or growth of indigenous Taiwanese consciousness. Similarly, despite Taiwan's de facto independence (in matters of institutional and social life) from the PRC since 1949, it was not until Presidential
elections in 2000 that all political parties in Taiwan actually recognized its
"political separateness" from the mainland, primarily as a means of deflecting the importance of countering China's right of sovereignty. In large part,
the Republic of China has still continued as a legal and institutional fact in
Taiwan long after it became a fiction in international diplomatic circles, thus
the deep ongoing investment in this fiction has been in the long run the
major obstacle to official recognition of its de facto political independence
in everyday social life.

The discursive fiction of the "Republic of China" as the protector of
traditional Chinese civilization (vis-à-vis the People's Republic) has also run
parallel to its other image as the embodiment of modern scientific values in
a Chinese context. Even more puzzling, the staunch monocultural nationalism that buttressed modern nation-state formation in postwar Taiwan has
run parallel to the KMT's ongoing defense of dual nationality (which may
be construed in literal terms as a recognition of multiple national identity).
In the context of the recent advent of transnationalism, it is significant to
carefully scrutinize how the coincidence of dual nationality with these other
forms of cultural conservatism has in fact exposed various contradictions in
Chinese cultural conceptions of identity and nationality (and its underlying
politics), which can in turn be used to shed new light on the current crisis
of multiculturalism in a newly transnational Taiwan.

The theme of Sinophobia seems to be a staple feature in (Western) textbooks of Chinese history, which has conveniently explained China's encounter with the West and the nature of its subsequent transition to modernity. In more recent times, it can perhaps be exemplified by the period of Maoist isolation and in the current renaissance of Chinese nationalist fervor. Such a concept of Sinophobia underscores a dualistic notion of us versus them, whether it be East versus West, inner versus outer, or native versus foreigner. No concept of nationality or citizenship can do without some basic notion of insider-outsider dualism that presumably corresponds with fixed definitions of boundary, and in the Chinese case one can easily sense an even sharper sense of cultural dualism. If anything, the concept of "foreigner" should be anything but ill defined. However, despite the rhetoric, there are many layers of ambiguity (or ambivalence) in cultural and legal terms that mark Chinese understandings of self and other, and especially in postwar Taiwan these ambiguities have provoked repeated attempts to institute a rational policy of nationality prone to heated contestation, irresolvable failures, and amendments of a patchwork nature.[9] In the final analysis, like the problematic notion of identity, these crises reflected less problems in definitions of "ethnicity" per se (which were fraught with enough inconsistencies of their own) than underlying (and often changing) political considerations that not only affected multiple boundaries that actually separated various notions of self from other but also highlighted the socially stratified connotations that were embedded in most, if not all, definitions of foreigner. Despite the legal clarity that typically cloaks a definition of citizenship (hence, by contrast foreignness), there is perhaps no nation in which the requisites of these definitions did not change, and continued change accented the fact that such laws regularly responded to changing political situations. Moreover, cultural definitions of self and other did not derive wholly from legal definitions; this was an added source of confusion.

A more appropriate way of explaining why Chinese might have a dualistic notion of self versus other that contributes (in an extreme case) to a sense of phobia would be to say that such dualism per se is more precisely the product (or the perception) of a colonial situation instead of an a priori cultural definition. If anything, such colonialism is largely political by nature and can be exacerbated by the imposition of other overlapping notions of boundary. The paradox that has ultimately confounded a national definition of Chineseness in the Cold War era actually has to do with the fictive status of the "Republic of China," which is a definition of political legitimacy instead of legality per se. While the international community may recognize the difference between a PRC and ROC passport, technically Taiwanese would consider it inappropriate to call people on mainland China "foreigners" (*waiguo ren*). If one adopted the official jargon at the time, they would be "Communist bandits" (*gongfei*), just as products originating from the PRC would be labeled "bandit goods" (*feihuo*) and the country Communist China (*zhonggong*). If the latter was a nation, it would be at best an illegitimate one and not an other. The neutral terms *mainland* (*dalu*) and *mainlander* (or *mainland compatriot, dalu tongbao*) were not considered acceptable until the late 1980s, after Cold War tensions had already waned and trade/contact restrictions were considerably relaxed.

The status of Hong Kong was perhaps even more ambiguous. While it was recognized to be under British control, it was not considered a separate nation by any official definition. Thus (prior to 1997), ROC citizens did not need to use a passport to go to Hong Kong, but they still needed a visa (issued by Hong Kong authorities). Like the PRC, Hong Kong was not considered a "foreign" country in either official or popular parlance, and its people were just called Hong Kongers, while neither of the dualistic terms used to describe being "inside the country" (*guonei*), that is, domestically, or being "outside the country" (*guowai*), that is, going abroad, was applicable to Hong Kong. One could only say that one is going to Hong Kong.

Legally speaking, possession of a national identity card (*shenfenzheng*) was probably the clearest proof of "citizenship," but possession of a card number was conditional on having permanent household registration (*huji*) somewhere, this being a survival of the Japanese colonial administration system. Citizenship, as inscribed on one's identity card or passport, was certainly one indicator of whether one was "foreign" or not, but it might not be the most important or relevant one. To a fervent nationalist, this status may be important, but in other contexts it was usually difficult to determine whether foreignness (or Chineseness) referred to one's nationality or cultural identification. For official purposes, since the ROC had always recognized dual nationality, one's nationality mattered less as a fixture of the person than as element of supervisory control. As far as Immigration and Customs Bureaus were concerned, the only thing that mattered was what passport one used to enter and exit the country. A condition of maintaining ROC citizenship was that one had to use an ROC passport to enter and exit Taiwan, and control over exit and entry permits was what kept citizens in line, as long as they were in the country. In the same way, attaining citizenship was just a prerequisite for registering one's household residence (*huji*), which was in effect the agency for monitoring one's movements within the country.

This might then lead one to ask: Who is eligible to attain ROC citizenship? At the risk of pushing it to the extreme, one can say generally that it is unusual for non-Chinese to apply for or to be granted citizenship. This obviously raises the sloppier question of how one defines being

"Chinese." In legal or other terms, there have never been good, unequivocal criteria for determining who qualified as being Chinese, but this was another way of saying that any acceptable standard (blood or descent tie) only constituted a *minimal* criterion for attaining citizenship. Given that there were Chinese everywhere (PRC, Hong Kong, and overseas), ethnicity was obviously a minor, if not insignificant, criterion for determining citizenship *in the long run*. If a wealthy overseas Chinese businessperson wished to become a legislator, or if a Hong Kong scholar was offered employment as a professor in a National University, they would generally find it easier (if not automatic) to obtain citizenship than a transient laborer. Thus, civil servants and those with official capacity in government service were expected to become citizens, but this was a means of invoking privileges as well as of maximizing control over those in roles of official responsibility. Otherwise, the rules and conditions for other kinds of people have always been complex and ever changing, depending on one's original abode, occupational status, length of residence, and so on. Rules were obviously different for mainland Chinese, Hong Kongers, and other overseas Chinese, and they have always changed to reflect changing political situations and exigencies. Being quintessentially political, nationality was hardly a good criterion of "Chineseness."

As far as Chineseness is concerned, it mattered little whether an overseas Chinese was a Chinese national or not, since overseas Chinese was an independent legal status, which was determined in part by whether one "identified" as such and in part by residence conditions that stipulated whether such a person was entitled to remain in Taiwan (for work, study, or other purposes). Those who opted to be overseas Chinese (regardless of citizenship) were in turn regulated by the Bureau of Overseas Chinese Affairs, and "Chinese" who held a foreign passport had an option of identifying as an overseas Chinese or foreigner. This might be a matter of ethnic pride for some, but it was more likely the case that people chose on the basis of whatever benefited them most. Yet most importantly, one must stress that the very term *overseas Chinese* was not just simply a Chinese who happened to live abroad, but rather a category of persons, which by virtue of historical origin had unavoidable social connotations that could change over time but did not guarantee to be value-free or timeless. This term originated in the late nineteenth century and was related to the rise of nationalism. Its political association with patriotic, diasporic Chinese has been waning over time to the extent where Chinese abroad have begun using more neutral terms, such as *huaren* and *huayu*, to denote Chinese people and Chinese language. Associations with migrant labor in a particular era of global capitalism have also stuck with the term to the point where it seemed inappropriate to use *huaqiao* to represent high-tech Chinese professionals working in Silicon Valley who have been enticed by the reverse brain drain to return to Taiwan in an elite or privileged capacity.

The use of *huaqiao* by the Sinocentric center to denote Chinese overseas will without doubt continue, despite its decreasing popularity among overseas Chinese themselves, for the simple reason that it enhances the Sino-center's sense of ethnic pride, even though the ties of political solidarity are dubious. Thus, the achievements of ethnic Chinese Corazon Aquino and Michael Chang have continued to be embraced fervently and heralded by the media, even though the source of their fame and success probably had little or nothing to do with their Chineseness. With regard to countertrends, the handover of Hong Kong by Britain back to China in 1997 resulted in the abrupt abolition of overseas Chinese status for Hong Kong and the adoption of Immigration and Customs rules that made it more difficult for Hong Kong "Special Administrative Region" passport holders to enter or travel through Taiwan, which reversed trends in the post–Cold War era. Similar arrangements then made it equally difficult for Taiwan citizens to travel to Hong Kong. For a while, it was easier for Taiwan citizens to enter PRC as "Taiwanese compatriots" (*taiwan tongbao*) than it was to go to Hong Kong, but in the long-term transition, which accepted the PRC's eventual international legitimacy, Hong Kongers traded their ambiguous status as overseas Chinese to ambiguous citizens of the PRC.

In recent years, the debate over official recognition of dual nationality has intensified. It may seem ironic, especially in light of the KMT's extreme cultural nationalist construction of the polity (as Republic of China and defender of traditional Chinese culture and civilization), that it would tacitly accept dual nationality. Such a policy was not simply to accommodate Chinese everywhere, regardless of nationality. As previously noted, nationality was guided less by ethnic principles than political imperatives. While presenting a monocultural face to the masses, who could not for the most part (at least during the Cold War era) travel in or out of the country easily, dual nationality in essence enabled privileged elites, whether they were overseas Chinese who were assimilated into civil service or children of high-ranking officials (as well as wealthy businesspeople who had the means to go abroad) to retain an exit ticket to a political safe haven in the event of war. With the explicit attempt by the government in the early 1990s in a reverse brain drain to attract Chinese abroad to return to the motherland to serve as chaired academics, technical elites, and ministers, the numbers of such dual nationals, especially in high positions of government, created an apparent crisis of identity that became increasingly inconsistent with a gradual trend toward indigenization and ethnic renaissance.[10]

In short, more important than the existence of multiculturalism itself were the strategic intents that drove the system and its policies. If anything, ethnic categories and rhetoric were superficial notions that by themselves explained little. In the final analysis, the ambivalent status of overseas Chinese could be viewed in two different ways: because ethnic Chinese can always be embraced as Chinese nationals, an option that is not open to non-Chinese, it makes the nation-state more of a primordial community that contradicts its constitution as a modern entity. Yet, on the other hand, dual nationality served in another sense to guarantee privileges of cosmopolitan multiculturalism to overseas Chinese as well as local elites seeking a safe haven on the outside, which at the same time prevented it from becoming an asset accessible to the masses, as though invoked by identity (which one expects from notions of citizenship). The political intents that drove the system also made it prone to changing needs and times.

Invasion of the Invisible Others in the Advent of Transnational Labor

Even before the advent of transnational capitalism, there had been a steady presence of "outsiders" into postwar Taiwanese society, if one not only included the gradual absorption of overseas Chinese (including from Hong Kong/Macau), but also the marginal existence of longtime resident foreigners (many of whom married local spouses, were employed and well settled). To this, one could add in recent years the massive influx of contract laborers (Filipino maids, Thai construction workers, PRC immigrants, expatriate businesspeople, technical experts, etc.), as well as increased numbers of Chinese abroad lured back by super-salary jobs and Chinese youth raised abroad who "returned" to exploit a growing niche of professional work requiring English-language fluency. All contributed in different ways to a diversified and transnational local Taiwanese economy, albeit accommodated within an ongoing stratified system.

In making sense of nationality issues and immigration policy in postwar Taiwan, one must first of all acknowledge Chinese cultural definitions of "Chinese" and "foreigner." As previously noted, while ethnic notions of Chineseness were intended to include all Chinese (however imperfectly defined), regardless of nationality, they overlapped with practices of nationality that were in essence politically motivated and largely exclusive of "foreigners." The dual nationality issue was in this sense less a debate about purging foreign status and multiculturalism per se than about purging the possible conflicts of interest precipitated by cosmopolitan elites within officialdom who held dual nationality. This predicament was the result of government policies that had from the beginning welcomed multiple "identities" into its top ranks. On the other hand, the consequences of dual nationality for average citizens and overseas Chinese were less important, except in a general discourse of national identity.

In the context of nationality, there were many kinds of foreigners, and they tended to be guided by different principles. As in English, different terms for foreigners reflected different social connotations. An "expatriate" tends to be understood, generally speaking, as a skilled technician who is sent in by a home office of a corporation or government to perform a task that a "local" is for most part incapable of performing. This term is largely the product of a colonial age, as it is normally expected that an expatriate will eventually be repatriated, thus will not (seek to) be a permanent fixture in that society. On the other hand, a foreign laborer invokes a somewhat different connotation of foreigner. Foreign labor in general is not a new phenomenon to global capitalism, which was in fact responsible for orchestrating the first major waves of ethnic migration in human history. However, the role of foreign labor has clearly been transformed by the current phase of *transnational* capitalism, characterized by disorganized flows of capital and labor, borderless economies, and the withering away of nationalist protectionism of various sorts, not to mention the most recent evolution of supra-national economic zones, such as EEC and NAFTA. The ramifications of such developments have been experienced in different ways in different nations of the world. The impact of transnationalism on the perception of national identity and national borders, insofar as it has led to a wider conscience of inseparable linkages within the global economy is, moreover, *analytically distinct* from the sentiments that have given rise to multiculturalism everywhere. The former is in essence a product of what Appadurai aptly called functional "disjunctures" inherent to the mutating world system; the latter is, on the other hand, a product of the *cultural decolonization* attributable to changes in modern nation-states typically founded on cultural nationalism, ethnic assimilation, and adherence to these standards. Former colonizers, such as Britain, have embraced multiculturalism as a way of life, rejecting assimilation to a dominant English culture. Australia's multicultural "postmodern republic" is another similar example.

In the transnational global economy, contrary to Appadurai's overt focus on its intrinsic "disorganization," flows of capital and labor have tended to be unequal in force or unequally determined by hierarchies of power. While it is assumed that transnational labor circulation follows the needs of capital, in fact different countries have, through control over boundaries and immigration, responded differently to transnational labor flows. Some have been open to the influx of human capital and their long-term integration, while others have been less so.

The election of Chen Shui-bian, the first DPP president of Taiwan, has given, especially after decades of ethnic oppression and struggle, the impression that a nation of Taiwanese has finally come to fruition. The wave of indigenous ethnic consciousness that fueled in part the acceptability of an "independent" Taiwan, if not in political practice then simply in cultural spirit, has breathed life into local indigenous movements of all kinds. The aboriginal rights of Taiwan's Austronesian peoples (represented by the cultures of its "nine tribes," *jiuzu*) have become mainstream issues in politics that have been elevated to the status of first principles.

One should not dismiss the general importance of multiculturalism, whatever its actual meaning, but I argue more importantly that it has been the product of indigenizing sentiments, which had a particular history in Taiwan, and should not be confused with multiculturalism in a transnational context, as prompted by the decline of the imperialist modern world system and "the end of organized capitalism." If Chinese cultural nationalism of the sort that brought about a Cold War defense of traditional Chinese culture as the legitimate front of a "Republic of China" can be seen as an indigenizing consciousness in the context of global imperialism, then the indigenization fueling first peoples' movements globally can be seen as a celebration of essentially the same consciousness as well. Not coincidentally, the "sinicization of social sciences" (*shehui kexue de zhongguohua*) movement, which constituted the major intellectual trend in mainstream Taiwan academia during the Cold War era from the late 1970s to early 1980s, whose most active contingent was in psychology, became reinvented in the mid-1990's as "indigenous psychology" (*bentu xinlixue*), with no change in content.[11] While "indigenous psychology" continued for most part to focus on Chinese conceptual and textual sources of a native (as opposed to Western) psychology, it was obvious that by the '90s the word *Chinese* had assumed different political overtones and that the same intellectual mind-set could easily be subsumed under the rubric of indigenization. The gradual replacement of "Chinese" labels with "Taiwanese" everywhere mirrored the shifting reference of Chinese to mean "mainland."

From the perspective of indigenization, it would be more precise to say that the political shift from the KMT's cultural nationalist view of "Republic of China" to the DPP's cultural independence position of "Taiwan for Taiwanese" represented a basic continuity instead of radical discontinuity in mind-set, insofar as it could be seen to promote the same essentialist modern project of a typical cultural nationalism. The emergence of Taiwaneseness has made it possible to view China as an "other." Domestically, while the embrace of aboriginal causes and the plight of minority ethnic groups seemed to reflect the official recognition of "multiple identities" and a turn toward hybridity of a kind championed by various genres of postmodern theory, it was still in essence a multiculturalism that did not include outsiders (foreigners) and made no attempt to absorb foreign labor in a way that was by nature blind to ethnicity, which should be indicative of transnational movements in an age of disorganized capitalism, driven by needs of the global market rather than by the interests of global imperialism or national protectionism. The essential distinction between these genres of multiculturalism, no matter how they appeared on the surface, is crucial, since it can explain why significantly increasing transnational flows of outsiders into present-day Taiwan has continued to be marked by their discursive *absence* or marginalized existence in relation to the constitution of mainstream society. If anything, the dominant discourse of indigenization conflicted fundamentally with the view that contemporary Taiwan was really, if not primarily, the product of its role in the global economy, driven by the easy flow of transnational capital and now by the transnational flow of human capital. Taiwan has *in fact* never been monocultural, if one takes into account the long history of Han-aboriginal interaction, interlude with European traders, the Japanese colonial interregnum, and postwar influx of overseas Chinese. But through the processes of historical erasure, political assimilation, and official elitism, the modern KMT nation-state has managed to absorb such outside influences and *discursively* portray them as the achievements of a monocultural state, while at the same time marginalizing "foreign" influences per se. Yet throughout the postwar era and accelerating in an open global economy, the growing influx of transnational human capital in particular has highlighted even more explicitly, in my opinion, the essentialist nature of the Taiwanese state, much like Japan, where "foreigners" (by Asian cultural definition) will forever be considered ephemeral fixtures of mainstream society, no matter how assimilated they happen to be. Ironically, even with the superficial embrace of multiculturalism and ethnic hybridity in Taiwan today, the blind eye that "indigenization" has turned to the increasing transnational multiculturalism that has resulted from the opening up of a global economy may in the long run represent a form of *erasure* that will belittle the violence of the modern nation-state, by contrast. Will this new wave of multiculturalism turn out to be the most *exploitative*, despite its emancipatory claims of "hybridity"?

The point here is that, while the cultural ideal of multiculturalism has been embraced everywhere as a keyword of our postmodern times, few if any countries have *fully* embraced transnational multiculturalism as a way of life, for this would engender a postnationalism or transnational nation that does not yet exist. The evolution from a modern world system to transnational capitalism is the product of many complex political and economic factors that have shaped the course of nations everywhere, yet even fewer nations can be seen as products of transnational capitalism itself. In fact, I would argue that Taiwan comes close to being a "postnation." Who says that the victory of an independent Taiwan is the result of its sudden cognizance of its *indigenous* reality? The reality is more like the following: Taiwan's sudden recognition in the international arena was the product of its success in a transnational economy at a time when its existence as a nation had been threatened by its expulsion from the United Nations. Its success had little or nothing to do with its success as a nation, and more likely *in spite of* it. The increasing turn toward indigenization was then, if anything, a step backward. In light of its renewed confrontation with the PRC, its hopes of gaining formal status as a nation in the United Nations on the basis of its independent cultural existence are close to nil. The PRC's track record in defending its nationalistic sanctity is evidenced enough by its ongoing border wars with India and its stern determination to keep Tibet "autonomous." If it could wait 50 years for the return of Hong Kong to the motherland, it could just as easily wait 500 years for Taiwan's eventual reunification. This is a drop in the bucket in the *myth* of China's long, "unbroken" lineage of history and civilization.[12] Taiwan's possibilities for true independence would stand a better chance, if it embraced transnationalism as a way of life in a way that more accurately reflected its actual emergence in the late modern global economy.

In the diplomatic arena, criteria for political independence are marred by contradictions of their own. There are limits to cultural autonomy and rights of political self-determination as principles for official separation. In any event, the very notion of the modern nation-state has been challenged even less, *especially* in this new era of transnational globalization.

The Primordial Imagined Community and the Limits of Global Multiculturalism

Human history has to some extent been the history of globalization. Even if one does not subscribe totally to Eric Wolf's (1982) dictum that there have never been any societies without History, globalization and multicultural interaction have long been staples of human existence that have had long and significant impact on social processes and political institutions.[13] Needless to say, the rapidity and degree to which globalization has affected contemporary life has been in part the consequence of time-space compression, in David Harvey's terms.[14] Yet, like the transformations of colonialism within a global context, the underlying process within political relations and institutional change should perhaps been seen more significantly as a function of newly emergent ideologies and geopolitical changes of power. Such paradigmatic shifts and discontinuous phases are a product of simultaneous imposition of hegemonic forces acting from above and local cultural processes acting from below. Within this *longue durée*, the mutations of global capitalism are only one element in this complex interactive process.

It is easy to write a history of globalization and multicultural interaction in Taiwan. It is a well-documented fact that, in addition to the several millennia of settlement by indigenous Austronesian peoples in Taiwan, settlement by Han Chinese has had a history of over 400 years, which might presumably include two periods of colonial rule by the Dutch (38 years) and Spanish (18 years), 268 years of imperial rule by the Qing dynasty, and, finally, 50 years of Japanese rule. In addition to these colonial encounters, there have been encounters between Chinese settlers and Austronesian aboriginal societies, not to mention complex interactions between various aboriginal groups and between diverse Chinese dialect groups.

Yet such accounts say intrinsically little about how such ethnic groups and boundaries are discretely defined and how they may soften, harden or mutate as a result of various kinds of power relationships. More importantly, the reason why one tends not to write history as a long, uninterrupted stream of globalization is that the frames of sociopolitical reference are constantly altered by changes in discursive perception (and their underlying politics). Just as we can be altered by global hegemonic changes from above, local perceptions of these same processes alter the way in which societies constitute, reconfigure, and interact with diverse agents in an ongoing political and social competition for power and survival.

Perhaps a more constructive point of departure for writing a history of this emerging era of transnational globalization is to take seriously in what sense transnationalism is a product of a changing nationalism, a mutating capitalist system, ongoing political imperialist orders and their impact on a differential hierarchy that increasingly dichotomizes cosmopolitanizing sites (like cities) as against nativistic, provincial survivals, and market-induced class divisions both within and across societies. The dominant focus on borderless economies and chaotic flows of capital and people in most accounts of transnationalism has accented in large part the changing practices of global capitalism that have transformed previously bounded notions of political identity, cultural substance, and regulated flows of people, media, and technology. The accent on the market has in turn made *disorganization* and *hybridity*, among other things, key words for our times. However, markets act in conjunction with and in competition with states, and a more complex equation is needed to explain how these two forces interact. In the global hierarchy of places, it is clear that this equation functions differently everywhere, because different places react according to their relative position in a geography of power. These relations are mediated by ongoing cultural discourses and local systems of meaning.

Borderless economies and disorganized capitalism have broken down prior relations of core and periphery in the modern world system, while at the same time replacing the cultural imperialism of that older capitalism with something else. But one might question whether such cultural hegemony has disappeared altogether or simply mutated into something more sublime and complicated. In many quarters, despite the changing face of global capitalism and increasingly apparent penetration of the global market into the pulse of everyday life (to wit, the domino effect of the recent Asian economic crisis of 1998), globalization has still been perceived as a force that is fundamentally extrinsic to society, if not something that is inherently culturally Western. Despite its best intentions (in deliberate blurring boundaries), it still creates differences, not only between rich and poor countries or cosmopolitanizing and indigenizing centers but also between rich and poor classes. The disjunctures of the "system" that have produced unstructured flows of capital are nonetheless analytically distinct from the *effects* of the system that may engender sharper social divisions. How else can one interpret the recent escalation of social movements against free trade globalization (as though the latter solely represents large corporate interests against the average citizen and the dispossessed)?

The intervention of states in the management of supply and demand in the global market can also differ widely in different countries; it may act not simply on the basis of economic calculation but also in order to protect national and vested class interests or to conform to accepted cultural rules. In some respects, Taiwan is remarkably globalized in ways that have already irrevocably altered its social and economic landscape. In addition to the ubiquitous institutional existence of Japanese consumer products, mainstays of American culture such as McDonalds and creolized forms of such institutions, few people have remarked that there are probably more 7-Eleven-type convenience stores in Taipei per capita than anywhere else in the world. The reasons for its acceptance are many, but it has even more remarkably and swiftly eradicated once commonplace neighborhood family stores and street kiosks that had been extolled by many sociologists as the "traditional" icon of Asian enterprise. Without a doubt, "convenience" and rational calculation have played an important part in this demise, but at the same time the lack of social resistance to the fate of small business is a function as well of the state's traditionally laissez-faire attitude toward the Chinese private economy and the tendency of small business to turn over with the times. In contrast to the easily commoditized nature of capital, the social movement of people in the global labor market has always been subject to differential rules not only within, but between societies as well. The creation of supranational entities such as the European Union has facilitated freer movement across once-rigid national borders, but they operate in conjunction with restrictions regulating the inflow, immigration, and naturalization of outsiders. Most such laws are necessarily discriminating in social terms in ways that respond to prevailing economic demand and political priorities.

From the position of the state, all flows of capital, information, and people are regulated, albeit according to different needs and standards. In the short view of things, Taiwan has in the last decade considerably liberalized the inflow of foreign labor in order to make up for a shortage of labor in specific sectors in order to minimize the outflow of industries in constant search of low labor costs. At the same time, it has adopted a stratified policy toward different classes of labor. Transient or unskilled labor is subject to short-term contracts and restrictive conditions that are always prone to revision, while those in more highly skilled professions or government related institutions are subject to more liberal laws. The large increase in foreign labor of all kinds in the last few decades eventually prompted the first major revision of the Nationality Law (*guoji fa*) in seventy-one years, put into effect on February 9, 2000, which restructured categories of residence by foreigners and instituted modified procedures for processing visas and stays of residence. In a longer view of things, while such revised laws were implemented to accommodate the flow of foreign labor for purposes of residence, they did not radically alter existing laws with regard to Dual Nationality and the inability of non-Chinese to gain permanent residence for purposes of citizenship. The latter ultimately impinged on cultural notions of primordial "community." Although not immutable, they defined certain limits to which notions of hybridity and (transnational) multiculturalism could be applied. If anything, the experience of cultural nationalism, while historically brief, has at least in Asia hardened the primordial constitution of the nation as an imagined ethnic community, while secularizing its apparatuses of state, which have rigidified through law its cultural boundaries.

In content, there should be as many different imagined communities as there are different historically and culturally constituted societies. Many are built on an ethnic ideal, others on different cultural principles, such as religion or ideology that may ultimately transcend local, ethnic, or class traditions.[15] Some are relatively open to absorption by outsiders, while others are firmly established in inherently closed communities. Regardless of ideal, almost all nation-states are fraught with internal tensions that make the nation-state an unstable entity, not to mention being transformed by transnationalism. The hybridity of people and practices, which has always been part of multicultural consumption, has in an era of transnationalism evolved to a new phase.[16] Flows of people cannot create glocalized multiculturalisms except by altering the fabric of society or its underlying values. Even then, this will not prevent multiculturalism from being what Nederveen Pieterse (2001:393) calls "a moving target."

Part Two

Hong Kong Betwixt and Between

The Liminality of Culture Before the End of History

It could be said that there has been in Hong Kong a true marriage of Confucian values and British colonial ethics. Indeed, the application of the principles of nineteenth century *laissez faire* and, in more recent times, positive non-intervention by the Hong Kong government has provided an ideal environment for business, and thus for Hong Kong as a whole, to prosper.

—Alan Birch, *Hong Kong: The Colony That Never Was*

Prologue

Despite the provocative title of Birch's book above, the book itself was an illustrated history of colonial Hong Kong, prompted by the eventual disappearance of it after its return to China or its change of fate. The title hinted at the author's nostalgia for a place soon to be lost in history. But it was tempered also by the recognition that Hong Kong was an atypical colony that had already transformed itself into a cosmopolitan city. In this regard, the government's laissez-faire or noninterventionist policies reflected to some extent this exceptionalism. In fact, official policy in the last few decades of the colonial era was to refer to Hong Kong as a territory, not a colony, as if to suggest the inapplicability or irrelevance of colonial domination.

The discursive disappearance of coloniality in Hong Kong is hardly an irrelevant factor; it is part and parcel of the colonial regime's ongoing mutation in the larger scheme of things. Ackbar Abbas (1997:7) depicted Hong Kong's culture as one "from reverse hallucination, which sees only desert, to a culture of disappearance, whose appearance is posited on the immanence of its disappearance." Caught between the tensions of a floating identity that saw itself in essence as the product of a cultural desert and the need to construct an explicit identity under conditions of political uncertainty, Hong Kong saw "an expansion of culture throughout the social realm," amounting to an "explosion." This culture of disappearance created in actuality a misrecognition of presence, where ephemerality, speed, and abstraction confounded the senses in a way that reflected the ambiguous crisis of late colonial modernity.

It is easy to find disappearance in the cultural spaces of film, architecture, and writing in this liminal transition to 1997, but I argue that the discourses and practices of disappearance have been a staple feature of Hong Kong's entire colonial history. Subjective effacement, institutional codification, and political sublimation became techniques with which the colonial government systematically downplayed or silenced the existence of conflict, rationalized its own actions, and then negotiated the many contradictions in practice that legitimated the rule of law, indirect rule, free market rationality, and diverse forms of disinterested domination. The more colonialism was seen not to exist or be replaced by its status of territory, ruled by value-free systems of justice or administration and transformed by the utilitarian rationale of modern capitalism, the more one would remain blind to real colonial difference, polarizations of a market class economy, and the disciplinary consequences of legalist and social regulation.

Chapter 4

Hong Kong Before Hong Kongness

The Changing Genealogies and Faces of Colonialism

The Nineteenth-Century Imperial Archive from the
Politics of Difference to the Sociology of Modern Power

Hong Kong was ceded in 1841 as a result of the Sino-British Opium War. The New Territories was leased from China to Britain in 1898 for ninety-nine years as an extension of the colony for purposes of military defense. Hong Kong was "no more than a barren isle" when the British took it over. The New Territories was, on the other hand, a larger land mass with settled rural communities. In a sense, the history of rule in the New Territories elucidates more clearly the changing nature of colonialism. At the outset, it aimed to be a model of indirect rule, based on the maintenance of local tradition and put into practice by the rule of law and its enlightened governance. In this regard, one may question the objective and invisible nature of this rational administration even as in the long run the New Territories became absorbed into the general colonial rule of Hong Kong and its mode of colonial governance appropriated by modernity, state power, and the free market. At the same time, Hong Kong was transformed not only by its status as a colony but also in the way its existence transcended its liminality between two Chinas. In short, colonialism in Hong Kong was a cultural project that contrasted with colonialisms elsewhere, which remade itself with parallel geopolitical forces that in the long run engendered distinctive societal consequences.

Much important work on colonialism and culture has appeared recently in the historical and social scientific literature. Scholars writing from the general vantage point of cultural studies have distanced themselves

---

This is a significant rewriting of "Colonial Govern-*Mentality* in Transition: Hong Kong as Imperial Subject and Object," *Cultural Studies* 14(3–4):430–61, published originally in 2000.

from a prior generation of scholars that has for the most part focused on the economic and politically exploitative dimensions of colonialism. This is, of course, not to downplay the obvious effect of domination and destruction that has characterized colonial rule and which capitalized on the creation and maintenance of difference in social, racial, and other terms, but rather to highlight the role of explicit practices and their underlying mentalities in legitimizing and normalizing the colonial project. Studies have diversely pointed to the positive effects of diverse colluding factors such as religion, language, history, and ethnicity that have made the colonial project a quint-essentially civilizing as well as routinizing process in ways that have ulti-mately contributed to the efficacy of rule. By cultural project, one can mean many things, of course. Anthropological interest in the role of Christian missions has situated colonialism within a wider civilizing process while at the same time accenting the importance of symbolic systems in the political process as a whole.[1] Others have noted the strategic use of language in the construction of colonial power.[2] The emergence of discursive fields such as historical writing and Orientalist writing can also be viewed as products of colonialism, whereby the meaningful construction of knowledge constitutes an integral part of an ongoing cultural struggle.[3] To such examples of cul-ture, one can add other forms of narration and representation, like travel writing and art, as phenomena that emerge out of a colonial context.[4]

The collusion between colonialism and culture can be understood not only in terms of how colonialism may be constituted as a cultural project, but also as a function of the way the colonial experience has given rise to the phenomenon of culture. Asad (1973:115), for example, has suggested that, in addition to glossing over the disruptive effects of colonial domination through recourse to images of functional integration, the cultural objecti-fication implicit in ethnographic writing today reflects to a large extent a situation of "routine colonialism." Similarly, Dirks (1992b:3) has noted that modern notions of public culture, of the kind that typically invoke some systematic unity of language, race, geography, and history, may also have been literal products of nationalism but were in essence claims encouraged and facilitated by a history of colonialism. Without denying the utility of the diverse notions of culture that have been invoked by recent writings on colonialism, there is another aspect of culture implicit in the practices themselves, a kind of *mentalité*, which can be seen as guiding the actions of concrete agents and behavior of social institutions that shed significant light on the nature and meaning of colonialism.

Thus, how one understands that culture (as *mentalité*) depends on how one understands colonialism. Despite calls from certain quarters of literary criticism to rally around the general label of "postcolonial" theory, rightly criticized by Gates (1991) as a kind of "critical Fanonism," colonialism in this context must be taken in the first instance literally as a historical phenomenon. Whether or not it is desirable for us in the final analysis to produce localized theories rather than general laws of colonialism, it is necessary, methodologically speaking, to situate the colonial experience in its proper geohistorical context. There are many kinds of colonial experience, not only because different kinds of colonial agents inevitably invoke different kinds of cultural and sociopolitical baggage, but also because, in each specific situation, colonialism inevitably changes as a result of interaction with local forces in ways that demand ongoing syntheses and shifting strategies. Each colonial experience is in other words a narrative in itself. But this does not mean, on the other hand, that such narratives should be understood only at the level of events. On the contrary, one should understand such events in the context of an interpretive framework by viewing action, discourse and practice both in terms of their underlying motives and intentions and as a function of inherently cultural rules and assumptions.

I think many of the essentializing tendencies of postcolonial theory stem from a misleading preoccupation with explaining the politics of "difference." Thus, racism has been conveniently viewed as a tool for making manifest a process of political domination and cultural construction of alien others, which appears to be universal to colonial regimes everywhere. It is as though colonial institutions are themselves contingent on such sentiments, cultural in origin, for their continued sustenance in sociopolitical terms. Noting that it is something of a paradox that racial differences between colonizer and colonized should become most prominent in precisely that period of the late nineteenth century when technologies of disciplinary power were deployed in the service of the colonial state, Chatterjee (1993:10) extends this "rule of colonial difference" even further to explain the inner dynamics of anticolonialism, nationalism, and postcolonialism. On the contrary, I think it is easier to show that racism or ideologies of racial difference are common to all cultures and are, if anything, analytically distinct from the formation of colonial regimes.[5] By noting in turn how "the *quality* and *intensity* of racism vary enormously in different colonial contexts and at different historical moments," Stoler (1989:137) makes it possible to suggest that the polarization of racial and other differences are instead arbitrary signs or dependent variables of a sociopolitical institution whose nature is grounded in specific places and times.

The same criticism can be brought to bear against Said's *Orientalism* (1978). Much more attention has been drawn to the objectification of the other in the construction of hegemonic discourses than to the more important point that such discourses have been made possible by the prior existence of an "imperial contest." Yet while Said has been content largely to concentrate predominantly on texts of high colonialism and the production of metropolitan knowledge, he has said much less about the institutional realities of colonialism that have given rise to these possibilities of discourse as well as those native realities that have been effectively obscured and objectified by both the discourses and practices of colonialism.

If one can view the institutional realities of colonialism as an appropriate point of departure for understanding the underlying *mentalité* of (local) colonial regimes and the way it may differ from the *mentalité* of native institutions and practices, one must then necessarily ask, what kinds of colonialism are there, and how does the Hong Kong experience contrast with other examples in reference to (cultural) origins and (historical) specificity? What is it about the underlying *mentalité* of Hong Kong's colonialism that sheds light on its cultural uniqueness and makes it relevant to anthropological misunderstandings of Chinese traditions?

At the risk of essentializing the nature of British colonialism in Hong Kong as a bounded category (vis-à-vis French colonialism or the experience of British colonies elsewhere and at other times), one must nonetheless admit that it shares certain features of colonial experience found elsewhere. Perhaps the most obvious was the implementation of what has been referred to in the literature as the policy of indirect rule. Hong Kong society may have been built from scratch since its cession by China in 1841, but given the settled population of Kowloon, ceded in 1860, there was much more to suggest that the overall disposition of the place resembled that of other treaty ports in China than colonies like the Falkland Islands. This became even more the case after the lease of New Territories in 1898. Even though in strict legal terms, Hong Kong (and Kowloon) was a colony in terms of its outright cession, while the New Territories was just a temporary lease, where the colonial government assumed the role of manager-cum-taxlord, in practice, this distinction eventually became blurred and for all intents and purposes nonexistent. The New Territories may have been in fact a lease, where the colonial government attempted to administer the territory in accordance with native custom and tradition, but this policy of indirect rule was in principle no different from that which guided administrators elsewhere in the British empire. This being said, however, the faithfulness to which individual colonial administrators regulated society in accordance with local custom varied considerably, largely as a function of how strictly policy was carried out.[6] In the New Territories, indirect rule was largely guided by purity of purpose but for complex reasons became subverted as a result of many other mitigating factors. Given that colonial policy was as a matter of principle guided by the aim of preserving traditional practices on the basis of local custom, one can then ask to what extent did the colonial government accurately understand the nature and operation of traditional custom, and what were the consequences of its particular implementation of tradition on the actual state of those beliefs and practices? Such questions have been posed already in the burgeoning literature on Fiji and India in particular, but local historians and anthropologists of Hong Kong have almost without exception taken the appearance of "traditional" custom and social organization at face value.[7]

The flip side of the colonial government's effort to administer society on the basis of local tradition was the emergence of modern institutions, most notably the state itself, that necessitated the disciplinary regulation of those same local social organizations and practices. In a Fijian context, Thomas (1990:170) has argued that colonialism was a "contradictory" project that, on the one hand, encouraged nonintervention in the maintenance of a customary order, yet, on the other hand, necessitated intervention to subordinate that order to the disciplinary designs of the state. Similarly, in his study of law in colonial India, Dirks (1986) has shown how legal efforts to codify and legitimize existing institutions led to subtle changes in rural society yet at the same time constituted the major failure of rural society to effect a complete and fundamental change. Contradictory as it seems on the surface, I argue that the aim to preserve tradition, which was a culturally arbitrary feature of nineteenth-century British colonial policy, was ironically part and parcel of the state's hegemonic and disciplinary designs. More than simply preserving tradition, it was the state's implicit goal to systematize and rationalize it, using the entire technology of modern objectification at its disposal (law, statistical knowledge, economic management) to make it optimally effective as a means ultimately of regulating it. At the heart of the colonial regime and its desire or mandate to rule then was the notion of governmentality (in a Foucaultian sense).

Chatterjee (1993:26) attempts to explain the essence of colonial rule largely as a function of its inherent project to perpetuate cultural difference and through the imposition of categories that mark the duality of colonizer and colonized, such as tradition and modernity. He notes that from a European point of view, colonial rule was usually never about the imposition of its own political institutions onto the other but the promotion of native self-government; it really aimed toward the preservation of local tradition instead of its destruction in the face of modernity. These claims that colonial rule was always about "something else," as if to deny the obvious fact of political domination, was according to him a persistent theme in the *rhetoric* of colonial rule (my emphasis). This has then coincided with his observation that the more nationalism (anticolonialism) tried to contest colonial power in the outer or material domain of politics, the more it met with efforts by colonialists to harden the boundaries of cultural difference to keep the inner or spiritual domains of self and other separate and sovereign.

Scott (1994) has tried to extend Chatterjee's view of colonial governmentality by showing how its intrinsic politics of cultural difference and reconstruction is really the evolution of a rule of modern power. The implicit contradiction that Chatterjee sees between the inner and outer domains of colonial politics becomes in Scott's terms a basic change in governmentality, where modern power is characterized by its shift in point of application from the economy to the body social, which includes customary or disciplinary life routines invoked by tradition and modernity.

There is indeed much one can say about the "rhetoric" of denial pointed out by Chatterjee as being fundamental to the contradictions of colonial rule. While the masking of domination is an element of colonial governmentality that is intrinsic to the efficacy of any kind of hegemonic presence, in Gramscian terms, this deliberate process of cultural mystification is in my opinion general to the emergence of state power rather than peculiar to the colonial regime. Contrary to Scott, I regard the nature of the modern project inherent to late-nineteenth-century British colonialism to revolve around its *discursive content* and *practical instrumentality* rather than its point of application. Without denying that all of society becomes the site of power, much like the way anthropological views of a total and systemic society later become galvanized through reference to the conceptual interlocking of "social structure" and "function," what needs to be explained in my opinion is why tradition, which is a culturally *peculiar*, hence symbolically *arbitrary*, aspect of nineteenth-century British colonial *imagination*, suddenly becomes incorporated into the colonial state's project of modernity, and then how the content of tradition becomes reconstructed and given new meaning in light of the various technologies of legal codification, administrative practice, and policing. It remains now to show how this field of discourse is demarcated, then spell out in what sense it entailed modern interventions through routines of state.

To reverse the Gramscian order of things, I argue then that the empire is basically a (cultural) fiction whose reality is intertwined with the process of state legitimation and methodologically put into practice by its technology of legal apparatuses and disciplinary institutions. Richards's (1994:6) observation that the nineteenth-century British "imperial archive was a fantasy of knowledge" and that it was a "paper empire" united not by force but by "information" is quite germane in this regard. It was not really the need for information that kept the empire unified in lieu of actual control but rather the Victorian project of positive knowledge that was appropriated within the overall colonial project. Institutions such as the British Museum, which served as monument for the accumulation of artifacts and documents, were clearly the product of this imagination. Likewise, the exhibitionary complex, which viewed the world as taxonomy, was what Mitchell (1988) in an Egyptian context called "colonizing."[8] As Cohn (1984) noted in his study of the census and social structure in late colonial India, this process of objectification was part of the colonial government's need to define the nature of society as a prerequisite for administering it in its own terms. In broader terms, one can argue that this imagination of the universe as ordered taxonomy that had to be made visible through the accumulation of information in order for it to be regulated systematically or efficaciously was a peculiar kind of world ethos or cultural vision that deeply influenced the conduct of government and by implication made all dimensions of social routine subject to what Corrigan (1990) aptly called "moral regulation."[9] Rather than being peculiar to colonial governmentality, it was fundamental to the governmentality of modern society in ways that became easily appropriated by the state. As Cohn (1988) phrased it, the emergence of the state created its own forms of knowledge, necessitating incessant accumulation of documentation in the genre of reports, investigations, commissions, statistics, histories, and archaeologies. Such knowledge then complimented various imaginations of the social invoked by myths of sacred origin, icons of national identity, shared values, ethnic traditions, and political thought.[10] This need to know, document, and imagine provided a basis for its capacity to govern by classifying social spaces, separating public from private, demarcating frontiers, standardizing language, defining national identity, and licensing the legitimacy of certain activities over others. It was an intrinsic part of the state's project to legitimize its emerging vision of rational order.

In order to govern efficaciously, it was necessary to "know"; the content of such knowledge was made possible by an ensemble of methodologies that made visible the "structure" of society and put into functional operation various components of social life. If colonial governmentality was part and parcel of the state's project, it also had to be to some extent intertwined with the very conduct of a modern, disciplinary society. In this regard, law played an important role, not only in terms of its ability to objectify in reference to "value-free" codes and rules but also by virtue of its institutional link to power. Far from being an "objective" institution, as perceived by those in power, it should be the very source of conflict with "native" reality. As Dirks (1986) notes for India, rule of law was the main reason why the British failed to alter the basic character of society (through preservation of tradition) yet explained why the (modern) changes that came about were

actually achieved with so little major disruption. The dual consequence of
legal rule is the ultimate source of contradiction that lies at the heart of
British colonial governmentality.

Land as Constituted: The Changing Mythologies of Local Rule in the New Territories of Hong Kong

It is possible to view the experience of British colonialism in Hong Kong
from the late nineteenth century on as the playing out of a contradiction in the colonial state's effort to institutionalize the content of tradition
using the methodology of a modern, disciplinary society. This interaction
between colonizer and colonized was mediated by culture and manifested
in shifting contexts of power over time. The unfolding of events themselves
then became the medium on which second and third order narratives of
Hong Kong history and society were constructed. These latter narratives
then became in turn reifications of "routine colonialism."

The territorial imperatives of local rule cannot be taken lightly. Colonial domination has usually been viewed as the administration at a local
level of global policies that have explicit roots in political theory of the
time. Much less has been said, however, about the local practices themselves and the underlying *mentalité* invoked at a more unconscious level
of routine control. They constitute the taken-for-granteds of colonial rule
that are manifestations of a different kind of historically constituted global
ethos. At one level of generality, land and its people constitute an object
of knowledge and structuration in a system of control. At another level
of generality, the colony becomes an object of gazing and policing within
changing utopias of the "empire."

The problematic nature of indirect rule, even in the "leased" New
Territories (as opposed to the *terra nullus* status of Hong Kong and Kowloon), exemplified the kind of administrative control central to the late
nineteenth-century imperial archive that entailed an imagination of both
land and people. Simply stated, land demarcation and village surveys were
not just prerequisite for the collection of tax revenue; they were the basis
of effective and orderly local administration in all other respects. As time
went on, the function of land in relation to the maintenance of the status
quo may have changed, but the extent to which the colonial government
regulated affairs of local society reflected the importance generally of native
knowledge to efficacy of rule.

One of the priorities which the British set out to accomplish immedi-
ately after occupying the New Territories was to undertake a detailed survey

of individual land ownership and tenure for each village in the territory. The survey involved using specially trained Indian surveyors, assisted by Chinese coolies, working continuously over a period of three years from June 1900 to June 1903. A map was drawn for each demarcation district, showing physical boundaries for each plot of land. Each unit of land was categorized, numbered, and registered in the name of a person or group that held a claim and could furnish the proper deeds. On submission of the deeds, the colonial government issued in return a Crown Lease or "license" (*zhizhao*). These demarcation maps and the particulars of landownership provided the basis for the Block Crown Lease, a land register numerically ordered by lot for each demarcation district, and the Crown Rent Roll, which became the instrument for tax collection. It took another two years to get the land registers in order. All unclaimed land not duly registered was then declared property of the Crown. Ordinance 18 of 1900 established a Land Court to hear disputed landownership cases.

In his 1899 Report on the New Territories, J. H. Stewart Lockhart summarized the task of setting up a system of land registration as follows: "a perusal of this memorandum (on Chinese land tenure) will, I think, show that, though the Chinese system may be excellent in theory, it has not been well carried out in practice, with the result that the land question has proved one of great difficulty" (RNT 1900:253). In other words, the complexity of the Chinese land system in theory represented less of an obstacle than the laxity and failure of the Chinese government to properly "operationalize" principles, which led to widespread abuse and confusion in the system. The British were frustrated by the state of affairs in the Xinan County Land Registry, which registered only deeds and not titles to land. The deeds never delineated exact land boundaries, peasants were often not able to document rights to land, and sometimes two parties would claim ownership rights simultaneously to the same piece of land (RNT 1900:278). Meanwhile, large clans and rich landowners made it a practice to bribe corrupt land officials so as to underreport actual ownership. Chinese also lacked the custom of making wills, probates or other documents to verify succession to property, and it was rare for one to officially register transactions with the Land Registry for the purpose of documenting customary arrangements between two parties. It was in reference to such haphazard practices and the bureaucratic problems implicit therein that the colonial government focused their energies on, when they set out to "operationalize" the land system on the basis of local custom, in accordance with "the lease."

However, after land surveys got underway, other problems slowed up the progress of work. Reporting the results of the Land Court from 1900–05, J. R. Wood cited several major problems (RLC 1905:146).

Excluding trivial problems of language barrier between Indian surveyors
and Chinese staff, general uncooperativeness of peasants, especially during
ritual and harvest seasons, and the problem of absentee landownership, the
British discovered that large clans often claimed tracts of land for which
they either had no documented proof or paid a small percentage of taxes
(RNT 1901:10). Second, peasant cultivators were often found exploiting
plots of land on the less productive periphery of the village for which they
had no titles and generally refused to register with the new government
(RNT 1902:559). Finally, and most importantly, cases of dual ownership
of land were found to be a common occurrence in the New Territories and
became a point of dispute between actual peasant cultivators and taxlords,
both of whom claimed to be the legitimate owners. Gradually, it became
apparent that these disputed instances did not represent conflicting rights
to the same piece of land but rights to distinct parts of the soil, namely
the "surface" and "subsoil," which was exacerbated by the fact that the new
government could only recognize a sole legitimate owner. The actual situation was complicated when one or the other side was unable to produce the
proper red deeds (to the subsoil) or white deeds (to the surface), and when
the colonial government was put in a situation of having to subjectively
decide who should be the real, legitimate tax-paying owner. The problem
of dual ownership, taxlordism, or perpetual lease ultimately frustrated the
British for a long time and became the subject of intense discussion by later
scholars (Nelson 1969, Kamm 1977 [1974], Hayes 1976, 1977).

In sum, the government was confronted with three kinds of problems:
(1) the dilemma of perpetual lease or taxlordism: (2) problems arising out
of land registration procedures for routine transactions such as inheritance,
sale, and succession; and (3) rules pertaining to the adoption of Chinese categories of land tenure and taxation. The government's handling of the dual
landlord system (*yitian liangzhu*) was a complex affair that resulted ironically
in the abolition of the entire system, contrary to the government's principle of administering on the basis of Chinese custom (Chun 1990:401–22).
Nonetheless, what was noteworthy about the resolution of this problem was
the reasons for its abolition. Their inclination for bureaucratic expediency
eventually made the administrative problem of recognizing the existence of
two "owners," one holding title to the "topsoil" and the other to the "subsoil"
an unnecessary burden. Moreover, their assessment of the situation led them
to believe that the institution in many instances exploited tenant cultivators
according to terms that were set (as if by ascription) in perpetuity.[11] This
view was reinforced by reports that in almost all cases the actual cultivators had been more knowledgeable about the details of landownership than
subsoil owners and that in many cases much more land had been attributed

to the latter, usually absentee clan landlords, than they were paying tax on. Thus in the final analysis, recognition of the institution was tantamount to perpetuating a corrupt system that effectively coerced tenant cultivators into accepting what was *in practice* spurious claims to landownership. As Orme (RNT 1912:1) noted in his Report on the New Territories for 1912,

> Before the New Territory was taken over, many Punti villages were living on their capital, on 'squeezes' from their neighbors, and on pay received from the government for collecting taxes. Under British rule, these sources of revenue soon failed, and the older families became impoverished: but their frugal neighbors, especially the Hakkas, released from their former exactions, thenceforward increased rapidly in numbers and riches at their expense.

Regarding land administration, the colonial administration felt it urgent to set up procedures to register inheritance, succession, and conveyances of sale in order to keep track of all changes in landownership. The initial work of land demarcation and registration in the New Territories was then an important first step in maintaining an orderly system of land records. On the whole, the British were especially sensitive to Chinese customary laws pertaining to the devolution of property in land. However, given the high proportion of land owned by ancestral estates (*zu*) in rural areas, the government had to concede to Chinese custom one important aspect of English law, the Rule against Perpetuities. In order to accommodate this practice, certain stipulations were added to administrative procedures pertaining to land registration, which were subsequently written into the New Territories Ordinance of 1910. They included the following:

1. (By-statute 15) Whenever land is held in the name of a corporate group, a trustee must be appointed to represent it. The trustee would be legally responsible for the land, as if he were the sole owner.

2. (By-statute 17) The Land Officer is to ascertain the name of the person entitled to succeed before registering any succession.

3. (By-statute 18) Whenever land devolves on a minor below the age of 21, a trustee must be appointed who will be responsible for any transactions undertaken on behalf of the minor.

The second of these by-statutes did not exist in Chinese customary law and was stipulated simply to insure that all persons register transactions with the government. As for the other two stipulations relating to trusteeship, they enabled the government to accept the material existence of perpetuities such as ancestral estates in accordance with local custom. More importantly, the institution of trusteeship in administrative terms transformed the perpetuity into the status of a legal person by making the trustee legally responsible for actions of the entire group. For all intents and purposes, the three amendments to land administration practice did not really modify colonial policy on the basis of local custom and had the converse effect, that of accommodating local custom into a system that recognized only the legal status of individuals. In other words, the fact that the trustee in his role as a legal person properly represented the group meant that by the same token the perpetuity had no legal existence per se. Nowhere in the New Territories Ordinance does one find any legal definition of a *perpetuity*, which is after all a matter of custom. The trustee may be constrained by custom insofar as the decision making process was concerned, but this was distinct analytically from the requirements of the legal transaction itself, which held the person of the trustee solely responsible. Nelson (1969:23) characterized this difference between legal procedure and its customary referent accurately, when he stated,

> The New Territories Ordinance, which lays down that a manager shall be appointed for all property registered in the name of an ancestral trust, does not lay down the responsibilities of the manager to the other members of the *tso* (ancestral group). In fact, the ordinance stipulates that he shall be treated as sole owner of the property, subject only to the requirement that he give notice of any transactions relating to the property and the permission of the Land Officer for those transactions. . . . Any instrument relating to the *tso* shall, when signed by the manager, be 'as effectual for all purposes as if it had been executed and signed by all members' of the *tso*.

The process of accommodating custom into a system of law points to a central feature underlying the theory and practice of "indirect rule" in a colonial context. Far from being seamless or neutral, it was by definition an act of cultural translation that assumed the *value-free* nature of legal codes in the practice of custom. In theory, such translation was rarely perfect, but more importantly the process of legalization dictated that local custom conform to a set of procedures, which was by nature modern. When backed by state power, the legal machinery institutionalized with a vengeance the absorption of custom into law and tradition into modernity.

The colonial government's attempt to adopt Chinese categories of land as a basis of taxation showed how translation, even at a literal level, produced incompatibilities at a higher conceptual level. In an appendix to Report on the New Territories for 1899, Lockhart attached a précis on Chinese customary law, titled "Memorandum on Land." This and other Western scholarly sources provided the basis on which the British adapted Chinese notions of land taxation for their own use. First-class land (*shangtian*) included land near villages in fertile valleys with a good depth of soil and good water supply, producing two crops of rice annually. Second-class land (*zhongtian*) was rated less fertile, was generally situated higher up hilly slopes, did not have as good water supply as first class, and usually produced one crop of rice annually. Third-class land (*xiatian*) was situated on still higher slopes and tended to be far removed from good water supply. It was thus more suitable for the cultivation of peanuts, sweet potatoes, millet, and other crops, all of which required less water. In addition to the three classes, fish ponds paid a tax slightly higher than first-class agricultural land, burial grounds paid a one-time registration and stamp fee, while house land was exempt from tax altogether. Land officers also noted that hills and wasteland that were not necessarily cultivated were sometimes claimed by nearby villages or powerful clans in the area. Land along the seashore under water, on the other hand, was registered and taxed whenever they were put to productive use (such as salt making). Finally, the notion of "crown land" among the Chinese was vaguely defined, and wasteland surrounding villages, including large tracts of virgin territory granted to families by imperial or provincial decree, did not appear to be subject to land tax at all. In view of the above, the colonial government modified the Chinese three-tiered land tax system as follows: first-class land was to include choice paddy land and first-class house land; second-class land included less fertile paddies, dry cultivation, and less desirable house land; while third-class land included wasteland and residual categories of nonagricultural or minimally productive land. All unclaimed land was then declared "crown land." These hard-and-fast categories became "law" and were enforced by the land registration system.

In the process of "translation," the colonial authorities rigidified the categories and imputed rules of usage that did not exist within the system. Two notable revisions of the Chinese three-class tax assessment scheme was taxation of house land and the definition of crown land as that residual category of all nonclaimed land. Using fertility as the taxable value of land mirrored the Chinese emphasis on productivity, but the differences in practice became points of conflict in later years. In fact, the most expensive land was usually the middle grade and not the most fertile land (Rawski 1972:21, citing Yang 1925:48–50). Ch'en Han-seng explained it as follows:

> The share rent does not . . . depend on the fertility of the soil alone but largely on the respective amount of labor power and fertilizer which the tenant puts into the land. In this particular district, the tenant of good land often supplies more means of production per mow than other tenants because such an investment is certain to pay. Improving the soil, he is actually in a better position to bargain with the landlord who cannot afford to lease his good land to tenants who cannot or will not keep up the fertility of the soil. It is for this reason that the landlord gets less rent from the tenant of the best land, paradoxical as this may seem, than he gets from the tenant of medium grade land. (Ibid.:50)

The most sorely disputed point of difference between the government and rural inhabitants rotated around what the British called "crown land" and what inhabitants called "people's land" (*mintian*). The next most contested point of conflict centered on the government's decision to tax house land. Its definition of land classification produced a volatile situation that continued to reverberate for decades. Moreover, when disputes in this regard took place, the government refused to yield. As early as 1905, inhabitants of the territory protested against increases in Crown Rent, twice in the space of six years, as well as against the imposition of a tax on houses and buildings. As for increases in Crown Rent, the colonial secretary noted in correspondence with the Governor that the thirty petitions submitted by 296 villagers to the government reflected agitation by a few, not general dissatisfaction among the populace. Despite recommendations by the registrar general to lower taxes, he defended the increases, adding that "these people who are obliged to be overtaxed can afford to offer a substantial fee" (CSO 3120/06). On the subject of house and building tax, petitioners claimed that this tax had never been imposed and was thus unreasonable (CO 129/338). The governor, Matthew Nathan, countered by arguing that the novelty of a tax did not affect the validity of its imposition (CO 129/335). This position was explained by the colonial secretary in official correspondence with the governor as follows:

> There is a house duty in England on inhabited houses occupied as farm house, public house, copper shop, shop warehouse, lodging house, and I think on house let in tenements or flats over

certain amount. This is in addition to local rates. Unless we are to go on the principle that no taxes are to be levied in the New Territory other than such as were levied by the Chinese government, a house tax is a usual tax. All the other taxes mentioned are fair taxes. (CSO 3120/06)

The objection was circumvented and the complainants mollified in part by a proclamation issued on July 11, 1906, which promised not to raise Crown Rents during the term of the lease. Such a promise not only deprived the government of large sums in revenue; it was also contrary to specific instructions given in 1899 by Chamberlain, the former secretary of state, stating in effect that the land tax must be subject to periodic revision. Even when Crown Leases were renewed in 1973 after the initial seventy-five-year lease had expired, the Crown Rent remained unaltered with respect to most lots in the New Territories despite enormous increases in the value of land. In short, in order to compensate for what appeared to be a legal contradiction of the Convention, the government made a financial concession. But in order to compensate for the obvious loss of revenue to be suffered in the course of succeeding years, they would have to make further revisions and restrictions in land policy and administration. All of this produced a vicious cycle, the end result being the increasing rigidification of those categories of land use, which they first modified on the basis of custom then reimposed on an indigenous way of life.

Conflicts over land and housing policy became acute in the midst of rural industrialization, population expansion and rapid modernization that were endemic to the 1920s and 1970s. But more importantly, these crises were prompted by the nature of the *discourse*. Far from being givens of coloniality, as might be suggested by notions of colonial governmentality predicated on the inherent dualism between racial others, I argue, on the other hand, that the dualism pitting colonizer and colonized that epitomized the essence of indirect rule was generated in *practice* by the systemic differences between custom and law and ultimately between tradition and modernity.

These systemic differences should not be reduced to inaccuracies of cultural translation, although factual differences at this level no doubt served to exacerbate deeper conceptual and institutional conflicts. Value judgments by colonial authorities that led to the abolition of the dual landlord system and introduction of new land taxes were strictly speaking contraventions of the New Territories Lease that were neatly covered up or defended as actions that contributed to necessary rationalization of the system, both in terms of bureaucratic accounting and maintaining order. On the other hand, legal codification and administrative routinization unconsciously transposed new

categories of use onto the practice of custom that in the long run transformed the institution itself. In short, control over land was not simply a
tool of economic extraction but more importantly part of a total project of
policing that entailed the structuration of communities tied to land. It not
only transformed the relationship between land and its people but ironically
also facilitated the overhaul of those communities by disciplining the fabric
of society as a whole. In this regard, the state mediated not only in its role
as colonizing agent but more fundamentally by invoking in the process a
peculiar culturalizing ethos.

Land as Constitutive: The Ambiguities of Territoriality in the Changing Globalism of British Colonial Rule

By definition, colonialism is the product of a global order. The rise of imperial conquest, the modern world system and most recently transnational
capitalism represent different phases in the evolution of the global order
in historical terms. At the same time, there have been equally importantly
variations in genres of colonial rule that reflect specific globalizing visions.
In this regard, one can, of course, compare the British experience with
competing regimes as a function of relative repression or assimilation. The
technical challenges of achieving global domination led Cell (1970:220–53)
to emphasize the seminal role of communications. At the same time, the
evolution of colonial hegemony in various forms became in the long run
a practice that relied ultimately on a mixture of force, legitimation, and
assuagement, as Low (1991:4) phrased it.

  This intrinsic ambiguity of territorial rule was most evident in light
of the changing meaning of the New Territories "lease" and the changing
status of Hong Kong in a contracting "empire." The events surrounding
the occupation of the territory exposed all the different interpretations of
the lease held by each side. After initial jubilation among the British in
Hong Kong subsided over the signing of the New Territories lease on June
9, 1898, referred to as the Convention of Peking, many details of its basic
conditions were still pending resolution, including, for example, the precise
demarcation of the northern frontier, the operation of Chinese customs
stations, and military garrison at Kowloon City as well as the scope and
nature of colonial administration. The northern boundaries were accepted
somewhat reluctantly by the British only in March of the following year and
ended up dividing the Shenzhen Valley and the market town of Shataukok
in half. There was still much debate on both sides over the presence of the
Chinese military and customs stations in Kowloon City, which the Chinese

government insisted on, while military skirmishes took place throughout the territory over the construction of police matsheds prior to the formal hoisting of the flag on April 17, 1899, resulting in many deaths. Apparently, the Chinese provincial government failed to inform inhabitants that the territory had already been relinquished to the British over a year ago. Even after signing the treaty, the Viceroy at Canton continued to administer the territory for months as though nothing really happened (Endacott 1958:25). Literal miscommunication aside, the deeper meaning of the lease was still debatable.

As Wesley-Smith (1980:90) rightly cited, international leaseholds of the type imposed on China by foreign powers in 1898 were inventions—instant creatures adapted to the environment created by imperialist rivalry in the Far East. Their status and effect in international law had not been carefully worked out, but it was vital to colonial interests in Hong Kong that subsequent practice affirm that the leased territory be transferred to Britain in the same manner as Kowloon and Hong Kong. The New Territories was not to be just another part of China administered by a Western power, but an extension of Hong Kong; the convention was to be seen as a treaty for the extension of established colonial boundaries, not just for the lease of territory. Thus, the Colonial Office declared from the outset that both countries would be administered in the same capacity and with the full powers of legal jurisdiction. This "new" interpretation of the "lease" was a post hoc imposition on the original convention. While it did much to clear up whatever confusion the British initially had at the outset about the status of the New Territory, it effectively widened the gap on both sides on most of the other unresolved questions. After all, the Chinese still talked about the leased territory as a lease, and this explained their insistence on maintaining a military garrison, customs station, continued payment of land tax by residents to the provincial government, and sovereignty over land and its people. By this token, the Convention of Peking did little to change their "business as usual" attitude toward the territory. The British evicted the Chinese military and customs station at Kowloon Walled City later as being inconsistent with the defense of the colony, even though they continued to respect Chinese territorial sovereignty over the Walled City in other regards throughout the Lease, contradictory as it may seem. This intrinsic ambivalence of the lease paralleled the way in which the colonial government set out to administer the leased territory on the basis of local custom and through cultural translation.

However, as with the case of the colonial government's legal codification of Chinese custom, the nature of British administrative presence in the territory was considered by native inhabitants as being anything but a system of "indirect" rule. In this regard, the Chinese essentially viewed the terms of the lease as a kind of landlord-tenant relationship, not unlike a dual landlord system where the Chinese retained rights to the subsoil and jurisdiction over its inhabitants and then leased to the British rights to the topsoil.[12] Moreover, the British made repeated assurances in official proclamations not to interfere with local customs or routines.[13] More often than not, the British were perceived as doing the exact opposite, for example, by disrupting the local *feng shui* and imposing customs that most Chinese viewed as alien, such as levying poll taxes, house taxes, numbering houses, registering births and deaths, and erecting police stations (CREBC:261).[14] At the literal level, from a British point of view, the "lease" was actually a provisional cession of territory, and this peculiar understanding was attributable to a deeper ambiguity within British colonial policy as theoretically constituted. The need to acquire and control territory as a means of promoting trade interests was by the late nineteenth century a vestige of a dying mercantilism. If the acquisition of Hong Kong and the New Territories was necessary to protect trade interests in China, it was so only in the minds of the Europeans. The Chinese were willing to yield territory to the British in order to enhance their physical security, but it was highly unlikely that the Chinese understood how territoriality was logically related to the operation of well-defined trade relations. Changes in the international political environment that later witnessed the decline of empires, the rise of nationalism, Cold War divisions, and the advent of a free market global economy in the postwar era were in this sense events that influenced both Hong Kong and New Territories regardless of their literal existence as colony or lease, thus making these conceptions anachronistic over time.

The complex nature of indirect rule, which involved the collaboration and assuagement of local authority, produced in practice consequences that did not particularly protect the status quo, despite repeated claims of official policy, nor satisfy indigenous interests, which proved to be more nuanced than that presumed by the immutability of tradition and an undifferentiated Other. Matters pertaining to land and social organization generally rigidified the lease by dualizing the conflicting role played by British rationalization-cum-institutionalization of Chinese customary practice and inhabitants' claims to indigenous rights as protectors of the same "local tradition" (Chun 1991:309–29). In this sense, it is worth noting that colonial District Officers deliberately mimicked the authority of the Chinese local magistrate by acting as *fumu guan* (literally "father-mother officials"). The role of the British as parental guardians of "the system" became even more anachronistic during the postwar era, which called into question native claims to tradition.

Hong Kong continued to thrive in an era when the British empire was already in permanent decline. The peculiar ongoing status of Hong Kong in this evolving environment had much to do also with the relationship of Hong Kong and its inhabitants to China, British interests vis-à-vis China given the changing balance of power leading up to World War II and into the Cold War era, then Hong Kong's role as a free trade port in an emerging global capitalist economy. The imperatives of indirect rule that prioritized collaboration and assuagement in the context of the lease were much less important here than the hegemonic functions of colonial control that served ultimately to legitimize existing institutions of rule and their underlying value systems. Control over the colony became, as time passed, less a matter of Britain's military ability to defend the territory than a result of other factors, the most important of which was China's intentions toward the territory (or Britain's ability to deflect China's territorial concerns away from Hong Kong).

The two most significant events that shaped Hong Kong's peculiar existence as a colony and its developing nature as a society were the nationalist movements of the Cold War era and the process of economic growth after World War II. But unlike Britain's other independence-prone colonies, the predominantly Chinese population of Hong Kong had no independent national identity to speak of. Consistent with the colonial status of Hong Kong, the British administered it in accordance with their own judicial conventions, like any other colony. Yet in spite of its colonial status, there was no question as to the cultural identity of its inhabitants. Before 1950, most people just called themselves Chinese; there was not even a notion of being Hong Kongers. The border between Hong Kong and China was open, and there was little to differentiate Hong Kong from foreign enclaves in other treaty ports. The dualistic nature of Hong Kong's colonial society was then a function of the way in which the British demarcated the public and private spheres. There was a strict separation between official culture, which was carried out in the medium of English, and local culture, which was rooted in Chinese tradition. Social intercourse was segregated along ethnic lines, and the government did little to cultivate among the populace any national affinity to Britain. The ongoing connection with Chinese culture and Cantonese regional tradition also made independence inconceivable as well as unrealistic. The political rift between Nationalist and Communist China in 1949 transformed Hong Kong instead into a battleground for competing national identities. Polarization of sentiment along ideological lines peaked during the Cultural Revolution of 1966–67 and erupted in fierce riots.

The Cold War tensions eventually catalyzed Hong Kong's transformation into a free market port, which was a deliberate policy initiative by the colonial government. A major consequence of this change in social terms was the evolution of a utilitarian society that diverted energy away from competing nationalist sentiments and led to the emergence of a mass media culture in following decades that was deliberately apolitical, which made it immune to direct control by the state.[15] The colonial government in effect took an active role in promoting economic growth in Hong Kong during the early postwar era, not just for the sake of modernization itself but more importantly as a means of steering Hong Kong away from ongoing national-ist conflicts that had threatened at times to destabilize the colonial regime.[16] From 1967 to 1984, influenced by the turn of events during China's Cul-tural Revolution and distracted by material progress at home, nationalist sentiment began to wane to the point of not being anchored to any political homeland (either to PRC, ROC, or UK). This contributed to the rise of a peculiar kind of Hong Kong culture that was essentially syncretic in nature. The promotion of consumer utilitarianism as a way of life also broke down ideological distinctions between Chinese and Western culture. Thus, Hong Kong's hybrid culture, which effortlessly fused East and West, was brought about by unrestrained capitalism's wholesale demystification of those cultural barriers that had been fostered by an earlier "colonialism." Indeed, during this period of political alienation from the two Chinas, British colonialism softened considerably. The government facilitated the adoption of British nationality, and the enticement of British nationality increased as sentiment toward a remote Chinese homeland eroded and was combined with ben-efits of emigration. This liminal public sphere that gave birth to a Hong Kong "identity" ironically led in turn to the discursive disappearance of the "colony" as well. They continued to be part of the same collusive process.

Narratives of Tradition and Modernity in the Domestication of the Colonial Mind: Second- and Third-Order Abstractions

In the final analysis, the free market institution gave rise to an autonomous culture industry. This autonomy was based in essence on representations born out of a postwar media culture that was cosmopolitan and apoliti-cal in nature. But this autonomy in a sociological sense effectively created competing "imagined communities," which were based on mentalities and lifestyles that were divided on the basis of class and education. Those people identifying primarily with this cosmopolitan, apolitical culture constituted a liminal community vis-à-vis an older generation tied to a national Chi-nese homeland and others drawn increasingly to Britain. Ironically, Hong Kongers quite clearly had no identity *as a people* in the sense of sharing common ideologies and values. The vacuous social space so created as a result of Hong Kong's displacement from the Chinese political mainstream and its caste-like status within the colonial system facilitated in the long run its mutating and increasingly vague existence as a colony. Its increasing isolation from the Chinese cultural sphere was without doubt a factor that accelerated the development of an autonomous cultural identity that was rooted in the popular culture of the mass media. But the fragmented nature of its resulting public sphere accommodated continued coexistence among various competing communities precisely because of its cosmopolitan, apolitical disposition. In effect, radical transformations of a market society not only insulated Hong Kong from actualities of an enveloping nationalist conflict but also facilitated the illusion of colonial disappearance. During this era, the word *colony* was stricken from official texts and replaced by *territory*. The intrinsic ambivalence of its local public sphere made Hong Kong constantly prone to crises of identity caused by shifting geopolitical disjunctures and cultural discourses. In the culture of public spheres, new forms of identity consciousness mimicked the rise of new social mentalities and the waning of preexisting ones. The utilitarian, politically indifferent ethos of "Hong Kong Man" was a combination of Hong Kong's liminal status vis-à-vis both Chinas and the colonial sublimation of politics. Colonialism appropriated modernity and in so doing transformed itself.

The lack of a consistent cultural-political identity that could galvanize the formation of a unified, autonomous community of people vis-à-vis China or Britain meant that the fate of Hong Kong continued to be determined by the pushes and pulls of diplomatic interests originating from London and Beijing. The contraction of the British empire elsewhere did not necessarily, if at all, diminish its imperial aspirations. London's desire to regain British possessions in East Asia at the end of World War II was just a matter of prestige (Tsang 1988:13, Chan 1990:293). The advent of a communist regime on the mainland made territorial control of Hong Kong even more imperative. On the other hand, China's desire to recover Hong Kong appeared to be lukewarm, or in Chan's (1990:314) words, subdued. Nonetheless, it was potentially threatening enough to persuade London to recognize Beijing. Thus, diplomatic recognition of China was the result of Britain's desire to protect its commercial interests in Hong Kong, and its desire to preserve Hong Kong in turn was seen as a defense of Western interests against communism than as a defense of the empire itself. Maintenance of a colonial status quo received tacit support from the Chinese side during the postwar period well into the 1980s, largely in view of the role of Hong Kong as entrepôt in China's economy. As Tang (1994:334–35) argued, Britain's adamant defense of Hong Kong as a colony later retreated significantly in response to China's resurging nationalism and Britain's recognition of the growing importance of China vis-à-vis Hong Kong politically and economically, culminating in its decision in 1984 to return all of Hong Kong to China in 1997.

The changing colonial character of Hong Kong during the postwar era viewed in light of its discourses of identity constitutive of the evolving worldview of its constituent population, on the one hand, and the geopolitics of territorial control and trade domination, on the other, represented a frame of reference that revealed a rather different dimension to the history of modernization and democratization. Contrary to typical positivist readings of the contribution of Western progress and its influence on the history of Hong Kong culture and society advanced by most officials and scholars, the advent of the modern world system that gave rise to a free market society and its peculiarly depoliticized media-based culture during the postwar period was not just the natural outcome of a rational desire for material progress. Rather, it was the result of a systematically orchestrated strategy by the colonial government to carefully maneuver through an unstable global political context. During most of the Cold War period, microeconomic laissez-faire was conducted in the service of a highly regulated macroeconomic policy, just as the capitalist nature of media culture was fostered largely under the auspices of an autocratic political system that limited political rights in most other regards. The subjective effacement of a colonialism that now began to see Hong Kong as a territory in an era of progressive modernization in turn made utilitarian notions of culture so engendered once removed from the source of state hegemony.

Not unlike colonial discourses of indirect rule that claimed to have reproduced and put into practice traditional principles of land and social organization in the administration of the New Territories, narratives of unilineal progress in postwar Hong Kong showcased by government policymakers and echoed by social scientists waving various banners of economic modernization theory have in effect neatly masked the hegemonic consequences of autocratic rule characteristic of Cold War politics and exploitative consequences of class inequality partly responsible for the emergence of a fractured public sphere and competing cultural identities. While the images of political stability and economic prosperity have no doubt enhanced the successes of Hong Kong vis-à-vis its communist counterpart, fraught by endless power struggles and the disincentives of economic socialism, the promotion of such discourses in itself in public or academic circles reflected no less than in the case of structuralist or functionalist theories a situation of routine colonialism. King's (1975) focus on the "administrative absorption of politics" and Lau's (1981) emphasis on "utilitarian familism" were typical of efforts by Hong Kong sociologists to interpret the nature of Hong Kong culture and society. King's attempt to attribute Hong Kong's postwar political stability to the importance of co-optation as a grassroots political strategy was really a result in part of the growth of local administration during the postwar era and the government's effort to transfer the authority of official-mandarins to routine clerical-managers. Similarly, Lau's characterization of Hong Kong Chinese social relationships as an extension of utilitarian familism was less an essentialization of Hong Kong Chineseness than the successful adaptation to a peculiarly commercialistic, cosmopolitan lifestyle that came about only during the postwar era. More important than the accuracy of all these second-order abstractions of everyday life, ephemerally constituted in the sense of being moments of a particular time and place, such intellectual discourses also served a hegemonic role by sublimating the essential violence of colonial rule, the power of the state, and modern economic survival. As post hoc rationalization of a routine situation of stability and prosperity, which was hygienically purged of other inherent repressive and divisive elements of the "system," the authority of local social scientific discourse can be questioned in much the same way as the legal codes and administrative practices that the British used to operationalize Chinese traditional customs on the land and maintain the status quo. By refining the colonial *mentalité*, it had domesticated its very source of institutional violence.

In sum, Hong Kong's history is less the product of British-Chinese interactions per se than the consequence of overlapping colonialisms, nationalisms, and modernities. These overlapping processes made manifest, on the one hand, the complexity of changing global political forces that have given birth to these phenomena as well as the complexity of cultural conflict and interaction that has taken place in specific local contexts. In the case of Hong Kong, the ambiguities of colonial-cum-modern rule manifested themselves during the postwar era. At the same time, the blurred boundaries between these overlapping processes exposed the complex interrelationship between colonial discourse and practice that has been neatly purged and glossed over by simple unilineal narratives of economic progress and social stability inscribed in orthodox histories and prevailing theoretical accounts. This effacement at the level of writing, once removed from the level of events, has in turn obscured our perception of the complex changes in colonial discourse and practice that have occurred over the long term (as events twice removed from our present understanding). In terms of territoriality, which was supposed to be the essence of colonial rule, one of the ironies of Hong Kong and the advent of 1997 was that reality of colonialism has been absorbed by the fiction of the lease. The paradox of "indirect rule," even in the "leased" New Territories, has shown, on the other hand, that in addition to the various political machinations and cultural misperceptions at the time, both society and its people had already in fact been administered for all intents and purposes as a colony. Despite the brute force and hierarchical stratification that buttressed this regime, I argue that the effectiveness and pervasiveness of colonial rule began to change. It continued to evolve in the process of systematic codification and institutionalization as well as in response to changing global imperatives.

Far from being a simple phenomenon, the intertwined relationship between the political processes of colonial rule, their underlying cultural constructions and the embeddedness of both in specific historical and local contexts has scarcely been systematically or rigorously analyzed. Without interrogating the explicit nature of what constitutes nationalism or modernity, I think the question of what constitutes colonial rule in Hong Kong is problematic enough. It is necessary first of all to view colonialism, not as an abstract force but as the interplay of concrete discourses and practices. As a historical imagination, it shares common features with British colonialism elsewhere. It is important to see, at each point in time, how it was a product of global political forces, while invoking a global vision, as a precondition of its imposition in a specific cultural context. Yet despite the common conceptual and institutional framework, British colonial rule everywhere differed widely in its actual deployment. Uniqueness of experience was the result less of its confrontation with different cultures in different contexts but rather the specificity of diverse situations of practice, within which cultural perception was one of many relevant factors. In theory, the explicit nature of the lease should have made Hong Kong's New Territories no different from Weihaiwei (a territory in north China leased by the British in 1898 but abandoned and relinquished in 1930). Comparisons with imperialist or extraterritorial situations in other parts of China likewise made the Chinese cultural factor per se a poor constant in explaining the nature of this colonial experience. On the other hand, the role played by various agents in their specific interpretations of the situation on the ground underscored even more the negotiable and oftentimes negotiated quality of the events that have contributed to the manifest contradictions, deep seated ambiguities, and cumulative systematicity that eventually became institutionalized in everyday practice. Over time, it became impossible to isolate colonialism from other processes.

More than just the fact of economic exploitation or a product of ethnic discrimination, not to mention the imagination of postcolonial theory, the concept and practice of colonialism must be viewed literally, as a sociopolitical manifestation of a peculiar, ongoing global contest, whose mentalities and strategies are the end product of negotiated and culturally constituted actions. Yet despite the real violence characteristic of such rule (as though backed by the appearance or threat of force), even less has been said regarding its efficacy of governance, not only as a mode of subjection but also social and moral regulation. The hierarchical order so imposed seems quite contradictory at first glance, based at one level on a set of values that attempted to maintain separation between different classes of the population yet at another level on a civilizing ethos whose ultimate goal was the assimilation of citizens into a larger, all-inclusive polity. It would appear that, at some point, these implicit contradictions of politics and culture should have sown the seeds of its own self-destruction. Much can also be said about the peculiarity of a policy of indirect rule, which has likewise relied on the maintenance (if not invention) of tradition as a condition for success of its own existence. In sum, the uniqueness of Hong Kong's experience is rooted in part in the mutation of colonial rule and its appropriation of modernity, in many senses of the term. The evolution of the state apparatus altered the essential character of rule by replacing the spectacle of power with a system of local, routine control that was supposedly self-regulating in nature. The rise of a free market society radically transformed the contradictions of a system built on political difference and replaced it with class struggles based on differential access to capital. The discursive effacement that followed mutations of the colonial system in terms of official policy and popular identity, epitomized by self-congratulatory imperial histories that reproduced narratives of pacification or unbroken unilineal progress and scholarly analyses that extolled the pristine structures of local society, represented the final stage of "colonialism."

Chapter 5

Critical Cosmopolitanism in the
Birth of Hong Kong Place-Based "Identity"

To say that the 1980s spawned the advent of a unique Hong Kong culture and an intrinsically diverse way of life there is an understatement. There is already an overwhelming literature that attests to Hong Kong's paradigmatic development in urban, pop cultural, cosmopolitan, capitalistic, colonial, and postmodern terms, among others. Such developments have given rise to mind-sets and lifestyles that have begun to impact worldwide as well. I suppose much of this began to emerge in that era of Hong Kong that one has typically ascribed to its status as a free market port, but it was an era where one began to see the birth of a local (place-based) Hong Kong culture, that is, one constructed not only in the context of explicit Westernization but also in a liminal space between two nationalistic forces. To confront such a large topic would seem on the surface vague and overly ambitious, but I think there are many reasons why this evolution should be unusual, if viewed from the perspective of prevailing theories.

If tradition is ongoing, there would be seem to be every reason to believe that local Hong Kong culture and society is the result of intrinsic developments or extensions thereof instead of impositions from the outside. However, when placed in a historical context and at the apex of overarching political forces, there are actually many more reasons to believe that this emergence is a result of unlikely circumstances and global, nationalist struggles within which the impulses of self-determining autonomy are minimal at best. I would argue that much of this initially has to do with the

This chapter was first published in 2009 as "Sketching the Discursive Outlines of Cosmopolitan Hybridity in Postwar Hong Kong: City Magazine in the Emergence of 1980s Popular Culture and Culture Industry," *Journal of the Hong Kong Sociological Association* 4:189–213. Research on various aspects of City Magazine has benefited from conversations with Chan Koon Chung, Lui Tai Lok, Peter Wong, Leo Lee, and Cheung Likkwan.

situatedness of Hong Kong at the intersection of overlapping frames of reference or governance, one being colonial and the other being nationalizing.

Interstices of Colony, Nation, and Modernity
in the Making of a Popular Culture

To say that Hong Kong is/was a colony is to say little or nothing at all. In
both theory and practice, colonialism has always been an evolving institutional phenomenon. British colonialism may be intrinsically different from
French or Dutch colonialism in many respects, but it has also evolved as
the result of changing political ideological imperatives at home as well as
in nuanced response to expedience and feasibility in each colony in ways
that has had more abstract consequences for local culture and society than
just literal ones. In any case, it has been much more than just the politics
of difference, as postcolonial theorists argue. Hong Kong's colonial polity
was in many regards a caste society, especially in an administrative sense,
which allowed for peaceful coexistence with a majority of inhabitants who
still lived as though they were part of China. The borders were open until
well into the Cold War era, and the rise of Chinese nationalism, in many
senses, enveloped people in Hong Kong despite its colonial status. Region-
ally speaking, Hong Kong had been at best a marginal satellite of a Cantonese sphere of influence based in Guangzhou. In short, there were many
hegemonic forces working against the self-determination of a Hong Kong
culture, represented especially by the kinds of hybridized, pop cultural,
irreverent, and egotistical lifestyles and mind-sets that people now take for
granted and unabashedly champion. How then did this all come about?

　　I approach this question not as a historian but more as a culturolo-
gist. I think too many books are written about Hong Kong in the genre
of unilineal narrative of progress, triumph of Westernization, inevitability
of a free-spirited can-do determinism, and postcolonial liberation of various sorts. The formation of a Hong Kong identity and the evolution of a
mass culture, among other things, are all complex sociological phenomena
in their own right that are more importantly made possible by politico-
institutional transformations and corresponding change in the geo-cultural
landscape. They may be invoked from above, but they respond to local
needs. Men make history, as Marx astutely put it, but not necessarily of
their own free will.

　　At this point, one may ask, why cosmopolitanism? In this regard, I
am less interested in exploring cosmopolitanism as a theoretical problem
or general sociocultural phenomenon than in using cosmopolitanism as a

reference point for understanding the unique and complex changes that precipitated the rise of a place-based Hong Kong culture and identity during the postwar era. It does not comprise all the seminal transformations that took place, of course, yet on the other hand, the peculiarities of Hong Kong's experiences can also shed light on the content and form of the culture that ultimately emerged. In short, what is cosmopolitanism?

Needless to say, cosmopolitanism is not unique to Hong Kong. One can view it as an intrinsic feature of the global city, of which there is a long history and for which there are many prominent examples, even before capitalism. The very idea of a city as a cosmopolis suggests that its scope of ambition and imagination aims to transcend secular and territorial boundaries. Its quest of worldly consumption and sacred communion reinforces its political elitism or vice versa. It should in literal terms be something quite contrary to an indigenous identity and popular culture. In the context of Hong Kong, if its colonial governance counts for something, one cannot consider cosmopolitan or Western influences alien either. It was, above all, a trading entrepôt and a base of regular interaction between Europeans and Chinese at all levels. Hong Kong has a long history of cultural exchange, if this is cosmopolitanism, at least in part.[1] Yet, at the same time, there is a sense in which for a long time cosmopolitan exchanges neither fundamentally disrupted the caste-like relationships between Europeans and Chinese nor fundamentally changed cultural perceptions of the polity until much later.

In the long-term transition into the postwar era, many things changed. In addition to the task of reconstructing society from ravages of war and economic deprivation, the British Empire had already entered the final stages of an irrevocable decline. Despite its liminality, Hong Kong was a Cold War battleground for competing nationalisms. Whether colonialism was subsumed by nationalism or was eventually the pivotal factor that enabled Hong Kong to transcend nationalism is a matter of interpretation, but I mention these historical conditions to argue that these changes beneath the geopolitical ground ultimately played an important role in establishing the conditions by which a place-based Hong Kong identity was able to emerge and in carving out a framework within which cosmopolitan influences ushered in a new kind of popular culture. Within this geopolitical process, the concrete agency of institutions and the creative force of culture were important vehicles in defining new lifestyles and mind-sets, but I think it is crucial to dissect the complex interplay between them in its historical context.

My (Chun 1996) comparative analysis of the emergence of public culture in contemporary Taiwan, Hong Kong, and Singapore outlines for present purposes a framework for articulating a role for geopolitics.[2] Among other things, it shows how three Chinese-populated societies can have radically different notions of ethnicity and cultural identity, resulting from the way in which nationalism, colonialism, and market capitalism interact. In the case of Hong Kong, its transformation into a free market port was prompted by a colonial regime determined in essence to neutralize nationalist conflict in the territory. It brought about a depoliticization of public culture that spawned, among other things, the emergence of a mass-mediated Hong Kong cultural identity, but the way in which explicit Westernization formed in collusion with the evolution of a class-based, market society were unintended consequences of this kind of top-down state politics and were in actuality products of a different dynamic interaction. It is easy to say that utilitarian capitalism translates everything into monetary terms, but when culture begins to be seen as commodity in a kind of identity space that becomes deracinated from the politics of nation, strange things happen. For one thing, it makes possible forms of culture, ways of thinking, and lifestyles that are forced to negotiate themselves on the basis of some kind of transnational, intercultural logic, and this is the unique matrix of what I see as Hong Kong's diverse yet inherently fractured public sphere. Among other things, it is easy to understand why, by contrast, the sort of ethnic politics that characterized Taiwan is wholly absent. One tends to forget that, in terms of ethnic composition, Hong Kong and Taiwan are similar (25% of their postwar inhabitants are from other provinces of China), but in Taiwan everything (politics as well as culture) is ethnically dualized, or at least people seem to think so. In Hong Kong, "borrowed place and a borrowed time" is a cliché that reflects its liminal status vis-à-vis conflicting and overarching national spaces, but it ultimately marks the advent of a locally born generation increasingly estranged, on the one hand, from an older diasporic generation yearning to return to the motherland, and a growing proportion of people who, on the other hand, began to identify with Britain (mostly those who by class, education, political affiliation, or through migration benefited most from ties to Britain). The geopolitical spaces are important, but the way in which people negotiate these spaces is equally important.

Cosmopolitanism and cultural hybridity can in theory be the product of many possible reasons and intentions, but in practice they had to compete with prevailing cultural mind-sets in Hong Kong and in the end transcend or overcome the latter. As cultural agency, it is both the result of people being able to create new forms of cultural sensibility that can successfully capture elements of such a complex, unsettled space as well as the result of social institutions successfully targeting the tastes and interests of a newly emerging public. In this interaction between people and institutions, I think the discursive and representational aspects of such a changing culture are worth careful scrutiny. This is the point of departure for my analysis.

It is possible to produce an exhaustive list of unique features about Hong Kong's culture and diverse lifestyles in the early 1980s. This has already been the object of countless essays in a massive journalistic and scholarly literature. But since I began by focusing on issues of identity and how forces such as nationalism, colonialism, and capitalism can craft perceptions toward ethnicity, regardless of actual demographic origin, I think it is equally relevant to ask how and why certain forms of identity (especially politicized ones) find it necessary to invoke culture as an explicit label (and discourse), while consumption of culture in other respects (as goods, ideas, values, or lifestyles) does not necessarily invoke culture as a marked category. In short, I argue that cosmopolitanism and creolism are inherently different forms of cultural appropriation, as they differ less because of any inherent cultural attributes than because they represent different practical strategies of "culturalizing." To promote cosmopolitanism as the ethos of a mass culture should be a contradiction in terms, at least on the surface. One is an effort to maintain social exclusivity, and the other intrinsically sublimates difference.

I do not mean to say that cosmopolitanism is undesirable or impossible as cultural ideal. We all wish to be cosmopolitan, multilingual, multinational, and multicultural, all the while consuming the original and unique. Yet in real life, we all know that this is available only to a privileged few; otherwise we accept it as purely imaginative. On the other hand, creolism operates on a different cultural logic. Here, cultural mixing is a norm, but without regard to the conditions of use attached to it or nuances implied by its explicit marking. In practice, cultural interchange and hybridity of all kinds operate between both extremes, but I suggest that, rather than view them as different forms of cultural mixing, one can see them as diverse *strategies* of culturalizing, within which pragmatic intents and social meanings are implicitly embedded. For example, hybridity can be used to reinvent staple and nouvelle haute cuisine but the underlying strategies in each case are quite conscious of their accommodation of local or original taste and the sacrifices involved in each case. The transformation of McDonald's from American hamburger to transnational staple is an example of *selective* accommodation.

Intellectual Salon "Culture" in the Transformation of the Public Sphere

Locating the discursive origins or representational aspects of cosmopolitanism or hybrid culture in Hong Kong involves in the first instance articulating the possible contours of that culture and secondly defining the agency of persons and institutions in that process of cultural construction. Culture is an ongoing phenomenon everywhere, and while it is not necessary to single out a culture's uniqueness in order to recognize the nature of its existence, it is fair to say that Hong Kong's imagined community as a culture began in large part with a growing awareness of its autonomous identity. Like Anderson's (1983) abstract nationalism, it can be seen as a positional break vis-à-vis given sociopolitical frames of reference, but positional autonomy can be a function of many situational forces.[3] In this case, rootedness in the local imposed by its deracination from traditional frames of reference cultivated the formation of a liminal identity space that then cultivated assumed sharedness through a colloquial language, mass media, and other popular values rooted in the ongoing present. Despite the liminal nature of its identity, this was not unlike the way the consciousness of shared nationhood eventually occupied through the spread of mass literature and colloquial language the empty, homogenous time-spaces of Anderson's imagined communities. That Hong Kong culture became firmly rooted in a concrete sense of place or locality should not be regarded as a natural given, but rather as the end product of ongoing sociopolitical forces and strategic practices by people to define and reshape mutating life conditions. The complex of institutions that one has typically associated with this newly emerging Hong Kong culture, without a doubt, produced novel mind-sets and life practices that later became a cultural hub for "Greater China," but this novelty, at least at the outset, along with its appeal to cosmopolitanism and modernity, was more precisely the apt confluence of factors that actively induced or prompted the autonomy of a depoliticized, colloquially local culture in ways that contrasted forcibly with hegemonic, nationalist cultures rooted in ethnic and other orthodoxies of state-based identity prevalent elsewhere in Asia. Consonant at the same time with the evolution of cultural institutions, lifestyles, and behavior that broke away from traditional spheres of influence typical of Chinese societies elsewhere was thus the conscious emergence of an indigenous Hong Kong (*bengang*) identity. Insofar as it reflected the subjective autonomy of a shared community vis-à-vis the outside world, identity was by definition a conscious and unconscious set of life choices and value judgments that had to negotiate between alien and native, elite and popular, old and new. Some distinctive features or institutions often noted in this regard include its utilitarian commercialistic ethos that in many ways devalued cultural markers and national origins, a depoliticized mass culture rooted in a popular media industry that was deracinated from historical or intellectual tradition, finally the advent of Westernized influences that reiterated through its modernity the disappearance of colonialism. In such a cultural terrain, cosmopolitan and hybrid processes occupied many niches and assumed many forms. One paradigmatic textual representation of such culture is a trendy magazine titled *Haowai* (or *City Magazine*) that recently celebrated its thirtieth year of publication. From the mid- to late 1980s, it became a successful cosmopolitan lifestyle, youth fashion magazine, which especially attracted yuppie professionals among its staple readers. On the surface, it has similarities with high culture magazines like *Vogue* or *Cosmopolitan*, but it promoted an alternative, countercultural mind-set to fashion its views on media, arts, thought, and lifestyles.

The institutions, lifestyles, and behavior typically associated with the unique emergence of Hong Kong culture in the 1980s are themselves a product of complex changes, to say the least, but many aspects of this evolution can be reflected in the thirty-year transformation of *City Magazine* itself. Few magazines anywhere have undergone such radical transformation, not to mention enjoying such longevity or continued appeal, and distinctive features of its content and form are worth careful scrutiny. *Haowai* literally means "newspaper extra"; it was initially called in English the *Tabloid*, in the spirit of investigative reporting exemplified by the *Village Voice*. Its first issue appeared in September 1976 as a monthly journal in a newspaper format resembling the *Village Voice* or *Rolling Stone*, containing mostly essays, cartoons, and reviews of various sorts. In issue 7 the following March, it changed its English name to *City Magazine*. Over the first year, it began to establish a recognizable, systematic body of contents pertaining to intellectual currents, social criticism, reviews of music and fine arts, contemporary fashion, and other trendsetting cultural activities, both locally and abroad, while at the time expanding in pages as a full-fledged magazine publication. During its first five years, its profitability was marginal, if not consistently in the red.[4] Its elitist intellectual quality and critically progressive views on social issues made its appeal limited to a narrow readership that consisted of like-minded intellectuals with eclectic tastes or professionals with cosmopolitan values. Even while growing in sophistication, it lingered financially for many years, surviving mostly because of the monastic dedication of a core group of writers and its reliance on outside writers willing to forego payment for journalistic contributions. Its April 1982 issue was a turning point in the history of the magazine, when it completely revamped its design, doubling in size from A4- to A3-page format, adopted a glossy cover, enhanced its textual and spatial aesthetics, added numerous color illustrations, and generally restructured its appearance to match its outwardly cosmopolitan image, trendy outlook, and implicitly elite aspirations. The revamped format attracted advertising revenue in the form of full-page ads, which at the same time provided the magazine with a staple, sustainable revenue. Its commercial viability in turn allowed it to develop more fully and diversely as a trendsetting cosmopolitan cultural magazine. The next twenty years saw at least two succeeding generations of writers, and the successful marketing of the magazine established it in the long run as a systematic, important beacon of Hong Kong contemporary culture, with interests in all aspects of pop culture, mass media, fine arts, lifestyle, taste, and modern fashion. In a word, if any magazine exemplified the ongoing pulse of a uniquely Hong Kong culture, reflected most typically by the gradually dominant tastes, attitudes, and consumption patterns of locally bred Hong Kong people, this was definitely one, if not, it. There are without a doubt many features of *City Magazine* that deserve detailed attention in this regard, but the very evolution of the magazine in the context of larger ongoing social and political changes is itself a noteworthy development that ultimately has important resonances for understanding the profound formative relationship between culture and the public sphere as well as the seminal role of discursive and representational imagination in that social agency.

At least in its mature evolution, the magazine captured in many obvious respects diverse aspects of Hong Kong's newly emerging culture, namely its open embrace of a cosmopolitan ethos, its extensive appeal to latest currents in film, music, fashion, the arts, and other aspects of progressive (commercialist-oriented) culture and its inherent cultivation of a public culture identified with and intricately tied to a popular and Cantonese-speaking TV and film industry. In various regards, it overlaps with many competing publications. In terms of cosmopolitan appeal, it is probably not the first or most prominent magazine to promote elite Western tastes, if this is what cosmopolitan means. The *Hong Kong Tatler*, an English-language magazine published by and mostly for British expatriates, devoted primarily to reportage of happenings in the West and information about expatriate social events and culture in Hong Kong, has had a longer existence as a publication, but its relationship to the lives and interests of local Hong Kong people is minimal. While cosmopolitan in one respect, its definition and tastes tend to be exclusively colonialist in nature. *City Magazine* was not the first publication to promote cosmopolitan fashion either. *Style Hong Kong* (*shishi*) is a bilingual, largely women's magazine devoted to cosmopolitan high fashion with a long history of publication and broad commercial appeal. The Chinese edition of *Esquire* debuted in 1984, and clearly catered to cosmopolitan tastes of educated, professional males. Like the two other magazines, it was successful in attracting people with culturally eclectic taste and high-end consumer lifestyles. Yet on the other hand, the clientele drawn to such publications seemed limited to a privileged niche and did not seem representative of cultural sensibilities among the populace at large.

The role that *Haowai* has played in the development of local popular culture has already been discussed by various writers in the cultural studies literature on Hong Kong.[5] However, its significance must be seen first of all in the framework of the magazine's metamorphosis over the decades. The magazine began as something quite different from what it eventually evolved into, despite the continued guidance of the first generation of editors and writers for most of its initial decade. As mentioned above, it was founded explicitly in the style of the *Village Voice*, and its English title, the *Tabloid*, was meant to embody a socially critical ethos and its explicit penchant for countercultural currents and alternative intellectual perspectives, whatever their origin. The contents of its inaugural 1976 issue are illustrative in this regard:

1. **Featured Essays**
   a. *Tabloid Report*: "Maternity hospital makes wrong transfusion of blood, resulting in death"
   b. *Essay*: "The psychological burden brought about by super (successful) women"
   c. *Essay*: "Reflections of a methadone user"
   d. *Essay*: "Dale Carnegie should teach a course on how to deal with salesmen"
   e. *Essay*: "Local community support organizations—are they activist groups"?

2. **Centerfold** (Five short *columns*)
   a. Literary review
   b. Introduction to *yijing* hexagrams
   c. Survey of late night eating
   d. Listing of concerts, dance, film, and art events
   e. "Jest Set"

3. **Book Review Section**
   a. *Review essay* on Robert Heilbroner, *An Inquiry into the Human Prospect* and Gordon Taylor, *Rethink Radical Proposals to Save a Disintegrating World*
   b. *Review essay* of two novels by Zhou Shou-zhuan
   c. *Review essay* on critical theory titled "Some problems in Marxist theories of the state"

4. **Arts Section**
   a. *Review* of Art Garfunkel's album *Breakaway*
   b. *Review* of jazz albums by Gabor Szabo, Maynard Ferguson, Herbie Mann, and Pat Rebillot

    c. *Review* of an out of print album by Josh White

    d. *Commentary* on the creative syncretism of the Hong Kong Youth Ballet Theater Troupe

    e. *Commentary* on the past and future of domestic handicrafts

    f. Two *reviews* of the film *Tiao hui*

    g. *Essay* on the diverse uses of classical music in some films

5. TV Program *Commentaries*

    a. One titled *The Existence of Zhong Ding-dang*

    b. One titled *Let Go of Francis Lai*

A brief perusal of the above contents shows that it began less as a trendy cosmopolitan lifestyle magazine than as an intellectually flavored journal grounded in contemporary social and cultural currents, not unlike the Parisian *Le Nouvel Observateur*. If it was cosmopolitan in outlook, it shared little with the colonialist expatriate tastes of the *Hong Kong Tatler*. In cultural content, it was not exclusively devoted to fashion and fine arts of a kind that typically dominated women's magazines, such as *Style Hong Kong*. Even in its refined style, culture here appealed less to the professional elite who tend to read *Esquire* and catered explicitly to countercultural influences or alternative lifestyles. The five main essays also aptly reflected the socially critical and investigative spirit of its title the *Tabloid*. This was not a magazine for popular consumption that attempted to appeal to mainstream interests. Its readers were most likely intellectual eclectics who shared similar sociopolitical viewpoints. As a Chinese language publication, it was remotely distanced from the traditional and nationalist concerns that dominated most other Hong Kong intellectuals and activists. In such a context, it would have been difficult to imagine this magazine appealing to anyone who was not already highly Western educated, if not literate in English as well. In fact, when *Haowai* first appeared, it was viewed as perilously alien by students belonging to various nationalist (*guocui*) cliques.[6]

Thus, from the Chinese mainstream, it is easy to regard *Haowai* as a Western-influenced magazine with radically different cultural interests that did not seem relevant to Hong Kong at that time. If it was cosmopolitan, it should really be seen as an effort to introduce a larger worldly outlook into a Hong Kong context. Despite its attention to Western pop music and art, there was also little explicit concern to developments in local Hong Kong popular culture, which were firmly Cantonese, if anything. Western pop culture appeared here as an eclectic element from a Hong Kong cultural point of view and was something still alien to most there. Culture here was treated as largely literary and intellectual in nature; at least, its attention to more mundane aspects of lifestyle, most notably as fashion, cuisine, and material consumption of various kinds did not appear until somewhat later. Its subtle social criticism should also be regarded as a mind-set that deliberately set itself apart from the popular public or the mass, whatever that was. Even the satirical cartoons that were interspersed along with the essays resembled *manga* but probably took their inspiration more from the underground comics of R. Crumb. In short, its underlying cosmopolitanism and critical ethos set it *apart* from popular culture, as it had existed "locally" at the time, even as it appeared to articulate the grounds for a *different* kind of popular culture or everyday lifestyle. Yet more importantly, in assessing the nature of this cosmopolitanism, perhaps its most significant feature was the way in which it tended to routinely embrace both Western and Chinese culture as *equals*, with little attempt to dualize or categorize them separately. There was also little attempt to cultivate hybridity, through mixing; there is at least a clear sense in which both represented compatible elements within the larger view of things. Even in the texts themselves, English terms were routinely interspersed with Chinese ones (without translation or romanization), which was disorienting, if not unacceptable and incomprehensible as well, in terms of conventional Chinese writing.[7] In sum, at the time of *Haowai*'s appearance, there were many more reasons for viewing it as something consciously alien and removed from the mainstream than anything constitutive of a newly emerging popular culture or public sentiment. Many things changed in due course.

Over the next five years, *Haowai* expanded its cultural coverage to include fashion, fine cuisine, and subtle changes in the arts, most importantly developments in the emerging film and mass media industry. Attention to intellectual developments in contemporary theory continued to be strong along with reporting on social issues. The combination of its esoteric interests and concern with alternative cultural and social lifestyles was a potentially explosive mix, but what characterized its underlying ethos was a unique *mind-set*, perhaps best reflected in the keywords invoked throughout the magazine: fashion (*shizhuang*), consumption (*xiaofei*), vogue (*chaoliu*), sensuality (*qingse*), culture (*wenhua*), middlebrow (*zhongchan*), style (*zitai*), perspective (*jiaodu*), objectivity (*zhongxing*), high class (*guizu*), taste (*pinwei*), form (*xingge*), image (*xingxiang*) and brand respectability (*qipai*).[8] In terms of content, it was probably the first magazine in Hong Kong to directly address and openly discuss topics such as 1960s counterculture, the disco scene, homosexuality, feminism, not to mention sexuality in general, and other explicitly irreverent issues, including bad taste. It was very conscious of its contemporaneity, occasionally reflecting on the passing of *les temps perdu*, even speculating about the advent of upcoming times. In fact, the potpourri of essays and regular columns on diverse aspects of culture, from literary thought to practical lifestyle, reflected interest in a wide range of issues, but its manifest representations of worldly sophistication and progressive alterity were always driven by a distinctly *irreverent* attitude or ethos of nonconformity that seemed less driven on changing the public *as a whole* than on giving voice to a heretofore unrepresented *niche* community, while ramifying its worldview.

That niche community was, of course, a generation of Hong Kong–bred youth that was disenfranchised from the public by other more dominant sectors of the population, namely, the diasporic interests of a refugee constituency caught between two sides of a nationalizing Cold War, colonialist interests of the government and a resident populace that still viewed itself as a satellite city within Guangdong and its Cantonese sphere of influence, albeit in increasingly unsettling terms. *Haowai*'s cosmopolitan eclecticism was radical for its time, and one can ask whether it actually influenced the emergence of new cultural sensibilities or just blended in with the times. Over time, I argue that prevailing nationalizing forces, traditional spheres of influence and diasporic ethnic elements began to wane not because of any inherent demise but because of fundamental paradigmatic shifts toward a geopolitical ground that necessitated a new place-based imagination. Whatever these cosmopolitan forces were, in the long run they had to be accommodated by or assimilated in line with this emergent sense of community that was increasingly dominated by a locally bred population explicitly *identifying* with Hong Kong as its primary cultural frame of reference. In short, postwar Hong Kong was a setting that witnessed diverse, competing cultural forces and had ramifications in all aspects of local thought and lifestyle, but what impacted the most were those elements that eventually melded best (most successfully) into the institutions and mind-sets of that emerging public culture.

The Aesthetics of Cultural Eclecticism
in an Emerging Culture "Industry"

The early evolution of *Haowai* invokes a familiar question prompted first by Habermas's *The Structural Transformation of the Public Sphere*, namely, what is the role of the salon and critical discourse in the creation of a space of rational communication that eventually became the basis for the emergence of a public sphere by galvanizing a practical field of opposition to hegemonic domination by the state and other vested interests in society?[9] In many respects, *Haowai* seemed to provide a discursive space for such critical communication, whether or not it actually was able to promote effectively the content of this ideology. Its later evolution, if anything, manifested growing interest in and cultivation of a locally emergent popular culture influenced heavily not only by cosmopolitan ideals, utilitarian values and modern lifestyles but also by identification with a mass media industry that gradually became the "colloquializing" framework for a new public and its imagined sensibilities. In this regard, the transformation of the magazine was perhaps significant less for its change in content than in form. A major turning point that propelled it into a successful widely read magazine and firmly established it as a representative voice of a newly emerging public culture was a decision by the editors in April 1982 to radically alter the magazine's design from a text-based journal focused on the literal content of its essays, printed in A4 format, to a glossily illustrated magazine, doubled to A3 size, with restyled headers and a considerably more spacious aesthetic look. A crude comparison of the two issues before and after the new design exemplifies the essence of this structural change. Another significant outcome here was a marked increase in full-page ads.

March 1982 (Issue 67)
Number of pages devoted to the following content categories:
Text-based essays: 59 pages
Noncommercial promotion (mainly public service announcements,
    event listings): 8 pages
Feature cartoons: 4 pages
Full-page photographs: 5 pages
Full-page commercially paid advertisements: 4 pages

April 1982 (Issue 68)
Number of pages devoted to the following content categories:
Text-based essays: 41 pages
Noncommercial promotion (mainly public service announcements,
    event listings): 5 pages
Feature cartoons: none
Full-page photographs: 23 pages
Full-page commercially paid advertisements: 13 pages

The number of full-page ads in issues 69–71 occupied 11, 22, and 20 pages, respectively, and continued in general to increase in subsequent issues. Full-page photographs increased many times over and became a staple feature of its new look. The number of pages devoted to text essays tended to decline slightly as a result of the new design, but this was offset also by its switch to A3 format. Equally importantly, the proportion of pictures to text in essays increased drastically from 20 percent to 30 percent in the old format to 40 percent to 60 percent in the new format, with blank space accounting for 20 percent on average (as aesthetic enhancement). While font size remained the same, the amount of space and pictures that occupied each page, more than the number of pages itself, tended to overwhelm the impact of the text on the page. The table of contents, which usually appeared just inside the cover, was now also buried inside the magazine, under six to eight pages of full color picture ads, mimicking standard commercial magazines. Whether this revolution in form fundamentally changed the impact of the magazine in substance can be debated, but it is clear that the feel of the magazine altered by its format changes introduced subtle changes in the way the magazine (as writers, editors, and owners) perceived its relationship to the kind of cultural values, trends, lifestyles, and institutions that it actively wrote about and promoted.

Without a doubt, the new format magazine sold well, and its commercial success was the most important factor that guaranteed its continued survival. In comparison to competing magazines at the time, *Haowai* was much less commercial. The April 1982 issues of *Style Hong Kong* and the *Hong Kong Tatler* devoted the same overall number of pages to essays, while carrying fifty-one and eighty-four pages of full-page ads, respectively, and burying their table of contents under sixteen pages of ads. The proportion of illustrations to text in essays tended to average 30 percent to 40 percent in the latter two magazines, which should have made *Haowai*, with its more aesthetic format, even more out of character with the supposedly serious, intellectual content of its writings. Its trend toward aesthetic appeal was inextricably related to a greater reliance on commercial appeal as a principle of operation, and both factors had inevitable and subtle influences on the content and form of its writing in the long run. As the baton passed to succeeding generations of writers and editors, the commercial viability of *Haowai* allowed it to expand in volume as well as to intensify its focus on high fashion, haute cuisine, cutting-edge technology, and esoteric dimensions of the good life in general, all driven by urban chic, trend pacing, heuristic consumption, and cosmopolitan eclecticism as the ethos of the new age. While its editors proclaimed in March 1982 that *Haowai*'s eccentric worldview would remain unchanged, in the long run one could unavoidably witness a gradual disappearance of writing on trendsetting developments in intellectual theory and the blunt investigative journalism that had represented a more staple presence in its early issues. What does all this really mean?

The constraints of space cannot do justice to the complex evolution that *Haowai* actually underwent during its heyday in the latter half of the 1980s and into the 1990s. By 1988, one might venture to say that it became a full-fledged commercial enterprise, after its conscious editorial makeover to promote a haute couture cosmopolitan lifestyle that was combined with the advent of computerized typesetting and its embrace of digital technology as the staple of everyday life. Surveys conducted by the magazine also revealed that its readers tended to be predominantly yuppie professionals, with many of them claiming to drive BMWs.[10] It also underwent several organizational changes, witnessing a change of publisher from Seven Hills, Ltd. to City Howwhy, Ltd. in 2000, then its purchase and absorption by the mainland Chinese conglomerate Xiandai Chuanbo in 2003, which made it a flagship publication within a family of magazines devoted largely to modern life-styles. In content, one witnessed without doubt a refinement and expansion of existing coverage in cultural tastes and social lifestyles that it had already promoted extensively since its inception, even though the relative proportion of attention to various fields of interest changed gradually in the long run. One might also say that the change in form primarily enhanced the appeal of such interests to a wider readership. However, in attempting to appeal to that broader public, one can question whether its success was really the result of its aesthetic and sophisticated effectiveness in promoting the critical, intellectual values that primordially drove its writing or whether it success-fully transformed itself in a way that made it acceptable and digestible to an emerging public that was changing of its own accord. That is to say, who was accommodating whom, and what really changed in the process? Despite the many distinctive features of mind-set or ethos that characterized the early evolution of *Haowai*, as noted above, and appeared to presage the behavior, thought patterns, and practical outlooks that later became com-monplace in subsequent decades, I am more inclined to believe that the emergence of a new public imagination rooted largely in the development of a mass media industry provided the primary institutional frame of refer-ence through which new cultural sensibilities and practical lifestyles became galvanized. In this regard, one can also detect a subtle change over time in *Haowai*'s critical relationship to the rest of society and its emerging culture at large. As cosmopolitan thinking and commercial consumption became more socially commonplace and extolled as the new gods of everyday life (as a result of depoliticizing tendencies of unregulated utilitarian capital-ism and moves away from prevailing nationalistic struggles), the critical sharpness that initially characterized *Haowai* (represented by differences that it cultivated vis-à-vis the mass) softened correspondingly, too.

One can undeniably say that *Haowai* continued to promote (even more successfully) the inherent interests, tastes, and values of a locally bred generation of Hong Kong youth who at the same time were increasingly distanced from an older generation of diasporic residents, on the one hand, and those people associated primarily with a mutating colonial regime and other expatriate interests, on the other hand. However, rather than directly influencing this new local generation, it appeared that the latter matured of its own accord and that its interests became shaped largely by a (politically desensitized and commercially oriented) mass media industry. This locally bred generation embraced many of the interests, tastes, and values promoted by *Haowai*, and *Haowai* in turn successfully transformed itself by accommodating those interests, tastes, and values and shaping them into a systematic worldview *at the expense of* other interests, tastes, and values that happened to reflect its more socially activist, critical intellectual perspectives.

Haowai actively embraced and inevitably became an integral part of that popular culture emerging from this new entertainment media and film industry, which cultivated a distinctive Hong Kong style or ethos of its own. Such a culture industry may or may not have entirely resembled that archetypically described by Horkheimer and Adorno, but it played to a large extent an important role in commoditizing a heuristic, mass-mediated lifestyle that served as a "standard linguistic community" for local culture.[11] Unlike elsewhere, this popular culture served in the absence of a political community, defined typically by common citizenship and shared social values. By virtue of its being an object of popular veneration and commercial consumption, driven by the imperatives of profit maximization through mass appeal, such a culture was correspondingly less moved by esoteric, intellectual trends or fine-tuned aesthetic norms. Thus, was commercial desirability or viability the new guiding principle that in the long run softened the critical edge and eclectic quality that epitomized *Haowai's* initial years and subtly transformed the underlying mind-set of the magazine in subsequent phases?

Subjective changes of mind-set are difficult to gauge and interpret, but it is clear that the gradual shift in *Haowai's* detached eccentricity or eclectic intellectualism inherent before the 1980s contrasts with its progressive posture in promoting the film and mass media industry in later years and collusive involvement in its institutional development. This gradual shift in subjective positioning was in effect a direct consequence precipitated by the radical changes in format and aesthetic design that restructured the magazine in 1982, changes that apparently took on a life of its own. At this point, one should ask in what sense this burgeoning mass media entertainment industry was able to represent an emerging "public" sensibility, which at the same time served as a standard lingua franca for a distinctive "local" cultural imagination.

In many respects, the development of Hong Kong film and TV captured public appeal in terms of broad popular acceptance and its ability to transcend class differences and political ideologies. Insofar as depoliticization of culture was implicitly enforced by colonial policy, one can say that a certain kind of public already predicated to some extent a certain genre of cultural landscape. At the same time, the development of the local was less a rediscovery or invention of such traditions than an explicit break away from prevailing national and regional spheres of influence. In the case of film, Hong Kong "style" established itself in contrast to Mandarin and Cantonese genres while at the same time rooting itself either in the place-based contemporary or in abstract mind-sets peculiar to Hong Kong sensibilities. TV also emerged at a time when the mass media began to play a dominant role in establishing a standard public community and institutional frame of reference for a shared culture. That both TV and film adopted Cantonese as their lingua franca was not an insignificant factor, even as the content of popular culture was continuously drawn from the outside and its constructive synthesis of many unlikely elements. *Huanle jinxiao*, a nightly entertainment show, was by far the most heavily watched TV program in Hong Kong in the 1970s and '80s, and perhaps best epitomized the cultural sensibilities of Hong Kong's general populace. Cosmopolitan influences were certainly one aspect of this creative mix but so were commoditizing forces imposed by the ethos of a market-dominated way of life as well as nomadic or liminal impulses derived from living in a borrowed place and time that glossed over a surreal, apathetic political worldview.

The commercial superficiality of popular culture cultivated by the mass media has been criticized typically as an intellectual desert, and this contrasts with the intellectual seriousness (albeit irreverent) that has always been characteristic of *Haowai*, but the media industry drew on mind-sets, behaviors, and values that happened to connect with a newly emerging cultural landscape that was already in the making as a result of diverse and complex forces. Like the mass media, *Haowai* also connected with part of that landscape of public imagination, which it iconically defined as synonymous with the "City." In the process of successfully tapping into these currents, it began deliberately or unwittingly to transform itself. It lent a uniquely sophisticated voice in promoting this City lifestyle and ethos, to say the least, but its collusive relationship with the evolution of mass-mediated popular culture made it an inherent part of the latter's development as a mainstream that contrasted with its critical distance in an earlier era and contributed in the long run to a subtle metamorphosis in its overall guiding principles.

The geopolitical creation in Hong Kong of a depoliticized public paved the way for the wholesale transformations spawned by utilitarian capitalism and its commoditizing ethos as a staple lifestyle, which in turn enabled Hong Kongers to redefine themselves in multicultural terms and through cosmopolitan consumption. These developments were consonant with an emerging consciousness of a local Hong Kong identity. Like all the above, this identity was not just a realization of its place-based existence or a discovery of its indigenous essence but rather a complex subject positioning that by force of circumstances made peculiar life choices in a process of strategic rationalization or selective accommodation. Although the invention of the local was not the product of intentioned free will, the advent of such an identity as well as the processes by which it became discursively articulated and institutionally disseminated took on a dynamic of its own that transcended simple appropriations of the global order.

The Birth of "Local" Popular Culture in the Context of Cosmopolitan Hybridity

On the occasion of the thirtieth anniversary of *Haowai*, Joint Publishing Co., Ltd. compiled a three-volume selection of exemplary essays and materials from its thirty years of publication.[12] Edited by Lui Tai Lok, a senior sociologist at the Chinese University of Hong Kong, who was an avid reader of and keen contributor to the magazine throughout its history, this collection of material and supplementary commentaries provided rich insights into the complex, diverse history of the magazine and its extensive connections to Hong Kong culture and society. An artistic collage reproduced from issue 225 (1995) prefaced one section, titled "Hong Kong Style." Perhaps more interesting than the collage itself, which was meant clearly to reflect the inherent hybridity of Hong Kong culture, was an editorial footnote: "Finally, *Haowai* is a Hong Kong magazine."[13] Echoing Lui's introductory essay in the three-volume set, it was as if to suggest that, despite the magazine's explicit focus on cosmopolitan hybridity and its claim to represent a local generation of Hong Kong and Hong Kongers throughout its long history, it was only in the mid-1990s, according to Lui, that the magazine had accomplished this vision in practice. What cosmopolitan hybridity really means in a Hong Kong context and in what senses this has come about is, rightly so, a question of interpretation and continuing debate. It is possible to read the magazine's overt representations as well as the intentioned meanings of its writers in many ways, especially after the fact.[14] Among other things, the long list of contributors to the magazine have gone on to other ventures, while moving on to other related publications, evolving into important commentators on Hong Kong pop culture and society in general, and becoming involved in other media institutions, such as filmmaking and TV.

Underscoring Lui's argument is less the claim that contemporary Hong Kong society is rooted intricately in its hybridity that his questioning of whether cosmopolitanism, especially of the kind espoused by *Haowai* in its early years, was really consistent with its intention to fashion a uniquely Hong Kong culture. As Peter Wong, one of *Haowai*'s later editors, aptly remarked, in relation to the magazine's routine usage of bilingual heteroglossia in its writing, its founding editors, Chan Koon Chung and Peter Dunn, in particular, usually thought things out in English and wrote them out in Chinese.[15] Much of how they viewed the direct import of things Western onto the Hong Kong scene can thus be interpreted in the same vein. On the other hand, the question of how they actually thought is in my opinion less relevant than our understanding of social processes underlying such cosmopolitanism. Even if the hybrid nature of their writing was a result of their ambidexterity in English and Chinese, one cannot say the same for a later generation of Hong Kongers who adopted linguistic heteroglossia as a routine mode of communication; likewise for the trend of youths to adopt English names and other hybrid practices. The latter were consequences of a broader mind-set that was already in the making and was not necessarily the product of cosmopolitanism, strictly speaking, or *Haowai*'s radical chic, which was truly premonitory in many senses. It is not surprising that, especially in its early years, *Haowai* was more often viewed as culturally elitist. Many of its cosmopolitan tastes were simply alien to those less sophisticated in general and could not have been viewed otherwise as long as such culture remained objects of limited (esoteric) consumption.

Orlando Patterson's work on Jamaican "cosmopolises" provides a contrasting reference point.[16] By focusing on an alternative facade of Gilroy's Black Atlantic, namely, the role of West Indian black intellectuals in the development of British philosophy and their active promotion of colonialist lifestyles there, Patterson has instead emphasized the overlapping coexistence of all kinds of cosmopolitan and transnational worldviews.[17] This has contrasted with the inherent creolism of working-class lifestyles. The development of reggae, which began as bad imitations of African music, then evolved into a hybrid cultural creation of its own and became exported globally as a genre of popular music, followed a different ideology of "mixing." Nonetheless, both approaches to intercultural practice coexisted as local cultural lifestyles but remained sociologically distinct.

In the context of Hong Kong, the transformation brought about by its development into a free port has been universally acknowledged as a seminal factor underscoring the utilitarian radicalization of local lifestyles and social values in general, but this in turn enabled, through market accessibility to foreign goods and ideas and commoditized consumption, the inherent demystification of cultural dualisms and nationalist markers.[18] Cosmopolitanism ushered in hydridity as an acceptable way of life, but the degree to which a cosmopolitan-based cultural ethos or indigenous syncretism prevailed was still a function of differential access to cultural consumption. That *Haowai* positioned itself both in relation to cosmopolitan values and the emerging sensibilities of popular culture makes its perspective on "cosmopolitan hybridity" ambivalent and prone to differing interpretations. With the growing affluence of the general public, one can see a general embrace of cosmopolitanism as well as a tendency to define the local in such terms, the latter being, in strict terms, a geopolitical product of identity position.

In assessing the important contributions of *Haowai*, Lui's problematizing of whether it played in fact a direct role in the formation of a locally bred, uniquely syncretic Hong Kong culture is probably relevant but is not necessarily the right question to ask. One should ask whether the force of ideas and culture alone, either through rational discourse or imaginative representation, can actively transform the public sphere and the popular landscape. Despite *Haowai*'s relatively late embrace of the notion of hybridity in the form of "Chinese-barbarian half breed" (*bantangfan*), attention to the Hong Kong scene had always been an intimate concern of the magazine since its origin.[19] If anything, it had always promoted a clear social realist stance combined with an articulate intellectual viewpoint and a flair for cultural eccentricity, which can be regarded as primordial elements of a socially critical imagination. Its concern with the practice of contemporary life was probably what distanced it from serious, scholarly journals, but it certainly did not lack in intellectual content or wit. Its intellectual qualities and esoteric remove from the tastes of a general populace tended, if anything, to guarantee it a niche readership. The magazine's transformation over the years was indeed complex, but the context in which it was embedded was more complex and deserves primary consideration, in my opinion. Despite the many growing linkages between the magazine and the emerging popular culture it seemed to nurture, one can ironically witness a gradual decline of precisely those elements that made it an intellectually critical and eccentrically positioned magazine to begin with. This was implicitly also part of Lui's chagrin in selecting presumably the most exemplary essays over those thirty years, which tended to favor the high-minded writings of the early years over the staple, well-known, and more widely read writings that established it as a successful, long-running magazine. The question of who really championed hybridity in the birth of the uniquely local pales in comparison to the way the eclectic, intellectual qualities of the magazine were in the long run sublimated and disappeared in the formation of the popular culture industry, dominated largely by the imagination of various mass media institutions.

The ways in which such institutions eventually define the cultural landscape and capture the public imagination thus represent the framework within which one can appropriately ask, what is cosmopolitan hybridity in a Hong Kong context? Its process of cultural negotiation is predicated first of all on complex changes in the geopolitical landscape that make possible the acceptability of different cultural forms, which then invoke the agency of various kinds of institutions and its vested interests, within which discursive imagination plays an important albeit lesser role in the long run. Cosmopolitan hybridity ultimately takes on different forms, and perhaps more importantly they all have different sociological functions and ramifications. In this regard, nouvelle haute cuisine and McDonald's are both cosmopolitan hybrid in their approach to cuisine. Both respond to local acceptability, albeit differently classed niches of the local. Cosmopolitanism functions differently in each case, and the nature of their hybrid practices, both explicit and implicit, is determined by the way it perceives culture as an object of promotion and consumption. Both can make equally strong claims of being local in ways that implicitly accent different definitions of uniqueness. In the final analysis, the important issues center not on how prevalent cosmopolitan hybridity is, or even whether, as a concept, it is worth championing, but rather the ways in which it has complexly shaped social processes.

Chapter 6

Hong Kong's Embrace of the Motherland

Economy and Culture as Fictive Commodities

History is what hurts, it is what refuses desire and sets inexorable limits to individual as well as collective praxis, which its "ruses" turn into grisly and ironic reversals of their overt intention. But this History can be apprehended only through its effects, and never directly as some reified force.

—Frederic Jameson, *The Political Unconscious:*
Narrative as Socially Symbolic Act

1997: A Year of No Significance

The renowned sociologist Wong Siu-lun (1999:181) opened his essay, "Changing Hong Kong Identities," by declaring, "the year 1997 is a year of significance for Hong Kong. The long anticipated rite of passage is over. With the change of flags at the handover ceremony on 1 July of that year, Hong Kong ceased to be a British colony. It acquired the new status of a Special Administrative Region [SAR] of China." As if to point to the subjective complexity underlying an objective reality, he cited remarks made by Chief Secretary Anson Chan, who, in reflecting on personal experiences gained in the first year after the handover, said, "[the] real transition has been much more complex, subtle and profound . . . That is because the real transition is about identity and not sovereignty."[1] In other words, real identities lurk beneath. One might then wonder what is so fictive about sovereignty that makes identity so real.

This is a rewriting and significant update of "Hong Kong 'Identity' after the End of History," which appeared in *Contemporary Asian Modernities: Transnationality, Interculturality and Hybridity*, eds. Chu Yiu-wai and Eva Kit-wah Man, Bern: Peter Lang (2010), pp. 167–90.

I argue on the contrary that history is in the first instance more about fictions than about realities. The historical irony of Hong Kong's official handover to China on July 1, 1997 (or "return to the motherland," depending on one's point of view) was that the future of Hong Kong, which had been a cession in perpetuity, was made to coincide with the end of the ninety-nine-year lease of the New Territories. Few people remember anymore that the New Territories was supposed to be administered as an extension of Hong Kong, with due respect to native (presumably unchanging) tradition, even though the reality of modern expansion effectively incorporated it later into the larger colonial history of Hong Kong. One might add to this the mystery of why the Chinese government, on the other hand, continued to play along with the official reality of the lease, denying all the while the validity of Hong Kong's status as a ceded colony (being the result of a treaty signed under duress). It not only made Handover Day a Chinese national holiday, whose media hype became an industry in itself, moreover the coincidence of Hong Kong's celebration of Queen's Elizabeth's Birthday on the eve of the handover canonized the five-day weekend into an event of unreal proportions many times over. Thus, the reality of Hong Kong's colonial existence, already mystified by its official disappearance, was suddenly resurrected by the fiction of a lease that had been meaningless, if not long dead. If sovereignty is rooted in such a fiction, then how unreal can identity be?

Identities can easily be driven by illusions, and postwar Hong Kong is an ideal example of how identities have been constantly made and remade. With ties to a culture industry and other institutions of authority, the history of Hong Kong identity(ies) can be seen in some instances more fittingly as a history of hype. As we all know, public sentiment in Hong Kong has always been prone to what Gustav Le Bon once called "the psychology of the crowd" (*la psychologie de la foule*), which can perhaps be deliberately misread as a crude pun on mass mentality. The stock market has been known to plunge drastically during moments of mass hysteria, and the slightest rumors of scandal have been known to cause a run on local banks, with nervous clients lining up for days to empty their savings accounts. Sentiments can swing from one extreme to another. Anti-PRC sentiment was, of course, strongest in reaction to the Tiananmen Incident of 1989, but it has been countered also by waves of nationalistic fervor, judging at least from the euphoria created by Beijing's almost successful bid, in 1994, for the (Sydney) Olympics. In the long run, these moments are precisely that; that is, they come and go. But more importantly, the volatile and fragile nature that seems to characterize Hong Kong public sentiment (of which identity is a specific politicized manifestation) is as much a reflection of its arbitrariness or unpredictability on the surface as a function of an institutional system that appears to make real the collective ramifications of individual desires and fears. The market has made what Hong Kong is today, where utilitarian rationality is not only an economic logic that drives the value of commodities and property but also a kind of ethos that dictates entire lifestyles, even though we tend to forget that global politics of the 1960s was what really transformed Hong Kong into a market society. In this sense, fear of capital flight that often epitomizes the seeming fragility or ephemerality of Hong Kong's economy is really a function of the absence of a place-based rural or industrial infrastructure that is the basis of economies elsewhere. In other respects, microeconomic laissez-faire is tempered by macroeconomic state intervention. The volatility of the HK dollar in 1984 led eventually to its currency peg to the US dollar, while the colonial government's regulation of land policy became a crucially important aspect of Hong Kong's planned urban and industrial modernization.

In short, the more one has been led to believe that identity in Hong Kong is a product of inherently individual desires and rational intents, the more it tends to take on, on the contrary, a fictive character. In the pre-1997 era, one has been led to believe that a concrete Hong Kong identity exists or is important in some respect, even though we all know that this identity is an invention that is less than fifty years old. Its distinctiveness is in effect less a product of its unique inventive quality than, in the first instance, of a changing sociopolitical landscape that has defined its parameters and shaped its possibilities of meaning. Moreover, in order to ask what post-1997 identity is or whether it exists at all, one must first ask whether 1997 really marks a significant change in sociopolitical terms. This remains a matter of debate and interpretation.

1997 is a year of no significance, it can be argued. Or to put it in another way, it is one that marks a potentially significant transition but at a deeper underlying level masks sociopolitical processes whose nature is still unclear or in the midst of being played out, in my opinion. In actuality, the hype of 1997 did not begin in 1997, or in the carnival atmosphere that led up to its ritual handover on July 1. It had been thirteen years in the making. Some of the changes in mind-set that predicated this new identity had been put into place during the "transitional" years, and to some extent have simply continued into the post-1997 era. But the sociopolitical circumstances of the transition itself in the larger flow of things have been unpredictable and are worth careful scrutiny. They are the end point of analysis instead of its point of departure.

Not surprisingly, the most heated debates and crises over identity took place in the mid-1980s, then again in the year leading to the handover itself. Nonetheless, in the entire transitional era, one can detect a subtle shift of sentiment with regard to definitions of the self that have been cultivated and reproduced in different regimes of subjective identification and cultural representation. This has already been the subject of many surveys as well as semiotic analysis of various kinds. It is not my intention to review the literature in this regard, except to say that all these popular discourses and analyses focus too much on deconstructing in a literal sense the superficial definitions of Hong Kongness vis-à-vis China and the West in order to uncover the underlying substance of these identities. In the final analysis, the existence of colonialism and nationalism is always inferred but never directly confronted as an institution of practice. In what senses do the facts of colonialism depend on its fictions, and vice versa? In what senses is nationalism dualistically opposed to colonialism, and in what senses is it a neo-colonialism? The transition signified by the year "1997" invokes many possible political processes, but in order to understand colonialism and nationalism it is necessary to unpack the relationship between their ongoing discourses and practices in a Hong Kong context.

The ethos of utilitarian familism and the myth of apolitical man tend to be the most often cited metaphors (myths) to characterize the culture and lifestyle of people living in postwar Hong Kong.[2] Without a doubt, the utilitarian lifestyle for which Hong Kong is so famous was largely the product of the 1970s. However, the free market economy that gave rise to this lifestyle was also the consequence of a complex political struggle to transcend the nationalist strife that enveloped Hong Kong, as well as a moment in the evolution of the modern world system. The fact that we view this utilitarian ethos merely as a manifestation of the modern life-style is at the same time a fiction that has neatly disguised the exploitative aspects of the capitalist system. Eugene Cooper (1982:25) perhaps phrased it best, when he said that free market development in Hong Kong was "a veritable proving ground for Marxist theory, where the enterprising student of Marxist political economy can literally watch chapters of *Capital* unfold before his eyes." The assertion that the typical Hong Konger was apolitical was also without doubt a product of that same modern, materialistic era, but few people note that this apolitical façade was strictly enforced by a colonial government bent on deflecting nationalist conflict from the territory to the extent of suppressing all political dissent. The institutionalization of an apolitical mentality and lifestyle had the ultimate goal of deflecting the essential violence of colonial power that maintained the system, like the way the virtues of modernization have obscured the exploitative dimensions of capitalism. One cannot in practice neatly separate colonialism from national-ism or modernity. I submit that their mutually collusive nature constitutes its sociopolitical ground, which in the final analysis engenders "identity."[3]

People who write about identity speak as if we are ipso facto supposed to have one; if not one, then many. Life is thus a process through which we negotiate on the basis of our presumed identity(ies). Yet it is harder to systematically say precisely when and why we should invoke identity(ies), *if at all*. We *think* we know who we are, when in fact our situatedness within a larger geopolitical order of things limits our scope of choices and strategies rather than vice versa. Unlike history, in Jameson's formulation, we can consciously apprehend identity only through its reified forces while being in turn transformed unconsciously by its effects.

"Postcolonial" Hong Kong: What's Culture Got to Do with It?

In the year preceding the handover, after years of official disavowal by the government of Hong Kong's colonial existence, a large stream of publications in both the English and Chinese scholarly literature appeared, dealing precisely with topics in relation to colonialism. Whether this explosion of interest was an attempt to cash in on a trendy topic in the wake of colonialism's demise or the result of other more serious intellectual concerns is anyone's speculation, but it was also without a doubt fueled to some extent by corresponding realizations of cultural difference. I hesitate to say that such discoveries of difference are sentiments of nationalism, but it is clear that the appearance of an explicit positionality about colonialism as a real (discursive) other marks a subjective distance or removal from its object, as though the latter can now be "gazed," both in light of impending transition and people's attachment or identification to it. It is as if one said, "colonialism has now become history." Thus, the end of history marked (if not championed) the arrival of a different future while at the same time relegating colonialism to its destined fate in the sociopolitical evolution of things.

The plethora of retrospective publications on colonialism that appeared in anticipation of the handover actually covers a wide range of critical perspectives. In addition to books that dealt with issues of sovereignty, the "one-country, two-systems" framework, Hong Kong Basic Law, and calls for democracy, there was no shortage of publications in English alone ruminating on the historical legacy of colonialism in Hong Kong, both positive and negative.[4]

Colonial difference aside, it is important to note that the inevitability of 1997 in the years leading up to the handover did indeed invoke attempts by China, at least rhetorically, to cultivate nationalist sentiment at a local level as well as attempts by institutions in Hong Kong to cultivate favor with its Chinese counterparts, in the interest of future constructive engagement. Needless to say, the resurgence of cultural nationalism in China in that last decade had often become the source of the government's appeal to popular support among its masses. While sometimes seen as a heavy-handed tactic in a Hong Kong context, the rhetoric of nationalism also had to be viewed in the manner it overlapped with the discourse of democracy and the collusion of capitalist interests. As constructive engagement, conformity to nationalist pressures (imagined or real) had not just taken the form of positive initiatives, as evidenced by the fast-growing numbers of PRC scholars invited to and students enrolled by universities in Hong Kong prior to the handover, but had also taken the form of negative sanctions, evidenced by the increasing prevalence of self-censorship that was imposed during the same period within media, political, and intellectual circles. In this sense, increasing pressure to conform, whether one called this explicit or implicit nationalism or not, already began to be rooted in pre-handover Hong Kong, and this trend corresponded simultaneously with a phase of overt anticolonialism or impending postcolonialism.

Thus, nationalizing sentiments in the transitional era leading up to 1997 had as its goal the objectification of colonialism as a real other and the inculcation of a different kind of identity. In effect, some sense of identity had to be heightened, not only in reference to a newly objectified other but also in contrast to an apolitical other of the prior era, which became a source of cultural ambiguity during the transitional era.[5] But more importantly, with these nationalizing sentiments came the *fiction* that identity was somehow necessary for survival in the inevitable future. There are no hard-and-fast rules that dictate that identity is necessary for the survival of anything; it is a function of "the system" per se. Western identity was not necessary for people's survival under a colonial system that tried in fact to maintain the separations of social hierarchy. Similarly, the absence of a higher abstract identity in the apolitical 1970s may have been a cause of what some saw was the source of Hong Kong's cultural and intellectual desert, but in another sense it served as an appropriate vehicle for institutionalizing another kind of social system driven by divisions of class and differential access to cultural resources. Impending nationalism played on the resurrection of a colonial other and incipient cultural identity, not because political change was inevitable but rather because it *viewed* shared identity as a necessary foundation for that new political order.

Yet the question is not why or if identity is *really* necessary, but rather *what is it for*? One might also add, who is it for and to what extent do alternative notions of culture provide the basis of effective counteridentities? I think the developmental trends leading up to 1997 that invoked a nationalistic mind-set were enough to presage the order of things to come. In the waning years of the transition, different rhetorical contests were played out on different levels that continued well into the post-1997 era. Aside from the debate over how and to what extent the one-country, two-systems rule would be implemented, the other debate that invoked much discussion involved the rule of democracy. The notion of identity impinged on both debates but in different ways. Seen from the perspective of "one-country, two-systems," culture appeared to enjoy some kind of autonomy, in the sense that it only seemed to be a matter of political affiliation and not a matter of social and economic lifestyle. However, in the context of democracy debates, culture seemed to be an irrelevant factor, secondary to the criterion of political participation, which was seen as the defining characteristic in relation to the perceived importance and continued maintenance of local autonomy.

One can debate at great length as to whether the principle of "one-country, two-systems" actually guarantees autonomy of the political sphere from the economic. However, the great tide of nationalism that continued to swell in the waning years leading up to 1997, manifested in overt discourse as well as in implicit action (through constructive engagement of various kinds and the imposition of self-censorship), should have indicated that, if anything, the post-1997 years would see more of the same. In light of the resurrected anticolonialism, the label "Royal" had already begun to be deleted from all government and other affiliated institutions, sometimes amid the clamor of protest to replace all icons of colonial legacy with Chinese ones. In the aftermath of the "glorious restoration" (*guangfu*) of Taiwan by China, the KMT government renamed all the major streets there with names extolling Confucian virtues, such as *Renai* (benevolence) and *Zhongxiao* (loyalty) Road, or with names memorializing Chinese places and people. Nationalist revolutions everywhere else caused streets to be renamed, routinely, one might add. This systematic swelling of nationalist sentiment that was being cultivated in the transition years should have easily spilled into the educational sphere, with increased emphasis on learning Chinese language and history.[6] Given popular acceptance of the handover's inevitability and the change of political sovereignty, the mood should have been ripe for the imposition of a new, if not different, "identity." Indeed, several writers have gone further by predicting the radical penetration of Party, military, and other bureaucratic institutions after the handover.[7] Jamie Allen (1997) perhaps put forward the most pessimistic view, when he predicted that, after the Party sets up shop, the party would be over.

Despite the inevitability of the handover and presumed public acceptance of the change of sovereignty, if not identity as well, one might wonder why, on the contrary, so little has changed in post-1997 Hong Kong. The People's Liberation Army, under the intense scrutiny of the handover media, entered Hong Kong, but little else to signal the advent of military or Party domination materialized.[8] Despite the fears of political oppression that prompted the media to adopt self-censorship, the relative freedom of the press in airing critical views of official government policy after the establishment of the SAR regime ran counter to all the trends anticipated by this heightened nationalism, which was supposed to be the point of departure for other all institutional changes.[9] If all these changes predicated by the end of colonial history and advent of a new cultural identity failed to materialize, then one might ask further—what, if anything, does culture have to do with "postcolonial" Hong Kong? Even the nationalizing rhetoric seemed to diminish accordingly.

Culture is rarely a politically neutral entity; identity is even less so. Rising nationalist sentiment in mainland China has often served an important function, especially in recent decades, in providing necessary popular support for the government's actions and policies. In the case of Hong Kong, it could have effectively served to facilitate political integration.

The Public Sphere in Search of a "Structural" Transformation

One can easily speculate on the possible reasons why so little has changed in the sociopolitical order of things, especially in light of various indicators to the contrary. The Chinese government made several official proclamations, perhaps in countering fears of anticipated suppression of press freedom, that it would adopt a position of noninterference in local affairs. In light of assorted events that have taken place in Hong Kong after 1997, there will always be disagreement on the degree to which Beijing is perceived to have or has actually interfered in the running of Hong Kong. It is not my intention to offer any interpretation of these events; rather, I merely wish to point out that things could have radically changed just on the basis of the critical mass that had accumulated to disassemble the legacy of colonial culture, install new beginnings by gradually reorienting Hong Kong back to its political roots, and institutionalizing the means by which a newly emerging identity could be fostered and put into practice. All these things had already been successfully inculcated into individual thought and behavior long in advance of the handover. Why did the government then kill the momentum that would have facilitated such (presumably desirable) integration?

In support of Beijing's noninterference policy, many observers had also hinted that the insistence on keeping a good face on the "one-country, two-systems" rule had to do instead with the PRC's attempt to woo the confidence of people in Taiwan to return to the motherland under the same kind of setup. This is rather dubious, as Hong Kong was the not the first or only example where the PRC has claimed to guarantee local "autonomy" (Tibet being the other), and because its hard line tactics, which threatened Taiwan militarily in the event of independence, were largely inconsistent with its soft-sell pitch. Besides, political priorities can always change China's view of or policy on anything, as has already been demonstrated on many occasions during the past few decades.

In all this, the democratization movement in Hong Kong government seemed to have an uncertain future. Thanks to the colonial legacy of autocratic rule in Hong Kong, the post-1997 administration found it more convenient to maintain the status quo, while championing the rule of Hong Kong by Hong Kongers. Efforts to demand increased direct democratic participation in the election of legislators and running of government continued to be fought for and frustrated, and such efforts have mostly been pursued without regard to culture and identity issues. In other words, unlike Taiwan, where the national independence movement had derived its energy from efforts to demonstrate the existence of a separate Taiwanese ethnic-cum-cultural consciousness vis-à-vis Chinese ethnicity, the democracy campaign in Hong Kong had largely been a political or legal issue, devoid of cultural content. This also colored the way in which issues regarding the public sphere have developed, in contrast to Taiwan. In Hong Kong, there was a sharper contrast between the state (and its functional interests) and elements of a public effectively excluded from democratic participation. In Taiwan, ethnic coloration of political issues was largely a survival of a cultural nationalist policy of the former KMT regime that can mutate, if ideological difference between various parties becomes articulated in increasingly political terms. Moreover, in Hong Kong, there was no firm indication that local identity could or would ever have useful political leverage.

I deliberately point to the question of identity, the principle of local autonomy, and issues of democratization to show that, in discussions of the Hong Kong public sphere, they are and have been seen largely as mutually distinct factors. They tend to represent different struggles and were not mobilized to influence each other, whereas in other venues, such as Taiwan, it can be argued that these factors have always been mutually intertwined (if not hopelessly entangled). Moreover, I would argue that the cultural arbitrariness of Hong Kong's situation is a discursive *fiction* that obscures other facets of institutional reality that are relevant to the emergence of a very different kind of structural transformation in the public sphere.

First, whatever role a "new" national identity was meant to play or could have played after 1997 was effectively undermined by the Asian financial crisis in late 1997, which continued well into 1998. At least in a political arena, identity issues receded far into the background with the onset and deepening of economic recession that made societal survival the prime substance of public discourse. In the face of international attacks on the Hong Kong dollar, which threatened to destabilize the Asian economy, Beijing allied with the Hong Kong government, but primarily to present a unified political front that was based solely on economic considerations (such as defending the currency peg). The pivotal position of Hong Kong in insulating mainland China from the Asian recession strengthened, if anything, the autonomy of the Hong Kong government in establishing policy and controlling the fiscal crisis. The Tung Chee-hwa administration suffered a sharp loss of confidence during this crisis, but it probably had more to do with his performance in handling political affairs than attacks on the nature of his autocratic rule. In effect, issues of identity, local autonomy, and democratic rule would appear to be distinct, discursively speaking, but their significance in any political context can and does *in fact* change vis-à-vis other issues.

Official noninterference in the media had also appeared to enhance the existence of Hong Kong autonomy, but this was actually only a partial reality that disguised the changing nature of Hong Kong's "public" sphere. The fiction that contributed to the notion that Hong Kong was an autonomous "region" was reflective to some extent of the PRC's position that, at least in some functional respects, Hong Kong could be seen as separate from China. Economically, China was linked integrally to the global economy through Hong Kong, and the most recent fiscal crisis had demonstrated that Hong Kong still played a major role in this regard. But in social and local political matters, Hong Kong's autonomy impacted less on developments on the mainland. As long as the ongoing state of political affairs favored the appointment of Beijing-sympathetic cliques in power, media opposition was a matter for local government to handle and did not directly impact Beijing. However, freedom of the press was curiously enough restricted only to "local" affairs. As Frank Ching (1998:50) keenly noted, the Hong Kong media tread more cautiously in news pertaining to China, or, to be more precise, news and information requiring the cooperation of Chinese agencies and China-backed companies. Some topics were too sensitive or were seen as totally taboo, such as the activities of official agencies that fronted for the Communist Party. As Michael Curtin (1998:288) also noted, the boundaries of media openness and closeness were a function of the fact that the Hong Kong media was not a local entity but one whose market depended on expansion into China. As he put it, "this strategy of expansion into the mainland market thus requires the cooperation of government officials, if the industry is going to reap the benefits of its popularity." The principle of media freedom was thus compromised to satisfy the reality of market access and control. This reinforced the necessity of self-censorship as well.

In short, business interests have in fact always been intertwined with politics in ways that influenced *at an underlying level* support for or compromising of certain ideological principles (whether it be identity or democracy). This realization then solidified "the rules of the game." This complicit relation of power (and *guanxi*) is in the end the largest threat to the emergence of a democratic public sphere. This is the *real* face of post-1997 Hong Kong.

Apprehending History Through Its "Effects"

One of the strange surprises of a short visit I made to Hong Kong in November 1994 during the intense bidding for the 2000 Olympics (which was eventually won by Sydney, Australia) was not so much the fact that once "apolitical" Hong Kongers now seemed to be awash in a euphoric patriotic fervor but rather how all this came about. It surprised me even more that a politically neutral Hong Kong friend, who was a long-term Australian resident, was also swept up by the prevailing current of opinion and media hype to admit as well that Beijing would almost surely win the Olympic bid. Of course, the intensity of "nationalistic" sentiments had its roots in a rising and ongoing renaissance of Chinese consciousness that covered the transitional era, which ranged from a quiet resurgence of interest in lost historical and intellectual roots to overt expressions of political solidarity. Yet, one should also not lose track of the fact that this sudden outpour of nationalist sentiment was as much the product of an inherent Chinese consciousness that Hong Kongers have *always* had (even during the colonial era) as it was the machination of sophisticated media hype. Hong Kong business interests had the most to gain from a successful bid by Beijing to hold the Olympics, and it was essentially the same interest that drove them to seek *guanxi* alliances with important officials and entrepreneurs in the PRC. In other words, they were not simply motivated more by profit motives than nationalistic feelings per se, but more importantly they were quite able and often willing to manipulate such sentiments (up and down) purely for the sake of self-interested commercial gain. Hence, the economy's new tie to culture.

Thus, it is not really surprising, in retrospect, that the first people who ardently supported reunification of Hong Kong with China or at least expressed confidence in the future of a postcolonial Hong Kong were rich capitalists. At the same time, these same people were most likely to steer clear away from any overt conflict with Beijing, especially in the face of democratization movements and campaigns for increased local autonomy. In this context, unlike the "apolitical" capitalism that was characteristic of the 1970s, capitalist interests of the postcolonial era may have been driven by the same purely self-interested profit motives of capitalists found elsewhere, but in a Hong Kong context specifically it was clear that such capitalists would knowingly, if not willingly, subordinate democratic ideals and manipulate nationalist sentiments in order to protect their own vested interests, if necessary. This *unholy* alliance between business and the new regime was not only designed to be the foundation of the new order. More importantly, its success depended on suppressing those (democratizing) forces that represented a challenge to this power relationship.

Quite clearly, the kind of structural transformation that was required in order to give rise to a democratic public sphere in post-1997 Hong Kong involved not only the advent of open, rational communication, but more importantly a challenge to the various forces that had resulted in the institutional collusion of big business and political bureaucratic interests. The predominance of commercial interests in government was nothing new to Hong Kong, given its founding in the history of global trade and the strong representation of major corporate interests in the colonial government, but the policy of the SAR government to divide legislative representation according to functional constituencies at the expense of direct democracy thus insured corporate interests a direct and omnipresent role. In the era leading up to 1997, nationalistic fervor was a useful mode of representation to promote their own interests as well as to curry favor with counterparts within the PRC. In the ensuing Asian recession, the mood of societal survivalism forced the government to prioritize purely economic interests at the expense of other values but in a way that made identity, among other things, secondary concerns. Moreover, not unlike the market sensibilities that had forced the media to mute its criticism when transcending local boundaries, the expansion of Hong Kong corporate interests into China that had co-opted them into toeing the line in Hong Kong also showed that the domain of the public sphere had effectively transcended a local Hong Kong context. Despite its fictional autonomy (under the one-country, two-system scheme), the reality of its post-1997 existence thus thrust Hong Kong society into a mutually dependent economic and political relationship with the PRC. The Hong Kong media (and film industry) now had to expand its market into the PRC just to survive locally, and Hong Kong corporate interests viewed control of the PRC market in turn as a larger priority than the local Hong Kong one. In short, the reality of this larger sphere of economic and political dependence was eventually the bottom line that in turn forced compromises made at a local level. In the final analysis, who cared about identity, as long as everyone could make ends meet and got what he or she sought, despite the various facades?

At one level, the appearance of official autonomy did not prevent Beijing from trying to impose laws to repress acts of dissent or seditious behavior. Pro-democracy forces could also counter by rallying in the streets, especially if they were stifled in efforts to make changes in the system, but strategies of collusion have inculcated a new mode of dependency relations.

To call this newly evolving system of social relations *guanxi* capitalism would be overly simplistic. As a mode of capitalism, it was driven by a utilitarian logic that understands the dominant power of the market in controlling the flow of capital. China is consciously aware that it was at the center of an expanding global market, both in terms of outsource production for the developed nations and the consumption of global products, and this awareness has in turn allowed it to use its pivotal role to control people's access to desired resources or benefits of the system by making people conform to the rules of the game in all other respects. Thus, the media has learned that it is free to print whatever it pleases in matters pertaining to Hong Kong (and, hence, is autonomous), but that in matters involving China or cooperation with Chinese agencies it is forced accordingly to toe the proper ideological line as one's price of admission. Increasingly, they toe the line, especially when they discover that the economic survival of their own enterprise is dependent on expansion into the China market. The willingness of Western global media, such as STAR-TV, to censor BBC news and other programs, when they comment unfavorably on China, as a condition of their continued access, demonstrates that it was not just a local policy specific to Hong Kong. Taiwanese businesspeople, entertainers, and professionals of all sorts have learned to mute any expressions of or sympathy for Taiwanese independence so as not to jeopardize their own prospects for cashing in on the lucrative China market, especially when it has become obvious that this market is much richer than their own. PRC authorities also revoked a tourist visa to Hong Kong for Taipei Mayor Ma Ying-jeou for making politically incorrect remarks. Such sanctions seem superficial and frivolous, but they underscore the main point that, while the market is in principle open, people are free to make money, and there is no attempt by the government to control the redistribution of income, as has been the case of old socialist economies, access to the market is in practice a privilege that can be politically controlled, if deemed desirable or necessary. Hence, the economy's new tie to political ideology. To say the least, it is clearly antidemocratic as well.

More fundamentally, the subjective positioning behind this new capitalism is hardly the kind one would expect from a poor Third World nation.

China is supremely confident in its ability to pull the strings behind the whole system and in the process protect its own sense of ideological purity. The continued flow of global investment attests in part to their faith in this regard. Driving this subjective centrality is an imminently real nationalistic fervor (or deep-seated cultural arrogance), which matches the size of its ambitions to rectify centuries of imperialism and political shame. Ultimately, the biggest fiction is that of "one-country, two-systems." The ritual facade of the handover has marked the fictive significance of 1997, and the fiction of Hong Kong's autonomy in a meaningless ideological framework has reset the clock again on its eventual integration with the mainland. In the PRC, continued emphasis on "socialism with Chinese characteristics" has amplified its ideological purity. In Hong Kong, embrace of the motherland has instead refined institutional capitalism to new heights.

What Is (Post)Colonial "Modernity"?

The history of Hong Kong, both in its evolution as a colonial city-state and its post-1997 transformation as special administrative region of China, should have relevant and significant things to say about the nature and operation of colonial modernity. It should lead one above all to question what coloniality and modernity are as well as the collusive relationship between the two. Coloniality should be questioned not only for how it exists in fact (as a mode of political practice) but also how it portrays itself as representation (through cultural discourse, subjective narrative, and (re) writings of history, ritual, or other codifications of memory and fictive denials). These same forms of coloniality can also be used to legitimate the existence of other forms of political institutions not termed colonial, strictly speaking. If so, then the continued existence of colonialism can easily transcend its explicit change of political status, because it is in effect a matter of interpretation. Modernity deserves questioning in the same way. Far from being an autonomous and value-free entity, it is, on the contrary, something that is put into practice in the service of that same political evolution. Global capitalism is in this regard not only the abstract operation of a market society, as though a realization of utilitarian ideals, but also the end product of its own ongoing historical process. In the context of the colonial development of Hong Kong into the post-1997 era, one can witness its subtle and complex transformations. More importantly, these transformations are part and parcel of its necessarily collusive relationships to changing policies and governmentality in the abstract.

The work of Bernard Cohn (1984) on late colonial India offers a useful parallel into the collusive relationship between the cultural sociology of the state, structurations of modernity, and constructions of identity. His observations about cultural and social objectification that he argued were seminal to British colonial rule in India has proved to be broadly endemic to diverse forms of modern govern-"mentality" throughout the world. More than just castes of mind or imagined communities in the making, identities have always been cultural fictions predicated on the assumption of real roots and the need to reaffirm them. The tendency to objectify "ethnic" identity in particular has been in effect symptomatic of attempts to define the illusory nature and form of such an *ethnos*, but it is perhaps characteristic of society's need to inculcate the *ethos* of its own modernity, whether it is encoded in the rule of law, civilizing imperatives, moral regulation, personhood or the etiquette of everyday interaction. Such changing discourses of identity supplement (rather than conflict with) the extraordinary extent to which state apparatuses have labored to compel people into "becoming their ID." Taken as an entire cartography of power, they freeze us, as Corrigan and Sayer (1985:211) phrased it, through these programs of power, "into mythic statuses of sedimented language." *Why identify?* I personally do not believe that it is necessary to identify with anything. Yet, people everywhere go to great lengths to prove that identities are real, even worth dying for.

If identity, like Cohn's colonial impositions of caste and social structure, are fictions or inventions, then history must be seen as the ongoing institutional and political embodiment of fiction as fact and the constant interaction of discourse and practice. Fictions can run deep, and it is in the process of institutionalization that its political violence becomes "normalized." Hong Kong Colonial Secretary of State, Philip Haddon-Cave, joked in 1985 (Birch 1991:1):

> When Sir John Bremridge [the Finance Minister] came to see me about the [Chinese] banks he was in a rage.
>
> "I've told them," he spluttered, "they've got to toe the line, otherwise . . . otherwise, we'll *nationalise* them!"
>
> "Oh, no Sir John," I said, "you *can't* say 'nationalise'—we're not a nation."
>
> "Well, we're a colony, aren't we?" he said, "so we'll *colonise* them!"
>
> "Oh *no*, Sir John," I explained, "you *can't* say that, we *never* refer to Hong Kong as a 'colony' these days."
>
> "Well then," he replied, "what *are* we called now?"

"Well," I explained, "these days we call ourselves a 'territory.'"

"Right then," said Sir John, "we'll *terrorise* them!"

Statements about what is or what is supposed to be, when Hong Kong was literally a colony, should raise similar questions about what post-1997 Hong Kong is or is supposed to be after the end of colonialism. Names are only part of the story, but they are an important preamble to how people construct their identities, and then in turn tie them into the practices and politics of a deeper struggle to define and regulate a particular ethos of life or mode of survival.

Underlying these complex interactions between culture and politics, facts and fictions, and strategic intents of agents located within this geometry of power, colonialism can be regarded here *above all* as a regime of political practice that depends to some extent on the efficacy of modernity as culture. The dynamics of this power geometry requires a critical epistemology that can transcend the rhetoric of colonialism, nationalism, capitalism, and the ends of history.

Part Three

The Reclamation of National Destiny

On the Unbearable Heaviness of Identity

Because China is so vast, its successes can be attributed to whatever your pet cause is. Do you oppose free markets and privatization, like John Ross, former economic policy adviser for the city of London? Then China's success is because of the role of the state. Do you favor free markets, like the libertarian Cato Institute? Then China's success is because of its opening up. Are you an environmentalist? China is working on huge green-energy projects. Are you an energy lobbyist? China's building gigantic pipeline projects. Are you an enthusiast for the Protestant work ethic, like historian Niall Ferguson, who describes it as one of his "killer apps" for civilizations? Then credit China's manu-facturing boom to its 40 million Protestants—even though they're less than 5 percent of its 1.3 billion people.

—James Palmer, *Washington Post* Opinion

Prologue

China claims to be the longest continuous civilization in the world. Its aura of legitimacy and destiny is to a large extent invested in the mandate of an unbroken history. In light of this kind of tradition, or the perception of it, Chinese unsurprisingly tend to think that it is not possible to understand its culture and society without reference to its civilization as a whole or the weight of its influence up to the present. Equally unsurprisingly, courses on Chinese culture and civilization are taught precisely in this way. The same sense of Sinocentrism is also the basis of which we tend to view Taiwan, Hong Kong, and other Chinese communities, that is, primarily in reference to that shared legacy or as a link/break to/with a common lineage.

Continuity with a shared legacy would be incompatible with an approach that views the history of an ongoing present as a function of

141

distinctive epistemic or geopolitical moments. On the contrary, there is no reason why one's embeddedness to an ongoing globalized context might not serve as a more appropriate frame for discrete localizing experiences. If colonial rule in Hong Kong can be seen as a juncture for situating the course of its latter formation, parallel to other frames, one can also view the formative experiences of the PRC and ROC as a primary function of its opposition as modern nation-states in a Cold War setting. Without denying their common legacy, one could question to what extent culture as shared substance, even if it happens to be represented as tradition, serves in fact as a continuity or extension, instead of as a dependent factor within a discrete formative frame. In postwar Taiwan, the revival of Confucian tradition was at best an invention of tradition that serviced an emerging cultural nationalism. Similar things can be said about culture in the PRC's formative regimes.

Much can be said about the evolution of the PRC from the Maoist era to its subsequent transition under the aegis of Deng Xiaoping and beyond. Perhaps the single most dominant force within this transition was not the emergence of market capitalism itself but the collusion of government policy and oligarchic entrepreneurial interests to consolidate domination by a single-Party state, reinforced at a popular level by a resurgent cultural nationalism. National identity has in effect played a legitimating role in filling the void created by the demise of socialist-class values.

Chapter 7

From the Ashes of Socialist Humanism

The Myth of *Guanxi* Exceptionalism in the PRC

The publication of Mayfair Yang's (1994) book on *guanxi*, or what she calls "the art of social relationships in China," can be viewed as a landmark study of a changing PRC. If anything, it sparked an awareness of an increasingly omnipresent social phenomenon in China, which in turn created a burgeoning social scientific literature on it. A conference in March 2015 at UC Berkeley on *The Field of* Guanxi *Studies* shows that both the phenomenon as well as attention devoted to it has grown rapidly in recent years, which has also spawned comparison with similar phenomena elsewhere. Without a doubt, *guanxi*, especially in combination with corruption, has proliferated with the opening up of a market economy in the post-Deng era, but despite the seemingly unique attributes of the term, there is little to suggest that the kind of social relationship invoked by it is in actuality a distinctively Chinese phenomenon and more to indicate that it is the product of institutional incongruences that are common to many, if not most, societies. The problematic of *guanxi* has in fact a long history in the sinological literature in Taiwan, Hong Kong, and overseas Chinese business culture. More importantly, as part of a cultural complex, I argue that *guanxi* is only one of three seminal concepts in a Chinese power theory of culture, not even the most important one of them. This chapter is in essence a thick description of that cultural complex. On the basis of this interpretation, one can meaningfully infer on the problematic of *guanxi* in the PRC today as a crisis rooted along institutional fault lines, which in turn reflects directly on capitalism with "Chinese" characteristics.

This is a revised adaptation of an essay published in 2002 as "From Culture to Power (and Back): The Many 'Faces' of *Mianzi* (face), *Guanxi* (connection), and *Renqing* (rapport)," *Suomen Antropologi* 27(4):19–37.

From *Mianzi* to *Guanxi* to *Renqing*:
Outlines of a Power Theory of Culture

In his treatise on "the native's point of view," Geertz (1974) argued that the uniqueness of social experience and organization resides ultimately in our understanding of its primordial constitution in culture and language.[1] In this regard, I argue that the literature on *mianzi* ("face"), *guanxi* ("relationship"), and *renqing* ("rapport"), which has been the object of heated debate by psychologists, sociologists, and anthropologists of Chinese society, represents an ideal case in point for bringing to the fore our understanding of cultural meaning within the primary context of practice and ritual behavior. Sinological experts have tended to view the meaning and operation of the above concepts as characteristic of behaviors and institutions unique to China, thus unwittingly highlighting the marked or distinctive features of culture, when it is in fact the institutional and perceived practices of power interaction that situate cultural meaning that are unique. The semantic or epistemological specificity encoded in such terms presumably provides the key for understanding the uniqueness of experience in any particular society. What is interesting about the three terms discussed here is that, to any native Chinese speaker, they are easy enough to define and use. More importantly, the sociological significance that resonates from such notions as public face, moral rapport, and social networks should be familiar to many other societies as well. But a brief look at this literature will show that there is much more than meets the eye, even in semantic terms. The fact that these terms routinely appear italicized in scholarly writings on China reiterates a cultural specificity that is difficult to translate. The practical difficulty in interpreting these notions, on the other hand, is that they constantly overlap in usage and that they can all invoke each other at some more abstract level. Contrary to Geertz, I also argue that it is impossible to explain the nature and process of social relations invoked by these concepts simply on the basis of their symbolic negotiation as primordial meanings. The systematic interrelations of social or institutional-qua-political practice offer instead a more useful framework of analysis that not only explains possible permutations of meaning in any concept, but also determines why certain concepts are relevant for invoking specific kinds of behavior in a given context.

There has been most recently, especially from contemporary work done in the People's Republic of China, a virtual explosion of writings focusing on *guanxi*. In actuality, it is probably more accurate to say that, over the past few decades, there has been increasing attention devoted to the phenomena of *mianzi, guanxi*, and *renqing* in the social science literature that has broadly encompassed Chinese society in general but has witnessed different disciplinary perspectives grappling with different combinations of issues. The evolution of this literature as a whole is noteworthy in the sense that it reflects different problematics that have in turn shed increasingly clearer light on the subtle semantic relationships between these concepts. However, in taking stock of many of the issues therein, I would argue that we are perhaps looking at something larger than the sum of its component parts. In synthesizing different disciplinary perspectives on the matter, it is important to understand the nuances between these concepts as a further function of how we understand their possible systematic interaction in the context of practice. However contrary to prevailing views in the literature, I submit that our ongoing failure to recognize the salience of contexts of practice (driven by intentionality and power) in determining meaning and engendering social relationships based on these concepts has in turn led us to underestimate the dynamics of subjective perception in dyadic interaction. I conclude that such a sophisticated framework of pragmatic meaning, more than "webs of significance," can explain the problematic crisis of *guanxi* in the PRC today.

At first glance, the semantics of the three concepts seem to be somewhat unambiguous and unproblematic. *Mianzi* literally means "face" (as in saving or losing . . .), *renqing* means "human emotion" or moral rapport, and *guanxi* means "relationship" or connection (i.e., in the sense of network connections).[2] To the average native Chinese speaker, it is easy for one to spell out what these terms mean literally and recognize which terms should be used in which contexts of speech. Their literal meaning differs little from their equivalent English counterparts. At the same time, it seems that at a deeper level of comprehension each term involves specific cultural rules about the conduct of social behavior, exchange, and etiquette. In other words, at one level, the field of linguistic usage invoked by these terms seems to be clearly demarcated, but at the same time the scope of social behavior, exchanges, and etiquette that engender these notions in fact overlaps considerably. That is to say, if one turns the question around and asks instead, which of the various kinds of behaviors, exchanges, and etiquette are relevant to face, moral rapport, and social connectedness, respectively?, one will discover that these concepts are not easy to distinguish. Similarly, if one probes the average Chinese speaker beyond the usual conventions of speech and practice by delving precisely into the cultural specificity, social rationality, and ethical values underlying these concepts, he or she not surprisingly gets lost. In posing the question in this manner, I do not mean to be evasive but to suggest instead that, from the recent literature on *mianzi, renqing,* and *guanxi,* one can clearly see that each of these terms is a permutation of a larger complex of cultural rules. The question then is, how can one understand this larger complex, and how does it invoke the appropriate conduct of behavior in different contexts of social practice? In order to answer this question, I think it is necessary first to look at each of these concepts in their respective discourses of analysis then show how, despite what one sees on the surface, everyone has been pointing to the same interrelated nature of culture and power in Chinese society.

The Chinese concept of face (*mianzi*) has long been an object of scrutiny by sinologists. As if to emphasize that Chinese notions of face are anything but superficial, writers usually begin by asserting that there is more than meets the eye. Thus, Lu Xun once wrote, "what is this thing called face? It is very well if you don't stop to think, but the more you think about it, the more confused you grow." Similarly, Lin Yutang argued that face was impossible to define. Being "abstract and intangible, yet it is the most delicate standard by which Chinese intercourse is regulated."[3] Perhaps contrary to its literal reference to egoism, Hu Hsien-chin (1944:45) stressed the socially normative aspect of face. It "represents the confidence of society in the integrity of ego's moral character, the loss of which makes it impossible for him or her to function properly within the community." In other words, face is a prestige or reputation achieved through success and its display; it is the projection and maintenance of a public image. The linguistic permutations of the two Chinese terms for face (*mianzi* and *lian*), both literal and figurative, are endless, but it is clear that the focus of attention is on the processes of saving and losing face and the way that they invoke underlying moral or ethical codes of behavior. Thus, face is, crudely speaking, less psychological than sociological in function, and there have been tendencies by some to overemphasize the status maintenance aspect of face, especially given the hierarchical nature of Chinese society, such as when Stover (1962:375) noted, "face is the social ideology which legitimizes status rectitude." At other times, subsequent commentators point to what Erving Goffman would have called the social interactionist dimension of "face-works." David Ho, a social psychologist, has taken the discourse on Chinese notions of face a step further by arguing that face is not simply a personality variable, as though a pure attribute of individual behavior, nor is it simply a status maintenance mechanism, as though people are expected to conform to ascribed or invariable social standards. There is always in essence an intertwined relationship between these two aspects of face in the same way that shame is both an attribute of individual behavior and the product of moral or public values.[4] Ho then negotiates between the individual and social by emphasizing the reciprocity of social expectations (*bao* in Yang Lien-sheng's [1957] terms), or what Ho perceives to be the binding aspect of social control. There is the appearance of subjective volition, but this is really circumscribed in or constrained by social expectation. This is the reason why there is generally more concern with losing face than gaining face.

Psychologists in Hong Kong and Taiwan have devoted much attention to discussions of face. They note, first, that like the Confucian concept of *li* (ritual propriety), face has two mutually intertwined aspects, a ritual-symbolic one that internalizes ethical or moral norms and an external one that conforms to the expectations of social status and political authority. But, as if to counter the excessive emphasis placed on social factors that seem to force the individual to conform to the expectations of public performance, psychologists have tended to stress the interpersonal dependence that allows for the individuality of others in society to express their public face. In other words, part of the interpersonal performance of face-works is the need to give *other* people face, namely by suppressing one's own egoism. Or as Zhu Ruiling (1988:243) has neatly phrased this, "the essential feature of *mianzi* is its interdependent nature; it functions by responding to intercourse with others or a public audience. In this process of mutual interaction, there is no such thing as an absolute face (as though fixed and predetermined); the owner of that face is not just a social role player."[5]

The focus on social interaction explains why psychologists have tended to view face ultimately in terms of a kind of egocentric, decision-making model of behavior, one that effectively gives primary weight to individual selectivity and strategic control. Thus, it should come as little surprise that, when Hwang Kwang-kuo (1985, 1987) interprets face and favor as "the Chinese power game," he is implicitly intersecting with the writing of scholars studying similar related concepts of Chinese social behavior, notably *guanxi* and *renqing*. For Hwang, social behavior can be reduced to a dyadic interaction. In an actual interaction, which may involve two or more people, each party holds the power of allocating some kind of social resource that may satisfy the needs of the other, while each dyad expects the other to distribute resources under his or her control in a way that is favorable to the allocator. The individual's reason for employing this power to influence other people lies in the desire to obtain social resources controlled by reciprocating others. Likewise, others consent to ego's influences, because the allocator can foresee that this strategy will in turn bring a certain reward or help in evading some kind of punishment. In this model, Hwang not only deals with face, which is a superficial aspect of this interaction, but more significantly tries to incorporate related notions of *guanxi* and *renqing* within the total picture of social relations. He recognizes that this interaction can be driven either by (1) expressive or socially altruistic ties; (2) instrumental or utilitarian-individualistic ties; as well as what he terms

(3) mixed ties, controlled by *renqing* or the need to maintain social rapport.[6] What is noteworthy about *renqing* here is that it is ambivalent; that is to say, it can cut both ways. Hwang understands *guanxi* in this model in its broad denotation as a moral desire to establish and maintain ties or social connections with others. Without these implicit relationships, there can be no dyadic interaction to speak of. One can perhaps rephrase Hwang's model as follows: face-work is an important way of showing off one's power. As a strategy for manipulating and allocating resources to one's own benefit, it is basically a *power* game played out in Chinese *cultural* rules. Although he does not say so, the focal element driving the system at an underlying or abstract level is the dilemma of *renqing*. Although he is able to define *renqing* in terms of its implicit moral sentiment or need to maintain favors in ongoing, reciprocal relationships, his dilemma of *renqing* is something that is calculated ultimately in terms of its cost-benefits from an egocentric, decision-making perspective. There is little consideration by Hwang of the concrete, sociological factors that influence *renqing* or in contrast to other sociopolitical values. We get instead the ego making rational sense of the world around him on the periphery.

Psychological models of this sort have their utility, but I have deliberately exaggerated their methodological individualism to suggest also that these models lack much that requires qualification too. Without doubt, certain important trends in this discussion of face carry over in actuality to a discussion of other related concepts in a constructive way. First of all, face has aptly highlighted the importance of reciprocity as a seminal aspect of Chinese social relationships, at least vis-à-vis modern individualism. Second, Hwang has introduced the existence of power as a primary force that drives the process of reciprocity. Third, Hwang sees all of the above as embedded at a more abstract level in *renqing* or the need to maintain moral rapport. These three themes pervade the literature on *guanxi* as well, but I think it is necessary to rephrase the present discussion and ask at this point, what are the differences between face and *guanxi* in terms of *renqing*, or what are their effects on *renqing*, and how does one define *renqing*, not so much in terms of semantic or cultural substance but rather in the context of practice or as a negotiation of competing values and institutional forces? As a footnote to the literature on face, one should mention that Hwang, King (1988, 1991) and others emphasize that these notions are everyday values that ultimately owe their ideological substance and social legitimacy to Confucianism and other jewels of civilizational thought. Needless to say, such concepts are rooted in intellectual tradition and embedded in culture, but in my opinion their inherent relationship to social exchange, the practice of power and embeddedness in moral rapport invoke more important theoretical issues that have never been posed in the literature. A power theory of culture opens up an even larger Pandora's box.

Guanxi as Phenomenon versus Guanxi as Problematic

First, one must point out that the concept of *guanxi* being invoked in the literature is less the broader notion of "relationship" or network ties per se than the more instrumental or utilitarian denotations of *guanxi*, in the sense of relying on personal connections.[7] *Mianzi* and *guanxi* do not contrast directly, but it is useful to note that, as mechanisms that cultivate implicit social bonds in order to gain or wield power, they both have significant superficial differences. *Guanxi* has negative connotations that one does not find in *mianzi*. Because face is largely a response to social expectation, having too much face is not necessarily a bad thing. There are some who would literally "die to obtain face" (*siyao mianzi*), but excessive egotism in this regard is not necessarily the same as selfishness. On the other hand, the connotation of gaining connections by pulling strings suggests a kind of back-door facade that is anything but public or openly cultivated (as a self-interested act). The open denial of self-interest, even though people cultivate *guanxi precisely* for instrumental reasons makes it by nature a private rather than public act. In other words, it is not important whether the gift-giving and other forms of amicable exchange that are employed often to cultivate *guanxi* relationships are openly seen or practiced; it is more important that neither of these parties publicly recognize them as deliberate acts of favor that mask an instrumental intent. This back-door dimension (which face does not have) also implies that *guanxi* is really a tie that is always something *other* than what is desirable or relevant in a given context of speech or practice. That is to say, kinsmen have kin relationships (*qinshu guanxi*), but in a context that requires display of kin solidarity, saying that one is "pulling on a connection" (*la guanxi*) is somewhat nonsensical. On the contrary, pulling on my kin connections to get my friend a job means that I do not have the required criteria or resource to do this in the proper context of employment, and that is what *guanxi* is for. Network building may be a desirable feature of social relationships everywhere, but the *discursive* focus on *guanxi* in the social scientific literature is largely or solely based on the *pejorative* aspect of personal connection in the context of a given institutional framework defined *normatively* by *other* sociological criteria.

There has been a long-established cottage industry of scholars studying Chinese business organizations, focusing on the predominance of family ties.[8] The ubiquitous usage of the term *guanxi* to depict these relationships in its personal, connective sense is not inaccurate here, but it highlights in effect the cultural uniqueness of the "Chinese" enterprise in contrast to economic organizations that are *normatively* defined by *other* econometric or sociological criteria. A paradigmatic example of the way *guanxi* has become a framework for explaining Chinese social institutions and behavior comes from the political science literature. Bruce Jacobs, in his study of Taiwan local politics, was perhaps the first person to make this term fashionable. Jacobs was not trying to inject a pejorative view of Taiwanese politics, but his characterization of these particularistic ties as *guanxi* marked the cultural uniqueness of the phenomenon vis-à-vis his own (structural-functionalist) expectations of political behavior.[9]

Related to and feeding on the initial impetus that has led one to focus on *guanxi* as a culturally specific and pervasive phenomenon in Chinese society is the recent explosion of writing on the contemporary PRC that has viewed *guanxi* as a phenomenon intrinsic to or deeply rooted in the fabric of social and political life there. Andrew Walder's (1983) classic study of work and authority in post-Maoist mainland China is clearly an early and systematic analysis of the way *guanxi* has tended to work in the institutional setting of a workplace. In the workplace, *guanxi* aptly represents what Walder calls "private strategies," as opposed to public strategies of the official reward system. He remarked that Chinese employees tended to perceive the formal hierarchy of offices as a hollow shell, overlaid with networks of *guanxi* and feelings of *renqing* that determined the actual operation of the organization as well as the way in which social interaction was conducted, how decisions were made, if not also who got what. A worker stated, "this kind of thing, using human sentiments (*renqing*), is common. It is a form of 'going through the back door' (*zou hou men*). This sort of practice influences everything, including raises, bonuses, and promotions."[10] While Walder does not assert that *guanxi* wholly dominates the workplace, he pits private cultivation of *guanxi* against what he calls *biaoxian*, literally performance. Work performance here can concretely mean many things, ranging from actual work achievement to performance as a kind of acting or going through the motions. The reason Walder chose to preserve the Chinese term rather than to gloss it in English has little to do with the semantics of the word, whose meaning is unambiguous. The uniqueness of *biaoxian* in the Chinese context has to do with the fact that the system of rewards and punishments that epitomizes the work regime is based not only on objective merit but more often on "subjective" factors such as work attitude, political correctness, going through the motions, and displaying the proper deference to authority. In sum, being *rexin* (fervent) in one's work are expressions of *renqing* that make the system run.

However, what I find particularly noteworthy in Walder's description is that *biaoxian* is not all that dissimilar from "face." In a work context, one's face, from the perspective of the system, is in short the product of one's *biaoxian* in all the above senses, and it is important to give each other face. But the point that I wish to make ultimately is this: in any context of practice, face and *guanxi* operate in distinct but parallel niches; what ties them together is that they are simply different strategies for cultivating rapport (*renqing*). What determines how important *renqing* is or what area it should be applied to has nothing to do with the intrinsic meaning of the terms and has more to do with the definition of that underlying context of practice. While I think that the importance of *guanxi* is prevalent in all Chinese societies, I also think that the heavy attention paid to *guanxi* in studies of PRC society in particular is warranted as well. That is to say, there is something peculiar about the nature of the *guanxi* phenomenon in PRC society that explains why it has attracted so much attention there and relatively less discursive attention in Taiwan or Hong Kong, by contrast. The question, then, is what? Walder has already hinted that the flexibility of work reward systems provides fertile institutional ground for the growth of informal *guanxi* ties, in addition to the fact that the work regime in PRC, at least vis-à-vis other societies, is highly dependent on the general maintenance of tight interpersonal ties. But rather than characterizing the system as being "neo-traditional," in the sense of having constructed socialist institutions on the backbone of traditional (hierarchically ascribed) social relationships, I tend to see the growing prevalence of the *guanxi* phenomenon in the PRC as a by-product of those changing *regimes* themselves.

At this point, one cannot overlook the fact that the three most important ethnographies to appear in recent studies of PRC society happen to be on *guanxi*. I refer especially to works by Mayfair Yang (1994), Yan Yunxiang (1996a), and Andrew Kipnis (1997). There are many merits to Yang's book, but the single most significant factor in my opinion has to do with the line of analysis that begins with making sense of the proliferation of a complex discourse called *guanxixue* ("*guanxiology*"), then links the production of this discourse to the intricate micropractices of *guanxi* found in her case study, and finally juxtaposes the ritual construction of this *guanxi* subjectivity against the institutional practices of the Maoist and post-Maoist state. As Yang (1994:286) articulates it, "*guanxi* subjectivity does not oppose the state directly, but forges a multiplicity of links through and across state segments."[11] Juxtaposed against Walder's analysis of the work regime, her analysis of the pragmatic etiquette and strategies of *guanxi* offers a much more fertile ground for explaining the complex relationship between the official regime of institutional practice and the space of personal power games encompassed by *guanxi*. Viewed in this light, I see the emergence of *guanxi* less as neotraditional in Walder's terms and more as *radically reappropriating*. This radical transition has less to do with the substantive nature of *guanxi*, which has, of course, deep roots in Chinese social relations, than with the radical changes at the level of macro-institutional values and practices after the Maoist era that enabled *guanxi* to take on a life of its own as an acceptable tactic of survival or desirable mode of instrumental gain.[12] On the twentieth anniversary of Ezra Vogel's (1965) "From Friendship to Comradeship: The Change in Personal Relations in Communist China," Thomas Gold (1985) remarked on the radical changes that emerged after the Cultural Revolution in an essay appropriately titled "After Comradeship." Of course, the changes described there did not simply involve changes in personal relations per se but encompassed more precisely a complex series of institutional changes in the everyday regime of life that was the consequence at a macrosocial level of engagement between the state's redistributive economy and commodity capitalism. Gold singled out from this entire social complex as the predominant characteristic of personal relations in PRC the rise of instrumental ties in the form of *guanxi*, but somewhat disappointingly, like Walder, he concluded that these changes revealed the staying power of a revived traditionalism.[13] As Gold (1985:674) explained it in cross-cultural perspective, "traveling in Chinese societies with diverse economic and political systems, such as the PRC, Taiwan, Hong Kong and Singapore, the striking thing is not the difference but the similarity of personal interaction despite other variances."

His empirical observations may be correct, but theoretically he misses the point totally. *Guanxi* relations are ubiquitous in Chinese-speaking societies, such as Taiwan, Hong Kong, and Singapore, thus it is more pertinent to ask, why has the *problematic* of *guanxi* become so acute in present-day PRC in a way that is totally absent in these other "Chinese" societies?[14] In other words, especially given the ubiquitous existence of the phenomenon everywhere, the absence of this unusual discourse of *guanxixue* is not a trivial matter. If *guanxi* (in the sense of personal connection) is a dirty word in common parlance, it is an even dirtier word in light of the kind of sociopolitical and value changes that these other societies are undergoing.[15]

In Taiwan, which claims to be the most "traditional," *guanxi* proliferates in the same institutional cracks that Walder observed was part of the flexible system of rewards in a work regime. This is a general rule that explains the proliferation of *guanxi* in a Chinese cultural context. Especially in a society that emphasizes the importance of Confucian benevolence and morality, what outsiders might call *guanxi*, Chinese in Taiwan would just call *renqing*.[16] Even in a professional context, the rapport runs deep, but these relationships can still be and are very often a power game. In Taiwan, people prefer generally not to do things according to hard-and-fast rules, because official bureaucracy tends to be inflexible and impersonal. Imperfections in the system can be smoothed over by personal negotiation, but this "humane" intervention also has a dark side.[17] When one says, "I do you a favor," and "you do me a favor," it makes everything prone to manipulation. More importantly, the *very* insinuation that these relations are actually *guanxi* runs counter not only to traditional ethics but also the ethics of modern society. With increasing emphasis on professionalization, especially in an evolving service economy, relying on *guanxi* connections in routine life has likewise been regarded unfavorably, which may differ from the high life of business and politics.

In quintessentially modernizing Hong Kong and Singapore, *renqing* in actuality still runs deep in many quarters, but it has been also appropriated by the norms of modernity, or at least one of its variants, namely British legalism. The existence of the *guanxi* phenomenon (as connection) here is in turn no different from that found elsewhere in the Chinese world, which demonstrates that such kinds of relationships are important everywhere. However, whether such behavior is termed *guanxi* or *renqing* is in fact an important consideration, since it reflects the kind of normative value that *predicates* the context of social practice and *underlies* the strategic choices that makes such behavior appropriate or not. One person's *guanxi* may be another's *renqing*, but its meaning is hardly a function of the *acts* themselves.

In comparing the broad range of Chinese "societies," I argue instead that the kinds of institutional and other changes that have contributed to a proliferation of *guanxi* relations as a way of life in PRC contrast with different institutional trends taking place in other Chinese societies and that the *latter* can explain the absence of a *guanxi problematic* there. As a corollary, I think *perception* plays an important role here too. In the strict sense, *guanxi* is a *value judgment*. Only when *renqing* becomes perceived as being negative or inappropriate is it termed *guanxi*. I find *guanxi* easier to interpret than *renqing*. I do not know of any actual *guanxi* tie that is not at the same time an attempt to cultivate *renqing*, no matter how instrumental its intent. It is harder, on the other hand, to determine when *renqing* is in fact an attempt to cultivate *guanxi* (instrumentally) or just a friendly act, since it is a value judgment.

Culture as Meaning Versus Culture as Practice

Returning to the PRC literature, due to the acute problematic of *guanxi*, I sense a certain danger toward *guanxi* overdetermination. I have serious reservations about Yang's dualism of *guanxi* and *renqing* as urban/rural or even male/female phenomena, partly because it is a value judgment, as noted above, but I sense an even greater danger of viewing everything as a function of *guanxi*. Yan's (1996a) work is an attempt to show that *guanxi* is a ubiquitous aspect of rural life, among other things. The pervasiveness of *guanxi* in diverse aspects of local social life there is indisputable. Yan focuses to a larger extent than Yang on exchange, which is indeed a clear and significant expression of *guanxi* or *renqing* relationships. There are some differences in the approaches adopted by Yan and Yang with regard to exchange theory, but there is especially in Yan's case a danger of reading social reciprocity and gift giving solely through the eyes of *guanxi*. The intensity and complexity of gift giving in his village case studies are indisputable. As one reads his monograph, one gets the impression that gift giving is a systematic, widespread social practice that is driven at an interpersonal level by *guanxi* networks and at an ethico-moral level by abstract notions of *renqing*. But in a later paper, Yan (1996b) terms gift exchange as the "culture" of *guanxi*, which appears to reiterate the sociological functions of the latter. Kipnis (1996:301) is even more to the point in characterizing gift giving as a "language" for "managing" *guanxi*. As he puts it, "the first point that could be made is that the closer the *guanxi* the bigger the gift. Close relatives tended to give more than friends, and those who wished to claim a close friendship gave more than those who didn't." It is important to point out that, when Kipnis says "the closer the *guanxi* the bigger the gift," he is referring to *guanxi* in its *general* sense as "relationship." Chinese have a more precise term for "closeness," namely *qin*. Close relations are generally expected to give proportionately more. This is straightforward customary practice in almost all other societies as well. Especially on ritual occasions such as weddings and funerals, it is necessary to know what the norm is in relation to one's closeness and other considerations, such as relative wealth or personal affinity. Giving beyond the scope of customary norm will raise suspicions about instrumental intent, thus when Kipnis says, "those who wished to claim a close friendship gave more than those who didn't," this is really the realm of *guanxi* in the *strict* sense alluded to in the literature. In the contemporary PRC, the pervasiveness of *guanxi* as a tactic of social relations that straddles all walks of life seems to have taken on a life of its own to a point where we see everything in terms of *guanxi*. In other parts of the Chinese-speaking world, the *same* acts of gift reciprocity are just called *custom* or the norm, not *guanxi*. *Guanxi* is *not* the custom. By its very instrumental intent, *guanxi* represents an attempt to cultivate favor *beyond* the scope of existing customary and other social ties; this aberrational strategy and its widespread acceptability is the product of peculiar *institutional* changes in PRC. Gift giving is an obvious manifestation of *guanxi*, but too much attention has been devoted to using exchange as a way of magnifying *guanxi*, when in fact gift giving is a key constituent of many aspects of Chinese social life. Even given our more immediate concerns, I think that it is more difficult to distinguish when gift giving is an expression of *renqing*, an act of *guanxi* or a bribe.[18] That which is being circulated here is not just *things*, but the *perception* of things.[19] The efficacy of the gift as pure *renqing* is dependent on the degree to which one recognizes or is willing to admit the instrumental nature of the act. The ability to *recognize* it as an altruistic or instrumental act is a significant one, because they can ultimately distinguish between different kinds of social relations. Anyone who has lined up to visit a doctor in China will know that one way of getting to the head of the line is to grease his palms with a carton of cigarettes. Although this may be perceived as an explicit bribe, showering a surgeon with liquor (and money) to ensure success in a life-threatening operation is not normally viewed in suspicious terms and can be viewed both as *guanxi* or *renqing*.[20]

Thus, the key to understanding *guanxi* should really be a function first of our ability to *interpret* its implicit intentions and strategies and differentiate it from other kinds of relations, not just by reference to its semantic meaning or literal manifestations. *Guanxi* is a peculiar kind of social relationship that inculcates a peculiar kind of behavior. If I wish to cultivate favor with someone for instrumental purposes, I may go to great lengths to mute criticism of that person for fear of damaging these ties, even go out of my way to keep up a nice facade.[21] There are complex permutations of such behavior that transcend mere gift giving. More importantly, the efficacy of such ties will also depend on their acceptability in a particular social-political-institutional context vis-à-vis other kinds of behavior. The problem with gift giving, on the other hand, is that it has existed long before *guanxi* and is analytically *distinct* from it. It is not just the language of social relations. Gift exchange is the basic structure of social organization and ritual process. In this regard, there are significant differences in the way anthropologists interpret social exchange that can easily highlight the multifaceted complexity of the phenomenon. Jonathan Parry (1986) has distinguished between "the gift" and "the Indian gift" to accentuate the sociological and cultural dimensions of exchange. Marshall Sahlins (1972) has, in reinterpreting "the spirit" of the gift, on the other hand, been less interested in gift giving per se than in showing how exchange engenders social structure itself. In this context, I am less concerned with showing how *guanxi* or *renqing* has invoked all manner of gift exchange than in showing how it is a complex and pervasive kind of ritual act whose permutations of behavior must be seen as a function of perceptions and intentions, *not just* material transactions. More than the literal calculus of social relations, exchange is a constitutive element of the ritual process. The symbolic complexity of gift exchange in domestic rites did not begin in post-Maoist PRC, as though discovered by a recent explosion of writing in the social scientific literature. Most contemporary customary practices pale in complexity in contrast with the esoteric ritualism of gift exchange in late traditional China.[22] *Nowhere* in this literature are they referred to as *guanxi*; they are customs par excellence.

Exchange as Ritual Behavior in the Interpretation of Practice

Marcel Mauss's classic book *Essai sur le Don* was less about *The Gift*, as it was literally translated into English, than about the morally obligatory nature of reciprocity in exchange or acts of donation (hence, *le don*). Acts of gift giving, even donation, demanded reciprocal acts or gestures; this was the nature of social solidarity. Chinese customs were predicated on gift giving, typically of cash. To say the least, commoditizing customary gift giving as *guanxi* is a gross mischaracterization. Chinese refer to gift giving literally as *song liwu* ("give material gift") and *sung li* ("give ritual"), where *li* can mean both gift and ritual. The equivalence of gift giving as ritual etiquette and social reciprocity lends a different spin to the *renqing* (rapport) that inherently drives such acts. Mauss begins his book with a quote about friendship.[23] It would not be inaccurate to render it into Chinese as "what is *renqing*?" To infer that an act is instrumentally driven by *guanxi* has less to do with its nature as custom than the field of relations within society or politics that makes gift giving an acceptable mode of strategically manipulative behavior. At issue in this regard are the various permutations in a specific context of practice (in the PRC, Taiwan, or Hong Kong) that situate these acts.

In a context of practice, the issue is not just one of deciphering the meaning of *renqing* but also unpacking the ensemble of acts and behaviors associated with "acting like a person" (*zuoren*). In the abstract, *zuoren* may mean that "he understands the principles of cultivating *renqing*"; in the concrete, it may just mean that "he knows how to go through the motions." To use an academic example, one might ask, "What does it take to get tenure"? In Chinese, one might say knowing how to *zuoren*. Concretely speaking, that might mean, in addition to publishing the right stuff (an esoteric book produced by a university press or papers, ideally in refereed international journals), performing visibly on the conference circuit, altruistically "making contributions" to administrative work, and placating influential senior professors. I would call this *biaoxian* in Chinese. How is this any different from the Communist Chinese work regime that Walder has described, with its emphasis on work attitude, going through the right motions, and showing the proper deference to authority? Without a doubt, there is also a difference of quantity as well as quality, but degree of rigidity in the system would determine to a large degree the appropriateness of various interpersonal strategies and demeanors.

Whether one begins from the principles of moral-ethical necessity, which invokes social and transactional behavior, or the acts themselves that implicitly cultivate moral rapport, it is clear that in a Chinese context *renqing* and *zuoren* are inextricably linked as permutations of culture and practice (or culture into practice and vice versa). The moral weight of *renqing*, expressed in large part by the quantity and intensity of its acts of "doing," is an important basis for understanding in turn the cultural specificity of social exchange and face relations in a Chinese context. On the other hand, institutional regimes of power predicate these social relations by transforming goal-oriented behavior into survival strategies within a framework of practice. In this sense, moral exchange can be transformed by inherent tensions of power.

In sum, it is futile to debate whether face, social relations of *guanxi* and its complex acts of material and symbolic exchange are really about culture *or* power. In a Chinese context, one should say that these actions and behaviors are in essence about cultivation of *renqing* and that what constitutes friendship (or power) is in actuality a matter of value judgment and perception. The principles are the same everywhere, but the terms and primordial meanings still constitute an important basis for assessing the variability of possible intentions.

The ambivalence of friendship and power in a Chinese cultural setting means that one can *never* be sure of an actor's intentions and meanings, despite the neat picture of social interactionist strategies depicted by psychologists, and this is precisely the cause of social tension in practice. In professional settings, such as one of work, where determination of merit is based on ethical standards of behavior that contribute to social rapport, in addition to objective markers of achievement, it is difficult for all intents and purposes to determine whether work performance (in the maintenance of the institution as a whole) is a power game (as might be fought between cliques competing to cultivate favor) or simply a matter of doing one's job. Not only is there a thin line between altruism and egotism in the cultivation of *renqing*, but this basic tension mirrors in a similar way the ambivalence of face relations. This tension is not inherently Chinese, as though cultural in origin; it is a problematic of practice.

The ambiguity of cultural terms has important theoretical ramifications for reassessing the sociological nature of exchange.[24] Perhaps contrary

to Mauss's (largely Durkheimian) assumptions about the necessity of reciprocity in society (as social solidarity), which became the platform on which
later anthropologists posited the (structuralist) rationality of kinship systems
and other elaborate ritual institutions, one can cite the Chinese case as a
paradigmatic example of how sophisticated and prone to endless interpretation and manipulation simple acts of reciprocity and exchange can be,
even when they are cloaked literally in the language of etiquette. Who says
that societies in general, and social institutions in particular, must intrinsically be built on principles of social solidarity, without which they would
dissolve into dysfunctional or structural chaos, this being the imagination
of grand theories predicated on the existence of sociocultural "systems"?
Changes in contemporary Chinese societies are shaped by different sociopolitical conditions and as a result of negotiation within intrinsic systems
of values and by people in relation to institutions. They reflect as well as
disguise intentions and strategies for which we still lack a clear framework
and language of practice.

By shifting the basic framework of reference to these ongoing regimes
of practice, the main epistemological problematic is one of identifying the
locus of institutions that produces a field of distinctive behaviors and visible actions, of which terms such as *renqing*, *guanxi*, and *mianzi* are specific expressive manifestations or cultural rationalizations. I do not think
that the *problematics* that have arisen in debates regarding *guanxi* or *biaoxian* are exclusively Chinese, in a cultural sense. Dilemmas engendered by
"connections" are no different from endemic crises of bribery and crony
capitalism in the Third World or scandals that plague the conduct of high
politics in "civilized" countries. Each must be viewed in the context of its
own ethico-institutional framework, where guidelines of acceptable behavior
may not always be unambiguously defined. In any case, the perception of
"corruption" is in essence a value judgment. Even if *guanxi* is the same
everywhere, the extent to which *guanxi* is construed as a problematic must
first be viewed as a function of prevailing values and practices. Such actions,
exchanges, and relationships then constitute a staple framework on which
one can ultimately assess the processes of cultural desire, social cohesion,
and will to power.

The *Guanxi* Problematic in the Fault Lines
of an Emerging Capitalist Regime

The immense sinological literature on *guanxi* can easily attest that network
relations in general have always been part of Chinese everyday life, especially

within its business culture. Even if, according to interdisciplinary studies, it has attained a high level of sophistication, as a general mode of sociality, it should be more sociologically universal than cultural peculiar to the Chinese. The pejorative manifestations of *guanxi* behavior as instrumental, calculated strategies of personal gain have also been amply documented in Taiwan, especially in relation to politics, and to a lesser extent in Hong Kong. But *guanxi* behavior in this regard clearly declined in these places over time as a result of broader societal transformations. ·Whether we call them the advent of a market based utilitarianism, the ethics of a new service economy or the rule of law, it is apparent that *guanxi* became incompatible with emerging life regimes. In the PRC, *guanxi* was not problematic during a Maoist era dominated by its socialist class ethics. Even when it emerged as an increasingly prevalent strategy of social survival in the post-Deng era, it was clearly not an evolution of its inherent nature as custom—neotraditional as Walder and others put it—but a radical break with, if not then perversion of, the past.

The sociological literature has perhaps played a key role in making *guanxi* studies on the PRC into a major cottage industry. A volume of essays edited by Thomas Gold et al., *Social Connections in China* (2002), attempted to highlight what they called "the institutional turn" in analyses of *guanxi*. Without rejecting overly cultural perspectives, they argued that the emergence and ubiquity of this phenomenon had more to do with structural and institutional conditions in society. Instead of being autonomous, *guanxi* was embedded in practices and tended to be a product of the latter. Thus, the focus in these essays was on the production or practice of *guanxi* relationships, power asymmetries within the political economy, external or "third-party effects" on dyadic relationships, the function of *guanxi* in the context of business relations, the use of *guanxi* ties as practical strategy in job finding and mobility, *guanxi* in the formal practice of law and as network tool in gossip communities, and so on. While it has been easy to dualize culture to accent concrete institutional realities, the book's exclusive focus on the PRC raises obvious questions about its *general* sociological conclusions for other Chinese-speaking societies that have undergone different sociopolitical changes. Lin Nan (2001), for example, has viewed *guanxi* as a lens for comparing institutional differences in the PRC, Taiwan, and Hong Kong. The general appeal of Gold et al. to social structural networking is reductionist and simplistic; at the same time its narrow focus on literal aspects of institutional practice overlooks at the same time deeper epistemic transformations within its broad regime.

A recent exhaustive review of 200-plus works on *guanxi* in the social scientific literature by Chen et al. (2013) demonstrates the extent to which *guanxi* has become an object of analytical overdetermination. Starting from the literature on Chinese management and organization, it is not surprising that the basis on which it conceptualizes a *guanxi* frame of analysis is built mainly on its networking ties, the nature of social capital and the role of cultural and ethical values in reinforcing these various relational processes and practical strategies. From the perspective of business management and entrepreneurial relations, the focus is largely on its impact vis-à-vis other aspects of economic performance and organization. While noting that attention to *guanxi* as widespread phenomenon has increased exponentially in recent decades, it attempts primarily to develop a comprehensive framework for understanding it by showing how it is essentially an outgrowth of traditional Chinese social practices and cultural values; it is less concerned, on the other hand, with showing how the phenomenon, as practiced, is in fact the consequence of broader underlying social transformations that have given rise to it.

Other works have attempted to transcend the framework of *guanxi* per se to elucidate the broader sociological ramifications of its inherent principles. Lo and Otis (2003) attempt to explain how the market in postsocialist China has been redefining *guanxi* and in the process provides something analogous to a culture of civility. In the historical long-term, the market expedited the modularization of *guanxi*, transforming its "generalized particularism" from its ritualistic nature in a Confucian moral economy and its informal workings in a Maoist society into a flexible regime of practices that has had clear social ramifications beyond the economic realm, allowing it to flourish in extra-institutional domains. I have strong reservations about how the authors view this modularization as a gradual emergence of informal social relations in the Maoist economy, much less a continual adaptation of a Confucian moral practice in the context of market modernity. The idealization of such flexible relations as a kind of civility also ultimately accentuates the authors' normative view of current developments in the PRC. On the other hand, Qi Xiaoying's (2013) effort to view *guanxi* as a social capital theory in a globalized social science highlights an attempt to broaden the relevance of culturally specific concepts to other societies. While recognizing *guanxi*'s conceptual embeddedness in other concepts, such as *renqing* and *xinyong* (trust), the author less convincingly reconciles its dual aspects of "notoriety and nobility," opting to distinguish instead its generality in principle and particularity in form, ultimately reflecting a normative approach to this "globalized" theory.

In accenting China's transitional economy, Chang Kuang-chi (2011) develops a slightly different sociological approach to the above literature. Noting that the literature is divided among culturalist, institutional, and network theory paradigms, he differentiates between three *guanxi* strategies that inherently invoke them. He calls the instrumentalist *guanxi* associated most with bribery an "accessing" strategy, the general network *guanxi* indicative of business relationships based on personal trust a "bridging" strategy and the *guanxi* seminal to complex institutional relationships such as in a capitalist economy an "embedding" strategy. He then shows in the context of China's changing economy how each strategy responds to different actor-centered decision making rationales. In the context of his historical evolution, *guanxi* forms change generally from the prevalence of accessing strategies to embedding ones. The transformation that he envisages conforms intricately to his interpretation of the institutional history but is inconsistent with the blatant reality of instrumental *guanxi* that is intricately tied to the growth of corruption in China's emerging capitalism. The *guanxi* problematic in the PRC is different from its relative demise in other Chinese speaking societies and is endemic to the institutional context that gives birth to it. As a private nepotistic strategy, it contrasts with the institutional economy and is more importantly a product of its systemic fault lines.

In retrospect, much of the confusion pertaining to our understanding of *guanxi* derives from the hysteria created by the prevailing literature about its problematic exceptionalism. It just means "relationship"; there is nothing in the meaning of the word that justifies glossing it in Chinese to denote a uniquely cultural concept, much less a philosophy, as though rooted in Confucianism. As a cultural code of conduct in a Chinese setting, the concept of *renqing* is what regulates *mianzi* and *guanxi* in a power theory of culture; *renqing* is what initiates and maintains the exchange relationships that define *guanxi* in the concrete. Its association with *bao* makes such exchange relationships no different from others found elsewhere; reciprocity or the commitment to it is what makes social exchange ongoing, regardless of instrumental intent. The inherent association of gift giving and ritual in most traditional Chinese customs has made it a ubiquitous staple from the outset, not a recent invention. If it has always been customary to give gifts on ritual occasions, since when did it become a matter of *guanxi*? It is necessary first of all to understand its cultural meanings before articulating its functions. In terms of cultural substance, the function of *renqing* (or *guanxi*) is actually *no* different for a businessman building relationships of trust and someone engaged in gift giving as a bribe. As a strategy for cultivating favor, it is by nature politicizing. It is also possible, of course, to view its instrumental intent as strategies of accessing, bridging or embedding, in Chang's terms, but this is above all a *value judgment* on the part of the analyst, not something that the participant need readily concur with. Nonetheless, it is apparent that a diversity of *guanxi* behavior characterizes different Chinese speaking societies as well as changes within them.

The early literature on Taiwan, Hong Kong, and elsewhere has been full of references to the rampant existence of *guanxi*, whether it be in the form of vote-buying in politics or norms of doing business. What deserves mention is not just the demise of *guanxi* in the historical long-run but more importantly the basic transformation of the societal or institutional ground that made *guanxi* incompatible with normative life strategies. In other words, this was not simply the product of changes in *guanxi* alone, as though evolution sui generis. Whether it is attributed to the advent of a service economy or system of governance, it should prompt us to assess the sociopolitical ground that *frames guanxi* and other life practices. In the PRC, it is obvious that a different set of sociopolitical transformations has grounded the emergence of *guanxi* as a dominant or prevalent life strategy. *Guanxi* seems exceptional, but it is merely a surface phenomenon that epitomizes the rumblings of a deeper transformation. What needs further scrutiny is the advent of nepotistic forms of *guanxi* from general ones. It paralleled the demise of Maoist era society and polity as well as the rise of the post-Deng economy; the focus of discussion should really shift to articulations of the latter and their systemic regimes. Ultimately, *guanxi* in its pejorative sense is not a Chinese phenomenon per se. It can be found in any society, marked by a variety of local terms and practices, where the institutional fault lines allow for it.

Chapter 8

A New Greater China

The Demise of Transnationalism and Other Great White Hopes

The term *Greater China* was used primarily in the 1980s to denote a newly emerging China spawned by Deng Xiaoping's policy of economic liberalization and the diverse transnational influences to follow. Hong Kong and Taiwan became major sources for a renaissance of all sorts, economic and cultural. Greater China thus represented this greater cultural-economic domain that seemed to transcend political boundaries, but it was an entity centered outside China or between "the triangle." Reference to Greater China has gradually faded out, while giving birth ironically to an even "greater" China. The nature of this social transformation is without a doubt worth investigating, not simply in the context of broader geopolitical changes but more importantly with reference to the embeddedness of theories in geopolitical practice.

East Asian Fantasies in Perspective

It is difficult to view the development of China apart from its inclusion within a wider regional sphere. Its civilizational ties to Korea and Japan were perhaps the closest, but it has also enjoyed centuries of trade with Southeast Asia, prior to mass emigration of laborers from southeastern China from the nineteenth century. In past decades, (Western) scholars have looked at China and East Asia in general from a variety of regional or global lenses. Such

This is a revision and expansion of a paper, first published in 2007 as "What Happened to 'Greater China'? Changing Geopolitics in the China Triangle," *Macalester International* 18:28–44.

societies, especially in the postwar era, have been the foci of what William Callahan (2004) has called "social science fantasies." The rise of "miracle economies" in East Asia, first Japan, then Taiwan, South Korea, Hong Kong, and Singapore gave birth to the so-called The Four Little Dragons. Since this rise corresponded closely with the stagflation of Western capitalism in the 1970s, many scholars singled out culture as a prime determining factor in this distinctive development. Peter Berger (1987:7) coined the notion of economic culture. In a book (Berger and Hsiao 1988) titled *In Search of an East Asian Development Model*, he noted the "comparative advantage of Sinic civilization," but the first to underscore the role of Asian values in the rise of East Asia was the political scientist, Roderick MacFarquhar (1980), who wrote an essay in *The Economist* titled "The Post-Confucian Challenge." Models of East Asian capitalism filled the scholarly literature in the 1980s but shifted in the '90s to focus more on overseas Chinese capitalism, which corresponded, on the one hand, with the bursting of the Japanese economic bubble followed by a rise of transnational Chinese capitalism throughout East and Southeast Asia. At the same time, scholars began to compare Japanese models of capitalism with Chinese ones, but all of these discussions hinted at distinctive features, that is, unique ideologies, institutions, and practices that supposedly drove these discrete economies. As variations on the theme of this Sinic mode of production, there were diverse tendencies as well. Gordon Redding (1993) has taken Berger's notion of economic culture most seriously, by attempting to show how distinctive ideologies or institutions can be elucidated to shed light on Chinese business organizations and practices everywhere. Gary Hamilton (1996:331), on the other hand, while recognizing the relevance of cultural influences on Chinese economic organization, has argued against the danger of relying on a sociocentric model, noting that "Chinese capitalism cannot be understood apart from the dynamics of the global economy, because . . . Chinese capitalism is not a domestic capitalism (i.e., the product of indigenous economic growth), but rather is integral to world capitalism itself." Ezra Vogel (1991), a sociologist, has tended to see a balanced role between culture and sociopolitical context, which can be used to contrast the industrializing experiences of Hong Kong, Taiwan, South Korea, and Singapore, while anthropologists Aihwa Ong and Don Nonini (1997), from the vantage point of Southeast Asia, have viewed the success of Chinese capitalists mostly as an extension of inherently transnational tendencies and skills. Finally, there have been many scholars who take seriously the role of Confucianism in the development of capitalism, either in Weberian or other terms. In the 1980s, even the Singapore government actively explored the applicability of Weber's Protestant ethic to Confucianism, which helped to promote the primacy of Asian values in cultural policy, in the form of ideology or religion, as a prime mover in economic development. In raising all these examples above, I am not particularly interested in pursuing any of these complex themes, any of which can easily be the subject of separate books. My point is to suggest, by way of background discussion, that the way in which scholars look at China is often the product of inherently larger concerns. The debate regarding East Asian capitalism is as much reflective of a deeper debate about the nature of capitalistic development as it is inflective of the way scholars generally perceive the role of culture in constituting society or driving institutional life practices. In the end, they are not end points in themselves but are intended to have ramifications that disguise the way that we contrast the relative economic and political potentialities of East versus West (or what Samuel Huntington [1996] has ominously called "the clash of civilizations"), while serving as foci for extending academic debates over the nature of capitalism or revitalizing Confucianism.

Greater China as Transnationalizing Imaginary

The concept of Greater China is a product of somewhat different concerns and different circumstances. Since I already mentioned the ominous specter of Samuel Huntington, it is not by coincidence that he also happens to have a position on Greater China. He (1996:238) has argued that, through what he calls "Greater China and its co-prosperity sphere," "China is resuming its place as regional hegemon, and the East is coming into its own." It reflects also a Yellow Peril Orientalism that was promoted avidly by Cold War–era polemicists and now by their descendants in the CIA and Pentagon. On the other hand, Greater China, as I understand the term here, was initially coined in the 1980s and became popular in the '90s to represent what seemed to be a newly emerging phenomenon at that time. A major journal on contemporary Chinese affairs, the *China Quarterly*, devoted a special issue to this in 1993. As its editor, David Shambaugh (1993:653), neatly put it, "Greater China is a complex and multifaceted phenomenon which exists even if the term to describe it is not entirely apt." In effect, the phenomenon that Shambaugh alludes to here refers not just to the face of a newly emerging China, as though it is the product of its own internal political struggles and social transformations. I would say also that this newly emerging phenomenon took on distinctive meaning in the context of subtle unconscious changes taking place at the same time within the modern world system, during which one can also see a renewed importance in the role of cultural forces and relationships. I deliberately phrase my description of the phenomenon in this way, because, first, I think it is crucial to explain what was really old or new about it; second why we tend to see the inherent influence of cultural factors; and third what happened when use of *Greater China* began to fade into obscurity toward the end of the millennium.

One should begin with the phenomenon itself: it is generally recognized that, in the 1980s, one began to see growing interactions and interdependencies between China and its neighbors, Hong Kong and Taiwan, initially, then broadly expanding outward in Asia through links with other ethnic Chinese. Harry Harding (1993) notes that first reference to a notion of greater China most likely occurred in journalistic articles in Taiwan and Hong Kong, that foresaw and advocated the emergence of a "Chinese common market" that would link Taiwan, Hong Kong, Macau, Singapore, and PRC, using terms like *zhongguoren gongtongti* (*Chinese communal entity*) and *zhongguoren jingji jituan* (*Chinese economic corporation*). I emphasize the advent of the phenomenon as described above and initial attempts to characterize it as a term rather than the appearance of the term itself, because I do not think that the term for Greater China, at least in Chinese (*da zhonghua*), was ever popular or useful in Chinese intellectual circles, unlike in the West. One can debate the hypothetical question of whether Greater China is actually an Orientalism, but the phenomenon itself is real. As cursory attempts to phrase it suggest, the phenomenon began initially in earnest with the increase of economic flows and relations between China and its neighbors. These economic bonds developed into a broader community that encompassed common cultural interests and political sentiments. In other words, it became more than an EU- or NAFTA-like common market. Its multidimensionality also raises obvious questions about its ramifications for other domains of life, society, and polity. At the same time, while one can recognize that this is a complex economic, cultural, and political phenomenon, our attempts to understand it functionally have invoked debate and confusion about the concepts and interpretations used to define the term. In other words, are we looking at interaction, integration, or reunification? This confusion in conceptualization in functional terms underlies the controversy over Greater China as a problematic idea, much more than the understanding of what constitutes "Greater" and why. In geographical terms, the nucleus of Greater China has been unambiguously Hong Kong and Taiwan, but how far one can extend it elsewhere in Asia through the network of Chinese is a matter of definition.

Nonetheless, the phenomenon of Greater China emerged clearly in the 1980s and into the '90s, followed by a growing awareness and attention to it in intellectual circles in the '90s. In economic terms, we see in this period of expansion greater flows of capital between the three places that constitute what I prefer to call the China Triangle, and the nature of these flows is very uneven. In the post–WWII era, Hong Kong had always been heavily engaged in and dependent on trade with PRC for goods of all kinds, principally for subsistence, while serving as an entrepôt for China trade going to and from the rest of the world. But active investment by Hong Kong entrepreneurs in China was made possible in the post-Maoist era by the change in policies initiated by Deng Xiaoping. This coincided symbolically with the Sino-British agreement in 1984 to return Hong Kong to Chinese sovereignty in the sense that it ironically signaled the opening up of capitalism in China and Hong Kong's role in it. This change in policy not only opened the floodgates of capital but also opened up flows of people and other things between China and Hong Kong. Most of the movement was unidirectional; special economic zones in Shenzhen (bordering Hong Kong), and then elsewhere, acted as magnets to attract Hong Kong investment, which in later years spread everywhere else in China. The outflow of capital from Hong Kong to China has continued unabated to the present to the point where Hong Kong manufacturers today employ more workers in south China than in Hong Kong itself. How it has changed the existence and operation of Hong Kong's manufacturing industry, among other like industries, does not require elaboration here. The case of Taiwan is slightly different. In 1981, the PRC's no-tariff policy for Taiwan imports, followed by the creation of a special economic zone in Fujian, served as initial incentives to attract Taiwanese investment. The flow of Taiwan goods and capital into China was mostly unidirectional too, in the sense that the KMT government on Taiwan was slow to open up its Cold War embargo against PRC goods until much later. But like in the case of Hong Kong, the opening up of economic trade on both sides eventually increased the flow to the point today where it is getting just bigger and bigger. So on the economic face of things, Greater China is supposed to be getting greater and greater. More interaction should bring about more dependence, but does this bring about more integration, and is more integration the backdrop eventually for more reunification, as though to suggest that this is really what PRC had in mind when they first coined such meaningful terms as *socialism with Chinese characteristics* and *one country, two systems*? The interface where phenomenon meets concept is unfortunately also the interface where fact meets (discursive) fiction. At the outset, I deliberately set aside this problematic, because this is where the confusion starts, and this is where the phenomenon starts to get complicated, beyond anyone's imagination, in my opinion. If we stay only at the descriptive level of phenomenal change, Greater China has never stopped getting greater, but this already contradicts our later discovery that the concept has most recently faded away.

The cultural phenomenon of Greater China moreover referred in the 1980s to the emerging popularity of Hong Kong and Taiwanese pop culture, despite official disdain by the CCP. Canto-pop and Mando-pop have diverse, complex origins in Hong Kong and Taiwan. One should not assume ipso facto that they are just indigenous creations of an ongoing folk culture. In an early essay, I (1996) have argued that popular culture in both places is in fact the unique consequence of changing geopolitical forces. The advent in the 1970s and '80s of what we recognize today as Hong Kong and Taiwan pop culture was made possible by overt depoliticization of the cultural domain; mass-mediated culture emerged against the current of more dominant forces like Mandarin and Cantonese cultural spheres, as well as Western ones. But despite its actual origins, the cultural face that was presented in the context of PRC took on a different tune. Pop culture was not just the conduit for the influx of modernity; its political subversive nature made its channels even more blatant than those of the informal economy. The cultural flows that defined Greater China in this regard were without a doubt unidirectional, almost exclusively. Thomas Gold (1993) correctly called this Greater China culture *gangtai* (literally, Hong Kong–Taiwanese). Perhaps even more so than in the case of Greater China's economy, the cultural affinities were more apparent. The fact that it was a Chinese language medium culture made the cultural content of this Greater China unabashedly modern, if not Westernized. Reverse cultural flow from PRC back to Hong Kong and Taiwan did not occur until much later, and this was obviously a consequence of the emergence of pop culture in China precipitated in part by *gangtai* culture. One can ruminate on cultural developments in this regard, which as in the case of the economy will inevitably invoke questions of presumed integration, synthesis, and resistance, but it was clear that economy and culture did not seem to work in exactly the same way, and thus should have different implications for a Greater China.

An interesting spin-off from the cultural dimension of Greater China described above is the idea of cultural China invoked by Tu Weiming (1991). Although his use of cultural China was not meant to coincide with Greater China, it was motivated by the same perceptions that saw a greater community of mind that transcended China per se and by values that advocated a renaissance from the outside that could serve as paradigmatic model for "a declining core." As a neo-Confucian intellectual historian, he was not referring to pop culture as the great synthesizer but a set of civilizational values that could in theory unite Chinese and Sinophiles everywhere and whose center of gravity was perhaps closer to Cambridge, Massachusetts, that is, in the global center.

The political dimension of Greater China, in contrast to the economic and cultural, was perhaps the most dubious, but if one reads the literature, one gets the sense that the political is unavoidably intertwined with other dimensions of Greater China. On the surface, Greater China is not about political relations binding PRC, Hong Kong, and Taiwan. If anything, it is a communal entity built on informal, extra-political, or transnational ties relying on concrete economic and cultural bonds that simultaneously seem to have political ramifications. The diverse politicized readings invoked by the literature were really a function of how diverse people read the significance of its economic and cultural relations. The astute sinologist Harding (1993:673) concluded his analysis of Greater China by saying: "the re-creation of a global Chinese culture has been a natural process: the product of a common ancestry, facilitated by modern communications." At least in cultural terms, the institutional developments in relation to a more universalistic Chinese culture seemed to suggest that increased communicability could lead to dissolution of physical and bureaucratic obstacles, while linguistic and cultural affinities between people could also exploit common values in tradition or interests in modernity to create such a global village. More importantly, the cultural aspect of Greater China seemed to have only positive effects that would facilitate any eventual reunification. In the realm of economy, Harding (1993:666) argued that the emergence of a transnational Chinese economy was not just about the progressive embrace of a capitalist way of life to raise one's standard of living and that its political strategies in Greater China were played differently by all sides of the China Straits:

> From Beijing's perspective, economic interaction is viewed as a way of facilitating the eventual political reunification of China. The mainland Chinese government has therefore adopted a series of policies to stimulate commercial relations with Hong Kong and Taiwan, most notably the creation of special economic zones directly opposite them, for political as well as for purely commercial reasons. Hong Kong, in turn, regards economic ties with the mainland as a way of cushioning its return to Chinese sovereignty in 1997, in that they will give Beijing a large and direct stake in preserving the territory's political viability and economic prosperity throughout the transition. On Taiwan, in contrast, economic interaction with the mainland is seen in the short term as a lever for extracting political concessions from Beijing, especially with regard to renouncing the use of force against the island and allowing Taiwan a larger

voice in international affairs, and possibly a way of promoting democratization.

I think that the complicated relationships that Harding projects reflect less the complex nature of the phenomenon than the complicated nature of his thinking. More importantly, it is not possible to divorce his complicated logic from his political reading of real or imagined intents of policy strategy on different sides of the divide. I do not deny that there is politics in the way policies are practiced on all sides of this battle; I spell them out merely to suggest that there are other kinds of politics at work here too, that is, a more abstract kind of geopolitics.

At this point, it might be useful just to underscore and problematize certain aspects of Greater China, as depicted here. First, it is without a doubt a transnational phenomenon, but I would argue that this is the product of changes in both the local and global environment. To be sure, none of this would have been possible without the post-Maoist transition in PRC that not only gave rise to capitalism but also actively engaged interaction with the rest of the world. This change of policy garnered the active support of rich Hong Kong capitalists who ended up being the biggest promoters of reunification with the motherland and toeing the line to suppress democracy. However, in its overt transnationalism, scholars tend to neglect that the border-crossing nature of Chinese capital and people is no different from the transnational transformations of Western capitalism seen elsewhere. That is to say, in the demise of Cold War and imperial politics, the opening up of the market in China has generally followed the path, at first glance, of what Lash and Urry (1987) called "disorganized capitalism," or "disjunctures" in Appadurai's terms. Flows were not literally random or chaotic, but this implicit decentralization effectively broke down standard norms of political, economic, or cultural affiliation, and this is what Greater China predicated, namely a mobile transnational cultural economy defined by porous borders and free flow of people, ideas, and capital. What Greater China was supposed to signal was the breakdown of closed, traditional identities through constant deracination and hybridization, which in turn constituted the engine of change for the rest of China. Second, despite the cultural facade of Greater China, I argue that the unifying effect of a common culture was highly exaggerated and played at best a secondary role. I doubt that a common pop culture could unify anything political (Tu's Confucianism actually stands a better chance), and nepotistic ties that bound Chinese entrepreneurs to their ethnic origins were equally exaggerated. Chinese businesspeople, like those Chinese traders who dominated commerce for 300 years in Southeast Asia, were, according to Wang

Gungwu (1991), penultimate multiculturalists. Successful survival required adaptability to diverse local conditions, including assimilation, if necessary. The first principle of any entrepreneur, even in multinational corporations, was usually to exploit the markets that were most familiar. In this sense, the rapid expansion of overseas Chinese interests into Greater China was simply a natural reaction prompted by the dismantling of political or bureaucratic barriers. Third, I think that an obvious feature of Greater China that happened to be more salient than culture itself was its center of gravity. Whether it is economic, cultural, or political, its critical mass was always centered outside China, if not in Hong Kong then somewhere within the Triangle (and presumably rooted in modern values).

In short, I would argue that, whatever made Greater China what it was, its driving force, however defined, was in essence located outside the PRC. More importantly, the thing that created this gravitas was not any one factor, although scholars usually underline the economy. It was more precisely the unique confluence of both local and global forces: on the one hand, the ideological or political forces transforming PRC society and polity as a whole and, on the other hand, the changing face of transnational capitalism that in many senses accommodated the fluid nature of transborder flows globally, which nurtured in turn the informal economy and hybridized identities that began to develop and mutate in PRC, expanding back outward.

At this point, one must really ask, does Greater China exist anymore? If we define the phenomenon superficially as that transnational entity characterized by increasing cultural and economic flows between extrapolitical Chinese-speaking societies, then Greater China should, if anything, be greater and greater. But this does not accord with the declining popularity of the concept itself. Without a doubt, something else has fundamentally changed. *The center of gravity has clearly shifted.* Hong Kong and Taiwan no longer represent the driving force or foci behind the system, as though they were models for "a declining core" in Tu Weiming's terms. The center has definitely moved into the PRC itself, and the rules of the game that define the system have been rewritten. In the year leading up to the Hong Kong handover of 1997, while many have been debating the future of capitalism and democracy in Hong Kong, others have been debating whether Hong Kong would maintain its status as an important hub of capitalist development and pivotal entrepôt for international trade. Some argued that the continued support for capitalism in PRC policy would ensure Hong Kong's ongoing dominant role. Others argued that Hong Kong would eventually be overshadowed by Shanghai's rise.

Shanghai's rise to prominence as an unrivaled cosmopolitan center is a story in itself, but I think there is much substance to the contention that

Hong Kong has already lost its role as prime mover within Greater China. I would argue that much of it has to do with a simple fact: the development of capitalism in China. It is not just that capitalism was transforming a traditional way of life. Capitalism itself has taken on a life of its own, and in rewriting the rules of the game it has in the process increasingly sucked in the rest of the world. One of the things that drives the logic of this new capitalism can be summarized in Reaganite terms: It's the market, stupid. The way in which the centripetal pull of a limitless market has been wielded to make people conform to political correctness should make utilitarian theory proud.

The Changing Geopolitics of the China Triangle

In any event, the geopolitics of the China Triangle has continued to mutate to a point which eventually brought about the demise of (transnational) Greater China as a phenomenon. These underlying processes in essence transcended the apparent features of Greater China as an ongoing regional entity per se. Moreover, in my opinion, the fundamental transformation in geopolitical relationship between Hong Kong and PRC presaged best the evolving nature of PRC capitalism, in general, which in the long run has not only formed the basis of political economic relations with Hong Kong and Taiwan but ultimately the rest of the world as well.

Most importantly, these processual developments ran counter to explicit policy positions and scholarly assessments that served in effect as convenient fictions. The first such fiction involved the relative autonomy of "one country, two systems." Much of the energy devoted to the Sino-British Agreement in 1984 to guarantee the preservation of its capitalist economy for fifty years after its repatriation to China proved to be a futile exercise. The commitment in post-Deng PRC to liberalize the market economy made the maintenance of a capitalist system in Hong Kong a moot point. What started as free trade zones in Shenzhen, Xiamen, Zhuhai, and so on simply expanded elsewhere to become the standard mode of production in China. The relative autonomy of Hong Kong (and Taiwan) vis-à-vis China was never a significant point of contention. Hong Kong's economic influence or dominance in this regard began to be challenged at the same time by the rise of Shanghai. At least, the economy in a superficial sense did not represent obstacles to a transnational Greater China characterized by free flows. Whether this was a consequence or attribute of "one country, two systems" is another matter.

The second fiction was the anticipation of socialist or nationalist integration. In fact, the mood in Hong Kong prior to 1997 for eventual repatriation in a cultural sense was rather accommodating. The transitional era from 1984 to 1997 may have been marked by Hong Kong's discursive "disappearance," in Abbas's (1997) terms, but it was also characterized by a search for lost or forgotten cultural and historical origins brought about by a previous decade or more of overt Westernization and modernizing hybridity. The momentary euphoria of the impending Beijing Olympics further enhanced cultural sentiment into nationalizing ones. This may have been combined to some extent with decolonization in a literal sense, but the media even adopted self-censorship in order to accommodate increased ties with the mainland and offset potential political repression. Ironically, few of these developments continued after 1997. The People's Liberation Army, under the intense scrutiny of the media, entered Hong Kong, but little else to signal the advent of military or Party domination materialized. Despite all the fears of political oppression, the relative freedom of the press in airing critical views of official government policy after the establishment of the SAR regime ran counter to the trends prompted by heightened nationalism, which was supposed to be the point of departure for other all institutional changes. Policies to increase the use of Mandarin in general and reforms to change the educational system to make it more "inclusive" of national culture and history inevitably provoked local reaction and debate, but all of this arrived somewhat later.

The fiction contributing to the notion that Hong Kong was an autonomous "region" was reflective to some extent of the PRC's position that, in some functional respects, Hong Kong could be regarded as separate from China. Economically, China was linked integrally to the global economy through Hong Kong, and the 1998 Asian recession had demonstrated that Hong Kong still played a major role in this regard. In social and local political matters, Hong Kong's autonomy impacted less on developments on the mainland. As long as the political scheme of things insured the appointment of Beijing-sympathetic cliques in power, media opposition was a matter for local government to handle and did not directly impact Beijing. Yet freedom of the press was ironically restricted only to *local* affairs.[1]

The third fiction involves the emancipatory and colonizing potentialities of the capitalist revolution in transforming China, which implicitly hinted to some extent at the demise of the socialist regime. Foreign capital and enterprises in PRC continued to grow unabated during this period, but its effects on transforming other aspects of society and politics were to say the least debatable. On the other hand, Law Wing-sang's (2000) "northbound colonialism" was a projection of capitalism's advance into the mainland and its exploitative consequences for class conflict and future social relations. None of this seems to have panned out, however.

One way to transcend the inadequacies of the above fictions is to examine the nature of evolving capitalism in the PRC as more than just an economic mode of production. Beyond the surface, it was always from the outset linked to political control. Betting on the shifting center of the global market, the government was able to convert its new rules of the game into political leverage. Hong Kong and Taiwan were the first to witness the immediate effects.

There has been a long, established literature on the origins of capitalism in China, roots of its historical divergence with the West and comparisons with other East Asian experiences. It is possible to view these economic developments in the historical long-term or as inherent to deeper civilizational processes. Arrighi's (2007) eloquent "Lineages of the 21st Century," which underscore his analysis of China's recent economic ascent, is not simply the aftermath of the "Long 20th Century," but another chapter in classical economic debates between Smith and Marx. The ascent of Asia comes only in the last quarter of this *longue duree*, which by the time of Deng's liberalization of the market economy then becomes a battle between Smith and Friedman (flat globalization). There is an attempt inevitably to view this ascent within a broader geopolitics, which for Arrighi refers mainly to the global politics of a modern world system instead of the power dynamics that bind economic domination to political hegemony. Other versions of this neoliberal debate abound. I see it as a different collusion between the economy and politics, which in the context of the China Triangle has inevitably engendered a new paradigm for geopolitical relations, gradually following the shifting center of the market.

Oligarchic Capitalism as Antidemocratization and Anti-Autonomy

Most of the media attention in Hong Kong has turned to the plight of democratization, but few people see its failure as a consequence of the *institutional* entrenchment of capitalism, that is to say, the collusion of oligarchic interests and central government policy in exchange for the former's guaranteed political representation at the local level. The historical inability to institute a truly democratic government in post-1997 Hong Kong has mainly to do with the legacy of British rule. The governor and members of the legislative council were appointed. Chris Patten's attempts to introduce fully free elections in the post-1984 transition were, contrary to rhetorical fanfare, primarily facetious last-ditch efforts by a colonial lame duck administration to frustrate Communist takeover. Corporate interests were then guaranteed a proportional functional constituency in the post-1997 legislature. This was the cost (and benefit) of being able to do business in PRC. In the transformation of Hong Kong's public sphere, the political free rein given to oligarchic capitalist interests facilitated suppression of democratic opposition. The same could be said about the operation of capitalism in China.

In short, business interests were in fact intertwined with politics in ways that influenced *at an underlying level* support for or compromising of certain ideological principles (in this case, democracy). This collaboration increasingly solidified "the rules of the game." This complicit relation of power (or *guanxi* connections) was thus the *real* face of Hong Kong capitalism after 1997. This then became the model for doing business generally in China, regardless of with whom. Yahoo, Star-TV, Microsoft, and Google have all given way to political correctness as the price of admission to the China market. While this did not affect global capitalism, as practiced elsewhere, its ramifications for Greater China, where culture and the economy were defined by increasing flows of capital and people as well as ever-increasing bonds of interdependence, cannot be understated. What can this say about Greater China as an ever-mutating entity?

To call its mode of operation *guanxi* capitalism (pejoratively, crony capitalism) would be too simplistic. China was consciously aware that it was at the center of an expanding global market, both in terms of out-source production for the developed nations and the consumption of global products, and this awareness then in turn allowed it to use its pivotal role to control people's access to desired resources or benefits of the system by making people conform to the rules of the game in all other respects. Thus, the media has learned that it is free to print whatever it pleases in matters pertaining to Hong Kong (hence is autonomous), but that in matters involving China or cooperation with Chinese agencies it is forced to toe the proper ideological line as one's price of admission. Increasingly, they toe the line, especially when they discover that the economic survival of their own enterprise was dependent on expansion into the China market. Similarly, Taiwanese businesspeople, entertainers, and professionals of all sorts have learned to mute any expressions of or sympathy for Taiwanese independence so as not to jeopardize their own prospects for cashing in on a lucrative China market, especially when it has become obvious that this market was much richer than their own. These sanctions underlined the point that, while the market was in theory open, and people were free to make money, there was no attempt from above to control the redistribution of income, which had been the case with orthodox socialism. On the other hand, access to the market was in practice a privilege that could be politically controlled, if deemed desirable or necessary. In policy terms, this could be called socialism with Chinese characteristics.

If the advent of a new kind of capitalism was the real engine that drove both China and Greater China at the core, at least in economic terms, one might then ask, what ramifications did this have for the politics of Greater China, if not for the rest of the world? In fact, are there intended or potential ramifications for Hong Kong's eventual reintegration and the prospects of Taiwan's reunification, independence, or its continued ambiguous status vis-à-vis China? Despite the rhetoric of one country, two systems, which has as its ultimate goal reunification, economic power nonetheless plays a crucial role in leveraging political interests of the center.

In the evolution of Hong Kong's Occupy Central movement, what began as a critique of global capitalism and of issues central to its emergence in a PRC context eventually mutated to become the platform for its democratization movement. Taking its cue from the Occupy Wall Street movement, through its demands for universal suffrage, it directly challenged the politics of Hong Kong's presumed autonomy in a system where oligarchic economic interests were already firmly entrenched. The latest metamorphosis in 2014 of the occupy movement into the Umbrella Movement might seem on the surface to be the natural culmination of Hong Kong's campaign of antiglobal capitalism and a link to its ongoing democratization struggle.

To say the least, international media coverage of Hong Kong's Occupy (Umbrella) sit-in has heightened exponentially parallel to one's general hostility toward PRC rule or the latter's domination of Hong Kong's "autonomous" governance. But the democratization movement in Hong Kong has had a long history, with roots in the late British colonial era, and escalated in the wake of the June 4, 1989 Tiananmen suppression, memorialized by yearly vigils in Victoria Park. More importantly, this struggle for democratization had always been a purely political movement, with little connection to culture or Hong Kong's autonomous identity in any sense. Nonetheless, the process that brought together democratization in general and its renaissance in alliance with the Occupy Central demonstration is worth further scrutiny, if just to question whether its prime objective was motivated by anticapitalism, democracy, or both in tandem.

The Occupy Central movement officially began in October 2011, and its first occupying protests were forced to disband in September 2012. The second movement began in 2013, eventually became labeled the Umbrella Movement and ended in December 2014. The two movements differed in content, despite the continuity in name. The first was similar to the Occupy Wall Street movement. Its occupation of Central District, Hong Kong's financial hub, represented a direct confrontation with "Central District Values," the strong governance policies of Hong Kong's previous Chief Executive Donald Tsang. Its object of criticism was the exploitative consequences of neoliberal capitalism, as reflected mainly in growing income inequality between the rich and poor. It was generally perceived to be a politically radical movement and did not really achieve a mass following, which could make the problem attributable to society-at-large.

The second movement gradually became dominated by pro-democratization forces as a referendum on universal suffrage in Hong Kong. Its tie to the Occupy Central movement was its appropriation of its tactics of protest resistance and mass demonstration to galvanize widespread political support in the name of democratic freedom and universal human rights. In practice, its object of attack was the determination of legislative seats based on functional constituencies, which favored corporate interests with ties to the PRC's central government.

One might ask in turn whether the democratization movement's cooptation of Occupy Central resulted in the lifting of antiliberal capitalist critique to a higher level or subsumed it for the purpose of promoting its own cause. From the point of view of democratization, it is clear that the oligarchic corporate interests that dominate the legislature represent a real threat to democratic ideals and aspirations, but it is unclear to what extent Central District Values in fact represent a threat to its own ideology of governance, economic policy, and societal norm.

In the midst of its metamorphosis in the Occupy Central movement, democratization has ironically taken on an explicitly cultural tone. As a political battle, it has become the literal front for a direct confrontation between Hong Kong and PRC, a conflict between local and national interests and an incommensurable difference in cultural mind-sets or traits. Cultural differences have exacerbated Hong Kongers' criticisms of uncivilized behavior by mainland tourist "locusts" and their mundane habits, which are equally countered by mainland Chinese criticisms of Hong Kong people as corrupted by Western values that require moral correction. In other words, it has increasingly evolved into a minor and dualistic clash of civilizations.

One should contrast the rise of anti-PRC sentiment in Hong Kong with that in Taiwan. Against a preexisting backdrop of tension between calls for independence versus reunification at a rhetorical level, which has intensified the trend toward the autonomy of Taiwanese cultural consciousness vis-à-vis a mainland that is viewed as "Chinese" in extreme circles, this trend has in general heightened the significance of indigenization as a cultural norm in many senses of the term. The explicit emphasis on Taiwaneseness and concern with the rights of ethnic Hakka and indigenous peoples, combined with recognition of the historical legacies of Dutch, Spanish, and Japanese colonialism, thus underscore the primordial existence of Taiwan prior to Chinese domination, contrary to the sinicizing narratives of Chinese history and tradition propagated by early postwar KMT rule. This trend toward cultural autonomy has coexisted uneasily with the intertwined growth of Taiwanese capital and enterprise in Greater China. The advent of the Sunflower Movement, initiated by student protesters in 2014, was a protest against the implementation of the Service Trade Agreement proposed by the government of Ma Ying-jeou, which in the spirit of NAFTA called for deregulation of economic relations on both sides of the Straits. On the surface, this protest was not a demonstration against PRC political domination, as in the case of Hong Kong, but rather the veiled threat of increased political control by the PRC through the institutionalization of Chinese corporate interests in the Taiwan economy, which among other things would have allowed the ownership of stock in Taiwanese corporations and the establishment of Chinese banks and other vested interests.

Political movements in Hong Kong and Taiwan thus contested the penetration of Greater China in their local economy, politics, and society, but in characteristically different ways. If anything, the Sunflower Movement actually represented a more direct and salient attack on the collusion of big business and PRC policy that was the core of a newly emerging Chinese capitalism, through which the PRC central government disseminated and carried out political designs. This could hardly be called "soft power"; it was based on institutional leverage.

On the PRC front, support for the government's political and economic policies was also buttressed by a growing nationalist identity, something quite alien to an earlier era of Maoist class-based socialism. This kind of mass nationalist sentiment was anything but banal, to mimic Michael Billig's (1995) famous phrase. The search for national identity, which in its extreme forms of ritual effervescence gave way to patriotic fervor of all kinds, was inscribed in what Callahan (2010) aptly termed the cultural psychology of "the pessoptimist nation," which was ultimately driven by the manifest destiny of China's imperial civilization, which in its more recent historical manifestation exuded the subconscious desire and need to reverse the humiliation or shame brought about by a century of Western imperialist domination. If this is real face of the new Greater China, then what are the global ramifications of it all?

Chapter 9

Confucius, Incorporated

The Advent of Capitalism with PRC Characteristics

According to International Monetary Fund figures, China's gross domestic product has grown annually at an average rate of 9.91 percent from 1978 to 2012. At this rate, China will surpass the US in Gross Domestic Product within five years. The current fixation with the rise of China, especially after its transition to a free market economy, overlooks the fact that a long tradition of historical scholarship has always been concerned with the reasons for the rise and fall of China's civilization (and economy) over the last millennia of global history. The rise of the West in the nineteenth century may have given birth to the othering of Asiatic modes of production in the global scheme of things, but it is probably harder to show when there was ever a lack of such comparative gazing. Even Mark Elvin's (1973) *The Pattern of the Chinese Past* was less a civilizational discourse per se than a sophisticated effort to develop conceptual models for the rise and fall of the economy. In the PRC, in an attempt to offer a different spin on China's demise in the face of the West, Marxist historians engaged in debates on "the sprouts of capitalism" (that apparently failed to bloom). Later generations of theoretical discourse over the same terrain have seen the publication of Andre Gunder Frank's (1998) *ReOrient* and Kenneth Pomeranz's (2000) *The Great Divergence*, among many others. I am interested less in engaging in such economic debates than in interrogating the emergence of a particular regime marked by a policy of economic development linked intricately to the maintenance of a single-party state and its legitimation in the public sphere grounded in a nationalist identity.

The Renaissance of National Identity in the Politics of Colonial Difference

In *China: The Pessoptimist Nation*, William A. Callahan (2010) depicts China's national vision of itself in the world as one of "pessoptimism," an ambivalent facade more importantly rooted in deep-seated "structures of feeling." From a broader perspective, I think that this represents a more constructive approach to understanding its political, economic, and cultural dynamics, all of which tightly reinforce each other in policy and practice. A strong reading of the sustained interest in the liberalization of the Chinese market economy, especially as a Western-centered, inevitable process of globalization, is typically driven by an undercurrent of assumptions about the inevitability of a rule of law, political deregulation of the economy, the triumph of individual interest, and institutional rationalization in other regards. These are not unreasonable expectations, given transformations of the modern world system elsewhere.

China's "pessoptimism" is colored, on the one hand, by its belief in the manifest destiny of its long civilization and record of achievement then reflected, on the other hand, by the stain of "national humiliation" (*guochi*) inflicted as a result of imperialist domination and the loss of status, power, and economic wealth suffered in the process. Callahan documents in detail the myriad ways in which national humiliation has been instilled into narratives of history, the writing of educational textbooks, notions of territorial legitimacy, and the celebrating of national holidays. More than the overt promotion of patriotic fervor, there is a systematic investment into cultivating and sustaining such sentiments as part of a collective conscience. Although superficially similar to Raymond Williams's (1987) notion of "structures of feeling," Williams intended it to refer to the cultural existence of a popular abstract consciousness that was naturally opposed to representations of elite society or the institutional establishment, otherwise called hegemony. In the Chinese case, it was clear that this collective conscience was officially sanctioned and broadly promoted, even as social movement, if necessary. As official rhetoric, it seemed to hit a feverish peak during the late Qing and early Republican eras as well as from the 1990s, both paralleling a resurgence in nationalist identity as a whole.

The direct connection between the postcolonial trauma of national humiliation and the fermenting of national consciousness as general structure of feeling that transcended patriotic fervor and became the mental template for various genres of territorial boundedness or social belonging grounded ultimately in a common lineage of civilizational values closely mirrors the "the rule of colonial difference" that Partha Chatterjee (1993) argued was intrinsic to the birth of nationalism, at least in a Third World context. Rejecting the modular nature of the nation that Benedict Anderson (1993) argued made possible the widespread dissemination of nationalism, as though divorced from its inherent embeddedness in the politics of cultural resistance, Chatterjee's critical intervention can also be used to show the counterhegemonic roots of national imagination, even in its most abstract or neutral form. Moreover, I argue that national consciousness invoked as collective belonging and driven by the postcolonial politics of memory can and has been used in the context of China to galvanize mass support for state policy. The rise of China's economy in the global pecking order has also acquired the status of national obsession (and pride) in contemporary Chinese "structures of feeling." This has in turn enabled the state to use such popular support to reinforce political correctness in other regards, not as soft power but as part of a systematic regime of hard–ball domination.

The relative decline of humiliation as nationalist discourse in later Republican China in postwar Taiwan as well as through much of Maoist China can been explained as a function of larger geopolitical factors. In contrast to his anti-imperialist exuberance in the Republican era, Chiang Kai-shek's generally pro-Western stance in postwar Taiwan had much to do with maintaining the protectionist role of the US military, which has been tacitly supported to the present, despite the overt withdrawal of US bases and direct military presence. In the PRC, it can be argued that national identity was a relatively insignificant consideration in a Maoist socialist society vis-à-vis the formation of an egalitarian class consciousness. Especially in its purest ideological form, conformity to socialist values linked the destiny of workers of the world everywhere more than it separated nations on the basis of identity. Needless to say, all forms of traditional culture were denigrated as feudal and systematically purged. In such a mind-set, history and civilization played little or no role; identity was an empty signifier.

One of the least-noticed trends that paralleled Deng's liberalization of a market economy in China was the gradual renaissance of all forms of Chinese culture and civilization. It may be viewed as a symptom of the decline of socialist humanist ethics as political dogma but also a reversal of socialism's explicit suppression of "tradition," which above all represented a conflicting social ideology. The gradual emergence of "identity" can be reflected in the lifting of the taboos on tradition, history, custom, and most importantly, in their promotion as politically neutral or sociologically legitimizing attributes of the nation. The long-term investment made by the government in archaeological discovery and preservation became not only a showcase for domestic pride but also a powerful symbol of outward unity. This has been accompanied by an obvious intensification of patriotic fervor in politics and education and heightened anxiety over borders protectionist diplomatic policies. These were not isolated developments.

The fermenting of a new national consciousness was not a mover in the liberalization of the market economy, but it served as a crucial basis of popular legitimation in the aftermath of the economy's success. Policy did not have to be based on a belief in individual freedom.

Confucius Institutes in the
Cultural Policy of State: A Fatal Attraction

In a comparative study of cultural governance and place-making in Taiwan and PRC, Selina Chan (2011) argues that, contrary to expectation, Taiwan's government has generally used cultural policy to cultivate heritage and regulate locality, while the PRC has adopted a minimalist approach to the same. In many regards, these two divergent perspectives were in response to different sociopolitical transformations. Simply put, Taiwan's heavy-handed cultural policy was the evolution of a changing identity politics, whereas the PRC's approach facilitated the profiteering interests of its local residents in a way that was consistent with the values of its emerging market society. In the PRC case, heritage making resembled more a culture industry in a crass materialist sense that colluded conveniently with tourism. If it did not primarily serve to protect cultural interests per se, then it represented at best a front that benefited from official approval and sanction. While it is true that the PRC did not witness the kind of cultural engineering experienced in Taiwan that was driven implicitly by identity politics, heritage preservation and gentrification of traditional towns were equally prevalent in Taiwan and exploited by resident merchants in particular for the same commercial reasons. In each case, the government did not take a direct role in advancing economic interests, but to imply that economic promotion was a primary motivation is probably an overstatement. In the PRC, heritage making in general served the larger interest of promoting national identity. Heritage towns, ethnic cultural centers, and sanctification of Confucius's ancestral village are obvious exemplars amenable to the promotion of a culture industry, but other seminal aspects of cultural promotion have had a longer history, with less obvious or immediate commercial value. The time and money that has already been invested in archeologically restoring sites of historical importance, such as imperial tombs, ancient monuments, and so on will in the long run far surpass its commitments to other instances of superficial heritage preservation, and none of this was imaginable or possible in the Maoist era, where tradition was devalued and taboo.

I argue that culturalizing as a mode of politicizing has been as inherent in the promotion of state policy in the PRC as Taiwan, if not even more prevalent and hegemonic. A scathing article by Marshall Sahlins (2013) on Confucius Institutes aptly illustrates the extent to which culture represents a front for the promotion of state interests. In this instance, the Confucius Institute is less an instrument of cultural policy than an instantiation of culturalizing within the politics of the state. Sahlins's critique of the way Confucius Institutes act as a front for coercing host institutions to toe the political line focuses primarily on the threat to academic freedom that such Institutes pose to the university within which they are directly situated. In the long run, however, its underlying politics has been rooted in a broader, ongoing regime.

Since the Confucius Institute program was launched in 2004, there are now about 400 Institutes worldwide as well as 600 "Confucius classrooms" in elementary and secondary schools. It provides accredited Chinese language instruction and sponsors activities relating to Chinese culture and sinological scholarship. Unlike other cultural foundations, such as Goethe-Institut and Alliance Francaise, the Confucius Institutes tend to have a direct presence on the campuses that they occupy and have been known to wield strong opinions in matters pertaining to China, sometimes backed by veiled retaliatory threats and negative sanctions.

Needless to say, the Confucius Institutes are directly subsidized by the PRC government, and the extent of their funding often commands respect for their opinion in matters that they perceive as impinging on their national authority. In those universities that host a Confucius Institute, an official organization referred to simply as Hanban regulates matters pertaining to classroom instruction, including the appointment of teachers, use of textbooks and design of the curriculum in all courses that they sponsor. Cultural promotion as a mode of cultivating political favor is typically termed *soft power*, but the extent to which Hanban influences all matters pertaining to China on their host campuses has frequently taken the form of hard sell.

Sahlins notes that the precise agreement that Confucius Institutes enter into with specific universities vary in fact, but all contracts are enforced by strict confidential, nondisclosure conditions. The University of Sydney was pressured by its Confucius Institute to move an event involving the Dalai Lama off campus. Other universities have been threatened with retribution for sponsoring pro–Falun Gong activities. It is possible to add to this list other taboo topics, such as the Tiananmen Incident and Tibet/Taiwan independence, then reinforce these taboos with a strong atmosphere of self-censorship. Although Confucius Institutes involve Chinese language and culture, it could just as easily be about heritage protection. What drives the institution and its policies is a deeper-seated ethos and a distinctive regime of politicization.

As Christopher Hughes (2014) has argued, one must distinguish the political mission of Confucius Institutes from its cultural mission, at least in the formation and practice of policy. In content, it is easy enough to spell out the academic nature of the Confucius Institutes and the general importance of cultural dissemination in government policy that has motivated the promotion of such exchanges. To characterize this as "soft power" in Joseph

Nye's (2004) terms has been really to suggest that the Institute and its practices have primarily been based on goodwill, assuagement, co-optation and various forms of positive persuasion rather than force, coercion, and other more hard-ball political tactics. Funding for educational programs and support for academic research have without a doubt been substantial. On the other hand, its political mission or protection of its political interests has also influenced its scope of operation in ways that have transcended the literal wording of their institutional contracts to "not contravene concerning the laws and regulations of China." In practice, the coercive tactics that Institutes have applied to protect their political positions in relation to China have, on the contrary, been anything but soft. Is this just a difference between policy and practice, literal content and actual intent, or ideal principles and ulterior motives?

Heritage, culture, Confucius: does it matter?[1] The example of Confucius Institutes can be used to demonstrate the soft side of political aims, insofar as it involves the role of culture. But more importantly, it underscores the fictions that drive policy discourse and the widening gap with practical reality. No one seems to take seriously the resurrection of Confucius and the relevance of Confucian ideology in the operation of any Confucius Institute in the same way that no one takes seriously the ongoing salience of socialism with Chinese characteristics in a society increasingly dominated by crass materialism and unimpeded capitalist oligarchy. The point regarding culture is that its power was never soft. Far from being a neutral entity, both national identity and Chinese studies served as tools for enforcing political correctness.

The Great Collusion: Capitalist Oligarchy and Party Domination

As Rajesh Venugopal (2015:165) interestingly put it, "neoliberalism is everywhere, but at the same time, nowhere." The role of government in the rise of the Chinese economy has invoked much discussion in the literature about the relevance of neoliberalism. If anything, the debate over neoliberalism as a recent phenomenon in the West, especially in the context of a mutating modern world system, made comparison inevitable. Like earlier discussions of Greater China, which implicitly promoted the power of transnationalism in China through Hong Kong and Taiwan, the application of neoliberalism in a PRC context masked indirect concerns with the nature of government intervention in the market economy. However, the literature on neoliberalism was clouded by its own conceptual ambiguities. In a strict sense, as Ha-joon Chang (2003:47) correctly defines it, neoliberalism was "born out of an unholy alliance between neoclassical economics and the Austrian-Libertarian tradition." This strict definition of its school of thought overlapped over time with political ideological trends in the 1980s that began to favor market deregulation, privatization, and retrenchment of the welfare state. This represented a convergence between the phenomena of free market capitalism and state control, which were typically viewed as dualistic opposites, but it resulted in divergent theoretical approaches, one focused on newly emerging capitalist systems per se and the other focused on regulative aspects of governmentality. In this regard, the "millennial capitalism" of Jean and John Comaroff (2000) and Colin Crouch's (2011) evolution of the corporate state differ from approaches accentuating free market trade that have centered more on the broader restructuring of regulatory processes of the state and regimes of fiscal discipline, for example, Gordon Burchell (1993), Nikolas Rose (1993), and Pierre Dardot and Christian Laval (2013).[2] Yet despite the unambiguous relationship between market deregulation and governmentality, the literature on neoliberalism has been fraught with conceptual ambiguities and conflicting generalizations. Perhaps to defy systemic totalization, Jamie Peck (2010:7) has argued that neoliberalism is a decentralized force that produces heterogeneous outcomes and "can only exist in messy hybrids." Aihwa Ong (2007:1) similarly emphasizes that it is an amorphous phenomenon, "a migratory set of practices . . . that articulate diverse situations and participate in mutating configurations of possibility." But decentralization and heterogeneity ultimately beg the question of whether it is driven primarily by the market or its regulatory institutions.

In the context of China, Ong, and Zhang (2008) seem to be the most ardent supporters of the position that China is a mix of privatization and state control in the sense that the state requires neoliberalism to be managed by socialism "from afar," as though indirectly. On the other hand, Kipnis (2007) follows from his comparison of neo-Marxist cultural neoliberalism (especially of the Comaroffs' millennial kind) and the governmentality approach to suggest that their symptoms, outcomes, and policies are mutually contradictory, thus criticizing in the process their confused application to the Chinese context. Nonini (2008) sharply criticized even more explicitly the applicability of neoliberalization to developments in China, arguing that the proliferation of *guanxi* has produced instead the blurring of state and market or public and private in the operation of capitalism. Economic growth as a result of free trade and an uninhibited market created instead a conflict between the interests of a new cadre-capitalist elite and the disposition of increasingly dispossessed classes of people. Contrary to the lack of state intervention, the belief in free markets led instead to the building of large state-owned enterprises. If anything, it facilitated the designs of an oligarchic corporate state. The state was not becoming a corporation per se, but was nonetheless buttressed by corporatization in the market economy. Rational utilitarianism of the market helped to regulate social interest.

Nonini's critique of neoliberalist interpretations of the Chinese economy and the role of the state has ironically accentuated the consequences of the free market economy in a classic Marxist sense, namely the political economic disparity between the haves and have nots. In the context of post-Maoist socialism, the tendency of the state to align itself with oligarchic capitalist interests over individual rights, especially in matters pertaining to development, has pit capitalism squarely against the ideology of socialism in a way that has set the scene for an impending conflict between the disenfranchised class and the state. This problematizes not only in short the fictitious slogan of socialism with Chinese characteristics but also reiterates the need to understand more precisely the nature of capitalism with Chinese characteristics.

Huang Yasheng's (2008) analysis of the transition from early private entrepreneurialism in rural China to a later phase of state-controlled urban-based capitalism, appropriately called *Capitalism with Chinese Characteristics*, provides in my opinion the basis for reconciling the seemingly overlapping aspects of this economy, which has been oversimplistically miscast in neoliberalist terms. Huang's empirical reconstruction of that economic growth was intended initially to highlight the success of initial rural reforms, while privileging the role of private, small-scale entrepreneurialism in the takeoff process. His criticism of state-owned, *guanxi* based enterprises or corporatist state capitalism of this genre provides a historical link to the emergence of *guanxi* as a prevailing practice of everyday life and more importantly the basis of corporate capitalism itself. It is obvious to Huang that corruption has also become part of a systematic feature of such capitalism, but he stops short of identifying corruption as a core element or distinctive feature of this *guanxi* capitalism. As a systemic phenomenon, he adds the persistence of pollution, corruption, inefficient capital use, and state expropriation of land.

In a scathing essay, Richard Smith (2015) begins with what he calls China's "ecological apocalypse" to uncover its causal roots in the political economy. In a radically different take on the nature of this capitalism-socialism, he argues that the dynamics and contradictions of China's hybrid economy have been the product of how market reforms have compounded the irrationalities of both the old bureaucratic collectivist system and a systemically corrupt "gangster capitalism." The consumption of planetary resources fueled in the first instance the first wave of China's unsustainable growth. The global relocation of manufacturing and assembly industries there made environmental pollution the major by-product of this industrial revolution. The production of cheap goods made in China has exacerbated the trend toward a disposable consumption economy, leading to more material waste. Government planners invested heavily into new infrastructure, new housing, and social support, but this has been characterized more by vanity, redundancy, overproduction, and waste to the point of unusable excess. Empty highways, high-speed trains, and subways have led to construction frenzies, ghost towns, and vacant office-commercial complexes, all waiting for the real estate bubble to burst. In short, this vicious cycle was driven by an out-of-control economy and state excess.

Private corporate enterprises have thrived, but they are still dwarfed by the domination of state-owned enterprises, whose viability and fortune often rests on ties to the government or Party. As Smith (2015:49) succinctly states it, "life in the Communist Party is not so different from life in the Mafia: it's a constant, treacherous, and highly dangerous non-stop factional struggle between crime family-based groupings in struggle with one another over top offices and treasure. The key to safety is building unshakable vertical and horizontal networks of support and protection—of *guanxi*. And the key to solidifying those networks is sharing the loot from corruption." China's economy mirrors its politics, not vice versa.

Smith then proceeds to extensively document the extent of collusion between business and politics. Those in government did not profit from or run enterprises directly, but it did not prevent family members to be appointed corporate heads and enjoy access to government funding and assets. The extent of connections to power and money exceeds all definitions of customary trust in Chinese business. If anything, the systemic corruption makes *guanxi* more than just an instrument of patronage. By giving priority to the state-owned economy, the aim of China's state-owned enterprises is not profit maximization. Their ultimate aim is the security, wealth, and power of the Party. Even the anticorruption campaigns have less to do with cleansing of corruption per se than the purging of competing, undesirable cliques. In short, it is superficial and misleading to describe the system as a socialist-capitalist hybrid. The market economy is free, but privileged access to its resources is politically controlled.

In my opinion, Smith's depiction of this political economic complex accurately captures the intertwined relationship tying rampant environment degradation, a *guanxi*-based corporate economy, and the state's overinvestment in infrastructure development, which has in effect exacerbated the cumulative crisis of an accelerated growth economy. More than the product of *guanxi* capitalism or neoliberal governmentality, it is a regime grounded ultimately in the continued maintenance of the state or Party. It did not invest directly into the economy, but it manipulated access to resources in the market in ways that ultimately favored and protected its own interests, which included above all its policy and political positions. In this regard, perestroika or democracy of any kind also represented an inherent threat to its viability.

From a larger perspective, the system in question involves not simply the economy or nature of governmentality but a set of relationships linking the work of economy and culture to the process of state legitimation. Socialism with Chinese characteristics is a fiction that obfuscates the existence of an endemically corrupt, *guanxi*-based regime. Confucius, Inc. may represent an equally fictitious depiction of capitalism with Chinese characteristics, but fictions nonetheless underscore the importance of culture in legitimating the system, not just as "soft power." Driving support for the growth economy is not simply state policy but also the "structures of feeling" associated with a reinvented national consciousness. The rising discontent from an impending bubble economy and environmental crisis may in fact counter in the long run the general mass support that the regime still seems to enjoy, but this popular support has served in turn to lend credence to the state's suppression of democratic dissent. This systemic regime has become most explicitly institutionalized in the PRC, but its effects can be seen in Hong Kong and other "autonomous" regions, even globally, as "Chineseness."

Part Four

Who Wants to Be Diasporic?

The Fictions and Facts of Critical Ethnic Subjectivity

The apparatus of sequestration must manufacture behavior that characterizes individuals; it must create a nexus of habits through which the social "belongingness" of individuals to a society is defined, that is to say, it manufactures something like norms.

—Michel Foucault, *Discipline and Punish: The Birth of the Prison*

Welcome to the desert of the real.

—Jean Baudrillard, "Simulacra and Simulations"

Prologue

The death of Lee Kuan Yew, founding father and first prime minister of Singapore, on March 23, 2015, marked the passing of a political leader who played a dominant and pivotal role in steering Singapore through its early years of independence, while shaping the blueprint and putting into practice the framework for its unique development as a modern city-state. The week of national mourning that preceded the funeral of state may have celebrated his life and accomplishments, but it was not difficult to read into them the personification of Singapore's history. The prime minister, president, and former prime minister were among the political dignitaries to deliver eulogies, but it was important above all to include one eulogy in Malay, Chinese, and Tamil. Lee Hsien Loong, the current prime minister and Lee's son, detailed Lee's life accomplishments, but it was remarkable for the times that he clearly referred to "Mr. Lee Kuan Yew" as distinct from "my father." They represented two faces of Singapore.

Contrary to the accepted wisdom of ethnic majority rule, where Chinese made up 70 percent of Singapore's population, Lee strived vehemently

189

for racial equality. Protection of Asian tradition and tacit promotion of its values was combined with the value-free adoption of rule by law, economic modernization, and progress. Asian values also had another face, one that prioritized social cohesion over individual voice. The nation was thus literally a search for modernity, but it was one that had to deny ethnic culturalism as a foundational principle. In many senses, Singapore fits Foucault's disciplinary society to a tee, even more so when it is viewed as a top-down state project. The relative effects of postcolonialism, nationalism, and social workfare ethics constitute seminal formative aspects in the state's project of modernity.

The distinctive features of Singapore's experience have important ramifications for the meaning of Chineseness in a non-Chinese context. Whatever it is, it occupied a dependent position within a nation-state driven by its primary identification with modernity. The idea of Asian values was also a selective definition, if not Orientalizing as well, which epitomized the priority of collective values over individualist (i.e., Western) ones. Appeals to Sinophone theory and a cultural China have explicitly emphasized the multiplicity of Sinitic voices and the priority of a transnational periphery over a Sinocentric core, but they still privilege above all the authority of voice over its embeddedness in a grounded context as a prime determinant in Chinese identity formation. To be or not to be; that is not the question, but why identify?

Chapter 10

The Yellow Pacific

Diasporas of Mind in the Politics of Caste Consciousness

The concept of cultural China has attempted to champion diasporic values in the construction of new Chinese identities, and, thus, resembles the cosmopolitanism of Black Atlantic, which has become Paul Gilroy's paradigm of countermodernity, both through its appeal to hybridity and the emancipatory power of culture. Despite superficial similarities between both concepts, the relevance of diaspora here resides less in its capacity to invoke ethnic realities than its particular situatedness in a field of sociopolitical relations. On the one hand, while Chinese, Black, and other diasporas differ with reference to their situatedness to a local sociopolitical ground, they expose, on the other hand, the general limitations of diaspora as a phenomenon engendered by the rigid peculiarities of a(n increasingly anachronistic) stratified society.

The Double Consciousness of a Transnational Modernity

> It is remarkable what an adaptable creature the Negro is. I have seen the black West Indian gentleman in London, and he is in speech and manners a perfect Englishman. I have seen natives of Haiti and Martinique in Paris, and they are more Frenchy than a Frenchman. I have no doubt that the Negro would make a good Chinaman, with the exception of the pigtail.
>
> —James Johnson, *The Autobiography of an Ex-Coloured Man*

This is a revision of a paper published in 2001 as "Diasporas of Mind, or Why There Ain't No Black Atlantic in Cultural China," *Communal/ Plural: Journal of Transnational & Cross-cultural Studies* 9(1):95–110.

In the progression from postmodern to postcolonial to transnational world, it is easy to track the plethora of concepts that have emerged, but it is somewhat difficult to determine whether the invention of these concepts has followed the manifestation of social phenomena or the other way around. As human beings, we live in the real world, but as intellectuals we articulate our relationship to reality in reference to those discourses within which we are embedded. As soon as one has been led to believe that multiculturalism was invented by postmodern theory, one has then been led to believe that postcolonial theory finally liberated the multiple identities in us all.

Like the assumption of shared values and a collective conscience under-lying the nation-state that has made culture, ethnicity, and national identity problematic issues, postcolonialism's need to recognize multiple identities in the present is, on the other hand, the recognition of an empire of mind that has subordinated and negated difference. In effect, if celebration of hybridity and championing of diasporic interests are a consequence of our need to *decolonize*, then one must first ask whether there are significant differences between our problematic need to invoke hybridity and diaspora and the phenomena that have given rise to them. Equally important, the *universalizing* tendencies of postmodernism, postcolonialism, or transnationalism as *theoretical* trends that have stemmed from an intellectual *mainstream* should make one highly suspicious of whether the meanings of these terms are similar to their usages in a local or indigenous context. The celebration of postmodernism, which gives the illusion that it can be transposed anywhere with the same effects, regardless of their cultural specificity, is an often-cited case in point.

Decolonization has similarly become a figurative code word for resis-tance everywhere, regardless of whether the context of its application is liter-ally colonial or not. Transnational capitalism, characterized by disjunctures in Appadurai's (1990) terms, has enjoyed the same trendy status, to a point where scholars have begun to see transnationalism in earlier historical eras too, before the rise of nations, strictly speaking. One can attribute the prob-lem to slippage between the concept as strictly conceived and actually used, but there are significant differences between various theories, all of which champion cultural hybridity and transnational identities in a postcolonial context. Theories represent different discursive *positionings* vis-à-vis dilemmas of culture, and it is equally important to spell out the underlying ground on which these terms are meaningfully invoked and strategically articulated.

Paul Gilroy's (1993) notion of "the Black Atlantic" offers a pow-erful counternarrative to Western modernity not only by challenging the dominance of cultural nationalism or ethnic absolutism as core metaphors or paradigms of that experience, but also by recasting in the process the centrality of (African) Black experience in the modern history of the West. Key to his examination of "double consciousness" among Blacks in the West is his celebration of hybridity, which he (1993:3) characterizes as "the stereophonic, bilingual or bifocal cultural forms originated by, but no longer the exclusive property of, blacks dispersed within the structures of feeling, producing, communicating, and remembering." For Gilroy, the need to break away from the discrete national dynamics of culture and the presumed integrity and purity of ethnicity in the construction of that culture was a prerequisite for understanding the Black experience and its impact on the process of Western modernity. Instead of monolithic modernity creating hybridity as its other, one sees hybridity giving rise to modernity itself.

Hybridity in this regard is not just the individualistic and arbitrary synthesis of cultural forms. Through his depiction of important Black writers and thinkers, Black hybridity can perhaps be best characterized as a historical transition from a conscious formulation of dual identities to one which in which the basic features of Black experience become stripped of their explicit ethnic qualities and dialogue with the philosophical and universalist languages of modernity. In other words, what begins as an essentialist discourse inscribed in racial or political terms becomes eventually an integral part of the structures of modernity.

But far from simply being appropriated by modernity, Gilroy argues that the Black experience becomes an alternate discourse that also influences the Western experience of modernity. Hybridity's relationship to diaspora is based on the latter's disposition within the context of social subordination, terror, and emancipation that evokes the articulation of allegorical forms and ideologies by expanding on the underlying structures of feeling, expression, and memory. This process of hybridity can be traced clearly in the literature and thought from W. E. B. DuBois to Richard Wright and in the evolution of Black music.

The transformative nature of that hybrid experience is described in detail by Gilroy and can be read in many ways, but it is clear that the formation of this Black "nationalism" has transcended the political boundaries of the nation-state, while at the same time it has become an integral part of the culture within which it is embedded. Moreover, this hybridity seems to be predicated less on the authenticity of its voices than on the ongoing interpretation of the structures of feeling in Black experience that later becomes the basis of a Black politics of authenticity. Gilroy thus views modernity as a quintessentially bottom-up process, one in which the local informs the global and where the polyphonic nature of Black social realities becomes the basis for an imagined community that is represented by the Black Atlantic.

The way in which Gilroy has championed hybridity and diaspora differs, on the other hand, from the genre of Chinese modernity characterized by Aihwa Ong and others in their volume of essays titled *Ungrounded Empires: The Cultural Politics of Modern Chinese Transnationalism* (Ong & Nonini 1997). Like Gilroy, by accenting transnationalism, Ong et al. point to the existence of forces intrinsic to the Chinese experience that have eluded disciplining by nation-states while building on relations that intrinsically differ from Western narratives of modernity. Underlying their narrative of transnationalism in a Chinese context as an alternative modernity is their attempt to view Chinese cultural politics as an extension of diasporic identities rather than as the diffusion of an essentializing hegemony. But unlike Gilroy's Black Atlantic, which overlaps with and is embedded within Western modernity, the Chinese transnational modernity envisaged by Ong and Nonini competes with its counterpart. Both celebrate multiculturalism, but the diasporic identity invoked in the Chinese case seems to be predicated less by a "double consciousness" that leads explicitly toward hybridity than by a determination to maintain autonomy vis-à-vis the Sinocentric core and its host society. Ungrounded and constantly shifting, Chinese transnational modernity, as portrayed by Ong and Nonini, resists the absolutism of the state yet maintains a collusive relationship with it in both Chinese and foreign contexts. Thus, hybridity is part and parcel of being transnational.

Transnationalism requires careful qualification here, but it is apparent that it differs from essentialist formulations of a pan-nationalist Confucian ethics in the emergence of East Asian economies. It is not at all evident at first glance if Ong and Nonini attribute the success of a Chinese transnational modernity to the recent success of Chinese transnational entrepreneurs or to the rise of a new global capitalism that has enabled such Chinese transnationalists to flourish. In their rhetorical emphasis on diaspora, they appear to favor the former by seeing Chinese transnational capitalism as the end product of ongoing cultural practices. After all, Southeast Asia has witnessed centuries of Chinese comprador traders. As Trocki (1997:71) argues for the early history of Chinese enterprise in Southeast Asia, "it was the British flag that followed the Chinese coolies," thus the key organizational structures that drove Chinese capitalism were built on multiethnic alliances well prior to the advent of British colonialism. If so, it would be possible to view the later development of large-scale Chinese capitalism as the basic extension of a multicultural mode of production, writ large. Ong (1997:171–202) expands this thesis into a full-fledged alternative theory of Chinese modernity that celebrates the flexibility of hybrid or multiple identities and the fluidity of constant deterritorialization.

Ong juxtaposes the PRC's state project of Chinese modernity against this moment of "triumphalist capitalism" and views the diverse experience in Asian modernity as the result of ongoing tension between these two forces. It is the influx of Hong Kong, Taiwanese, and overseas Chinese capital into the PRC that then represents the driving force behind another multinational entity popularly called "Greater China." In championing the "triumphalist capitalism" of transnational, multicultural Chinese entrepreneurs, she privileges a late form of global capitalism, which is the result of fundamental changes in the modern world system, thus anything but local and diasporic in origin, and omits a whole history of Asian capitalism that was not transnational. Chinese capitalism is not the end product of transnationalism.

It is easy to romanticize in our current climate of transnational capitalism tycoons such as Li Ka-shing and the Riady family, but early Republican China and postwar Taiwan were full of rich capitalists and large enterprises. Far from being the culmination in transnational terms of a kind of utilitarianism that begins as pariah capitalism in Weber's terms, it is easier to understand the emergence of Chinese transnational capitalism as an ephemeral moment made possible by the end of organized capitalism, which emancipated rational organization from the strictures of a nation-based cultural economy. Despite the rhetoric focus Ong et al. place on diaspora and hybridity, one should note how Chinese cosmopolitanism invoked by such modernity differs from Gilroy's Black Atlantic. Contrary to the bottom-up process that contributed to a Black Atlantic cosmology, the transnational modernity that Ong and others celebrate in fact is one where the global informs the local and where an imagined community of multicultural Chinese capitalists becomes the basis for an alternative Chinese modernity.

Diaspora: A Term for All Seasons?

Fascists operate from a narrow, limited basis; they preach nationality, race, soil and blood, folk feeling and other rot to capture men's hearts. What makes a Fascist and another a Communist might be found in the degree to which they're integrated with their culture. The more alienated a man is, the more he'd lean toward Communism.

—Richard Wright, *The Outsider*

I have deliberately contrasted Gilroy's Black Atlantic and Ong's Ungrounded Empire of Chinese transnational capitalism to suggest that hybridity and diaspora can mean different things, despite being celebrated by the same

postnational, postcolonial counterhegemony of multiple identities and deterritorialization. For Gilroy, diaspora represents the primordial situation of
deracination, inflicted through the common social reality of enslavement,
which bound the experience of Blacks in a transnational Atlantic. Despite
a common experiential framework, the culture that developed on the basis
of these structures of feeling is multivocal and decentered, thus eventually
contributing to intrinsic hybridity. This hybridity is less a function of identifying per se than of the social context of deracination and oppression that
shapes the marginality and double consciousness of Blacks. It is significant
also to point out that this cultural hybridity (of which Black music is an
example par excellence) is built on the social experience of enslavement and
alienation (and feelings thereof) rather than with reference to cultural traditions of an imagined homeland. This is a cultural nationalism that lacks a
political nation and can transcend it precisely because of its transnational
wanderings and influences, which then derives its identity by amplifying
diasporic sentiments rather than by exploiting its alienation from a presumed
cultural core. More importantly, its dialogue with modernity ties it more
intricately to the West than to a history of Africa.

Ong's example of Chinese transnational modernity differs from Gilroy's, in part because of the recent emergence of disorganized, transnational
capitalism that has made the success of Chinese transnational capitalists
prominent and in part because the history of the Chinese diaspora, especially in Southeast Asia, has been inextricably tied to its politico-economic
relationship to or imagined communion with a Chinese homeland, at least
until most recently.

The long history of Nanyang Chinese traders in Southeast Asia is
incontestable. Their separateness as ethnic group vis-à-vis Europeans and
indigenous populations is heightened by their attachment to their provincial
homeland as well as to their sojourning intentions as traders. Although Chinese ethnic settlements were established in major port cities, they were rarely
if ever accompanied by migration of women or families. Over time, there
were, of course, large numbers of Chinese who intermarried and became
indigenized, such as the Peranakans in Indonesia and Babas in Malaya, but
this simply accented the polarization of the Chinese population in contrast
to other ethnic groups. In fact, their separateness was not just a function of
ethnic differences but also their status as traders who operated in personal
networks. The preoccupation of Chinese with business in the Philippines
led Filipinos to use the Spanish term to refer to Chinese, namely *sangley*
("merchant" in Chinese). This was not unlike the pre-nineteenth-century
term *Malay* to denote the Muslim (Arab) trading diaspora.

The applicability of the term *diaspora* to describe Chinese in the Nanyang region, even during this premodern era, is debatable. In light of the heavily Biblical connotations of the Jewish diaspora, the notion of dispersal and forced exile from a sacred homeland cannot be avoided, not to mention the themes of suffering and social memory that have without a doubt parallels with the Black slave experience but have little in common with Chinese experiences, except to accent the element of detachment from a homeland and separateness vis-à-vis its host society. This sense of detachment or separateness that epitomizes an ethnic diaspora is similar to anthropological uses of the term, notably in Cohen's (1971:2) definition of trading diaspora as "a nation of socially interdependent, but spatially dispersed communities."

Yet, ethnic separateness in this regard is not merely the function of self-identification but can also be a function of external factors in society that aim to maintain a stratified hierarchy between groups or prevent their accommodation and integration into the polity at large. As Curtin (1984) has described in his study of cross-cultural trade in history, trading diasporas were a long staple phenomenon throughout world history, whose prominence began to decline with the domination of a modern world system and the spread of industrialization. In other words, the caste-like, marginal status of diaspora is as much the function of a social system that reifies and hardens ethnic boundaries as it is the product of ethnic identification.

The fictive quality of diaspora is best exemplified by the anachronistic nature of the Jewish diaspora today, especially in America. One may question its applicability to those persons who have consciously disavowed attachments to an ethnic or religious homeland or chosen to assimilate to the cultural mainstream of its host society. For similar reasons, it would be unusual to speak of an aristocratic French or Anglo-Saxon Protestant diaspora. If an ethnic group ceases to become diasporic, because it has transcended its socially marginal status, then there is nothing ethnic about diaspora. One does not call the capital that fuels corporate America diasporic, even if it happens to have Japanese or Jewish origins. Given the extent of foreign influence in Hollywood culture, one would not call it diasporic either.

Diaspora thus has its limits, even as an "ethnic" concept, which it is not, strictly speaking, as I have argued above.[1] Gilroy's appeal to diaspora was based on the development of a Black consciousness that was built directly on those experiential sentiments of political oppression and social estrangement and was not a function of territorial dispersal per se. Yet, the political connotations of diaspora are still evident today in the way contemporary postcolonial theory has tended to champion diaspora in order to emancipate the (suppressed) multiple identities in us all. Reid (1997:36) has also

noted, for example, that its popularity as a term to symbolize the condition
of Chinese everywhere (outside China) was heightened considerably during
the first International Conference on the Chinese Diaspora, in Berkeley,
California, in November 1992. Its reception of use was found to be more
favorable among North American Chinese than among the Southeast Asian
Chinese, where ironically diaspora was used first and most prominently to
depict the sojourning communities of Chinese traders. Its popularity now
is attributable to those conditions that have created barriers and alienation.

The historicity of the term reveals in the final analysis less the primordial semantic meaning of a term than the restrictions imposed on its use
by its underlying sociopolitical context, the latter being more important.
A clearer case in point involves the changing use of terms for "overseas
Chinese." In the premodern, prenational period, Chinese sojourners in the
Nanyang region were less citizens of some unified polity (speaking a single
language [Mandarin] and sharing ties to a civilizational ideal) than dispa-
rate dialect groups bound together by familistic ties and attachments to a
provincial homeland. As Wang Gungwu (1998:1) rightly pointed out, "the
Chinese never had a concept of identity, only a concept of Chineseness,
of being Chinese and of becoming un-Chinese." The concept of Chineseness at the time was not one invoked now by the politically neutral term
huaren (being culturally Chinese). Southern Chinese at the time referred to
themselves as *tangren* (people of the Tang dynasty) who spoke *tanghua* (Tang
language), which to them just meant "Chinese," when in fact they were
regional groups speaking local dialect. There was less a notion of overseas
Chinese here than just a notion of Chinese living overseas. The nationalistic
term *huaqiao* to denote "overseas Chinese" as a group did not appear until
the late nineteenth century.

During a premodern era, the multicultural skills of Chinese traders
were less a function of their multiple "identities" than of strategic qualities
based on occupational and political necessity. Success in social intercourse
and economic exchange demanded fluency in many dialects and languages,
as well as familiarity with many customs. As Wang Gungwu (1991:139)
aptly phrased it, "for most of these merchants and entrepreneurs, being
Chinese had nothing to do with becoming closer to China. It was a private
and domestic matter only manifested when needed to strengthen a business
contact or to follow an approved public convention." In the colonial era,
the role of Chinese as compradors tended to enhance their separateness as
an ethnic community. In this regard, the functional specialization of other
traders, notably Indians and Arabs, added to their separateness as diasporic
communities, not just their ethnic differences, the latter then becoming a
phenotypical marker.

The meaning and use of the concept of "overseas Chinese" also cannot be divorced from the conditions of global capitalism that brought about large-scale immigration of Chinese laborers to Southeast Asia, starting toward the end of the nineteenth century. Most of them had been sojourners, at least initially, and their identity as a group was galvanized by Chinese nationalist sentiment that began to grow during the early twentieth century and culminated in the 1911 Revolution that overthrew the Qing dynasty. Through education in standard Mandarin and learning of Chinese history and civilization, the overseas Chinese considered themselves, probably for the first time, as identifying as Chinese (despite regional and dialect nuances), not only vis-à-vis a national homeland but also in contrast to their host society. But the use of this concept changed over time, and its popularity waned during the Cold War, which not only fractionalized identity among Chinese along political lines but also saw sentiments to homeland and host society shift as a consequence of changing socioeconomic conditions. It continues to be used by Chinese at the Sinocentric core (PRC and ROC) to denote Chinese living outside its national boundaries proper, to which anyone of Chinese descent is eligible. Use by Chinese living abroad, however, tends to be a function simply of "identifying."

The nationalistic connotations of the term *overseas Chinese* (*huaqiao*), along with the changing perceptions of Chinese living in Southeast Asia vis-à-vis their host societies, have in recent years led Chinese elsewhere to increasingly use *huaren* to refer to ethnic Chinese who speak *huayu*, standard Chinese which is literally the same as the Mandarin referred to on mainland China as *putonghua* ("the common language") or in Taiwan (following Republican usage) as *guoyu* ("the national language"). In short, terms differ significantly, less because of their semantic content than because of their pragmatic context of use. This parallels the recent aversion by Chinese outside China proper to calling themselves *zhongguoren* (Chinese) who speak *zhongguohua* (Chinese language), because of the nationalistic, essentially patriotic, associations of *zhongguo* with the Chinese polity. In fact, the highest degree of resistance to both the old term *overseas Chinese* and new term *diaspora* comes from the Chinese living in Southeast Asia. As Wang (1995:13) argued, "I do not agree to the word [*diaspora*] being used for the Chinese because it has implications which may have applied to some aspects of the sojourners in the past but do not apply to ethnic Chinese today. In many ways, diaspora is a word that has the kind of political content comparable to the term *huaqiao*." Similarly, Leo Suryadinata (1997) also asked in more systematic terms whether it is more accurate to call ethnic Chinese in Southeast Asia overseas Chinese, Chinese overseas, or Southeast Asians.

It is clear in any event that those solidary sentiments that once bound Chinese together as a group in its overseas environment and in relation to a patriotic homeland had withered as a result of Chinese geopolitics and changes in Southeast Asian nationalism, especially in its sociopolitical accommodation of the Chinese. As Tan Chee Beng (1997) remarked in his comment on Suryadinata's article, it is not just a matter of possessing multiple identities, as if one could simply put on and take off different cultural faces. The divisions among Chinese themselves show that they make explicit choices in cultural orientation, and even more importantly these choices are grounded in a context of territorial settlement, cultural assimilation, or political incorporation to local society rather than in their diasporic extension to a previous homeland.

Celebrating Hybridity in an Era of Invented Indigenization

> It matters a great deal whether modern racial slavery is identified as a repository in which the consciousness of traditional culture could be secreted and condensed into ever more potent forms or seen alternatively as the site of premodern tradition's most comprehensive erasure.
>
> —Paul Gilroy, *The Black Atlantic:*
> *Modernity and Double Consciousness*

The current resistance to diaspora experienced by Chinese overseas on the immediate periphery, most notably Southeast Asia and Taiwan as well, is less a declaration of their changing ethnic "Chineseness" than a crisis of *identifying* in the sense of having been bound morally or politically to a cultural core. The tendency of Chinese to increasingly identify with their settled nation as citizens, despite their minority status and continued maintenance of cultural difference vis-à-vis their host culture, has important ramifications for the meaning and use of the term *hybridity*. Different from Gilroy's formation of a pan-national cultural consciousness, hybridity here is in essence an act of political decentering that will in the long run lead to the absorption of Chineseness into increasingly local or indigenous frameworks of meaning. Tan Chee Beng (1997:31) noted, "President Corazon Aquino has acknowledged that she has Chinese ancestry, and the Chinese press has written of her as if she is an ethnic Chinese. But how has she identified herself? Has she ever identified herself as an ethnic Chinese? As far as I know, she is just Filipino." This contrasts with the case of the Baba Chinese of Malaysia, whom Tan regards as Chinese, despite their heavily creolized lifestyle.

The (indigenizing) trend of Chinese outside China to *identify* with their settler societies, despite the ongoing tradition of ethnic Chinese culture there, should also make the kind of appeal that Tu Wei-ming (1991) has made to "cultural China," something that is hopelessly out of touch with the real world, despite its call for hybridity and for diasporic voices to offer new models for a declining Sinocentric core, spirited by the success of "neo-Confucian" East Asian economies and built on corresponding sentiments of togetherness.

According to Tu (1991:22), "cultural China" was coined in the late 1980s by concerned Chinese intellectuals writing in overseas journals. It consists of three cultural universes: the first encompassing societies populated primarily by ethnic Chinese, such as mainland China, Taiwan, Hong Kong, and Singapore; the second covering overseas Chinese communities, notably in Southeast Asia; and the third comprising scholars and professionals concerned with the Chinese-speaking world in general. However, in practice, it refers to a single community whose common interest in Chinese society transcends national boundaries and discourses, a kind of Yellow Pacific. In a changing global system that witnessed once-patriotic overseas becoming more permanently settled in their host countries and massive migration of Chinese professionals to the West, followed by decline of the Sinocentric core as a sphere of influence, Tu's message of multivocality has as its main goal a cultural renaissance at the Sinocentric core, as represented by the theme "The Changing Meaning of Being Chinese Today," which graced two special issues of *Daedalus* in 1991 and 1993. Whether this is an alternative modernity is dubious, to say the least, but it is founded largely on a nonexistent transnational community or collective consciousness.

In the context of "indigenizing" Chinese communities in Southeast Asia, it is clear that the nationalist imperative to identify has become problematic. Or to put it in a somewhat different way, it has become increasingly apparent that the maintenance of a bounded ethnic identity has been seen as an irrelevant, if not incompatible, aspect of the conduct of economic and political life in these various societies. Much of the success of Chinese entrepreneurs (past and present) in these Southeast Asian venues had been achieved through multicultural skills, more often by downplaying ethnic difference. In the political domain, cooptation and networking have been constant features of social mobility strategies by Chinese, even if it resulted in cultural assimilation. Successful examples of ethnic Chinese, such as Chuan Leekpai, the prime minister of Thailand, and the various tycoons who made their fame and fortune by cultivating favor with native elites, have shown that maintenance of ethnic identity and lifestyles is largely irrelevant, if not secondary, to these politico-economic concerns.

Divergent paths of cultural discourse in Hong Kong and Taiwan show how inaccurate ethnicity is in reflecting sociopolitical reality. In Hong Kong, despite the large proportion of non-Cantonese immigrants to the colony after the war (making up about 25% of the total population), regional ethnic nepotism has never been problematic. In fact, the emergence of a Hong Kong identity for the most part created divisions between older-generation refugees still attached to the motherland and a local generation raised in the liminal spaces created by Chinese nationalist conflict. After the Sino-British Declaration of 1984 leading up to 1997, Hong Kong underwent a phase of reverse indigenization, as though attempting to rediscover its lost Chineseness. The recent discovery of Hong Kongers that they are really Chinese is less a sudden *prise de conscience* than a reflection instead of the primary embeddedness of ethnic identity to changes in the underlying and constantly shifting sociopolitical ground.

In postwar Taiwan, on the other hand, the proportion of local versus outsider ethnic groups (75% Taiwanese vs. 25% from elsewhere in China) mirrored that of Hong Kong, but in the era of post–Cold War "democratization," Taiwan has largely been undergoing a process of ethnic decolonization. Their later rediscovery of Taiwaneseness parallels its hypersensitive aversion to Chineseness, which it currently associates primarily with mainland China.

The ironic fallacy of Taiwan's ethnic reality resides in the fact that it has been slow to recognize the existence of a Taiwanese consciousness, despite the obvious demographics. It has struggled to advocate a political platform of majority rule, when nations based on less dominant ethnic imbalances (such as the Soviet Union, Yugoslavia, and South Africa) have in fact achieved political independence. Either appearances are deceiving, or the possibilities of ethnic discourse in Taiwan have been complicated by a different kind of political reality. Contrary to the emancipatory claims of postcolonial theory, Taiwan has already undergone many phases of indigenization. The first, termed *sinicization*, was part of a broad defense of traditional China vis-à-vis both the West and the PRC. Native Taiwaneseness then, like its earlier phase, reflects less a discovery of ethnic truths than a changing political landscape.

Toward a New Politics of Place in the Cosmopolises of Changing Identities

There is in this a cruel contradiction implicit in the art form itself. For true jazz is an art of individual assertion within and against the group. Each true jazz moment . . . springs from a contest in which the artist challenges all the rest; each solo flight, or improvisation, represents (like the canvases of a painter) a definition of his [*sic*] identity: as individual, as member of the collectivity and as a link in the chain of tradition. Thus because jazz finds its life in improvisation upon traditional materials, the jazz man must lose his identity even as he finds it.

—Ralph Ellison, *Shadow and Act*

The question is not one of whether it is possible to have multiple identities or whether hybridity can create new identities, but whether one can justifiably understand them without reference to the sociopolitical structures that contain and define them *in fact*. The changing nationalist spaces of identity discourse along with the shifting parameters of ethnic-cultural boundedness that characterize the process of identifying have in recent years fundamentally altered the framework for place-based imagination that is really at the core of community and diasporic affiliation. It is not insignificant that Chinese in Southeast Asia have begun to see themselves increasingly as subject-citizens of their host settler societies, just as Taiwanese have viewed themselves in relation to a reinvented but still indeterminate sense of place (to replace the spaces of a polity, discourse, and culture represented by the "Republic of China"). These changes in *situatedness* have important ramifications for how new cultural discourses will form and what role hybridity will play in shaping the scope and relevance of identity.

Contrary to the imaginary transnational fundamentalism that Tu Weiming's notion of cultural China advocates, which seems to include Chinese everywhere, it is very easy to show how such an imagined community is really limited to a small group of diasporic intellectuals in the ivory tower and is really far removed from the diverse kinds of geopolitical shifts that have influenced Chinese in different social settings. The fictive nature of the nation-state, for one thing, has been problematized in different ways in different venues.

The more Chinese "identify" with the various national regimes in which their routine of life is situated, the less likely it will be in the long run that one can view them as being part of a single universe of discourse, regardless of the disposition of their ethnic culture. Even in the case of Taiwan, the possibilities for identity can change radically not just as a function of how native Taiwanese consciousness comes to be defined, but rather to the extent that it can alter its boundedness to the cultural nationalist framework in which its fate has now become hopelessly entangled. Appadurai (1991:209) attributes many of these shifts in situatedness to the recent effects of globalization or what he calls "genealogies of cosmopolitanism." In any ethnoscape (which may be discreet localities or higher level communities), genealogies can reveal the cultural spaces within which new forms are indigenized (Appadurai notes how tourism invaded the space of pilgrimage in India). While any one place can alternatively become the site of functional disjuncture or the object of appropriation by other disruptive forces, the flip side of this is to recognize equally that any one place can be imbued with multiple meanings. The nation can thus be for some people a source of roots in a historical or political sense and for others a convenient abode or place of exile. Similarly, sacred sites can be seen by some as objects of pilgrimage and by others a tourist attraction. The tyranny of a hegemonic, collective "identity" associated with homogenous nation-states has given place a fixed or incontestable meaning, while, on the other hand, the fact that places can under *different* sociopolitical conditions adopt multiple meanings makes the choice of identifying with different moral communities an even more strategic and context-sensitive one.

Multiple meanings of place differ from multiple identities in the sense that they accent the primordial importance of *context* rather than ethnicity or culture in the construction of identities. Rather than viewing the substance of one's ethnicity or culture as a natural point of departure, more importantly it is necessary to see how context invokes the relevance of culture, as function of strategic choice, to the processes of identifying. Positionality within a context then becomes the subjective framework of power. In this regard, perception also plays a salient role. It is and can become the very source of cultural diversity.

An alternative approach to a cultural study of place (and its ramifications for identity construction) comes from Patterson's (1994) concept of "cosmopolis." Although less celebrated than Gilroy's analysis of the Black Atlantic, Patterson's sociohistorical analysis of the origins of reggae in the complex interactions of global culture and in the formation of the American cultural cosmos shows how multiple flows (rather than the singular threat of a homogenizing cultural "imperialism") have contributed to the invention of new cultural forms, while at the same time calling into question the meanings of place accorded to fixed cultural origins, which casts in a rather different light the status of musical culture in both the American and Jamaican cosmos. Like Gilroy, Patterson clearly describes the formation of an alternative modernity, one in which working-class Rastafarian culture becomes a local site of hybridity, whose actual sources of influence are global. In tracing its external influences to the West, one discovers instead that this musical culture has become the site of a different kind of globalization and synthesis.

Patterson contrasts the local assimilative strategies of these working-class Jamaicans with the cultural cosmopolitanism of Jamaican intellectual elites. He resists characterizing the different sites of Black hybridity as collectively making up a single Black Atlantic, and instead argues that many cosmopolises overlap over a single terrain, thus making the idea of a single global system superfluous. Each cosmopolis is then defined by inherently different processes of cultural accommodation as well as strategies of sociopolitical positionality. Quite unlike Gilroy, whose Black Atlantic excludes the contributions of West Indian scholars to mainstream White intellectual discourse, Patterson's Black "nationalism" is, on the other hand, less a hybrid "collectivity" than one inherently divided by social class and represented largely by many incompatible cultural ethos. Patterson's "cosmopolises," by virtue of their overlap over a single terrain, lend themselves to political negotiation and conflict in ways that contrast directly with Gilroy's harmonious polyphony, especially with its experiential root in the social memory of slavery and the structures of feeling located therein. This should also have important ramifications for Chinese "cosmopolises." In the limited context of China, Hong Kong, and Taiwan, there are always avenues for fissions, fusions, and ambiguities that have constantly been made, unmade and remade, despite a common language and culture. Structures of sentiment, cultural or intellectual, can likewise always be created, spliced, and synthesized in ways that reflect the changing geopolitical order of the times. In contrast to the way Ong and others have championed the heroes of Chinese transnational capitalism, I would also argue that in any terrain there is more divisive friction than unity. In any local setting, the cosmopolitan ethos of a transnational way of life must always compete with other kinds of social values, which may be rooted in class, gender, or the virtues of indigenous authenticity, in addition to machinations of the state itself.

The recognition of different perceptions of place epitomized by one's sociopolitical positionality suggests then a politics of place that is mediated by these structures of meaning. There is a sense thus in which these different spaces of culture created over a single terrain are a function of the social location of people within society, or as Massey (1994:2) aptly put it, "the spatial is social relations 'stretched out.'" At the same time, it is really in reference to these discourses or universes of meaning that people articulate and affirm their relationship to place. These changing discourses are thus an index of the stability as well as the internal divisibility of place. They pit the desirability of one level of place (locality, nation, world) over another, but they also pit the relevance of place to different domains of the lifeworld (familial, moral, economic, political). On the surface, it is quite easy to sympathize with the postmodern or postcolonial appeal to diasporic resistance and cultural hybridity, but this appeal is often based on the a priori "naturalness" of ethnic sentiment or multiple identities, when in fact ethnicity (even indigenous ones) can be shown to be inventions and fictions that must be constantly created, legitimized, and institutionalized in social practice. Meanwhile, the applicability of multiple identities must be viewed within the specific confines of those institutional regimes that attempt to define and regulate them.

Diaspora is in the final analysis a concept whose origins and connotations show it to be the product of a stratified system, which is itself subject to ongoing institutional change. Thus, its appropriateness is largely a function of the power relations that effectively drive institutions and of the perception of people within that geography of power. Of course, one can champion the bottom-up process of hybridity as a means to decenter the hegemony of cultural authority, even to the point, as Gilroy does, of showing rather convincingly that the Black experience has contributed more to the construction of modernity than has previously been recognized by the center. But this will not detract from the other fact that, in the modern (and postmodern) world, there may always be tension between forces of hybridity and the need to establish orthodox authority (through maintenance of standards, canons of correctness, and lineages of purity). In *any* place, politics is not irreducible but certainly attempts to *present* itself as an a priori given. Yet like Patterson's notion of cosmopolis, there appears to be no a priori reason why one should believe that this coexistence of forces is by nature conflictual or must lead to the desirability of one over the other. Between the different social strata and the various domains of the lifeworld, there is always room for overlap, separation, and convergence. They are ongoing, changing products of subjective perception and political negotiation for which there can hardly be a priori rules.

The politics of place that give rise to cosmopolises in the above sense contrast with Shih Shu-mei's appeal to the Sinophone. The use of Sinophone in a literal sense to denote speech or writing especially in discussions of Chinese literature is standard, however, Shih is clearly motivated by other critical concerns. While Sinophone designates "Sinitic-language cultures and communities outside China where Sinitic languages are either forcefully imposed or willingly adopted" (Shih 2010a:36), Sinophone studies is more narrowly defined as the study of Sinitic language cultures "on the margins of geopolitical nation-states and their hegemonic production," which "locates its objects of attention at the conjuncture of China's internal colonialism" (Shih 2011:710). As a celebration of multiculturalism, transnationalism, and postcolonialism, it is inherently a critique of Sinocentrism, in fact all centrisms. Although Shih bases her critical intervention on the "misconceived" notion of diaspora, the real object of criticism is the Sinocentric, patriotic notion of *huaqiao*, with its implicit ties to a national homeland, which has reinforced racialized constructions of Chineseness. If anything, this notion of *huaqiao* is a peculiarly politicized term that hardly represents any of its strict usages (even as ethnic stereotype). Ironically, the concept of Sinophone has privileged what used to be called the study of Chinese literature in the diaspora by championing its sense of authority as a voice of Sinitic culture. As a voice of cultural authenticity, its authority would seem to be limited to literature, despite Shih's lofty intentions. In the realm of culture, which could include all genres of lifestyle, it would be difficult to justify the privileged status of language.

In a broader perspective, as a marker of identity, the Sinophone accents the overarching salience of ethnic consciousness. As speech act inextricably bound to meaning in language, can literature or cultural imagination ever transcend its Sinitic nature? Perhaps contrary to the place-based logic Shih attempts to invoke, there is a sense in which the Sinophone reifies the inherent relevance of ethnicity to all things cultural. In an essay titled "Theory, Asia and the Sinophone," Shih (2010b) explores the possibility of "Asian" theory (as opposed to Western universalism), informed by the critical intervention of the Sinophone as method. If she takes for granted that theory is by nature Orientalist, which invokes the need to reconcile its Asianness of place, when or how is it possible for knowledge to de-essentialize in ethnic terms? The problem of Chineseness involves in part the way in which we unconsciously (or presumably) view it as inextricably tied to all other aspects of culture. The Sinophone, as a concept, rightfully challenges its hegemonic constructions, as if to privilege the legitimacy of alternative voices and meanings, but as method it accents the disenfranchised, reiterating the marginal and the multivocal, instead of directly engaging the institutional (political) source of that hegemony. How does this significantly differ from Rey Chow's *Writing Diaspora*?

The mutation of the concept of diaspora from religious to ethnic and other caste status shows that it is intrinsically tied to perceptions of social marginality. Why is it necessary to invoke the Sinophone to reiterate the obvious, when the more important question is when and how people de-essentialize diasporic status through *identification*, prompted by the changing politics of place that Shih claims to be epistemologically privileged? Patterson's concept of cosmopolis shows that imagined communities need not be ethnic in nature and are more often than not class based, accenting the dynamics of social relations within a geography of power. Even the dynamics of settler identification have important ramifications for the relevance of Sinophone identity in literature. Should we classify Ha Jin's, or Kazuo Ishiguro's relation to literature in relation to who they happen to be ipso facto or how they identify? Ang Lee is proudly Taiwanese, but is there a point where his work transcends his presumed ethnicity (his direction of Jane Austen's novel *Sense and Sensibility* being an appropriate case in point)?

Chapter 11

Ethnicity in the Prison House of the Modern Nation

The State in Singapore as Exception

Singapore is a case of a reluctant nation in search of a cultural identity. Established in 1819 as a trading post, Singapore was a British colony until it was granted self-government in 1959, with Lee Kuan Yew as prime minister. The fact that Singapore was a small island with few natural resources for economic self-sufficiency made the very idea of political independence unthinkable. The vast majority of its inhabitants were ethnic Chinese in a region located in the heart of an indigenous Malay tradition. At a time when import substitution was the major development strategy of decolonized states, Singapore, faced with high unemployment and a rapidly growing population, needed a market larger than itself for its industrialization program. This market was supposed to be Malaya (Drysdale 1984:249). Its strategy was thus to try to seek membership within the Malaysian Federation. However, the Malayan political leadership was never warm to the prospect of a merger, which would have added a million Chinese to the Malayan population and exacerbate existing ethnic tensions. The presence of a Chinese-influenced Communist Party also represented a potentially destabilizing threat to the proposed federation. Singapore was included within the Confederation in 1963, but the strained relationship led to Singapore's expulsion in 1965 and a reluctant independence.

This essay is based in parts on "Discourses of Identity in the Changing Spaces of Public Culture in Taiwan, Hong Kong and Singapore," *Theory Culture & Society* 13(1):51–75, and "On the Politics of Culture, or the State of the State, in Singapore," *Australian Journal of Anthropology* 20:369–78.

The Invention of Nationalism

The nation there was forced to invent nationalism, where the basis of such consciousness did not appear to exist, contrary to the "normal" scheme of things, according to Gellner (1964:169). Perceptions held at the time that Singapore lacked a unique sense of cultural identity rooted in history and that the population was itself an immigrant society within a Malay environment made the possibility of a collective identity and consciousness an uncertain thing. Yet while a national identity had to be "constructed," the form of this constructed ideology and its process of institutionalization were still inextricably linked to the same kind of ideological project of state formation that has been described in the other previous cases.

The Singapore government took a heavy-handed approach to the promotion of culture by setting out explicit policy perspectives and actively launching mass campaigns in accordance with official government directives. There were roughly three phases of cultural discourse. The first, from 1965 to 1982, focused on promotion of values of "rugged individualism," which accentuated the cultivation of a disciplined, achievement-oriented work ethic. The second, from 1982 to 1990, was spawned by the search for an Asian ethic, using indigenous religion and ideologies as the basis for promotion of an Asian mode of modernization. The third, from 1990 onward, focused on "shared values" and attempted seriously to formulate in secular (value-free) terms a set of pan-ethnic social principles with which people could identify and on which one could construct a genuinely national identity.

Ethnicity in Place

The most problematic concern in defining culture as national identity in Singapore had to do with the constant need to address social issues in terms of the multiethnic composition of its population (Benjamin 1976; Chiew 1983; Clammer 1985:162). Despite the numerical superiority of ethnic Chinese (70%) in proportion to Malays (15%) and Indians (8%), it was necessary to openly recognize ethnic equality as a means of neutralizing ethnic nepotism in matters pertaining to national interest. While it would have been easy to deal with national issues in direct proportion to ethnic representation, there was the greater danger of being influenced by ties to a mother country as well as to communism, which made ethnic identity a potentially troublesome factor. Moreover, as Chan and Evers (1978:121) have pointed out, the cultural divide between Western-educated individuals and those educated in their native language and tradition often tended to be greater. Following independence, there was also a gradual trend among all ethnic groups to gravitate toward English-stream education. The complexities of the ethnic situation actually made it desirable for the government to promote economic utility, disciplinary work ethics, and pan-ethnic values during the early postwar decades as the basis of cultural identity (Chua & Kuo 1998:41). This pan-ethnic policy thus effectively relegated ethnic identity and matters relating to customary practice to the private realm of culture in spite of its explicit attention in national politics. Ironically, the excommunication of ethnicity from the public realm shows that it was hardly a neutral entity.

The adverse consequences of modernization as "Westernization," that is, liberal freedom, drug abuse, sexual promiscuity, and rampant consumerism, were of constant concern to the government, but it was not until the early 1980s that it proposed to actively promote an Asian ethic of modernization as a cure for this virus. Increased emphasis on multilingualism in education was one aspect of this indigenization policy (Kuo 1985). The introduction of mandatory courses titled Religious Knowledge in secondary schools as part of a larger program to strengthen moral education was another aspect of this policy. The promotion of religious knowledge and moral education was the result of a perception of incipient moral decay, which came about as a result of lifestyle changes stemming from rapid modernization and which prompted the need to boost pride in one's own tradition. Following a Report on Moral Education in 1979, efforts were made not only to promote changes in the secondary curriculum but also to initiate mass campaigns touching on ethical themes, like the National Courtesy Campaign, Senior Citizen's Week Campaign, and Speak Mandarin Campaign.

The Sterilization of Religious Values

As part of the promotion of religious knowledge and moral education, a more ambitious program was undertaken to revitalize Confucianism as an Asian ethic, in order to capitalize on the economic success of Asia's "four dragons" and with the hope of unlocking the secrets of this Asian spirit of capitalism. While not a religion per se, Confucianism was portrayed as a kind of secular ethical philosophy compatible with Christianity, Buddhism, Islam, Hinduism, and World Religion. Starting in 1982, overseas Confucian scholars were recruited to set up a conceptual framework for promoting Confucianism in ideology and practice.[1] The Ministry of Education organized a Confucian Ethics Project Team to oversee curriculum development in this field, and the Institute of East Asian Philosophies was established in

1983 with heavy government backing to sponsor intellectual research and activities on Confucianism.

From Singapore's attempt to Asianize the process of economic modernization, one can see that it has generally recognized modernity as the basis of its cultural identity. On the other hand, its fears regarding "Westernization" also show that its attempts to define cultural identity were at the same time a search for a sense of uniqueness that could make up for its lack of historicity in a way that would neutralize the potential divisiveness of its ethnic composition. Ten years of experimentation with indigenization as cultural policy eventually produced disastrous results. A Report to the Ministry of Community Development in 1988 on religion in Singapore showed a disturbing rise in religious revivalism, especially in New Christianity, which was attributable directly to government promotion of religious knowledge (Kuo et al. 1988) Moreover, despite the government's efforts to promote Confucianism in particular, only a small fraction (17.8%) of secondary students, almost all Chinese, actually chose Confucian ethics, in contrast to 44.4 percent for Buddhism and 21.4 percent for Bible Knowledge (Kuo 1991:16). Dangers of religious fanaticism combined with the government's failure to promote Confucianism as an appealing pan-ethnic cultural ideal for modern society led the government to scrap religious education from the curriculum altogether. The Institute of East Asian Philosophies was transformed into the Institute of East Asian Political Economies, and its library was dismantled accordingly. This policy reversal provided the point of departure for a later phase of cultural discourse centering on "shared values," beginning in 1990.

As a statement of policy, the aim of this National Ideology (later renamed Shared Values) was to sculpt a Singaporean identity by incorporating relevant components of various cultural heritages as well as attitudes and values that would help promote survival of the nation. On January 15, 1991, the government formalized a set of principles that could reflect traditional Asian ideas of morality, duty, and society while accommodating the face of changing society. The *White Paper on Shared Values* outlined five such values: (1) nation before community and society above self, (2) family as the basic unit of society, (3) regard and community support for the individual, (4) consensus instead of contention, and (5) racial and religious harmony. One might argue that it represented as much an attempt to abstract a general ethos of Asianism in ways that transcended its specific differences, especially in emphasizing the primacy of social collectivity, as a deliberate effort to spurn Westernized, individualistic versions of the same.

Discourses of Public Culture in
Comparative Geopolitical Perspective

Taiwan, Hong Kong, and Singapore depict three different ways in which public culture has been demarcated and defined in relation to language, historical origin, ethnic tradition, political ideology, intellectual expression, and various other traits. In each case, global political factors like the Cold War and regional ethnicity helped to play an important role in creating a "space of dispersion," in Foucault's (1991:55) words, which cultural discourses operated on and cultural policies aimed to institutionalize a particular utopian vision of a just, rational polity. These attempts to define the specific content of culture were predicated by the perceived necessity to impose a homogenous sense of national identity that could also engender social solidarity. This homogeneity was reinforced by the state's control over the media in a way that severely restricted civil participation in cultural discourse while at the same time framing the possibilities of alternative constructions of identity.

Somewhat like Taiwan, the Singapore government consciously attempted to construct a set of shared ideals that could absorb everyone regardless of ethnic disposition. This set of ideals was not prone to the latent contradictions that gave rise to ethnic fragmentation in Taiwan, because the hegemony of Chinese culture in Taiwan also happened to be tied to the legitimacy of a fictitious entity called Republic of China. Nonetheless, the lack of a shared past or civilization in Singapore meant that the legitimacy of this constructed culture had to depend on the legitimacy of social values that could not by definition be fixed to a sacred aura, and, thus, by nature were always changing in response to the possibility of change. Singapore's response to cultural syncretism was a function of its love-hate relationship with the West and its attempt to strike a meaningful symbiosis between indigenous values and material progress. Moreover, contrary to global trends, democratization has not followed economic growth in a way that generally defies Huntington's thesis. In light of the apparent authoritarian style of government and its continued reproduction, it suffices to say that the legitimacy of national culture in Singapore has always and will continue to be determined by the ability of public discourse to achieve consensus over the meaning of modernity, on which the government has placed considerable importance in its construction of the polity.

In sum, public culture has been crafted by certain unconscious designs of the state, in an era marked by the growing importance of civil participation in the construction of the public sphere in a Habermasian sense (through rational communication). It would appear that the possibilities for change must be viewed in relation, first, to the discursive relationships between various sorts of cultural statements, and second, to the way in which the actions of the author or agent are tied into the production of such statements in order to reproduce a certain power relationship. Culture is not simply a neutral marker of one's identity; in the hands of the state, it is the very mechanism by which meaning is given to the nature of the polity and legitimacy is given to the apparatuses and routines of rule.[2] In order for effective counterdiscourse to exist, one must first grasp the imaginative process of cultural authority.

The construction of identity is more precisely a process of identifying, where cultural notions are not just selectively constituted but deliberately crafted from given elements to convey a particularistic ethos. Circumstances of historical moment and geopolitical place may explain to some degree the nature of strategic possibilities, but they invoke a global framework within which local factors ultimately play a key and decisive role in determining the politics of choice. If one can view discourses of identity as interpretive mechanisms through which specific people, institutions, or cultures local-ize (or indigenize) diverse global flows in order to negotiate a meaning-ful life space or position themselves within a situation of power, then it would be possible to see how in different localities specific institutions and practices serve as strategic sites for meaning and power. In Singapore, the imposition of a standard mass media and the use of mass campaigns to promote a collective consciousness have in the final analysis made all man-ners of behavior, such as work ethics, courteousness, and health, along with social policy issues, including family planning, marriage, and housing, matters of "public" concern that impinge on notions of a shared cultural identity.

The diversity of cultural responses to conceptions of identity authored in Taiwan, Hong Kong, and Singapore and their choice of strategic imple-mentation in institutional terms show that culture and identity are much more than knee-jerk reactions to the homogenizing threat of globalization. Perhaps more than just a diversity of flows and disjunctures, it is equally important to understand how such diversity in cultural response is a func-tion of different modes of accommodation or negotiation.[3] Underlying characterizations of globalization and their inherent concern with homog-enization and heterogeneity, cores, and peripheries, or pushes and pulls is a somewhat skewed vision of the "world" from the center of things. There tends to be relatively less concern, on the other hand, with the diverse ways in which the same threats from the "outside" are locally synthesized in order to produce reactions as varied as ethnic nationalism, pan-national

fundamentalism, supra-nationalism, cult fanaticism, and cultural creolization, all of which impinge ultimately on notions of identity.

The State of the State

As a matter of general principle, public culture is in the first instance shaped
by certain unconscious designs of the state, but there is a sense in which
the state in Singapore plays an extraordinarily prominent role in all aspects
of societal life. The (omni)presence of the state is indirectly reflected in
three recent books on Singapore: Cherian George's (2000) *Singapore, The
Air-Conditioned Nation: Essays on the Politics of Comfort and Control*; Yao
Souchou's (2007) *Singapore: The State and the Culture of Excess*; and Wee
Wan-ling's (2008) *The Asian Modern: Culture, Capitalist Development, Singapore*. Each book presents in its own way a subtle interpretation of contemporary Singapore culture and society, with reference to the peculiarities
(or distinctive features) of Singapore society, seen in the context of historical
practice and epitomized by seminal forces that have driven these events
and their underlying institutions. At the same time, they challenge prevailing notions of modernity, nation-state, and ethnic identity inherent to the
theoretical literature, especially pertaining to Asia.

On the surface, the three books cover different topics. George's book
is a compilation of newspaper essays written as a journalist from 1990 to
2000, which dealt strictly with the Goh Chok Tong era. Capitalizing on a
remark by Lee Kuan Yew that "there are few metaphors that more evocatively
crystallize the essence of Singapore politics" than the air conditioner, George
argues that the evolution of Singapore was ultimately about the mastery of
nature, not only of the environment but of the human kind, that was in
turn predicated on the desirability of progress. Comfort and control went
hand in hand; one was the means to the ends, and the substance of the
book, in its ruminations on politics, was less about theory than underlying
mind-sets that guided concrete practices and contributed to the development of society/culture.

George's thematic focus on governmentality, the mind-sets and practices that guided its relationship with the political opposition, its handling
of the emergence of civil society and the debates over ethnic and national
identity substantiate the familiar images of Singapore as a cosmopolitan,
multiethnic city-state managed by a strong technocratic central government
and governed by an ethos of utilitarian efficiency through collective discipline. The state's domination has been, for most part, the single-handed
achievement of the People's Action Party (PAP). The PAP's "success" can be

seen as the result of its effective articulation, on the one hand, of a political ideology that best mirrored the ideals of its mass constituency and its ruthless ability, on the other hand, through legal and institutional manipulation to eradicate and assuage opposition. Journalistic commentaries on daily politics tend to represent narrow views on society fixated disproportionately on the actions of people and institutions in power, but George's account reveals salient aspects of the subjective identity of the modern nation-state at a deeper level of reflection that provide a common ground with the observations of Yao and Wee.

Yao Souchou's book is an overtly symbolic analysis of Singapore society that begins by acknowledging the influence of Marshall Sahlins, but whose polemic style resembles Roland Barthes's *Mythologies* more in its effort to isolate epitomizing spectacles of everyday mind-set and lifestyle, and then, through demystifying and destabilizing tactics of writing, unmask various fictions of culture routinely promoted by the State as taken for granted norms. Singapore may be epitomized by its culture of excess, but Yao's critical facades, which shift randomly from discursive deconstruction to psychoanalytic interpretation, Orientalist decolonization, and literary catharsis, are also modes of exaggeration that deliberately create spectacles of excess by exhaustively overdetermining such banalities of culture. Ironically, in contrast to George, who as a journalist writes more like an ethnographer, with his attention to factual and historical details, and from which he abstracts a generalized account of society and its culture, Yao, who is an anthropologist, writes more like Homi Bhabha or Michael Taussig. With clear disdain for official narratives and their perspectives, he tortures the reader with mind-blowing exegeses of events, ulterior motives, and acts of mental terror disguised as secular rationality.

Yao's object of criticism is clearly the State, insofar as its authority is forcefully stamped in the spaces of everyday culture. The culture of excess is thus the product of its excessive omnipresence in these spectacles of everyday life. Disciplinary control and smooth society in George's depiction of Singapore are replaced in Yao's by accounts of naked violence and hegemonic terror subjectively driven by psychological anxieties. To counter the depiction of a squeaky-clean society and the rationalist intentions of government policy, Yao calls this brand of governmentality "useless pragmatism." Having subjected his patient (and reader) to psychoanalytic shock treatment, the fact that pragmatism is useless is an understatement, to say the least. As a political ideology, it "conceals and mystifies," thus in the final analysis it "also blinds the State to its moral defects" (Yao 2007:186). Magic then becomes tragic.

In contrast, Wee's book is an ambitious attempt to rethink the crises of global capitalism or modernity in a Singapore context. Despite his thematic focus on Asia, the book is less about Asia per se than its recognition that Singapore's experiences are inextricably entangled with discourses on Asia or comparative developments therein. His focus on the modern is an attempt to confront the broader issue of modernity, as understood in the complex interplay between culture, economy, and politics. Wee's deep play on the changing terrritorializations of Singapore culture is rooted, on the one hand, in his discussions of ideological visions that drove state policies in various dimensions of economic development and social planning, as personified in part by the influence of influential figures in the PAP, such as S. Rajaratnam and Goh Keng Swee, and the work of urban planners in the Housing and Development Board (HDB), who transformed the city into what Rem Koolhaas called a "Potemkin metropolis," and his readings of literary syntheses of these cultural landscapes. In the end, he attempts to tie these developments to abstract crises within global capitalism.

For Wee, culture is in effect a space that comprises ethnicities, identities, representations, social values, political ideologies, and imaginations of all genres constituting the substantive logic that drives the quest for modernity. In its reterritorialization, culture is an active object of discourse and appropriation within a changing capitalism. As Wee (2008:105) phrases it, "capitalism must homogenize—it must deterritorialize—while also producing difference—it must reterritorialize—and become a 'multicultural' capitalism," echoing similar arguments put forth by Zizek on the cultural logic of multinational capitalism. In this regard, many kinds of reterritorialization seem to overlap and interact. Wee discusses here the advent of Asian values as a cultural discourse of modernity, the government's management of race or multiethnicity in a multinational capitalism, the imagination of national culturalism within the capitalist order, and the use of Asian religions to foster neotraditional links to modernity.

Despite the different approaches that each author takes in articulating certain distinctive features of Singapore's modernizing experience, the same subtext emerges each time. It is not enough to say that the state plays a domineering role In these developments; the state is in each case a prime object of gazing and critique. Each author confronts the state directly but stops short of theorizing the state in a Singaporean context. George's observations remain largely at the level of practice, and his abstractions remain close to the mind-sets of actors in power. Yao psychoanalyzes Singapore from afar, but his critique of state is personified for most part in his diagnosis of "the sick father" whose sickness is ramified through the excesses of culture and spectacles of society. Wee's account is discursively grounded, but his critique of state is embedded largely in society's entanglements with modernity as global capitalism.

A recent paper by Chua Beng Huat (2010) confronts state capitalism by characterizing it ideologically as "hegemonic liberalism." But despite the hegemonic facade, for Chua, the state's direct investment in enterprises and industries has been a success story, driven largely by its ethos of profit maximization and market discipline, which subsequently made possible and socially desirable its imperative of social communitarianism that underlay cultural policy in other regards. Such success suggests in turn that there are viable alternatives to Western models of liberal-democratic-capitalism that are typically characteristic of *the* modern state, but they coexist with, if not mutually reinforce as well, the taken for granted paternalism and authoritarianism of the state that subtly engenders and legitimates routinized cartographies of power endemic to those various mediations of modernity that equally effectively compel us, through identity, to conform to the norm, perhaps even more successfully than in *the* West.

The various debates that have energized the recent literature on "global" or "neoliberal" capitalism have accented important issues in the contemporary world, but reterritorialization in one sense is geographically literal. One may argue, contrary to Appadurai's depiction of transnational disjunctures, characterized by chaotic flows or scapes, while parallel more with Deleuze's smooth society, which presaged Hardt and Negri's "empire," that this transnational (multinational) capitalism produced a new form of imperialism.[4] How else do we reconcile the widening gap between rich and poor nations that has fueled anti-WTO movements everywhere? Yet how relevant is this mode of capitalism to the discourse and policy of the Singapore state? Despite Wee's (2008:148) contention that "the PAP government has acknowledged for some years that the Fordist-Taylorist machinery of disciplinary modernization that it had so successfully used was starting to creak," leading to greater investment in a knowledge economy, the machinery remains largely unchanged. In its enticement of foreign capital investment in exchange for tax incentives, second perhaps only to Dubai, Singapore seems to be a willing partner to free market capitalism, on the receiving end. Its prime minister earns a millionaire salary, closer to CEOs of major corporations, and is expected to run the nation like a business, which would make Reaganites or Thatcherites blush. Recently, the embarrassment of national wealth has aggravated the extreme gap between rich and poor to such an extent that it has prompted the government to defend even more the sanctity of its workfare (antiwelfare) policies. Shades of classical Marxism—there still seems to be a long way to liberal, not to mention neoliberal, capitalism. As Singapore moves into the next stage of economic development, much can be said about its strange combination of microeconomic laissez-faire, macrosocial regulation, and illiberal democracy, which are seminal constituents of its unique capitalist order, but to lump all of culture then recast it as reterritorializations of modernity is to overgeneralize the nature of the problem, which centers really on making sense of the distinctive features of Singapore.

As a theoretical problem, I think the experiences of Singapore have been overlooked in the literature. Dennis H. Wrong (1961) criticized sociological theory for its oversocialized conception of the individual, but he never looked at Singapore. Foucault's genealogy of the disciplinary society made it the paradigm of Western modernity, but few mention Singapore, where disciplinary regulation has been fine-tuned to a degree of efficiency unseen elsewhere, largely as a project of the State. Gellner's (1964) argument that nationalism creates nations where they do not exist finds a perfect example in Singapore, whose search for identity has prompted unending reconfigurations of culture in materialist and abstract senses. Singapore has in many cases worn out established theoretical paradigms of all kinds, while spinning life into higher states of unreality. Yet few scholarly observers seem to notice or care. While I appreciate Wee's ambitious attempt to conceptualize the broader ramifications of Singapore's experiences, I think he has misleadingly situated the heart of the problem in a crisis of global capitalism, which I tend to view, after Dipesh Chakrabarty's (2000) "Provincializing Europe," as a problem of a "local" West extending outward. Singapore, as other nations, is conscious of its "being in the world," in Friedman's (1990) terms, but an abstract understanding of its sociocultural processes should proceed from the ground up, distinctive excesses above all.

The experience of Singapore has been paradigmatic of many theoretical trends, despite being overlooked in the literature. To say that Singapore is a modern disciplinary society in a Foucaultian sense would be an understatement; efficiency is largely a project of the state. At issue ultimately are the nature of domination and the role of critical theory in unmasking, through cultural representation, the bases of social and political power. In Singapore's case, all roads lead inevitably to the state. For better or worse, the omnipresence of the state is the product of its specific formative history, the embeddedness of ethnicity, economy, and culture to each other and everyday life regimes have made the state part of a disinterested process of moral regulation, and its relationship to capitalism and democracy is correspondingly related.

Chapter 12

The Postcolonial Alien in Us All

Asian Studies in the International Division of Labor

This essay is a combination of two unlikely topics. One is a long commentary on the work of Naoki Sakai, presented at a workshop in Taiwan.[1] The other is a paper given at a *boundary 2* conference in Hong Kong, which was a critique of latent ethnocentrism in current notions of globalization.[2] It is not apparent at first glance why the two are related at all, but certain unsettling themes underlying both are tied together by a presumed reliance on the centrality of identity. In Sakai's case, his recent work has posited an implicit ethnocentrism in axioms of humanistic understanding that have become for him a basis for postcolonial sensitivity. The *boundary 2* conference was prompted by an endeavor to find common ground among intellectuals of apparently different identities. Both cases assumed identity's positionality without really problematizing identity's situatedness in other things. Identity issues are not irrelevant to other disciplines either. In anthropology, "writing culture" and similar debates surrounding the authority of native ethnographic voices has invoked the relevance of identity under different disciplinary contexts.[3] Identity politics in other fields have underscored the primacy of subjectivity of all kinds. I deflate the importance of identity in the short term here as a preamble for arguing that our identities have always been fictions that are shaped by underlying institutional forces; that is, contrary to what we think, these identities can change and are stratified less by the ethnocentrism in our concepts than our *institutional situatedness*.

Humanitas and Anthropos as a Problem of Epistemic Gazing

In my initial commentary, I countered Sakai's eventual call for postcolonial sensitivity, which mirrors similar sentiments, best epitomized perhaps in the

This essay originally appeared in 2008 as "The Postcolonial Alien in Us All: Identity in the Global Division of Intellectual Labor," *positions: east asia critique* 16(3).

work of Spivak and Bhabha, by concluding that Sakai was not one of "us" (Asians). I underscore "us" here, because the question that I wish to pose here is, who are us and them in this global division of intellectual labor? The hard-and-fast identities that characterize us all are a function of our institutional situatedness rather than ethnic affinity per se. Nonetheless, what polarizes our institutional positionality is an ethnocentrism that is largely rooted in ongoing institutional practices. In other words, the dualism of us/them is much more deeply rooted than one thinks, especially because it is *not* a matter of identifying choice. A division of labor that is maintained by an implicit ethnocentrism in its categories makes academia, as practiced, much more caste-like than one stratified by other forms of power, even global capitalism, which was the focus of Dirlik's critique of the "postcolonial aura."[4] There are ramifications for global capitalism as discursive imagination, but it is necessary, first, to explain how identities derive from our institutional situatedness, which is in my opinion anything but obvious or taken for granted.

The most seminal aspect of Sakai's (2001) essay, "Dislocation of the West and the Status of the Humanities" is his critique of an implicit ethnocentrism in *humanitas* and *anthropos*. It is a dualism that pervades not only the division between philosophy and anthropology or area studies as the other of the social scientific and humanistic self, but also the very notion that separates the West from the Rest, even us versus them. His central thesis/argument regarding the dislocation of the West and its mutual relation to the objectivizing gaze of Asia resonates not only in Asian area studies and civilizational studies in general but in most social sciences too. One cannot underestimate the impact of Said's critique of *Orientalism* in this sense, not only in his attack on the legitimacy of the author as writer but more importantly as a political and institutional agent of a colonialist imperative.[5] One can view the rise of Asian studies as a product of American imperialism in a Cold War era, and the extent to which the negativity that defined Asia as a mirror image of the West is dependent on and reinforces the hegemony and separateness of the West is worth debating. But as a critique of Eurocentrism in theory, he was hardly the first. In anthropology, the work of Lévi-Strauss (1963) and Dumont (1980), writing in a mode of cultural relativism, had made systematic critiques of precisely the same ethnocentrism. In large part, Sakai's (or Said's) critique has focused more on the way Asia in area studies has been constituted as objects of a Western gaze, then reflect back ultimately on its own *humanitas*, and less on the parameters of indigenous discourse in this imperial contest. The problem is, in essence, one of Eurocentric subjectivity. This epistemological dilemma of Asia then invokes a need to problematize the West and Western studies. Or as Sakai (2001:71) asks, why is there an "absence of any serious attempts to build ethnic-study programs dealing with Americans whose ancestors came from Europe"? Moreover, "why are there no urgent demands from European Americans for European American studies programs at universities and colleges in the U.S." (Sakai 2001:72)? Or to rephrase it in the line of thought that has predicated these questions, why hasn't the West and knowledge of the West been problematized in a way that by contrast gave rise to the Orient and Orientalism as object and discourse? As Sakai (2001:74) finally poses it, why is a Western *humanitas* dualistically opposed to the *anthropos* of the other in this stratified order of things, as though to suggest that its refusal to be gazed is really a function of its inherent subjective faculties, its authority to evaluate and its right to reflect?

The critique of Eurocentric *humanitas* as a hegemonic mind-set and unreflective ego is worthy, yet there is little effort by Sakai to view this Occidentalism as something more than just a problem of representation. Sakai's emphasis on the effects of speaker distancing that result in the mirror image of Asia serving as the prima facie discourse in Europe's hegemonic construction of self is in my opinion just a metaphorical device for explaining the imaginative quality of the discourse; it is no substitute for unpacking the institutional regimes of practice that ground these projections of meaning. In other words, I agree with Sakai that there is a curious absence in the West of any serious attempt both to objectify itself and to challenge the hegemony of its humanistic subjectivity. But he fails to ask further, what are the sources of institutional resistance in political practice to the above? It is not enough to attribute this to a failure of imagination. Second, authorial identity/subjectivity never goes away, in light of his enlightened, critical *prise de conscience*. Thus, his identity claim of being one of "us" is in turn relevant as well, which was something he parlayed into a later paper, called "You Asians: On the Historical Role of the West and Asia Binary," which was written initially for a conference held in Singapore in February 2000, appropriately titled *We Asians*.[6] In his later work, he tries to reshape his critique of Eurocentric subjectivity within a framework that accentuates the centrality of authorial identity. In my longer commentary, I problematize some of his efforts in this regard, partly because I think there are aspects he omits that others develop more fully and partly because there are contradictions in regard to his own identity. It is interesting to note that Chakrabarty's *Provincializing Europe* (2000) starts with a quote from Sakai, as if to suggest that the main challenge is one of regarding Europe as a provincial local, whose claims to historical destiny simply universalized its own cultural values into the status of theory and truth. Equally importantly, the enunciation "you Asians" does *not* necessarily assume a speaking position of "we Europeans." As Sakai (2000:811) clearly states, discourse can "be construed in many other terms than 'Western' as opposed to 'Asian.' It could be construed in terms of gender, economic status, profession, social class background, level of education, and so forth." It is easy to indict ethnic Western scholars for evoking "you Asians," but if one subscribes to the position that such enunciations are ultimately rooted in "the imperial contest," in Said's terms, then it would be more accurate to say that the institutional system in which we are embedded ultimately defines who "we" are subjectively and regardless of what we happen to be *ethnically*.[7] As an Asian studies scholar, Sakai is really one of "them" and cannot possibly be one of "us." I argue that there is a significant difference between the two speaking positions, which becomes evident, only if one can divest oneself of the *superficial* illusion that they represent two ethnic modes of subjectivity. The key to understanding this can be seen in Sakai's (1997) essay "The subject and/or *shutai*," where he distinguishes between two notions of subjectivity, the first reflecting the positionality of the epistemic observer (*shukan*) and the second reflecting the positionality of the practical agent (*shutai*). This is an important distinction, because among other things it can provide one with a way to transcend the Eurocentric hierarchical distinction between *humanitas* and *anthropos*. The epistemic observer and the practical agent do not refer to different persons, which is the impression that Sakai gives in his paper, but differ really as a function of the *quality* of their engagement with the context of speaking and practice in which they are embedded. Epistemic observers will think/act on the basis of their identity as both *shukan* and *shutai*, but it is more likely that their subjectivity will be the result of how they compromise the different interests and values that shape their identities for any particular context (which is the case of the native scholar). I shall raise concrete examples of this later.

The Complicity of Epistemic Identities and Discourses as Signifying Regimes

Let me approach this issue from a different vantage point. The *crisis of globalization* has become a seminal theme or fulcrum to characterize the recent dilemma that has plagued political economic relations between peoples in the world as well as between academics in different venues. When *boundary 2* held its conference in Hong Kong, one of many that it has held in various places in the world, it was an honest attempt to explore the future of humanities in dialogue with culturally diverse scholars, mostly in the literary field (English), but it too was predicated to a large extent on implicit differences of identity that separated its participants. In the *current* era of globalization, there are many incongruous elements. Despite debates about our understanding of the concept itself, I do not doubt that the *phenomenon* referred to here is a new one. If we view it in Appadurai's (1990) terms, as transnational disjunctures, prompted by Lash and Urry's (1987) "end of organized capitalism," then this globalization is fundamentally different from the modern world system, as coined by Wallerstein (1974), for at least two reasons. First, the center of gravity has shifted, or one is led to believe so, second, the cultural imperialism of an earlier era has been replaced by free-flowing waves of multicultural hybridity (or scapes in Appadurai's terms). Yet what is overtly paradoxical about the *discourse* of globalization, as seen from the periphery (global South), especially if one considers increases in anti-WTO movements that have surfaced, is that globalization is almost universally perceived as a new wave of cultural imperialism or *Western-ism*. This is paradoxical, because globalization as a general phenomenon in human history is not new; neither is capitalism—capitalism has always been global. Globalization should have little to do with Westernism, especially as a cultural force. I raise these incongruent perspectives, based on one's positionality in the global order, which Friedman (1990) aptly calls "being in the world," to suggest in the first instance that ethnic marking of globalization still has much to do with its implicit stratified hierarchy, contrary to the theoretical claims of disorganized capitalism and celebratory hybridity, and to suggest, second, that the Eurocentrism inherent in these concepts extends further than the meanings of these terms; they are part and parcel of the constitution of institutions that unwittingly tie all of us within a global division of labor.

I think there is more truth in Dirlik's (1994:328) facetious remark that the postcolonial began at a time when Third World intellectuals became embraced and celebrated in the First World, than many will care to admit. But if this defines the postcolonial moment, then what exactly is postco-lonialism? Is it defined by articulation of postcolonial discourse, as marked by one's identity, or is it really the content of postcolonial discourse? There is a sense in which it refers mainly to the former, but as I have argued elsewhere, it cannot be defined by identity alone.[8] On the other hand, the content of this discourse remains in my opinion ill-defined, if anything. I argue that the relevance of any identity, in this case postcolonial, is in the first instance a function of how one defines a (post)colonial situation. There is an implicit relationship between postcolonial identification and content of postcolonial thought, but identities are never ipso facto. They are invoked by context and change with changing situations. This same point can be applied to globalization and the question of who we are in the global ecumene. I find it ironic, especially in an age of increasing transnational flows and cultural hybridity, that identities (academic ones too) have hardened instead of softened.

To ask whether there are common themes of discourse, especially among those who share the same discipline but are divided by the identities of its participants, is really to imply that differences of identity or context are relevant differences. In questioning the suggestion, I am not directly questioning who we are per se. I am suggesting instead that the question is relevant in certain fields and perhaps less so in others. Or to rephrase it from a different vantage point, authorial subjectivity seems to be relevant for some and not others. We are also too familiar with the artificial boundaries that divide the disciplines within the academy, so much so that people do not find it necessary to overstate the obvious. In the social sciences, Wallerstein (2001) has argued that this division of labor is the creation of nineteenth-century liberalism, which is maintained with even greater force today by institutions that we now call academic capitalism. By contrast, how does one know that similar forces are *not* at work to maintain the hierarchical division of labor that positions academia in the West vis-à-vis the rest, one of which contributes to an implicit, lingering ethnocentrism, not unlike the kind that Sakai sees as being endemic to the humanities? *Do identities matter?* I would say, in theory, not necessarily, and where they appear, coded in terms of a celebratory multiculturalism and emancipatory postcolonialism in particular, they *disguise* potential inequities of speaking position that serve in effect to harden existing regimes of academic practice and discourse. The fact that people continue to talk in terms of hard-and-fast identities is a sign, in my opinion, that the implicit stratified hierarchy and imperialistic exploitation prevalent more typically to a classic-era of unfettered capitalism and colonial imperialism still thrive today, albeit in a more sophisticated or sublimated form.

The least convincing aspect of Sakai's (and Said's) critique of Occidentalism relates to the silent other. The other may have been silent but *only* in Western discourse, which is a valid critique of the latter, but it does not resolve the question of what indigenous discourse amounts to. The latter is hardly silent, it may be in many cases uninteresting and uncritical in theoretical terms; I would add that its authorial authenticity is probably the least significant aspect of it. I have explored this problem elsewhere (see Chun 1995). Nonetheless, native discourses, especially prima facie Oriental Orientalisms, deserve to be critically examined in the same manner that Said and Sakai have problematized Occidental ones. Anticolonialist nationalist discourse often takes the form of a prima facie Oriental Orientalism, however, the main difference between these two forms of Orientalism is that ethnocentrism tends to be implicit in one case and overtly (if not blatantly) politicized in the other. Despite superficial, discursive differences, the authorial functions within a larger regime of institutional practices are probably very similar. However, in my opinion, the institutional functions are primary, because they are the source of authorial subjectivities. One should really be deconstructing in turn underlying institutional regimes and not simply conceptual representations.

I deliberately juxtapose the epistemological critique of Occidentalism with its nativist counterpart not just to contrast such discursive forms as two sides of the same colonialist coin but more importantly to argue that the relationship between the two, as signifying *regimes*, is mutually *complicit*. While I understand the pragmatic arguments about speaker distancing, I would argue that there are limits to which one can extend the meaningfulness or usefulness of speaker positionality, or for that matter *any* kind of subjectivity. Any dualism is dependent on both sides playing the same game, or both sides accepting the terms of its rules, as well as their respective roles. In this sense, the recognition of the global should at the same time be reciprocated by some recognition that others knowingly or unwittingly play the role of local.

If Eurocentric constructions of Oriental others and Oriental constructions of a cultural self are inherently different, *as a function of speaking position*, should one conclude that they *must* be different? Sakai's paper "You Asians" was first written at a conference held in Singapore, and provocatively titled "We Asians," without a doubt to suggest there is a difference between the two. Is there thus a difference between you Asians and we Asians, when one is supposedly gazing at the same object, and more importantly why *should* there be? I do not necessarily think that there should be any difference, but not for the usual empiricist reasons. I eventually argue that Sakai, despite his native sensibilities, really speaks from the position of you Asians, hence my rude attack on his own subjectivity. But by subjectivity I refer here to the positionality of the epistemic observer, or what he has termed *shukan*, in contrast to the positionality of the practical agent, which he has termed *shutai*. We have all heard similar criticisms voiced by Indian scholars about postcolonial theorists like Spivak and Bhabha. A cultural critic Evans Chan (2000) has referred to Rey Chow as "an American of Hong Kong origin," which among other things problematizes her particular notion of diasporic identity.

In short, why do we continue to assume that our ethnic identity is what determines our authorial subjectivity ipso facto, especially as intellectuals, all the while turning a blind eye to the equally (if not more) relevant forces that have shaped our epistemic subjectivities as Asian studies scholars, literary critics, social scientists, and so on? In our current era of politically enlightened criticism, which has rightly exposed the illusions of a previous era of scientific objectivity and naïve liberalism in various forms, we advocate speaking from positions of gender, class, ethnicity, or nation, as well as any combination of the above, as a function of how we perceive the nature of our complex engagement with the practical lifeworld. This subjectivity operates at a different level from the critical engagement that defines our identity as epistemic observer. It is easy to recognize that the values that define our subjectivity as epistemic observer and practical agent are different (they differ as a function of the quality of their engagement with the *context* of speaking and practice in which they are embedded), but it is more difficult to ascertain how to negotiate these different value systems in any context, because these situations are in fact different for different people. Just as the subjectivity of a practical agent is the product of multiple interests and intentions, which can conflict in any context of practice, there are always conflicts of interest between the values that influence my position as epistemic observer vis-à-vis those that influence my identity as a practical agent in my own life world. Of the two, it is more difficult to demarcate and spell out the values that define the position of the epistemic observer, but in the end it is always a process of strategic compromise. In short, discursive content, subjective positioning and quality of engagement with one's life world are in practice intertwined, often hopelessly so. That is the crux of it.

Globalization and Ethnicization as Entangled Processes

It is not necessary to invoke complex Deleuzian arguments about smooth society here. As a layman, it is easy to raise a few incongruous examples of what I mean, as an entrée for more serious discussion. In the current debate over globalization, one seems to waver often between definitions that attribute the global to the nature of the phenomenon, as distinct from its mode of institutional operation. McDonald's seems to be the typical global phenomenon, but McDonaldization refers in actuality to a particular mode of operation, which results in a genre of standardization or commoditization that is quintessential to globalizing processes. In this sense, the expansion of IBM or SONY and their products can be rightly characterized as globalizing. More importantly, there is nothing explicitly cultural about this globalization. Cultural promotion does not seem to be a prerequisite for this kind of capitalism; if anything, its mode of operation seems to be pan-cultural and glocal. Yet, as we all know, hamburgers were not the first food phenomenon to spread globally. Chinese cuisine has spread to more places throughout the globe and much earlier in history than the Big

Mac. The spread of New World spices to the Old World and the diffusion of European food that followed the first global traders in a classic era of Western imperialism have brought about much more change in the nature of traditional cuisines everywhere in the world than McDonald's, so why does one continue to assume that McDonald's is the first or paradigmatic example of global food?

Even though hamburgers and hot dogs have become the quintessential American food, we all know that they originated from Germany. Their diffusion from their ethnic homeland to the United States would at best be called an example of ethnicization, their creolization into a generic fast food product might be called Americanization, while their mass marketing throughout the rest of the world is called ipso facto globalization. The transformation of pizza from Italian ethnic food to its dissemination as globalized Pizza Hut product is equally paradigmatic. In effect, there is little in their transformation of substance that distinguishes these processes, yet we seem to think that ethnicization and globalization are inherently different, so much so that they cannot be used interchangeably. Is it not like the dualism of *humanitas* and *anthropos*?

Even more disturbingly, one seems to know a priori what is global and what is local, even before the phenomenon is invoked. There are even many global phenomena that have literally become universal, but they are rarely characterized as such. One does not call cars or phones global, much less Western; they are just modern. We seem to think that Japanese *tempura* and *tonkatsu* are quintessentially ethnic, despite their European origin, but will sushi ever become global? Some people think so, and it is not just a matter of substance or ethnic origin. In short, there are implicit value judgments associated with global and local, despite our best attempts to define them in neutral, analytical terms. Their relative positional status is one that inscribes or reflects a caste-like hierarchy. One might add to this the question of why these rankings become ethnically marked or culturally coded, when they are clearly not.

The Identity Crisis of Asian Studies within the Postcolonial Aura

Shifting from thoughts of food to food for thought, I think it is fair to ask analogous questions. Who are we in this globalized arena? Who are they? Why does one think that it is still important to refer to speaking positions? Finally, what is one talking about, really? The postcolonial aura has given many a misleading impression that Third World intellectuals have never been embraced or celebrated in the First World. Of course, they have. We all know that there have been at least several generations of Third World academics in the First World. The vast majority of such people has always worked in the natural sciences and will continue to do so. But this is irrelevant to postcolonialism, since there should be something about the nature of knowledge that makes postcolonialism what it is, other than one's identity, even though one is still hard pressed to say what it is. But to cite the example of humanities and social sciences, we know that the vast majority of ethnic Asian scholars in the West have always played a prominent role in Asian-related fields. They are, after all, the native or local experts. Yet ironically, a survey of many Asians there teaching Asian literature and history now or in the past will show that many (if not most) of them more typically had backgrounds in Western literature or history than in Asian studies per se. In my own case, although my region of expertise happens to be China, I have never considered myself a student of anything other than cultural studies or social science, broadly defined. I have never taught courses on Asia, although in the West this would be my expected area of expertise. When I taught most recently in the UK, I was classed ipso facto into Asian studies. The novelist Wole Soyinka's story is better known. Cambridge's English department routed his position to anthropology. African literature is apparently more African than it is literature. Even professors who had supervised me in anthropology never thought twice about my choice of area study, since presumably I was the native expert. Ironically, in fact, if one looks at anthropology in most of the Third World, one will find that the vast majority of Third World anthropologists end up studying their own society. One textbook definition of anthropology is that it is the study of other cultures, yet why do native anthropologists actually study their own society? One way of rephrasing this would be to say, anthropology is typically the study of other cultures, but *only* if one happens to be a white European. For all others, once a local, always a local. In the final analysis, these examples are not about code switching. The same displacement that invites Third World anthropologists to study their own culture also legitimizes the epistemic authority of Western anthropologists to study other cultures. It is the *same* for area studies. In Sakai's case, the global displacement that casts me as an Asian studies scholar in the West can also transform an Asian studies scholar in the West into a theoretician in the context of Asia, regardless of what we actually teach, write, or think. I raise such trivial experiences to show that choice or intention in identity in the larger order of things probably *counts* for very little. The institutional regimes that produce such categories of meaning are powerful and can be deeply embedded, especially when intertwined with other regimes and practices.

In order to satisfy my curiosity about the role of native scholarship in the production of global knowledge, I surveyed the history of Chinese students in the West, in reference to both their backgrounds and later professional transformations. The bibliographer Yuan Tongli compiled several volumes listing PhD dissertations by Chinese students from 1905 to 1964 in the United States and Europe.[9] The vast majority of students pursued degrees in science and engineering, but from the titles of PhD theses in these compilations, it is possible to see what proportion of them in social science and humanities is China related, how this proportion changes over time and between different fields, and whether these proportions differ in different countries. I did a simple comparison of three countries (USA, UK, and France) in reference to historical change and discipline (see Appendix table 1). I take China related in its broadest sense to mean anything related to China. I displayed the ratio of China-related to non-China-related theses both over history and across different disciplines. In general, the ratio hovers around fifty/fifty, although the ratio in France has consistently been closer to three to one. One can speculate about numerical differences here, but it is possible to view these ratios as being high or low. If one takes for granted that people study fields that are most directly relevant to their own interests or fields of knowledge, then this ratio may seem normal or low. After all, I doubt if the ratio of US students studying fields outside their own history or society is more than 20 percent. I expected the ratio of China-related theses to increase in the postwar era as well, which parallels the rise of area studies in the West, but this was apparently not the case, at least for Chinese students.

The breakdown by discipline, however, is more revealing. First, I should point out that only one of Yuan's volumes was subdivided according to discipline, yet I thought the disciplinary distinctions important enough to warrant a subjective determination. I stress subjective here, because I had to force categories on it on the basis of perceived relevance, in spite of where the degree was offered. I tended thus to classify topics like international law in Confucian thought under philosophy and Feng Hanyi's *The Chinese Kinship System* under anthropology. In assessing disciplinary breakdown in Europe, where the primary distinction is between the faculty of arts and the faculty of law (which incorporates the social sciences minus history and anthropology), it was necessary to use US-centric definitions for the sake of consistency. So said, there are fields that tend not to invite particular relevance to native knowledge, such as psychology, economics, business, and law. At the other extreme, there are fields that encourage students to work on their own culture and society, notably education, history, sociology, anthropology, and geography. Last, there are fields that could go either way, for example, political science, philosophy, linguistics, divinity, fine arts, and literature. The case of anthropology is quite peculiar. As one knows, anthropologists in China work on non-Han Chinese cultures; technically, this is called ethnology, but scholars working on Chinese rural communities, especially those trained by Fei Xiaotong, Malinowski's student in anthropology at LSE, tend to call themselves sociologists. Even with the non-Han ethnographies, it would be unusual to know that most Chinese anthropologists still end up studying their own society, especially, since we all know that anthropology is the study of other cultures. I would go as far to say that 100 percent of Chinese anthropologists work on their own society, or, put another way, their research, regardless of whether it is on Han or non-Han minority culture, is driven more by its direct or integral relevance to their own society. Moreover, if a study on China's border minorities were actually classed under any other discipline, in the West one would call it China related. Even if 99 percent of Chinese anthropologists study non-Han minorities, I would call it an aberration, contrary to strict disciplinary definitions. This is akin to saying that 99 percent of US anthropologists study American Indians, to the exclusion of the rest of the world. I have explored this particular problem elsewhere.[10] Nonetheless, it suffices to say here that such instances of disciplinary cross-dressing are hardly trivial or exceptional. They are in fact central to contradictions within the disciplines and to the way we (are forced to) *identify*.

I leave further discussion of these and other statistics to scholars on Chinese education, which allows me to focus further on the fetish of disciplinary cross-dressing. It is surprising perhaps to note that many of the best-known sinologists in the United States were not originally trained in fields or topics related to China. The most prominent examples include the following:

> Ho, Ping-ti (professor of Chinese history, University of Chicago), 1952, *Land and State in Great Britain, 1873–1910*, PhD Columbia
>
> Hsia, C. T. (professor of Chinese literature, Columbia), 1952, *George Crabbe 1754–1832*, PhD Yale
>
> Hsiao, Kung-chuan (professor of Chinese history, University of Washington), 1926, *Political Pluralism: A Study in Contemporary Political Theory*, PhD Cornell
>
> Cheng, Chung-ying (professor of Chinese philosophy, University of Hawaii), 1964, *Pierce's and Lewis' Theories of Induction*, PhD Harvard

Mei, Tsu-lin (professor of Chinese linguistics, Cornell), 1962, *Towards a Foundation for a Logic of Grammar*, PhD Yale

Yang C. K. (professor of Chinese sociology, University of Pittsburgh), 1940, *Marketing Institutions in Jackson Trading Area as Agencies of Community Integration*, PhD University of Michigan

Tsou, Tang (professor of Chinese politics, University of Chicago), 1951, *A Study of the Development of the Scientific Approach in Political Studies in the US, with Particular Emphasis on the Methodological Aspects of the Works of Charles E. Merriam and Harold D. Lasswell*, PhD University of Chicago

Fei, John Ching-han (professor of Chinese economics, Yale), 1952, *A Diagrammatic Representation of Certain Problems in General Equilibrium Theories*, PhD MIT

I cite these examples less to underscore scholarly dexterity by academic superstars (I think the most enviable example is Chao Yuen-ren, the father of Chinese linguistics, who earned a BA in math at Cornell and PhD in analytical philosophy at Harvard), than to suggest, first, that their ability to switch to sinology had to come from other than their academic training, strictly speaking, which was facilitated to a large extent by their native expertise. Needless to say, the primitive state of Asian studies could have been a deterrent or opening. Second, and more importantly, I doubt whether their PhDs in those topics could have gotten them jobs in China, especially in Chinese history or literature, which were ivory tower orthodoxies in their own right. I am sure that the considerations that led these people to switch to sinology were complex, to say the least. The Cold War and anti-Asian racism that continued into the early postwar era were explicit factors that could have contributed to stratification in US academia, either by limiting their future in Western studies or by facilitating their entry as native experts into sinology, yet this was a clear instance where identity counted for something, *but only in a Western context*. The only Chinese-born academic in the West I know who excelled in a field not related to sinology is Tuan Yi-fu, a well-known geographer and spatial theorist, who ironically is little-known in Chinese academia.

A student at Teachers College, Columbia, Kao Lin-ying, undertook an informative PhD thesis called "Academic and Professional Attainments of Native Chinese Students Graduating from Teachers College, Columbia University, 1909–1950." Although his study was limited to graduates of Teachers College, his depiction of the backgrounds and career transformations of those students were broadly applicable to most Chinese students at that time. Especially in the early years, students going overseas for study tended to be from a coastal city in China, and attend a Mission school and/or Mission college. As undergraduates, they tended to major in education or English. Thus, in comparison with other students, they had a solid grounding in English and were more cosmopolitan in influence. English language competence cannot be underestimated, even in later years. Kao (1951:65) explained this logic bluntly: "a very good student in China might turn out to be a very poor student in the US, simply because of his lack of English, and the reverse might also be true." Of those who graduated then went back to China, ironically few returned to teach in secondary schools, which should have been their goal of professional training at Teachers College.[11] Many used their US degrees to gain professorial positions; others secured administrative headships such as dean, principal, or college president; some became government ministers.[12] Most who remained in the United States abandoned education for business careers, while many women became housewives.

In short, posteducation professional transformations of all kinds tended to be the *norm* rather than the exception, and not all of them involved social climbing. One of the surprises in my crude tabulation of Chinese PhD recipients in the West was my discovery that literature degree holders accounted for very few of them. Especially given the postwar advent of area studies in the United States, this meant that teachers of Asian language and literature had to be one of the more expansive fields. But who were these people, and where did they come from to get to where they eventually went? Unfortunately, given the lack of exact data from 1964 on, one can just speculate, but my intuitions mostly parallel Kao's findings. As we know, many of the native Chinese-language teachers who stayed in the United States did not initially have relevant degrees in language training, which is a recent development. Many were graduate students in diverse other fields who for equally diverse reasons gave up other professions to become language teachers. Similarly, many students who finished their degrees and eventually stayed in US universities to teach Chinese literature did not initially have degrees in Chinese at all. Many had degrees in foreign literature or comparative literature, arguably more than Chinese literature. Some may have switched from foreign to Chinese literature after the MA degree, but few of them were top students in Chinese literature for the simple reason that even fewer were good enough in both Chinese and English to pursue Chinese literature overseas. In the same way, graduates in English literature switching to social science or humanities of all sorts while studying overseas were not an uncommon phenomenon at all. These are not just cases of code switching. Identification in such cases is really a product of *institutional relevance*.

Let me cite one other set of examples about disciplinary cross-dressing. I mentioned that many of the "native" experts teaching various fields of Chinese language and civilization in the United States could have originated from fields other than sinology, even English, but what about the Chinese students who pursued degrees in European literature and civilization there then eventually returned to their home country? Many, as one might expect, did in fact teach their strict fields of expertise, but not all. Few of them have recently become "postcolonial" intellectuals. I say this *facetiously* in Dirlik's sense of it. These examples say much about the meaning of "postcolonial," of the kind that has been invoked in the aftermath of Said's brilliant critique of Orientalism and that has been rightly criticized by McClintock, Shohat, Dirlik et al. as that theoretical mind-set, which has in turn been used to invoke an emancipatory imagination of various sorts, ranging from subaltern studies to nativist literature and native anthropology.[13] First, the object of criticism was really a *narrow* mind-set in Western literature. Second, I argue that there is nothing *inherently* emancipatory about nativism. Many Asian academics in history and anthropology who advocate so-called indigenous points of view and practice typical sinological research also happen to be theoretically uninteresting and critically unreflective. For those of us (including myself) who tend to be classified as "postcolonial," it refers to a species of "native" academic who publishes on the international circuit (i.e., in English), and more facetiously walks the walk and talks the talk. If I identify as postcolonial in these terms, albeit reluctantly, then it is mostly out of aversion to what I perceive as nativism. At the same time, there is nothing privileged about native knowledge. In criticism also of Dirlik's "postcolonial aura," which gives the impression that Third World scholars are recent mainstays in the metropole, nothing is further from the truth. The West has had generations of native scholars. More importantly, even if they began in academia by pursuing universal knowledge, they *still* ended up playing the role of local scholar in the larger stratification of things. This stratification is not the function of an inherent dualism between *humanitas* and *anthropos* per se. It is in reality a function of the institutional web of power that situates us all in an ongoing, evolving international division of academic labor.

My personal aversion to anything global is thus related to my fierce refusal to accept the role of local. It is a curse created by the global. The very use of these terms in a dualistic sense unwittingly maintains the caste-like hierarchy that stratifies all of us in a larger global division of labor. It is also a trap played equally unwittingly on both sides. I have been to too many conferences in Asia, where "we" Asians complain incessantly about the fact that we are relegated to playing the role of local area specialists, while Western-area specialists are ipso facto considered theorists. That is not entirely true. Clifford Geertz has written more books on Java than many Javanese experts write in a lifetime, but no one has labeled him an area specialist, even though he is eminently qualified to be one. These labels are castes of mind; more importantly within a global academic regime, these mind-sets have in the long run an eminently *politicizing* function. Why does one need such notions at all? While critical subjectivity, of all kinds, does serve a seminal function, it must be tempered with a critique of the institutions that bind us, sometimes beyond our power and despite our best intentions. Why can't we all just be free-floating intellectuals, at least in the real world? (Forget identity.)

If one can move beyond the ethnic politics of identity, I wish to argue that the more seminal problematic involves those qualities of engagement that characterize our identities as epistemic observer vis-à-vis practical agent. Contrary to claims of naive empiricism, they invoke subjective values that are not mutually opposed. Despite Sakai's problematizing of *humanitas* and *anthropos*, he does not really propose any corrective to transcend this inherent Eurocentrism other than to call for critical self-reflection. As an Asian studies scholar, is he suggesting also that *even* non-European specialists, like Asian studies scholars, should have a right to pursue European studies? Following up on Chakrabarty's invoking of Sakai's work in *Provincializing Europe*, I do not think it is such a bad idea. After all, anthropologists can study other cultures, so there is no reason why other ethnic, political, or historical perspectives cannot be used as modes of critical reflection for a hegemonic center. To mimic Sartre, it is just "a question of method." In my opinion, the subjectivity of the epistemic observer and the practical agent are not unrelated; they are just different modes of reflecting and engaging. I would say that, in practice, they can be viewed along the same continuum. If there is no universal *humanitas*, Sakai is suggesting that we can ethnicize it and show how it is grounded in European culture as well. Tom Nairn once said this about the "ethnicity" of philosophy:

> The true subject of modern philosophy is nationalism, not indus-
> trialization; the nation, not the steam engine and the computer.
> German philosophy (including Marxism) was about Germany in
> its age of difficult formation; British empiricism was about the
> Britons during their period of free trade and primitive industrial
> hegemony; American pragmatism was about the expansion of U.S.
> democracy after the closure of the Frontier; French existentialism

manifested the stalemate of 1789 Republicanism after its 20th century defeats—and so on. What philosophy was 'about' in that sense has never been just 'industrialization' (*contra* Ernest Gellner) but the specific deep-communal structures perturbed or challenged by modernization in successive *ethnies*, and experienced by thinkers as 'the world.' (Nairn 1998:17)

Thus, to rephrase Nairn in Sakai's terms, I would add that what starts out as *anthropos* in the subjective reflection of *shutai* in their engagement with local life eventually becomes generalized or made worldly by *shukan* as *humanitas*. There are similar cases of epistemic transformation in every cultural tradition of thought. "Abstract" social theory also started out as reflections on capitalism and modern reality. *It is not enough to say that ideology is colonially hegemonic.* In the process of epistemic transformation, it is possible to discover the roots of cultural value and reflective standard. Cultural value is by nature egocentric but reflective standards can be sociocentric, hence neutrally defined. If there is any meaning to intercultural/ interdisciplinary dialogue, it is because the possibilities of method are limitless.

I would argue that we are far from determining the parameters of our epistemic values and standards, even for our own intellectual disciplines, because we are still too enmeshed in the overt ethnicization of intellectual identity, when it is *ultimately* about how our disciplines and specializations force us to "subjectivize" and "evaluate," strictly speaking. I think part of the problem has to do with the distancing mechanism that dichotomizes the cultural other as a means of underscoring the superiority of the subjective self, which by extension would make anthropology Orientalist by virtue of its reification of other cultures. Such criticism is misplaced. As Tzvetan Todorov (1988) aptly phrased it, the *distance* between observer and observed is analytically distinct from the *detachment* from one's personal or cultural values that the epistemic observer must have in order to evaluate the objects of one's observation or study. The teaching of theory in its own terms is predicated on detachment, not distance. Otherwise, one would call it politicization. Misplaced reification of this kind in the long run mystifies the real nature of subjective reflection—and most importantly its critical function.

Epistemic subjects in various places in the world will continue to be separated by their positionalities within a hierarchy of power. How one defines the nature of epistemic method will in large part be decided ultimately by how one is able to negotiate one's interests or aims within this larger order of things. Distancing is a given, but there is always space for critical reflection, if that is what cultural studies is about, crudely defined. In this regard, epistemic observers, *of all kinds*, continue to play an important role in this, arguably much larger than the identity politics of recent debates surrounding postcolonial theory would seem to suggest.

There are ramifications here for Asian studies. The Orientalizing of Asian studies has its limits, thus by implication postcolonial calls for critical reflexivity. On the other hand, one cannot deny the influence of a different kind of ethnicization that has marginalized Asian studies within mainstream knowledge and stratified identity within an international division of academic labor. I argue ultimately that critical epistemic reflection is a function more of our engagement with the minefields of our respective discursive niches than how we happen to be positioned as persons within "the world." In any event, discursive content, subjective positioning, and practical encounter with one's lifeworld will remain hopelessly intertwined.

Afterword

From Geopolitics to Geopragmatics as a Mode of Subjective Engagement

Regardless of how one views the world theoretically, one is inevitably positioned implicitly or explicitly with reference to existing genres of thought or interpretation. In 1996, when I advocated defining identity as a discourse for representing public culture, it went contrary to prevailing notions of culture as "native's point of view" or subjective realities in the politics of identity.[1] By arguing that culture was a discursive instead of analytical category, I was, on the one hand, implying that culture was politicizing in ways that were incommensurable with basic anthropological definitions and, on the other hand, suggesting that it was a fiction that was constructed less with regard to any rooted, taken for granted reality than to ever-changing sociopolitical formations or geopolitical regimes. These discursive constructions reveal at a deeper level subjectivities of rule while mapping out the regimes and routines that define one's imaginative possibilities of being and acculturative processes of becoming, otherwise called identification. In an institutional sense, the nature of these formative regimes invokes in the first instance questions of the state and governmentality. They are rooted globally, insofar as the geopolitics of the state, nation, and empire must inherently be viewed in such a context. At the same time, this geopolitics is always locally grounded and negotiated.[2]

The incommensurabilities of culture and identification across societal boundaries derive in large part from the diverse specificities of these historical experiences and local grounds. Nonetheless, much of Asian studies continues to be framed within variations of the same generalized paradigms. Tradition versus modernity and the West versus East have given way to the imposition of East Asian models and recourse to neo-Confucian influences. Even if it is possible to divorce societal experience from the lineage of tradition and place, the history of societal transformations everywhere has been inextricably linked to larger narratives about nationalism, colonialism, capitalism, and globalization, which have been fraught with their own inconsistencies of definition and uncertainties of relevance. It is possible at the same time to regard Hong Kong, Taiwan, PRC, Singapore, and elsewhere as venues for problematizing the above processes and their mutually collusive relationships. One should instead argue that each represents an exemplar in its own terms of the permutation of general processes. In many respects, Hong Kong's transformation as both imperial subject and object established a unique dynamic that molded changing relationships between the polity, economy, and culture. The same can be said for nationalizing regimes in Taiwan and Singapore or the evolution of capitalism with Chinese characteristics. At the same time, our attempts to understand these distinctive features of historical experience have been marred by Eurocentric projections and flawed "theories." The writing of Hong Kong postwar history as a unilineal narrative of progress has in many respects sanitized the violence of colonial rule in the same way that it now portrays post-1997 Hong Kong as the battlefield for an inherent struggle over autonomy and democracy. The advent of capitalism in the PRC is embedded in changing narratives of capitalist theorizing that straddle neoclassical machinations about the market to neoliberal projections about the role of the state and rule of law. In addition to superficial accounts of *guanxi* capitalism, they fail to capture the formation of institutional regimes in their own terms.

If anything, this institutional context provides the point of departure for understanding identity formations and its inherent politics, which in turn demarcates the possibilities for pragmatic engagement. The systemic inculcation of cultural nationalism in Taiwan as a life regime has in many ways hardened the avenues of engagement with the PRC. Even with the indigenization of Taiwanese cultural consciousness, the prospects for effective autonomy remain dim. But on the other hand, who says that this relationship must be discursively rooted in such "truths" and cannot be actualized in other more constructive ways? Post-1997 Hong Kong and its relationship to the PRC are defined by another kind of entanglement. The emergence of an explicit identity conflict where none has existed previously or where differences were encoded in other terms inscribes the consequences of a relatively distinct kind of geopolitical terrain. I submit that this entanglement should invoke a different kind of pragmatic politics, one that is not necessarily determined by dualistic opposition (as is often implied by the emancipatory trajectories of a pure democratization movement). In any case, the politics of the China Triangle has long transcended the era of a Greater China fueled by hopes of transnational hybridity and multivocal appeal to the margin. Needless to say, the main factor is the shift in gravity created by a newly emergent China. It is difficult to ascertain to what extent the system can successfully maintain its intricate balance between a growth economy and ties linking capitalist interests to the politics and policies of state. It is evident only that its operation is governed by a different set of rules. It is first necessary to wake up to Chineseness. On the other hand, the prospects for change still depend to a large extent on what happens at its center. If geopolitics engenders by definition the diverse specificity of historical experience and local ground, then the pragmatics of social action can only follow from similarly or alternatively grounded identity constructions and life strategies. They cannot be predetermined or imposed by principle. One can also ask in this regard to what extent identity, whether as ethnicity, class, or human being, is in fact relevant as a political factor?

From the perspective of critical cultural theory from multiculturalist identity politics to postcolonial theory, the pragmatics of cultural resistance is largely based on oppositional politics. I would argue that a geopolitical approach to culture suggests the need for more complex practical (pragmatic) strategies. It may be the case that the development of postwar Taiwan society has predominantly been conditioned by the imposition of monocultural nationalism and the transformation of KMT rule to the present, which can easily explain the rigid, still largely inflexible ways that ethnicity and national identity have become intertwined. This may in the long term limit the parameters of ongoing change, but none of it is structurally preordained. They were the products of systemic sociopolitical forces, and it would take as much to undo or redo them. There were opportunities in the past for the Republic of China to become politically independent, if this is what the current desire is, and each time the force of predetermined intentions and impositions worked against it. The first was in 1949, when it abandoned the mainland, the second was after its ouster from the United Nations, and the third perhaps was during the Cultural Revolution. In each case, Chiang Kai-shek's resolve to recover the mainland and reunite China was the obvious reason why they were unthinkable options, in which case Taiwan has no one else to blame for losing the future. The breakdown in the PRC of a Maoist society was the turning point for a resurgent nationalist identity, but this emergent mind-set is the basis of popular support against threats to its perceived unity, rooted now in 3,000 years of historical civilization. Against this kind of identity mind-set, the emergence of Taiwanese consciousness may have successfully emancipated Taiwan from its oppression by alien mainlander rule, where "Chinese" is increasingly synonymous with foreign. But the extent to which such indigenous emancipation can be parlayed into legitimation rationale for national independence is, at least in the current climate, minimal. As I have argued, there is no reason why the geopragmatics of culture should be determined by the prison house of history. It is not necessarily wedded to real roots; much of early KMT rule was its attempted legitimation of an illegitimate regime to a point where many, or most, Taiwanese have successfully inculcated the various fictions buttressing such rule. It is always possible to construct new discursive and institutional "realities," which should in this case be predicated by thinking beyond the box.

The threat of a new *greater* China is equally real for both Taiwan and Hong Kong, but Hong Kong differs in one important respect: Taiwan can at least claim to be de facto independent of China; Hong Kong cannot. The political history of Hong Kong, vindicated most recently by its return to the motherland, is a simple enough reason to believe that it has never been independent, despite the historical provisionality and corresponding illusions of colonial rule. The geopolitics of Hong Kong has created moments of liminality and ambivalence in the formation of identity, but its experience has been radically different from that of postwar Taiwan. Far from inculcating a rigid national identity, Hong Kong had been, during the early postwar era, the battleground for competing nationalist identities then, largely as a result of its changing colonial rule—one characterized by disappearance and liminality, before its eventual return in 1997. The gradual cultural embrace of Chinese nationalism has been complicated more by its politicizing nature than by the changing gravitas of a PRC-based capitalist market. Its status is more similar to Xinjiang than it is to Taiwan. The rise of Taiwanese consciousness can serve the cause of emancipatory independence to a limited extent, but the same cannot apply to Hong Kong. The geopragmatics of cultural critique must take into account the embeddedness of Hong Kong to the larger political context of the PRC. If anything, postcolonial critique must adopt a different strategic practice beyond oppositional discourse and based on new possibilities of institutional engagement.

Part of confronting the challenges of a new geopragmatics depends on how one understands and can engage with the advent of this new *greater* China, viewed not only as a capitalist regime but more importantly as a geopolitical regime, within which its domination of a capitalist market serves as leverage for its imposition of political correctness. In this regard, the threat of such a capitalist regime is not just the nature of economic exploitation but rather the politicizing nature of its expanding regional, ultimately global, ambitions. Imperialism in its classical definition is not the most exact term to characterize this regime. Its success in the market, backed by popular support at home, is in the long run the basis on which it legitimizes the political institutions in which its invests its power and ideology. Predicting the demise of the economic order of things is probably easier than directly confronting the institutional power that drives its politics. But the recognization of its inherent politicization is more relevant and seminal than the intense attention paid in the literature to the economic development of capitalism in the PRC or continued future in Hong Kong and the fictitious diversions of "one country, two systems," however defined.

The nature of geopragmatics ultimately should have ramifications outside a Chinese sphere; it should be equally applicable to everywhere else in the world, characterized by one's distinctive geopolitical constitution. Asian studies has been especially complicit in perpetrating the cultural community of East Asia, driven by fictive neo-Confucian lineages and other models of affinity. If it is more productive to view relations within an ever changing greater China in terms of their distinctive geopolitical formations than presumed cultural affinities, the same can then be applied to a transnational context. The challenge is ultimately one that necessarily encourages us to think beyond the simplistic cultural critique of prevailing identity politics and postcolonial theories. It has always been one based on the politics of place and discursive imaginations and is one that leads ultimately to open-ended, localizing and differentiated geopragmatic strategic practices.

Appendix

Table 1. Doctoral Dissertations by Chinese Students, 1905–1964

Year	US China Related	US Non-China	UK/NI China Related	UK/NI Non-China	France China Related	France Non-China
1905–19	22	15	1	1	5	1
1920s	70	73	3	4	51	15
1930s	95	104	16	13	156	44
1940s	104	77	9	16	33	17
1950s	149	138	20	7	25	16
1960s	69	80	1	1	1	1

Discipline	China Related	Non-China	China Related	Non-China	China Related	Non-China
History	95	14	15	5	36	4
Education	105	60	2	0	7	2
Political Science	88	95	9	8	68	23
Economics	88	170	6	8	50	13
Psychology	9	44	0	5	0	4
Sociology	29	17	1	2	17	6
Anthropology	11	0	4	0	3	0
Geography	8	2	5	3	4	1
Philosophy	33	19	0	3	15	9
Linguistics	5	6	3	0	8	0
Literature	12	19	0	3	21	6
Fine Arts	4	2	0	0	3	0
Divinity	5	5	0	0	0	0
Law	18	27	5	5	39	26
Business	0	5	0	0	0	0
Journalism	0	2	0	0	0	0
TOTAL	509	486	50	42	271	94

Notes

Preface

1. "Fuck Chineseness: On the Ambiguities of Ethnicity as Culture as Identity," *boundary 2* 23(2):111–38 (1996).

2. "Discourses of Identity in the Changing Spaces of Public Culture in Taiwan, Hong Kong and Singapore." *Theory Culture & Society* 13(1):51–75 (1996).

3. "On the Geopolitics of Identity," *Anthropological Theory* 9(3):331–49 (2009).

4. See Wang Gungwu, "The Study of Chinese Identities in Southeast Asia," in *Changing Attitudes of the Southeast Asian Chinese Since World War II* (Hong Kong: Hong Kong University Press, 1988), 1.

Chapter 1

1. Pierre Ryckmans (1980:20) wrote that the book was "300 pages of twisted, obscure, incoherent, ill-informed, and badly-written diatribe."

2. As Said (1978:4–5) stated, "we must take seriously Vico's great observation that men make their own history, that what they can know is what they have made, and extend it to geography: as both geographical and cultural entities—to say nothing of historical entities—such locales, regions, geographical sectors as 'Orient' and 'Occident' are man-made. Therefore as much as the West itself, the Orient is an idea that has a history and a tradition of thought, imagery and vocabulary that have given it reality and presence in and for the West."

3. In the case of China, Western Orientalist scholarship can be viewed in this light. Changing views of China from the Enlightenment onward were more often a function of changing views than of a changing China. The discourse of Oriental despotism and hydraulic society is a case in point (March 1974). Early views of civilized China were based on favorable reports by Jesuit missionaries. This enlightened view suffered an eclipse by the eighteenth century. During this era, China was increasingly seen as the mystical, unchanging Other, paralleling Said's observations on Orientalist writings on the Arab world (see Zhang 1988, Qian 1940, 1941a, 1941b).

4. The seeds of Said's full-fledged critique of the Orientalist literature can be attributed to the influence of earlier works by Abdel Malek (1963), Asad (1973), and Laroui (1976). See also the discussion in Said (1985:93).

5. Said elaborated on this point more fully in a later essay when he (1989:217) remarked, "in fact there is no way that I know of apprehending the world from within our culture without also apprehending the imperial contest itself." Fabian (1990:756) made a similar point when he said, "if representation has to do above all with power, then it may not only be thought of as praxis but it is praxis."

6. Clifford (1988:260) pointed out in his discussion of Said's Orientalism that Said differed here from Foucault by suggesting that there is a real Orient that is distorted and is denied the authority to speak.

7. In discussions of the Orient, the Orient is all absence, whereas one feels the Orientalist and what he says as presence; yet we must not forget that the Orientalist's presence is enabled by the Orient's effective absence.

8. Eric Wolf (1988, 755) remarked, for instance, "China constituted less a society than a cultural world order."

9. The implicit Sinocentricism of this middle kingdom stemmed from their own perceived separation from the barbarians situated on the outside or periphery of their world (see Wang Ermin 1972:2 for an extended discussion).

10. Hu Houxuan (1990:368) argued that, although *zhongguo* was a term coined by the Zhou, it originated from *zhongshang* to denote an alliance of states that traced their cultural foundation to the Shang dynasty. Thus, Cai Xuehai (1981:139–40) maintained that the terms *zhongguo* and *huaxia* were essentially coterminous in meaning.

11. It was for this reason also that Tu Wei-ming (1991:1–6) can talk about a "cultural China" that was both living and continuous with the past.

12. There is a considerable literature on this subject, stemming independently from the work of Hobsbawm and Ranger (1983), Eisenstadt (1972), Keesing and Tonkinson (1982), and Linnekin (1983), among others.

13. According to Peng Yingming (1985:9–12), composite definitions of the nation that linked people (*minzu*) and nationalism to the principle of a common people (*minzu zhuyi*) were spelled out explicitly by Liang Qichao and Sun Yat-sen and were later influenced by foreign writings, like those of Joseph Stalin.

14. This is similar to what Fox (1990:3) called "ideologies of peoplehood."

15. See Dirks (1990) for a similar discussion of modern historical writing.

16. See Corrigan and Sayer (1985), Benjamin (1988), Cohn and Dirks (1988), and Thomas (1990) and Keesing (1989) for thoughts on the latter.

17. I agree here with Thomas's (1991:5) interpretation of Said's Orientalism as a mode of writing, which in its language of neutrality and objectivity represented a rhetorical device for legitimizing the self and the authority of colonial dominance. The imaginative character of its literary imagery that contributed to the exaggeration of the Other was actually a secondary, if not superficial, aspect of Said's Orientalism (see Richardson 1990).

18. Cui Chuiyan (1979, 3) argued that the influences of pragmatism and empiricism were implanted in Sun's Three Principles as a result of his Western train-

ing overseas. Zhang Hao (1987:189) noted here that the Three Principles focused in large part on the revolutionary character of nationalism and anti-imperialism. In contrast, emphasis on democracy (*minquan*) and livelihood (*minsheng*) was second-ary. See Chen Yishen (1987:742–43).

19. For a discussion of the "corporatist" nature of the KMT government and its relationship to Sun's thought, see Shen Zongrui (1990:19–24). Sun's emphasis on centralized control was based on his belief in the ability of strong government to combat imperialism in the larger global struggle for self-determination.

20. This was most clearly spelled out in a 1952 lecture titled "The Essence of the Three Principles" (*sanmin zhuyi de benzhi*), an excerpt of which is reprinted in Chen Yishen and Liu Arong, eds. (1987:107–20).

21. The policy of using the Three Principles as an ideological weapon against communism followed the overall practice of "using ideology to decide policy and using policy to decide human affairs."

22. Taiwan Provincial Government News Agency (1970, section 18, p. 2). A collection of essays written on the occasion of the Chinese cultural renaissance movement is reproduced in Taiwan Provincial Government (1967).

23. See Taiwan Provincial Government (1978).

24. As Huang Chun-chieh (1992:218–20) pointed out, even Confucian aca-demic discourse in postwar Taiwan tended to rally around a search for cultural identity, with factual investigation being a secondary concern.

25. As Wu Kunru (1981:72) remarked, "the present situation underlying the philosophy of The Three Principles is that it clearly lacks a holistic systematicity. Its scattered texts were mostly of a style that was consistent with a (Western) philosophi-cal framework. They were assembled to put forth an epistemology, a core ideology and a philosophy of life, but there was never an attempt to view the substance of The Three Principles as a primary consideration and to abstract from it an inherent mode of philosophical thought."

26. For a view of the influence of Confucianism and science on Sun's think-ing, see Shen Zongrui (1986:89–145).

27. These included works of a polemical nature such as Ye Qing's *Sanmin zhuyi gailun* (A General Treatise on the Three Principles), Fu Qixue's *Sanmin zhuyi dagang* (An Outline of the Three Principles), and *Guofu yijiao gaiyao* (An Overview of Sun Yat-sen's Teachings), Ren Ruoxuan's *Sanmin zhuyi xinjie* (New Perspective on the Three Principles), Tao Tang's *Sanmin zhuyi zonglun* (A Synthetic Discussion of the Three Principles), Ye Shoukan's *Sanmin zhuyi tong lun* (An Introduction to the Three Principles), Liang Yaokang's *Sanmin zhuyi sixiang tixi* (The Intellectual Framework of the Three Principles), Zhang Yihung's *Sunxue tixi xin lun* (New Look on Sun Yat-sen's Thought), Cui Chuiyan's *Guofu sixiang shenlun* (A Treatise on Sun Yat-sen's Thought), Jin Pingou's *Sanmin zhuyi conglun* (A Comprehensive Account of the Three Principles) and others bearing general reference to Sun's thought.

28. According to Liu Arong (1987:765–66), the most noteworthy of these included Cui Daiyang's *Guofu zhexue yanjiu* (A Study of Sun Yat-sen's Philoso-phy) and *Guofu sixiang zhi zhexue tixi* (The Philosophical System of Sun Yat-sen's Thought), Jiang Yian's *Guofu zhexue sixiang lun* (A Discussion of Sun Yat-sen's

Philosophical Thought), Zhou Shifu's *Sanmin zhuyi de zhexue xitong* (The Philosophical Framework of the Three Principles), Jin Pingou's *Guofu zhexue sixiang tiyao* (A Synopsis of Sun Yat-sen's Philosophical Thought), Ren Ruoxuan's *Guofu kexue sixiang lun* (Sun Yat-sen's Scientific Thought), Jiang Yian's *Guofu kexue sixiang lun* (A Discussion of Sun Yat-sen's Scientific Thought), Lin Guibu's *Minquan zhuyi xin lun* (New Perspective on Democracy), Yang Yujiong's *Guofu de zhengzhi sixiang* (The Political Thought of Sun Yat-sen), Lo Shishi's *Minsheng zhuyi xin lun* (New Perspective on Livelihood), He Haoruo's *Minsheng zhuyi yu ziyou jingji* (Livelihood and Liberal Economics), Ren Joxuan's *Minsheng zhuyi zhen jie* (The Truth of Livelihood), Zhou Jinsheng's *Sun Zhongshan xiansheng jingji sixiang* (The Economic Thought of Sun Yat-sen), Zhou Kaiching's *Guofu jingji xueshuo* (The Economic Principles of Sun Yat-sen), Su Zheng's *Pingjun diquan zhi lilun tixi* (The Theoretical Framework of Equal Land Rights). There were many other scholarly works specifically covering sociological, educational, legal and historical aspects of the Three Principles.

29. Major compilations included those edited on the occasion of Sun's ninetieth and one hundredth birthdays, such as *Guofu xueshu sixiang yanjiu* (Research into Sun Yat-sen's Intellectual Thought), edited by the *Guofu yijiao yanjiu hui* (Sun Yat-sen Studies Research Committee); *Guofu sixiang yu jindai xueshu* (Sun Yat-sen's Thought and Recent Scholarship), edited by Zhengzhong Publishing Co.; and anthologies brought out by Wenxing Publishing Co. titled *Sunwen zhuyi lun ji* (Essays on Sun Yat-sen's Thought), *Yanjiu Sun Zhongshan de shixue yu shiliao* (Historical Studies and Documentary Materials on Sun Yat-sen), and *Sun Zhongshan minsheng yanlun* (Sun Yat-sen's Lectures on Livelihood).

30. In his discussion of the various methodological techniques employed by scholars to do textual analysis of the Three Principles, Ge Yongguang (1990:491–95) has suggested that the looseness of interpretation used to force a meaningful synthesis of Sun's scattered texts also permitted scholars in a subsequent era to conduct social scientific research in fields loosely subsumed under the name of the Three Principles where in fact little or no reference to Sun's work was ever made.

31. This was taken directly from Academia Sinica's *General Information Handbook* 1984 and 1988, published and updated regularly by Academia Sinica.

32. See the forum discussion in Hung Quanhu et al., eds. (1990:529–31).

33. The explicit emphasis in all these courses on cultivation of a higher national collective conscience cannot be understated. In chapter 72 of volume 6 of the textbook *Citizenship and Morality*, used at the elementary-school level, no less than 1,387 references can be found to words invoking nationhood, China, patriotism, society, and world (not even counting less exact references to Chinese culture, the people, etc.). In contrast, only 298 references were found to words invoking individuals and individuality (see Zheng Rongzhou 1989:40).

34. As Liu Dingxiang (1989:65) clearly noted, "from the goals and aspirations of this kind of education, it would appear that 'party-based education' [*danghua jiaoyu*] did not have a strong aim of creating an ideological regime; on the contrary, one could even say that the enlightenment of democracy [*minzhu qimeng*] and the development of rationality [*lixing de zhankai*] were the means to promote

the education of political liberation. In this regard, the primordial meaning of Party-based education was to view education as the agent of revolutionary change, democratization, scientific progress and socialization."

35. The influence of Chiang Kai-shek's particular focus on personal hygiene and practices of the body in relation to Sun's understanding of livelihood cannot be exaggerated. Perhaps not unlike Elias's (1978) understanding of the civilizing function of etiquette and manners, which prefigured the control of the emotions crucial to the evolution of a rational disciplinary lifestyle, clearly from an ontogenetic perspective, the health of the body was prerequisite to the practice of moral conduct and in turn became the basis for understanding civics and society.

36. Lin Yuti (1985:29) noted that merit points were earned on one's achievement report (*chengji kaohe*) for these two activities.

Chapter 2

1. In cultural studies, Willis's *Learning to Labour* (1981) is cited as a pioneering work in education, even though it was less about the school than the making of class culture in E. P. Thompson's terms.

2. The later work of Emile Durkheim (1961) stressed the moral nature of education, which explicitly accented its ethical content and disciplinary function. Shoko Yoneyama's (1999) study of school violence in Japan focused on authoritarian intensity rather than normative "rationality" as the inherent source of institutional domination.

3. As Weber (1976:332) pointed out for France, "we come to the greatest function of the modern school: to teach not so much useful skills as a new patriotism beyond the limits naturally acknowledged by its charges. The revolutionaries of 1789 had replaced old terms like schoolmaster, regent and rector, with *instituteur*, because the teacher was intended to *institute* the nation. But the desired effect, that elusive quality of spirit, was recognized as lacking in the 1860's and 1870's."

4. Paul Bailey (1990) aptly characterized the evolution of popular education in early Republican era China as one of "reforming the people," which underlined its focus on mass education. In this sense, education was not just nationalist in a broad sense but also Nationalist, insofar as it was interpreted and disseminated ideologically by the KMT, literally Nationalist Party.

5. Ruey Yih-fu (1972) once argued that *jiao* (education as "teaching") was an important counterpart to a Chinese understanding of culture, different from the term *wenhua* (which tended to invoke the notion of a literary based culture). Acculturation was not just dependent on concrete institutions of learning but more precisely education in the abstract, as ritually transformative practice.

6. For a detailed history of Chinese education from ancient to present times, see Cleverley (1991).

7. There were many ethnographic studies that have dealt with education in contemporary China, most notably the collection of essays by Liu et al., eds.

(2000). One can compare this with the essays in Postiglione and Lee, eds. (1998), which focused more on pedagogical aspects of school in Hong Kong.

8. Frederick Wiseman's film *High School* suggested that discipline is a staple fact of all schools.

9. Perhaps contrary to McVeigh's (2000) description of Japan's cult of school uniforms, students in Taiwan generally wore uniforms with reluctance and disdain associated with state control.

10. Schoenhals's (1993) ethnography of a school in the PRC has focused largely on face relationships and the way such cultural behavior complemented or stemmed from socialization within the family.

11. Following Corrigan's (1990) use of the term, *moral regulation* should be understood here in a Durkheimian sense, where the obligatory nature of moral rules necessitates social control.

12. See Hughes and Stone (1999:985–89) for an overview of policy changes in the curriculum.

13. It is difficult to translate the term *chengshi*, except to say that it means honesty in the sense of being sincere (as an attribute of one's moral behavior) rather than being epistemologically true.

14. The socializing role of schools was what Weber (1976:303) neatly called "civilizing in earnest."

15. Japanese scholars, such as Iwama (1995), reiterated the collectivist ethos of conformity. For China, Gardner (1989) reproduced the same kinds of dualisms between Western individualism and traditional Chinese discipline through apprenticeship and pattern maintenance.

Chapter 3

1. This was, of course, an extension of ideas initially presented by Claus Offe (1985). My usage of transnational capitalism follows from discussions therein. Contrast this with Held et al. (1999).

2. The DPP, founded largely in opposition to the ruling KMT (hence *dangwai*), was quite explicitly founded on a policy platform of "Taiwan for the Taiwanese." Without a doubt, factions within the DPP represent different variations of Taiwanese ethnic nationalism. On the surface of things, there has been much overlap in the ethnic positions advocated by both the KMT and DPP. This was partly a deliberate attempt by the (Taiwanese faction of the) KMT to co-opt "the middle ground" of the Taiwanese populace. The KMT has generally tended to view local culture and identities as constituent elements within a more inclusive Nationalist polity.

3. Ethnic indigenization started actually in the pre–martial law era during the presidency of Chiang Ching-kuo, who proclaimed himself to be Taiwanese, despite his ethnic roots in Zhejiang. He picked Lee Teng-hui, a native Taiwanese

(Hakka), as his successor in order to ease tensions between native Taiwanese (*ben-sheng ren*) and Chinese mainlanders (*waisheng ren*). Lee Teng-hui in turn organized a predominantly Taiwanese faction within the KMT, which for many years held ground against a DPP that was born from grassroots Taiwanese sentiments. Cultural centers devoted to the archivalization of Taiwan history and culture were created as part of larger efforts at social reconstruction directed by the Committee for Cultural Development (*wenhua jianshe weiyanhui*).

4. Following official directives by the Ministry of Education, departments for multicultural studies (*duoyuanzhuyi wenhua yenjiusuo*) were established in several teachers' colleges to promote the study of multiculturalism (which means here aboriginal minority studies), even though no one had ever been trained in such a discipline and its practitioners had come from various other fields.

5. The notion of borderless economies follows Kenichi Ohmae's (1990) usage. The term *glocal* has been used widely, but its actual or exact origins are uncertain. See Roland Robertson (1992).

6. The most comprehensive treatment of transnational migration is perhaps Glick-Schiller et al. (1994). While such transnational labor movement within Asia has also been intense, it has not led to the fluid migration patterns characteristic in the West. See, for example, essays in Kris Olds et al. (1999).

7. See Appadurai (1990) for a paradigmatic statement.

8. I have made this general point in a paper written in 1996.

9. It is interesting to note that, since the establishment of the Chinese Republic in 1911, there has only been one systematic revision of the Basic Nationality Law of 1929, this being in 2000.

10. Unlike the multiculturalism of marginalized "foreigners," such as Japanese spouses from the colonial era, who decided to settle down in postwar Taiwan and whose assimilative fate relegated them to a cruel nonexistence, the blind eye turned to the multicultural status of the privileged was designed to enable those at the top strata of society to maintain their cosmopolitan elitism.

11. The Sinicization of the social sciences movement first took off with the publication of a series of essays edited by Yang Kuo-shu et al. (1982). Psychologists have in recent years organized an ongoing forum on "indigenous psychology," with publications appearing in their journal *Bentu xinlixue*.

12. See my 2000 essay for full details of this argument.

13. See Wolf (1982). The problem of linkages is different from that of systemic transformation.

14. This oft-cited term first appeared in Harvey (1989).

15. Thus, the challenge of globalization and multiple or truly fluid nationalities is less a problem of realizing a global ideal than one of directly confronting deeply embedded cultural definitions.

16. In this regard, there is no reason to believe that even strict definitions of the bounded nation-state, which are a product of modernity, cannot be fundamentally altered in legal-political terms.

Chapter 4

1. Perhaps the most comprehensive of these studies is the two-volume work by Jean and John Comaroff (1991).

2. Representative works here are those of Fabian (1986) and Viswanathan (1989). Fabian is interested particularly in showing how choice of language was a means to maintain hierarchical distance between colonizers and colonized, while Viswanathan shows that literary study of English served technocratic, utilitarian and civilizing functions in the maintenance of colonial hegemony.

3. The work of Said (1978) has spawned a minor cottage industry that does not need elaboration here. Likewise, colonialism has made the writing of history and resistance to imperial history (as in subaltern studies) important and inevitable enterprises in the process of political legitimation and public reconstruction.

4. See especially the works of Pratt (1992) and Thomas (1994).

5. The work of Burrow (1966) and Stocking (1968) in particular shows that the Victorian concept of race has roots in ideologies and institutions quite independent of colonialism, although there can be no doubt that colonialism can be used to institutionally intensify racial differences, among many other things.

6. France's (1969) analysis of the changing discourse of land policy in the construction of a Fijian tradition shows how such indirect rule was the cumulative result of individual interpretations of policy principles and native custom.

7. In addition to the work of France (1969), Clammer (1973) has detailed the role of colonialism in inventing Fijian tradition on the basis of their perception of social organization and their synthesis of a unified set of customary laws. Also, Thomas (1990) has noted contradictions of the state's nonintervention in "preserving" Fijian custom and their intervention in the disciplinary reordering of routine life in other regards. In the context of India, Dirks (1992a) has emphasized that caste was a political construction of the colonial state, paralleling earlier arguments put forth by Cohn (1984) regarding the objectification of social structure in the census.

8. See Bennett (1988) and Stocking (1987) for different views on the evolution and function of archivalization and cultural classification, which emerged with the birth of the museum in the Victorian era.

9. According to Corrigan, this notion has roots in Durkheim's arguments about the obligatory nature of moral rules that are really at the heart of social norms.

10. As Corrigan and Sayer (1985:3) put it, "the state never stops talking."

11. The British were probably wrong in their "assessment." As Rawski (1972:19) pointed out, the longer the period of the lease and especially in the case of perpetual leases, the greater the degree of freedom exercised by the tenant over the land vis-à-vis the landlord. Economically, it provided cultivators with incentives to increase productivity, given guarantees of fixed rent for the duration of the lease (Kamm 1977:63, Rawski 1972:18), and politically it provided a high degree of autonomy and self-regulation in everyday affairs. This self-assertion and independence on the part of the tenant was a result of the contractual nature of

such a "one-field, two-lord system" (*yitian liangzhu*) and led Rawski (1972:20) to remark in conclusion, "custom was on the side of tenant and not the landlord."

12. The Chinese government repeatedly maintained that the leased territory had the same status as trade concessions or "settlements" at the treaty ports. It never relinquished its right of sovereignty over the territory and its citizens. As late as the 1930s, China continued to assert its "landlord" status, one instance of which involved the granting of mining licenses in the territory and fishing licenses in the waters of the Colony. Dr. Philip Tyau, special delegate for foreign affairs for Guangdong and Guangxi argued that the Chinese government held authority to grant licenses in both cases on grounds that the New Territories and Kowloon City were not part of the Colony proper of Hong Kong and that, as the British consul-general at Canton paraphrased him, "China has by no means forfeited all her rights *as ground landlord* in these territories, and the adjoining waters under the lease agreement" (Wesley-Smith 1980:167, compare to CO129/564, emphasis mine).

13. As Groves (1969:48) rightly pointed out, both the tone and content of these proclamations more often than not had an effect that was contrary to intended aims. Instead of advocating noninterference with local practices on the land, for instance, proclamations appeared to advocate more stringent control over them, and instead of advocating self-government they made village elders appear like pawns within an autocratic system of administration. Or as Groves (ibid.) put it, "control over both land and political institutions appeared to be at risk."

14. The reaction by Ping Shan villagers to an announcement of the construction of the first police station was explicit:

> It says that land, buildings, and customs will not be interfered with but will remain the same as before. Why should they therefore, when they first come into the leased area, wish to erect a police station on the hill behind our village? When has China ever erected a police station just where people live? The proclamation says that things will be as before. Are not these words untrue? (CREBC 1900:261)

15. See King's (1975) discussion of "administrative absorption of politics," which was quite relevant to the common perception of an innately "apathetic" political culture in Hong Kong, especially during the 1970s.

16. Law Wing-sang (1992:5) attributed the colonial government's policy of promoting economic growth through administrative efficiency and autocratic control to a strategy or rhetoric of "managerial-corporatism."

Chapter 5

1. Matthew Turner's "Made in Hong Kong" exhibit is influential in this regard (Turner and Ngan [1995], eds.).

2. My notion of geopolitics follows from the above.

3. The notions of imagined community and cultural identity here are intertwined.

4. See Kam Kin Hung (1988). In its early years, editors had ownership shares.

5. See in particular the special issue on Hong Kong culture edited by Leung Ping Kwan (1995) for *Haowai*, issue 226 that focused primarily on the role of *Haowai*.

6. See especially Siu Kwok Wah (1984). One could also call this "academic non-academicism."

7. See Yau Sai Man (1995).

8. One in-house ad is reproduced in Lui Tai Lok (2007), ed., p. 188.

9. Jurgen Habermas (1989). Gramsci resonates here too.

10. Chan Koon Chung (1988). The Attitude and Style Manual served as an editorial preface in each issue.

11. Max Horkheimer and Theodor W. Adorno (1989), pp. 120–67. Criticism focused on the inherent tendency within capitalism as industry to transform mass culture into objects of commoditized consumption.

12. Lui Tai Lok (2007) ed. This compendium was initiated by the publisher, not the magazine.

13. Lui Tai Lok (2007) ed., p. 238, originally *Haowai*, issue 225 (1995).

14. Lui is probably correct to argue that *Haowai*'s promotion of a uniquely hybrid Hong Kong culture was not an explicit program designed from the outset but rather something that became consciously apparent many years after the fact. See also Chan Koon Chung's (2007) essays.

15. Peter Wong (1992). Wong served as managing editor of the magazine for much of the last two decades.

16. See Patterson (1994). Any society can thus be viewed as a set of overlapping and competing cosmopolises.

17. Gilroy (1993) underscored the contribution of Blacks to the development of modernity in the West.

18. Leo Lee (1999) argues that Shanghai served as a nostalgic "other" for Hong Kong. Postwar Hong Kong was, in my opinion, largely a forward-looking entity; its cosmopolitanism transcended urban modernity.

19. Chan Koon Chung (1982); he has recently focused more explicitly on urban hybridity and cosmopolitanism.

Chapter 6

1. For a report on Chan's talk, see the essay by Chris Yeung titled "Role of Civil Servants Comes Under Scrutiny" (South China Morning Post, July 1, 1998).

2. In this regard, the most representative works are Hugh Baker (1993) and Lau Siu-kai (1981).

3. I have made this basic argument more systematically in a previous publication (Chun 1996).

4. Writings by Western authors can be divided into two camps, those sympathetic to the British legacy, such as Adley (1984), Lamb (1984), Johnson (1985), and Rabushka (1997), and those critical of the colonial sellout of Hong Kong, such as Nicholson (1992), Atwood and Major (1996), Thomas (1996), and Ingham (1997). Local writers, such as Wong (1984), Liang (1995), Kwok (1996), and Lau (1998), have, on the other hand, tended to be more concerned with the ability of Hong Kong to remain autonomous and threats of Chinese hegemony.

5. Much has been said about the search for an unknown Chineseness that dominated Hong Kong films in the transitional era as well as the sense of ambiguity that a generation of youth brought up in colonial Hong Kong felt in being forced to identify with an alien culture. On handover night (Lilley 2000:179), reported a fifteen-year-old girl's dream where "she is on stage about to sing the Chinese national anthem. She is holding a flag and the audience is muttering in *putonghua*. Suddenly she realizes that she knows neither the melody nor the words."

6. As a result of the Sino-British Declaration of 1984, the Hong Kong Education Department drew up guidelines on civic education, one in 1985 and another in 1996. The priority of more recent guidelines was clearly the inculcation of values pertaining to the national community. As a PRC educator, Li Yixian (1996:254), put it, the curriculum should be refocused to accent "love of the country and nation, as well as education in the proper social behavior." Hughes and Stone (1999) note important parallels in the relationship between nation-building and curriculum reforms in Hong Kong and Taiwan, despite their concrete differences. The implementation of the actual guidelines in Hong Kong during the post-1997 era remains unclear and unexplored, however.

7. Chinese dissidents represented the harshest critics of China's intentions, citing political motives of various sorts. See, for instance, Yao Biyang (1995) and Ho Ping and Gao Xin (1998).

8. Even Martin Lee, leader of the democratic movement in Hong Kong was surprised. In late July, he noted that Chinese government officials had been quiet on Hong Kong issues and "we no longer hear intimidatory remarks from Beijing as we did when the last governor was here."

9. Frank Ching (1998:218) noted that the preparatory committee created in 1996 to oversee the handover was abolished, as were other bodies that had been seen as potential instruments for interfering in Hong Kong affairs.

Chapter 7

1. Geertz's choice of terms such as *lek* and *nisba* to reflect underlying features of Balinese and Moroccan life, respectively, has underscored his primary emphasis on language as a methodological point of departure.

2. *Renqing* is similar to what Fried (1953) termed *ganqing* (sentiment in an emotive sense).

3. Both quotations were cited in Ho (1976:867).

4. The work of King and Myers (1977) is a paradigmatic example in this regard.

5. The ambivalence between altruistic and egoistic dimensions of face is typified by political leaders who claim to "serve the people," yet are at the same time "power hungry," for example, Willy Stark in the novel *All the King's Men*.

6. Hwang's (1987:948, fig. 1) theoretical model of face and favor illustrates the dyadic interaction between these kinds of ties, insofar as they are driven by what he calls "the dilemma of *renqing*."

7. In other words, if *guanxi* just refers to ties of personal trust, it would not be necessary to invoke its cultural specificity, because this sentiment is probably universally present in every culture. It would not be necessary to gloss it by highlighting the Chinese term. The sociological necessity of networking and moral sentiment has already been well articulated by social theorists beginning from Durkheim on.

8. See, for example, Hamilton ed. (1996), which epitomizes the efforts of many transnational projects. Other recent works include Redding (1993) and empirical studies in Yeung and Olds, eds. (2000).

9. Later works, such as Bosco (1993), reiterate the predominance of *guanxi* as a *phenomenon*.

10. Cited in Walder (1983:61).

11. Her argument in this regard is a significant expansion of an earlier paper (Yang 1989).

12. It is not my aim to speculate on the nature of this socio-politico-economic system, except to say that the use of *guanxi* in a newly emerging institutional regime is less a deliberate recourse to traditional ethics than a function of shifting spaces within the system that must be viewed as a synthetic response or attempt at reconstruction. Essays by Pieke (1995) and Dirlik (1997) offer differing views on the appropriateness of socialist capitalism, capital socialism or other terms to characterize the nature of this presumed "fit" between *guanxi* and capitalism.

13. Douglas Guthrie's (1998) counterargument that the *guanxi* phenomenon has actually declined in the period where others have seen a renaissance is bit misleading. His narrow focus on a privileged strata of modernizing state apparatuses takes Shanghai as the model, which is hardly representative of general patterns seen elsewhere.

14. This being the real topic of my essay, all of the above can be considered a long preamble.

15. The open and public nature of discussing *guanxi* strategies in newspapers, which then gave rise to the term *guanxixue*, is similar to the uninhibited nature of sex advice columns written by Ann Landers or Dr. Ruth. It is predicated on the acceptance of what was taboo behavior as now normal, if not morally condoned.

16. In my academic workplace in Taiwan, I am supposed to refer to my colleagues, especially in a public context, such as an Institute meeting, as *tongren* (the Confucian equivalent of comrade).

17. "Crony capitalism" is a paradigmatic case in point. The humane, "altruistic" intentions that drive the process of gift reciprocity should not detract from the fact that it is socially corrupt.

18. It is interesting to note that both Kipnis (1997) and Smart (1993) invoke Bourdieu, but in different ways. In my opinion, neither of them exploits successfully

the concept of practice to explain how *guanxi* is a function of changing contextual strategies *and* perceptual meanings.

19. The complexity of gift-giving behavior, even as *guanxi*, is attributable to the fact one can never be sure of the intentions of the other, yet the significance of the act depends precisely on claiming to be able to understand its intentions and meanings. Shifts between altruistic acts of friendship and attempts to gain instrumental favor are subtle, complicated by the fact that both are manifested by the same visible sometimes intense acts of gift reciprocity. See Smart (1993) for an account of gifts, *guanxi*, and bribes, from a "Bourdieuan" perspective.

20. To demonstrate the complexity of possible permutations, I can cite a personal experience. On the eve of an operation to remove a spleen from my sister-in-law, my father-in-law went to the house of the surgeon. Both were professors at the same university in Taiwan, but they did not know each other personally. In paying a personal call, my father-in-law exchanged courtesies and gave the surgeon two bottles of whiskey and a large sum of cash. Neither the gift nor money was considered an inappropriate thing to give a doctor in this context, as a matter of customary practice. While the surgeon accepted the gifts, that next morning his wife went to my father-in-law's house to return the money, because it was inappropriate in light of their collegial relation (as *tongren*). In Japan or Singapore, as in most modern societies, such gift-giving would be considered improper. In all the above, traditional custom is not a given fact but must always be viewed vis-à-vis professional and other ethics.

21. At academic conferences, it is common knowledge or accepted etiquette not to openly criticize colleagues, even if papers are bad, for the same reasons of saving face and maintaining amicable relations.

22. The ritual revivalism of late Qing Confucianists sparked a popular proliferation of customary etiquette handbooks, many of which prescribed in intricate detail the nature and precise amount of gifts that had to be given at particular stages of various domestic rituals. See the case examples presented in Chun (1992).

23. Mauss (1967, xiv) cites a passage from *The Havamal*, the first few lines of which read as follows:

> I have never found a man so generous and hospitable that he would not receive a present, nor one so liberal with his money that he would dislike a reward if he could get one. Friends should rejoice each other's hearts with gifts of weapons and raiment, that is clear from one's own experience. That friendship lasts longest—if there is a chance of its being a success—in which friends both give and receive gifts.

24. Despite Duran Bell's (2000) attempt to transcend a transactionalist approach to gift exchange, his emphasis on *guanxi* as a nesting of groups based on an extensionalist notion of relationship that goes beyond the personal scope of connection is misguided. First, I fail to see how tribute-for-protection is a general extension of *guanxi* relationships in any of the Chinese contexts that I am familiar with. He also fails to account for the dimension of power that is central to Hwang's analysis of face, which the latter sees as culturally motivated.

Chapter 8

1. As Frank Ching (1998) noted, the Hong Kong media tread more cautiously in news pertaining to China, that is, news and information that required the cooperation of Chinese agencies and China-backed companies. As Michael Curtin also noted, the boundaries of media openness and closeness was a function of the fact that the Hong Kong media was not a local entity anymore but one whose market depended on expansion into China. As he (1998:288) put it, "this strategy of expansion into the mainland market thus requires the cooperation of government officials, if the industry is going to reap the benefits of its popularity."

Chapter 9

1. As Kam Louie (2011:77–78) put it, "China's recent economic and political rise has produced a concomitant surge in interest in 'Chinese' culture. Into this discursive space, the government of the People's Republic of China (PRC) has offered Confucianism to domestic and international audiences hankering to locate 'China's uniqueness' as the key emblem of Chinese culture and paramount symbol of Chinese civilization. Confucius and Confucianism have become China's 'brand' in a world where national identity is marketed for political spin."

2. As Jamie Peck (2010:9) phrases it, "neoliberalism, in its various guises, has always been about the capture and reuse of the state in the interests of shaping a pro-corporate, freer-trading 'market order.'"

Chapter 10

1. James Clifford's "Diasporas" (1994) is an attempt to extend the usage of diaspora beyond its literal status to accent its role in articulating difference, suturing fractures, and engendering new connections and communities by celebrating its tacking gestures, border crossings, strategies of negotiation, and counterhegemonic challenges.

Chapter 11

1. Various Confucian scholars weighed in on the Asian values discourse and included, perhaps most prominently, Tu Wei-ming (see Tu Wei-ming et al., eds. 1992) and Wm. Theodore deBary (1998).

2. Or as Gupta and Ferguson (1992:19) aptly put it, in the context particularly of a culture industry dominated overwhelmingly by multinational corporate interests and promoted in the mass media, "the 'public sphere' is therefore hardly 'public' with respect to control over the representations that are circulated in it."

3. Friedman's (1992:360–62) useful attempt to schematize a panorama of cultural strategies represents an important contribution toward outlining how different local impulses, practices, movements, and strategies are implicated in global processes that distribute fields of immanent identification in the world arena.

4. See Appadurai (1990), Lash and Urry (1987), Deleuze (1988), and Hardt and Negri (2000), in particular.

Chapter 12

1. See Chun (2004).

2. See Chun (2006).

3. The most representative work is Clifford (1983).

4. See Dirlik (1994); the essay was reprinted in his book of the same name (Boulder: Westview, 1997), 52–83.

5. See Said (1979) (one of many versions).

6. See Sakai (2000) (first given at *We Asians: Between Past and Future: A Millennium Regional Conference*).

7. This term was articulated clearest in Said (1989).

8. Chun (1996); see last section in particular.

9. Yuan (1961, 1963, 1964); Li (1967).

10. See Chun (2001).

11. Kao (1951:97).

12. Kao (1951:98).

13. McClintock (1992); Shohat (1992).

Afterword

1. See "Discourses of Identity in the Changing Spaces of Public Culture in Taiwan, Hong Kong and Singapore," *Theory Culture & Society* 13(1):51–75 (1996). There are ramifications here also for the politics of difference.

2. Rather than view nationalism, colonialism, globalization, and capitalism as specific niche processes, I suggest viewing them as broader institutionalizing, acculturating, and normalizing regimes, which have ramifications for the nature of identification. See "On the Geopolitics of Identity," *Anthropological Theory* 9(3):331–49 (2009).

Bibliography

Abbas, Ackbar (1997) *Hong Kong: Culture and the Politics of Disappearance*, Minneapolis: University of Minnesota Press.

Abdel Malek, Anwar (1963) Orientalism in Crisis, *Diogenes* 44: 107–08.

Abrams, Philip (1988) Notes on the Difficulty of Studying the State, *Journal of Historical Sociology* 1(1):58–89.

Adley, R. (1984) *All Change Hong Kong*, Poole, Corset: Blandford Press.

Allen, Jamie (1997) *Seeing Red: China's Uncompromising Takeover of Hong Kong*, Singapore: Heinemann.

Anderson, Benedict (1983) *Imagined Communities: Reflections on the Origins and Spread of Nationalism*, London: Verso.

Appadurai, Arjun (1990) Disjuncture and Difference in the Global Cultural Economy, *Public Culture* 2(2): 1–24.

——— (1991) Global Ethnoscapes: Notes and Queries for a Transnational Anthropology, in *Recapturing Anthropology*, ed. R. G. Fox, Santa Fe: School of American Research Press, pp. 191–210.

Arrighi, Giovanni (2007) *Adam Smith in Beijing: Lineages of the Twenty-First Century*, London: Verso.

Asad, Talal (1973) Two European Images of Non-European Rule, in *Anthropology and the Colonial Encounter*, ed. T. Asad, New York: Ithaca Press, pp. 103–18.

Atwood, L. Erwin & Anne-Marie Major (1996) *Goodbye, Gweilo: Public Opinion and the 1997 Problem in Hong Kong*, Cresskill: Hampton Press.

Bailey, Paul J. (1990) *Reform the People: Changing Attitudes Towards Popular Education in Early Twentieth-Century China*, Vancouver: University of British Columbia Press.

Baker, Hugh D. R. (1993) Social Change in Hong Kong: Hong Kong Man in Search of Majority, *China Quarterly* 136: 864–77.

Basch, Linda, Nina Glick Schiller, & Cristina Szanton Blanc (1994) *Nations Unbound: Transnational Projects, Postcolonial Predicaments, and Deterritorialized Nation-States*, Amsterdam: Gordon and Breach.

Bell, Duran (2000) *Guanxi*: A Nesting of Groups, *Current Anthropology* 41(1): 132–38.

Benjamin, Geoffrey (1976) The Cultural Logic of Singapore's Multiculturalism, in *Singapore: Society in Transition*, ed. R. Hassan, Kuala Lumpur: Oxford University Press.

———— (1988) The Unseen Presence: A Theory of the Nation-State and Its Mystifications, Working Paper, Sociology Department, National University of Singapore.

Bennett, Tony (1988) The Exhibitionary Complex, *New Formations* 4: 73–102.

Berger, Peter L. (1987) *The Capitalist Revolution: Fifty Propositions About Prosperity, Equality and Liberty*, Aldershot: Wildwood House.

———— & Michael H.-H. Hsiao eds. (1988) *In Search of an East Asian Development Model*, Oxford: Transaction Books.

Billig, Michael (1995) *Banal Nationalism*, Manchester: Manchester University Press.

Birch, Alan (1991) *Hong Kong: The Colony That Never Was*, Hong Kong: Odyssey.

Bosco, Joseph (1993) Taiwan Factions: *Guanxi*, Patronage, and the State in Local Politics. *Ethnology* 31(2): 157–84.

Burchell, Gordon (1993) Liberal Government and Techniques of the Self, *Economy and Society* 22(3): 267–82.

Burrow, J. W. (1966) *Evolution and Society: A Study in Victorian Social Theory*, Cambridge: Cambridge University Press.

Cai Xuehai (1981) *Wanmin guizong: minzu de goucheng yu rongho* (Back to the Roots: The Constitution and Amalgamation of (Chinese) Ethnicity), in *Zhongguo wenhua xin lun* (New Perspectives on Chinese culture), ed. Xing Yitian, Taipei: Lianjing chuban shiye gongsi, pp. 123–70.

Callahan, William A. (2004) *Contingent States: Greater China and Transnational Relations*, Minneapolis: University of Minnesota Press.

———— (2010) *China: The Pessoptimist Nation*, Oxford: Oxford University Press.

Cell, John W. (1970) *British Colonial Administration in the Mid-Nineteenth Century: The Policy-Making Process*, New Haven: Yale University Press.

Chakrabarty, Dipesh (2000) *Provincializing Europe*, Princeton: Princeton University Press.

Chan Heng Chee & Hans-Dieter Evers (1978) National Identity and Nation Building in Singapore, in *Studies in ASEAN Sociology: Urban Society and Social Change*, eds. P. S. J. Chen and H.-D. Evers, Singapore: Chopmen, pp. 117–29.

Chan, Evans (2000) Postmodernism and Hong Kong Cinema, in *Postmodernism and China*, eds. Arif Dirlik & Zhang Xudong, Durham: Duke University Press, pp. 294–322.

Chan Koon Chung (1982) *Ban tang fan fengge* (Chinese-Barbarian Half Breed Style), *Haowai* 60.

———— (1988) Attitude and Style Manual (in Chinese), *Haowai* 146.

———— (2007) *Shihou: bentu wenhua zhi* (After the Fact: A Journal of Indigenous Culture), Hong Kong: Oxford University Press.

Chan Lau, Kit-ching (1990) *China, Britain and Hong Kong, 1895–1945*, Hong Kong: Chinese University Press.

Chan, Selina Ching (2011) Cultural Governance and Place-Making in Taiwan and China, *The China Quarterly* 206: 372–90.

Chang, Ha-joon (2003) The Market, the State and Institutions in Economic Development, in *Rethinking Development Economics*, ed. H.-J. Chang, London: Anthem, pp. 41–60.

Chang Kuang-chi (2011) A Path to Understanding *Guanxi* in China's Transitional Economy: Variations on Network Behavior, *Sociological Theory* 29(4): 315–39.

Chatterjee, Partha (1993) *The Nation and Its Fragments: Colonial and Postcolonial Histories*, Princeton: Princeton University Press.

Chen, Chao C. et al. (2013) Chinese *Guanxi*: An Integrative Review and New Directions for Future Research, *Management and Organization Review* 9(1): 167–207.

———— & Xiao-Ping Chen (2012), Chinese *Guanxi*: The Good, the Bad and the Controversial, in *Handbook of Chinese Organizational Behavior: Integrating Theory, Rsearch and Practice*, eds. Huang Xu & M. H. Bond, Cheltenham: Edward Elgar, pp. 415–35.

Chen Yishen (1987) *Zhengchi yishi xingtai de liubian—yi sanmin zhuyi wei li* (Shifts in Political Ideology—The Case of the Three Principles), in *Sunwen sixiang de lilun yu shiji—cankao ziliao xuanji* (The Theory and Practice of Sun Yat-sen's Thought—A Selection of Reference Material), eds. Chen Yishen & Liu Arong, Taipei: Hungwen guan, pp. 742–47.

Chen Yishen & Liu Arong eds. (1987) *Sunwen sixiang de lilun yu shiji—cankao ziliao xuanji* (The Theory and Practice of Sun Yat-sen's Thought—A Selection of Reference Material). Taipei: Hungwen guan.

Chiang Kai-shek (1987) *Sanmin zhuyi de benzhi* (The essence of the Three Principles) [1952], in *Sunwen sixiang de lilun yu shiji—cankao ziliao xuanji* (The Theory and Practice of Sun Yat-sen's Thought—A Selection of Reference Material), eds. Chen Yishen & Liu Arong, Taipei: Hungwen guan.

Chiew Seen Kong (1983) Ethnicity and National Integration: The Evolution of a Multi-Ethnic Society, in *Singapore Development Politics and Trends*, ed. P. S. J. Chen, Singapore: Oxford University Press, pp. 29–64.

Ching, Frank (1998) The Hong Kong Press: Will It Remain Free After 1997? *Asian Affairs, an American Review* 24(4): 217–25.

Chow, Rey (1993) *Writing Diaspora: Tactics of Intervention in Contemporary Cultural Studies*, Bloomington: Indiana University Press.

Chua Beng Huat (2010) Disrupting Hegemonic Liberalism in East Asia, *boundary 2: an international journal of literature and culture* 37(2): 199–216.

———— & Eddie C. Y. Kuo (1998) The Making of a New Nation: Cultural Construction and National Identity in Singapore, in *From Beijing to Port Moresby: The Politics of National Identity in Cultural Policies*, eds. V. R. Domínguez & D. Y. H. Wu, Amsterdam: Gordon and Breach, pp. 35–68.

Chun, Allen (1990) Policing Society: The "Rational" Practice of British Colonial Land Administration in the New Territories of Hong Kong, c.1900, *Journal of Historical Sociology* 3(4): 401–22.

——— (1991) *La Terra Trema*: The Crisis of Kinship and Community in the New Territories of Hong Kong Before and After "The Great Transformation," *Dialectical Anthropology* 16(3–4): 309–29.

——— (1992) The Practice of Tradition in the Writing of Custom, or Chinese Marriage from *Li* to *Su*, *Late Imperial China* 13(2): 82–122.

——— (1995) An Oriental Orientalism: The Paradox of Tradition and Modernity in Nationalist Taiwan, *History and Anthropology* 9: 27–56.

——— (1996a) Discourses of Identity in the Changing Spaces of Public Culture in Taiwan, Hong Kong and Singapore, *Theory Culture & Society* 13(1): 51–75.

——— (1996b) Fuck Chineseness: On the Ambiguities of Ethnicity as Culture as Identity, *boundary 2: an international journal of literature and culture* 23(2): 111–38.

——— (2000) Democracy as Hegemony, Globalization as Indigenization, or the "Culture" in Taiwanese National Politics, *Journal of Asian and African Studies* 35(1): 1–27.

——— (2001) From Text to Context: How Anthropology Makes Its Subject, *Cultural Anthropology* 15: 570–95.

——— (2004) *Lun guoji xueshu fengong zhong de 'women' yu 'tamen'* ("Us" and "Them" in the Global Division of Intellectual Labor), in *Wenhua de shijue xitong* (The Visual System of Culture), ed. Liu Chi-hui, Taipei: Maitian, pp. 301–17.

——— (2006) The Alien in Us All: Illusions of Ethnicization in the Global Division of Intellectual Labor, paper presented at *boundary 2* Conference on Thinking Common Problems: A Literary Critical Symposium, co-sponsored with the English Department, University of Hong Kong, Hong Kong, June 13.

——— (2009) On the Geopolitics of Identity, *Anthropological Theory* 9(3): 331–49.

Clammer, John (1973) Colonialism and the Perception of Tradition in Fiji, in *Anthropology and the Colonial Encounter*, ed. T. Asad, London: Ithaca Press, pp. 199–220.

——— (1985) *Singapore: Ideology, Society and Culture*, Singapore: Chopmen.

Cleverley, John (1991) *The Schooling of China: Tradition and Modernity in Chinese Education*, 2nd ed., Sydney: Allen and Unwin.

Clifford, James (1983) On Ethnographic Authority, *Representations* 1: 118–46.

——— (1988) *The Predicament of Culture*, Cambridge: Harvard University Press.

——— (1994) "Diasporas," *Cultural Anthropology* 9(3): 302–38.

CO 129 (Colonial Office Correspondence) [Hong Kong Public Records Office]

/335 (23 August 1906) "Nathan to Elgin."

/338 (8 August 1905) "Petitioners to Lyttleton."

/564 (30 September 1937) "Extract from Canton Intelligence Report for Half-Year Ended."

Cohen, Abner (1971) "Cultural Strategies in the Organization of Trading Diasporas," in *The Development of Indigenous Trade and Markets in West Africa*, ed. C. Meillassoux, London: Oxford University Press, pp. 266–81.

Cohn, Bernard S. (1984) The Census, Social Structure and Objectification in South Asia, *Folk* 26: 25–49.

———— (1988) The Anthropology of a Colonial State and Its Forms of Knowledge, paper presented at Wenner Gren Conference "Tensions of Empire."

———— & Nicholas B. Dirks (1988) Beyond the Fringe: The Nation-State, Colonialism and the Technologies of Power, *Journal of Historical Sociology* 1(2): 224–29.

Comaroff, Jean & John Comaroff (1991) *Of Revelation and Revolution: Christianity, Colonialism and Consciousness in South Africa*, Chicago: University of Chicago Press.

———— (2000) Millennial Capitalism: First Thoughts on a Second Coming, *Public Culture* 12(2): 291–343.

Cooper, Eugene (1982) Karl Marx's Other Island: The Evolution of Peripheral Capitalism in Hong Kong, *Bulletin of Concerned Asian Scholars* 14(1): 25–31.

Corrigan, Philip (1990) *Social Forms/Human Capacities: Essays in Authority and Difference*, London: Routledge.

Corrigan, Philip and Derek Sayer (1985) *The Great Arch: English State Formation as Cultural Revolution*, Oxford: Blackwell.

CREBC (Correspondence Respecting the Extension of the Boundaries of the Colony) (1900) Hong Kong, Correspondence (June 20, 1898 to August 20, 1900), Respecting the Extension of the Boundaries of the Colony, *Eastern* no. 66, Colonial Office, London.

CSO (Colonial Secretary Office) Files [Hong Kong Public Records Office]

CSO 3120 (1906) "New Territories: 1) Crown Rent, 2) Land, 3) Licenses; Submits Petitions of Various Districts Respecting . . ."

Cui Chuiyan (1979) *Sanmin zhuyi wei minsheng daode zhi biaoxian* (The Three Principles as the Manifestation of the Morality of Livelihood), in *Minsheng shiguan luncong*, ed. Qin Xiaoyi, Taipei: Jindai zhongguo, pp. 393–505.

Curtin, Michael (1998) Images of Trust, Economies of Suspicion: Hong Kong Media after 1997, *Historical Journal of Film, Radio and Television* 18(2): 281–94.

Curtin, Philip (1984) *Cross-Cultural Trade in World History*, Cambridge: Cambridge University Press.

Dai Jitao (1954) *Sunwen zhuyi zhi zhexue de jichu* (The Philosophical Foundation of Sun Yat-sen's Thought), Taipei: Zhongyang wenwu gongying she.

———— ed. (1978) *Sanmin zhuyi zhexue lunwen ji* (Essays on the Philosophy of the Three Principles), Taipei: Zhongyang wenwu gongying she.

Dardot, Pierre & Christian Laval (2013) *The New Way of the World: On Neo-Liberal Society*, London: Verso.

deBary, Wm. Theodore (1998) *Asian Values and Human Rights: A Confucian Communitarian Perspective*, Cambridge: Harvard University Press.

Deleuze, Gilles (1988) *A Thousand Plateaus: Capitalism and Schizophrenia*, London: Athlone Press.

Dirks, Nicholas B. (1986) From Little King to Landlord: Colonial Discourse and Colonial Rule, *Contemporary Studies in Society and History* 28: 307–33.

———— (1990) History as a Sign of the Modern, *Public Culture* 2(2): 1–9.

———— (1992a) Castes of Mind, *Representations* 37: 56–78.

—— (1992b) Introduction to *Colonialism and Culture*, ed. N. B. Dirks, Ann Arbor: University of Michigan Press.

Dirlik, Arif (1994) The Postcolonial Aura: Third World Criticism in the Age of Global Capitalism, *Critical Inquiry* 20: 328–56.

—— (1997) Critical Reflections on "Chinese Capitalism" as Paradigm, *Identities* 3(3): 303–30.

—— (1999) Place-Based Imagination: Globalism and the Politics of Place, *Review* 22(2): 151–87.

Drysdale, John (1984) *Singapore: Struggle for Success*, Singapore: Times International.

Duara, Prasenjit (1995) *Rescuing History from the Nation: Questioning Narratives of Modern China*, Chicago: University of Chicago Press.

Dumont, Louis (1980) *Homo Hierarchicus: The Caste System and Its Implications*, 2nd ed., Chicago: University of Chicago Press.

Durkheim, Emile (1961) *Moral Education* [*L'éducation morale*, 1925], Glencoe: Free Press.

Eisenstadt, S. N. (1973) Post-Traditional Societies and the Reconstruction of Tradition, *Daedalus* 102(1): 1–27.

Elias, Norbert (1978) *The History of Manners*, New York: Pantheon.

Elvin, Mark (1973) *The Pattern of the Chinese Past*, Stanford: Stanford University Press.

Endacott, G. B. (1958) *A History of Hong Kong*, London: Oxford University Press.

Fabian, Johannes (1986) *Language and Colonial Power: The Appropriation of Swahili in the Former Belgian Congo, 1880–1938*, Cambridge: Cambridge University Press.

—— (1990) Presence and Representation: The Other and Anthropological Writing, *Critical Inquiry* 16(4): 753–72.

Fitzgerald, John (1996) *Awakening China: Politics, Culture, and Class in the Nationalist Revolution*, Stanford: Stanford University Press.

Foucault, Michel (1977) *Discipline and Punish: The Birth of the Prison* (1975), New York: Pantheon.

—— (1991) Politics and the Study of Discourse, in *The Foucault Effect: Studies in Governmentality*, ed. C. Gordon, Chicago: University of Chicago Press, pp. 87–104.

Fox, Richard G. (1990) Introduction, *National Ideologies and the Production of National Cultures*, Washington: American Anthropological Association, pp. 1–14.

France, Peter (1969) *The Charter of the Land: Custom and Colonization in Fiji*, Melbourne: Oxford University Press.

Frank, Andre Gunder (1998) *ReOrient: Global Economy in the Asian Age*, Berkeley: University of California Press.

Friedman, Jonathan (1990) Being in the World: Globalization and Localization, *Theory Culture & Society* 7(2–3): 311–28.

—— (1992) Narcissism, Roots and Postmodernity: The Constitution of Selfhood in the Global Crisis, in *Modernity and Identity*, eds. S. Lash and J. Friedman, Oxford: Blackwell, pp. 331–66.

Fukuyama, Francis (1992) *The End of History and the Last Man*, New York: Free Press.

Gardner, Howard (1989) *To Open Minds: Chinese Clues to the Dilemma of Contemporary Education*, New York: Basic Books.

Gates, Louis Henry, Jr. (1991) Critical Fanonism, *Critical Inquiry* 17: 457–70.

Ge Yongguang (1990) *Sanmin zhuyi xueshu yanjiu yu jiaoxue de xin fangxiang* (New Directions in Scholarly Research and Pedagogy on the Three Principles), in *Zhonghua minguo de fazhan jingyan* (The Actuality of Development in the Republic of China), eds. Hung Quanhu et al., Hsinchu: National Tsinghua University, General Education Department, pp. 489–528.

Geertz, Clifford (1963) The Integrative Revolution: Primordial Sentiments and Civil Politics in the New States, in *Old Societies and New States*, ed. C. Geertz, Chicago: Aldine, pp. 105–55.

——— (1976) "From the Native's Point of View": On the Nature of Anthropological Understanding [1974], in *Meaning in Anthropology*, eds. K. Basso & H. Selby, Albuquerque: University of New Mexico Press, pp. 221–37.

Gellner, Ernest (1964) *Thought and Change*, London: Weidenfeld and Nicholson.

——— (1983) *Nations and Nationalism*, Ithaca: Cornell University Press

George, Cherian (2000) *Singapore, The Air-Conditioned Nation: Essays on the Politics of Comfort and Control*, Singapore: Landmark Books.

Gilroy, Paul (1993) *The Black Atlantic: Modernity and Double Consciousness*, Cambridge: Harvard University Press.

Goffman, Erving (1961) *Asylums: Essays on the Social Situation of Mental Patients and Other Inmates*, New York: Anchor.

Gold, Thomas B. (1985) After Comradeship: Personal Relations in China Since the Cultural Revolution. *The China Quarterly* 104: 657–75.

——— (1993) Go with Your Feelings: Hong Kong and Taiwan Popular Culture in Greater China, *The China Quarterly* 136: 907–25.

———, et al., eds. (2002) *Social Connections in China: Institutions, Culture and the Changing Nature of Guanxi*, Cambridge: Cambridge University Press.

Gramsci, Antonio (1971) *Selections from the Prison Notebooks*, eds. Q. Hoare & G. N. Smith, London: Lawrence and Wishart.

Groves, R. G. (1969) Militia, Market and Lineage: Chinese Resistance to the Occupation of Hong Kong's New Territories in 1899, *Journal of the Hong Kong Branch of the Royal Asiatic Society* 9: 31–64.

Gupta, Akhil & James Ferguson (1992) Beyond "Culture": Space, Identity, and the Politics of Difference, *Cultural Anthropology* 7(1): 6–23.

Guthrie, Douglas (1998) The Declining Significance of Guanxi in China's Economic Transition, *China Quarterly* 154: 254–82.

Habermas, Jurgen (1989) *The Structural Transformation of the Public Sphere: An Inquiry into a Category of Bourgeois Society* [1962 translation], Cambridge: MIT Press.

Hamilton, Gary G. (1996) Overseas Chinese Capitalism, in *Confucian Traditions in East Asian Modernity: Moral Education and Economic Culture in Japan and the Four Mini-Dragons*, ed. Tu Wei-ming, Cambridge: Harvard University Press, pp. 328–42.

———, ed. (1996) *Asian Business Networks*, Berlin: Walter de Gruyter.

Han Jinchun & Li Yifu (1984) *Hanwen "minzu" yici de chuxian zhi qi shiyong qingkuang* (The appearance of the Chinese term *minzu* and its circumstances of usage). *Minzu yanjiu* 2: 36–43.

Harding, Harry (1993) The Concept of "Greater China": Themes, Variations and Reservations, *The China Quarterly* 136: 660–86.

Hardt, Michael & Negri, Antonio (2000) *Empire*, Cambridge: Harvard University Press.

Harvey, David (1989) *The Conditions of Postmodernity*, Oxford: Oxford University Press.

Hayes, James W. (1976) Rural Society and Economy in late Ch'ing: A Case Study of the New Territories of Hong Kong (Kwangtung), *Ch'ing-shih Wen-t'i* 3(5): 33–71.

——— (1977) *The Hong Kong Region, 1850–1911: Institutions and Leadership in Town and Countryside*, Hamden: Shoe String Press.

Held, David, et al. (1999) *Global Transformations: Politics, Economics and Culture*, Stanford: Stanford University Press.

Ho, David Y. F. (1976) On the Concept of Face, *American Journal of Sociology* 81(4): 867–84.

Ho Ping & Gao Xin (1998) *Beijing ruhe kongzhi xianggang* (How Beijing Controls Hong Kong), Mississanga, Ontario: Mirror Books.

Hobsbawm, Eric & Terence Ranger, eds. (1983) *The Invention of Tradition*, Cambridge: Cambridge University Press.

Horkheimer, Max & Theodor W. Adorno (1989) "The Culture Industry: Enlightenment as Mass Deception," in *Dialectic of Enlightenment* [1944], New York: Continuum, pp. 120–67.

Hu Houxuan (1990) *Lun wufang guannian ji zhongguo chengwei zhi chiyuan* (On the concept of *wufang* and origin of the term "middle kingdom"), in *Jiagu xue shangshi luncong* (Essays on Oracle Bone Studies and Shang History), Shanghai: Shanghai Shudian, pp. 283–388.

Hu Hsien-chin (1944) The Chinese Concepts of "Face," *American Anthropologist* 46: 45–64.

Huang Chun-chieh (1992) Confucianism in Postwar Taiwan, *Proceedings of the National Science Council*, Part C: Humanities and Social Sciences 2(2): 218–33.

Huang Yasheng (2008) *Capitalism with Chinese Characteristics: Entrepreneurship and the State*, Cambridge: Cambridge University Press.

Hughes, Christopher R. (2014) Confucius Institutes and the University: Distinguishing the Political Mission from the Cultural, *Issues & Studies* 50(4): 45–83.

——— & Robert Stone (1999) Nation-Building and Curriculum Reform in Hong Kong and Taiwan, *China Quarterly* 159: 977–91.

Hung Quanhu, et al. eds. (1990) *Zhonghua minguo de fazhan jingyan* (The Actuality of Development in the Republic of China), Hsinchu: National Tsinghua University, General Education Department.

Huntington, Samuel P. (1996) *The Clash of Civilizations and the Remaking of World Order*, New York: Simon and Schuster.

Hwang Kwang-kuo (1985) *Renqing yu mianzi: zhongguoren de quanli youxi* (*Renqing* and *Mianzi*: The Chinese Power Game), in *Xiandaihua yu zhongguohua luncong* (*Essays on Modernization and Sinicization*), eds. Yang Guoshu et al., Taipei: Guiguan, pp. 125–53.

———— (1987) Face and Favor: The Chinese Power Game, *American Journal of Sociology* 92(4): 944–74.

Ingham, Richard (1997) *Hong Kong: City on the Edge*, Hong Kong: Agence France-Presse.

Iwama, Hiroshi F. (1995) Japan's Group Orientation in Secondary Schools, in *Japanese Schooling: Patterns of Socialization, Equality, and Political Control*, ed. J. J. Shields Jr., University Park: Pennsylvania State University Press, pp. 73–84.

Jacobs, Bruce (1979) A Preliminary Model of Particularistic ties in Chinese Political Alliances: *Kan-ch'ing* (*Ganqing*) and *Kuan-hsi* (*Guanxi*) in a Rural Taiwanese Township. *The China Quarterly* 78: 237–73.

Jameson, Frederic (1981) *The Political Unconscious: Narrative as Socially Symbolic Act*, Ithaca: Cornell University Press.

Johnson, Graham (1985) *1997 and After: Will Hong Kong Survive?* Toronto: Joint Center on Modern East Asia.

Kamm, John T. (1977) Two Essays on the Ch'ing Economy of Hsin-an, Kwangtung, *Journal of the Hong Kong Branch of the Royal Asiatic Society* 17: 55–83.

Kapferer, Judith (1981) Socialization and the Symbolic Order of the School, *Anthropology and Education Quarterly* 12(4): 258–74.

Kam Kin Hung (1988) *Haowai shier nian jinghua zongjie ji* (A Retrospective of the Best of *Haowai*'s Last 12 Years), *Haowai* 147.

Kao, Lin-ying (1951) Academic and Professional Attainments of Native Chinese Students Graduating from Teachers College, Columbia University, 1909–1950, PhD thesis, Teachers College, Columbia University.

Keesing, Roger M. (1989) Creating the Past: Custom and Identity in the Contemporary Pacific, *The Contemporary Pacific* 1(1–2): 19–42.

Keesing, Roger M. & Robert Tonkinson eds. (1982) Reinventing Traditional Culture: The Politics of Kastom in Island Melanesia (special issue), *Mankind* 13(4).

King, Ambrose (1975) Administrative Absorption of Politics in Hong Kong: Emphasis on the Grass Roots Level, *Asian Survey* 15(5): 422–39.

———— (1988) *Renji guanxi zhong renqing zhi fenxi* (Study of *Renqing* in Interpersonal Relations), in *Zhongguoren de xinli* (The Psychology of the Chinese People), ed. Yang Guoshu, Taipei: Guiguan, pp. 75–104.

———— (1991) *Kuan-hsi* (*Guanxi*) and Network Building: A Sociological Interpretation. *Daedalus* 120(2): 63–84.

———— & J. T. Myers (1977) Shame as an Incomplete Conception of Chinese Culture: A Study of Face. Chinese University of Hong Kong, Social Research Centre Paper.

Kipnis, Andrew (1996) The Language of Gifts: Managing *Guanxi* in a North China Village, *Modern China* 22(3): 285–314.

———— (1997) *Producing Guanxi*, Durham: Duke University Press.

———— (2007) Neoliberalism Reified: *Suzhi* Discourse and Tropes of Neoliberalism in the People's Republic of China, *Journal of the Royal Anthropological Institute* 13(2): 383–400.

Kuo, Eddie C. Y. (1985) Language and Identity: The Case of the Chinese in Singapore, in *Chinese Culture and Mental Health*, eds. W. Tseng and D. Wu, New York: Academic Press, pp. 181–92.

———— (1991) Confucianism as Political Discourse in Singapore: The Case of an Incomplete Revitalization Movement, paper presented at Conference on the Confucian Dimension of the Dynamics of Industrial Asia, American Academy of Arts and Sciences, Cambridge, MA, June 15–18.

————, et al. (1988) *Religion and Religious Revivalism in Singapore*, Report to the Ministry of Community Development, Singapore.

Kwok Nai-wang (1996) *1997: Hong Kong's Struggle for Selfhood*, Hong Kong: Daga Press.

Lamb, H. K. (1984) *A Date with Fate: Hong Kong 1997*, Hong Kong: Lincoln Green.

Laroui, Abdullah (1976) *The Crisis of the Arab Intellectuals: Traditionalism or Historicism?* Berkeley: University of California Press.

Lash, Scott & John Urry (1987) *The End of Organized Capitalism*, Madison: University of Wisconsin Press.

Lau Emily (Liu Huiqing) (1998) *Xianggang keyi shuo bu* (Hong Kong Can Say No), Hong Kong: Hongyeh.

Lau Siu-kai (1981) Utilitarian Familism, in *Social Life and Development in Hong Kong*, eds. A. Y. C. King & R. P. L. Lee, Hong Kong: The Chinese University Press.

Lavie, Smadar & Ted Swedenberg, eds. (1996) *Displacement, Diaspora and Geographies of Identity*, Durham: Duke University Press.

Law Wing Sang (1992) Discourse of Crisis and Stability: The Possibility/Impossibility of Community and Democracy in Hong Kong, Paper presented at the Conference on Cultural Criticism 1992, Chinese University of Hong Kong, Hong Kong, December 29–January 9.

———— (2000) Northbound Colonialism: A Politics of Post-PC Hong Kong, *positions: east asia critique* 8(1): 229–64.

Lee, Leo (1999) *Shanghai Modern: The Flowering of a New Urban Culture in China 1930–45*, Cambridge: Harvard University Press.

Lévi-Strauss, Claude (1963) *Totemism*, trans. Rodney Needham, Boston: Beacon Press.

Leung Ping Kwan, ed. (1995) *Xianggang wenhua teji* (Special Issue on Hong Kong Culture), *Haowai* 226.

Li Yixian (1996) On the Characteristics, Strong Points, and Shortcomings of Education in Hong Kong: A Mainland Educator's View of Education in Hong

Kong, in *Education and Society in Hong Kong*, ed. G. Postiglione, Hong Kong: Hong Kong University Press, pp. 253–64.

Li, Zezhong (1967) *A List of Doctoral Dissertations by Chinese Students in the United States, 1961–1964*, Chicago: Chinese-American Education Foundation.

Liang Fu-lin (1995) *Jiuqi hou xianggang qiandan* (The Future of Hong Kong after 1997), Hong Kong: Wide Angle Press.

Lilley, Rozanna (2000) The Hong Kong Handover, *Communal Plural: Journal of Transnational and Crosscultural Studies* 8(2): 161–80.

Low, D. A. (1991) *Eclipse of Empire*, Cambridge: Cambridge University Press.

Lin, Nan (2001) *Guanxi*: A Conceptual Analysis, in *The Chinese Triangle of Mainland China, Taiwan, and Hong Kong: Comparative Institutional Analyses*, ed. Alvin Y. So, et al., Westport: Greenwood Press, pp. 155–66.

Lin Yuti (1985) *Taiwan jiaoyu mianmao sishi nian* (Forty Years of Education in Taiwan). Taipei: Zili wanbao.

Linnekin, Jocelyn S. (1983) Defining Tradition: Variations on the Hawaiian Identity, *American Ethnologist* 10: 241–52.

Liu Arong (1987) *Jin liushi nian lai sanmin zhuyi xueshu yanjiu zhi shidai quxiang* (The Epochal Orientation of Scholarly Research on the Three Principles in the Last 60 Years), in *Sunwen sixiang de lilun yu shiji—cankao ziliao xuanji* (The Theory and Practice of Sun Yat-sen's Thought—A Selection of Reference Material), eds. Chen Yishen & Liu Arong, Taipei: Hungwen guan, pp. 748–76.

Liu Dingxiang (1989) *Zhengzhi yishi xingtai yu guomin zhongxue "gongmin yu daode" jiaocai zhi yanjiu* (A Study of Political Ideology and Textbook Materials in Middle School "Citizenship and Morality" Courses), M.A. thesis, School of Education, Taiwan National Normal University.

Lui Tai Lok, ed. (2007) *Haowai sanshi: neibu chuanyue* (*Thirty Years of Haowai: Internal Distribution*), Hong Kong: Sanlian.

Lo, Ming-cheng M. & Eileen M. Otis (2003) *Guanxi* Civility: Processes, Potentials and Contingencies, *Politics & Society* 31(1): 131–62.

Louie, Kam (2011) Confucius the Chameleon: Dubious Envoy for Brand China, *boundary 2* 38(1): 77–100.

MacFarquhar, Roderick (1980) "The Post-Confucian Challenge," *Economist* 9: 67–72.

March, Andrew (1974) *The Idea of China: Myth and Theory in Geographic Thought*, New York: Praeger.

Massey, Doreen (1994) *Space, Place and Gender*, Minneapolis: University of Minnesota Press.

Mauss, Marcel (1967) *The Gift*, I. Cunnison trans. New York: W. W. Norton.

McClintock, Anne (1992) The Angel of Progress: Pitfalls of the Term "Postcolonialism," *Social Text* 31–32: 84–98.

McLaren, Peter (1999) *Schooling as a Ritual Performance: Toward a Political Economy of Educational Symbols and Gestures*, 3rd ed., Lanham: Rowman and Littlefield.

McVeigh, Brian J. (2000) *Wearing Ideology: State, Schooling and Self-Presentation in Japan*, Oxford: Berg.

Mitchell, Timothy (1988) *Colonizing Egypt*, Cambridge: Cambridge University Press.

Nairn, Tom (1998) *Faces of Nationalism: Janus Revisited*, London: Verso.

Nederveen Pieterse, J. P. (1995) Globalization as Hybridization, in *Global Modernities*, eds. M. Featherstone et al., London: Sage, pp. 45–68.

——— (2001) The Case of Multiculturalism: Kaleidoscopic and Long-Term Views, *Social Identities* 7(3): 393–407.

Nelson, Howard G. H. (1969a) British Land Administration in the New Territories of Hong Kong and Its Effects on Chinese Social Organization, Unpublished paper given at the London-Cornell Project for East and Southeast Asian Studies Conference, Adele en Haut, August 24–30, 1969.

Nicholson, Brian (1992) *A Conspiracy to Destroy Hong Kong*, Essex: Bear Books.

Nonini, Donald M. (2008) Is China Becoming Neoliberal?, *Critique of Anthropology* 28(2): 145–176.

Nye, Joseph (2004) *Soft Power: The Means to Success in World Politics*, New York: Public Affairs.

Offe, Claus (1985) *Disorganized Capitalism: Contemporary Transformations of Work and Politics*, Cambridge: MIT Press.

Ohmae, Kenichi (1990) *The Borderless World: Power and Strategy in the Interlinked Economy*, New York: Harper and Row.

Olds, Kris et al., eds. (1999) *Globalisation and the Asia-Pacific: Contested Territories*, London: Routledge.

Omae, Kenichi (1990) *The Borderless World: Power and Strategy in the Interlinked Economy*, Harper Business.

Ong, Aihwa (1997) Chinese Modernities: Narratives of Nation and Capitalism, in *Ungrounded Empires: The Cultural Politics of Modern Chinese Transnationalism*, eds. A. Ong & D. M. Nonini, London: Routledge, pp. 171–202.

——— & Donald Nonini, eds. (1997) *Ungrounded Empires: The Cultural Politics of Modern Chinese Transnationalism*, London: Routledge.

——— & Zhang Li, eds. (2008) *Privatizing China: Socialism from Afar*, Ithaca: Cornell University Press.

Parry, Jonathan (1986) The Gift, the Indian Gift and the 'Indian Gift.' *Man* 21: 453–73.

Patterson, Orlando (1994) Ecumenical America: Global Culture and the American Cosmos, *World Policy Journal* 11(2): 103–17.

Peck, Jamie (2010) *Constructions of Neoliberal Reason*, Oxford: Oxford University Press.

Peng Yingming (1985) *Guanyu woguo minzu gainian lishi de chubu kaocha* (A Preliminary Analysis of the History of the Chinese Concept of *Minzu*), *Minzu yanjiu* 2: 5–12.

Pieke, Frank N. (1995) Bureaucracy, Friends, and Money: The Growth of Capital Socialism in China, *Comparative Studies in Society and History* 37(3): 494–518.

Pomeranz, Kenneth (2000) *The Great Divergence: China, Europe, and the Making of the Modern World Economy*, Princeton: Princeton University Press.

Postiglione, Gerald A., ed. (1996) *Education and Society in Hong Kong*, Hong Kong: Hong Kong University Press.

——— & Wing On Lee, eds. (1998) *Schooling in Hong Kong: Organization, Teaching and Social Context*, Hong Kong: Hong Kong University Press.

Pratt, Mary Louise (1991) *Through Imperial Eyes: Travel Writing and Transculturalism*, New York: Routledge.

Qi Xiaoying (2013) *Guanxi*, Social Capital Theory and Beyond: Toward a Globalized Social Science, *British Journal of Sociology* 64(2): 308–24.

Qian Zhongshu (1940) China in the English Literature of the 17th Century, *Quarterly Bulletin of Chinese Bibliography* 1: 351–84.

——— (1941a) China in the English Literature of the 18th Century (I), *Quarterly Bulletin of Chinese Bibliography* 2: 7–48.

——— (1941b) China in the English Literature of the 18th Century (II), *Quarterly Bulletin of Chinese Bibliography* 2: 113–52.

Qin Xiaoyi, ed. (1979) *Minsheng shiguan luncong* (Essays on the Historical Perspective of Livelihood), Taipei: Jindai zhongguo.

Rabushka, Alvin (1997) *Freedom's Fall in Hong Kong*, Stanford: Hoover Institution.

Rawski, Evelyn S. (1972) *Agricultural Change and the Peasant Economy of South China*, Cambridge: Harvard University Press.

Redding, Gordon S. (1993) *The Spirit of Chinese Capitalism*, Berlin: Walter de Gruyter.

Reid, Anthony (1997) Entrepreneurial Minorities, Nationalism, and the State, in *Essential Outsiders: Chinese and Jews in the Modern Transformation of Southeast Asia and Central Europe*, eds. D. Chirot and A. Reid, Seattle: University of Washington Press.

Richards, Thomas (1993) *The Imperial Archive: Knowledge and the Fantasy of Empire*, London: Verso.

Richardson, Michael (1990) Enough Said, *Anthropology Today* 6(4): 16–19.

RLC: (Report on the Land Court)

(1900) compiled by H. H. J. Gompertz, *Hong Kong Sessional Papers* 1901.

(1902) compiled by H. H. J. Gompertz, *Hong Kong Sessional Papers* 1902.

(1900–05) compiled by Cecil Clementi, *Hong Kong Sessional Papers* 1905.

RNT: (Report on the New Territories)

(1899) compiled by J. H. S. Lockhart, *Hong Kong Sessional Papers* 1900.

(1899–1912) compiled by G. N. Orme, *Hong Kong Sessional Papers* 1912.

Robertson, Roland (1992) Glocalization: Time-Space and Homogeneity-Heterogeneity, in *Global Modernities*, eds. M. Featherstone et al., London: Sage, pp. 25–44.

Rohlen, Thomas P. (1976) *Japan's High Schools*, Berkeley: University of California Press.

Rose, Nikolas (1993) Government, Authority and Expertise in Advanced Liberalism, *Economy and Society* 22(3): 283–99.

Ruey Yih-fu (1972) The Concept of *Chiao* in the *Chungyung* as a Counterpart of Culture, in his *Zhonghua minzu ji qi wenhua* (The Chinese Nation and Its Culture), vol. 2, Taipei: Yiwen Yinshuguan, pp. 637–54.

Ryckmans, Pierre (1980) Orientalism and Sinology, *Asian Studies Association of Australia Review* 7(3): 18–21.

Sahlins, Marshall D. (1972) *Stone Age Economics*. Chicago: Aldine.

——— (2013) China U., http://www.thenation.com/article/176888/china-u.

Said, Edward W. (1978) *Orientalism*, New York: Pantheon.

——— (1985) Orientalism Reconsidered, *Cultural Critique* 1: 89–107.

——— (1989) Representing the Colonized: Anthropology's Interlocutors, *Critical Inquiry* 16(4): 753–72.

Sakai, Naoki (1997) Subject and/or Shutai and the Inscription of Cultural Difference, in his *Translation and Subjectivity: On "Japan" and Cultural Nationalism*, Minneapolis: University of Minnesota Press, pp. 117–152.

——— (2000) "You Asians": On the Historical Role of the West and Asia Binary, *The South Atlantic Quarterly* 99: 789–817.

——— (2001) Dislocation of the West and the Status of the Humanities, *Traces* 1: 71–94.

Schluchter, Wolfgang (1979) The Paradox of Rationalization: On the Relation of Ethics and World, in *Max Weber's Vision of History*, eds. G. Roth and W. Schluchter, Berkeley: University of California Press, pp. 11–64.

Schoenhals, Martin (1993) *The Paradox of Power in a People's Republic of China Middle School*, Armonk: M. E. Sharpe.

Scott, David (1994) Colonial Governmentality, *Social Text* 12(4): 191–220.

Shambaugh, David (1993) Introduction: The Emergence of "Greater China," *The China Quarterly* 136: 653–59.

Shen Zongrui (1986) *Guofu duiyu rujia zhexue yu kexue sixiang zhi rongho* (Sun Yat-sen's Synthesis with Regard to Confucian Philosophy and Scientific Thought), Taipei: Zhengzhong shuju.

——— (1990) *Guojia jiaose yu shehui—shi lun tongho zhuyi de lilun yu yingyong* (The Role of the State in Relation to Society—A Preliminary Sketch of the Theory and Application of Corporatism, in *Zhonghua minguo de fazhan jingyan* (The Actuality of Development in the Republic of China), eds. Hung Quanhu et al., Hsinchu: National Tsinghua University, General Education Department, pp. 15–44.

——— (1991) *Yishi xingtai de gongwei yu danhua—poxi sanmin zhuyi yu guomindang de guanxi* (The Strengthening and Waning of Ideology—An Analysis of the Relationship Between the Three Principles and the Kuomintang), Conference on Sun Yat-sen's Thought and National Development, School of Law, National Taiwan University.

Shih Shu-mei (2010a) Against Diaspora: the Sinophone as Places of Cultural Production, in *Global Chinese Literature: Critical Essays*, eds. Jing Tsu and David Der-wei Wang, Leiden: Brill, pp. 29–48.

——— (2010b) Theory, Asia and the Sinophone, *Postcolonial Studies* 13(4): 465–84.

—— (2011) The Concept of the Sinophone, *Proceedings of the Modern Language Association* 126(3): 709–18.

Shohat, Ella (1992) Notes on the Post-Colonial, *Social Text* 31–32: 99–113.

Siu Kwok Wah (1984) *Haowai*'s Non-Academic Academicism (in Chinese), *Haowai* 100.

Smart, Alan (1993) Gifts, Bribes, and *Guanxi*: A Reconsideration of Bourdieu's Social Capital, *Cultural Anthropology* 8(3): 388–408.

Smith, Richard (2015) China's Communist-Capitalist Ecological Apocalypse, *Real-World Economics Review* 71: 19–63.

Stocking, George W. (1968) *Race, Culture and Evolution: Essays in the History of Anthropology*, New York: Free Press.

—— (1987) *Victorian Anthropology*, New York: Free Press.

Stoler, Ann Laura (1989) Rethinking Colonial Categories: European Communities and the Boundaries of Rule, *Contemporary Studies in Society and History* 31(1): 134–61.

Stover, Leon E. (1962), Face and Verbal Analogues of Interaction in Chinese Culture, PhD thesis, Anthropology Department, Columbia University.

Sun Yat-sen (1981) *Sanmin Zhuyi: The Three Principles of the People* (with two supplementary chapters by Chiang Kai-shek), Taipei: China Publishing Company.

Suryadinata, Leo (1997) Ethnic Chinese in Southeast Asia: Overseas Chinese, Chinese Overseas or Southeast Asians? in *Ethnic Chinese as Southeast Asians*, ed. L. Suryadinata, Singapore: Institute of Southeast Asian Studies, pp. 1–32.

Taiwan Provincial Government (1967) *Zhonghua wenhua fuxing lunji* (Essays on Chinese Cultural Renaissance), Taipei: Gaizao chuban she.

—— (1978) *Zhonghua wenhua fuxing yundong shi nian jinian quanji* (Commemorative Essays on the Tenth Anniversary of the Cultural Renaissance Movement), Taipei: Committee for the Promotion of the Chinese Cultural Renaissance Movement.

Taiwan Provincial Government News Agency (1970) *Taiwan guangfu ershiwu nian* (Twenty-Year Retrospective of the Glorious Restoration of Taiwan), Taichung: Provincial Government Printer.

Tan Chee Beng (1997) Comments on "Ethnic Chinese in Southeast Asia: Overseas Chinese, Chinese Overseas or Southeast Asians?" in *Ethnic Chinese as Southeast Asians*, ed. L. Suryadinata, Singapore: Institute of Southeast Asian Studies, pp. 25–32.

Tang, James T. H. (1994) From Empire Defense to Imperial Retreat: Britain's Postwar China Policy and the Decolonization of Hong Kong, *Modern Asian Studies* 28(2): 317–37.

Thomas, Nicholas (1990) Sanitation and Seeing: The Creation of State Power in Early Colonial Fiji, *Contemporary Studies in Society and History* 32(1): 149–70.

—— (1991) Anthropology and Orientalism, *Anthropology Today* 7(2): 4–7.

—— (1994) *Colonialism's Culture: Anthropology, Travel and Government*, Princeton: Princeton University Press.

Thomas, Ted (1996) *What's Going to Happen in 1997 in Hong Kong?* Hong Kong: Simon and Schuster.

Trocki, Carl (1997) Boundaries and Transgression: Chinese Enterprise in Eighteenth and Nineteenth Century Southeast Asia, in *Ungrounded Empires: The Cultural Politics of Modern Chinese Transnationalism*, eds. A. Ong and D. M. Nonini, London: Routledge, pp. 61–85.

Tsang, Steve Yi-sang (1988) *Democracy Shelved: Great Britain, China and Attempts at Constitutional Reform in Hong Kong, 1945–1952*, Hong Kong: Oxford University Press.

Todorov, Tzvetan (1988) Knowledge in Social Anthropology: Distancing and Universality, *Anthropology Today* 4: 2–5.

Tu Wei-ming (1991) Cultural China: The Periphery as Center, *Daedalus* 120(2): 1–32.

———, ed. (1996) *Confucian Traditions in East Asian Modernity: Moral Education and Economic Culture in Japan and the Four Mini-Dragons*, Cambridge: Harvard University Press.

———, et al., eds. (1992) *The Confucian World Observed: A Contemporary Discussion of Confucian Humanism in East Asia*, Honolulu: Institute of Culture and Communication, East-West Center.

Turner, Matthew & Irene Ngan, eds. (1995) *Hong Kong Sixties—Designing Identity*, Hong Kong: Hong Kong Arts Centre.

Venugopal, Rajesh (2015) Neoliberalism as Concept, *Economy and Society* 44(2): 165–87.

Viswanathan, Gauri (1989) *Masks of Conquest: Literary Study and British Rule in India*, New York: Columbia University Press.

Vogel, Ezra F. (1965) From Friendship to Comradeship: The Change in Personal Relations in Communist China, *The China Quarterly* 21: 46–60.

——— (1991) *The Four Little Dragons: The Spread of Industrialization in East Asia*, Cambridge: Harvard University Press.

Walder, Andrew (1983) Organized Dependency and Cultures of Authority in Chinese Industry, *Journal of Asian Studies* 63(1): 51–76.

Wallerstein, Immanuel M. (1974) *The Modern World-System*, vol. I, New York: Academic Press.

——— (2001) *Unthinking Social Science: The Limits of Nineteenth Century Paradigms*, Philadelphia: Temple University Press.

Wang Ermin (1972) *Zhongguo mingcheng suyuan ji qi jindai quanshi* (The origin of the term "middle kingdom" and its modern interpretation), *Zhonghua wenhua fuxing yuekan* 5(8): 1–13.

Wang Gungwu (1988) The Study of Chinese Identities in Southeast Asia, in *Changing Attitudes of the Southeast Asian Chinese Since World War II*, Hong Kong: Hong Kong University Press, pp. 1–21.

——— (1991) Among Non-Chinese, *Daedalus* 120(2): 135–57.

——— (1995) The Southeast Asian Chinese and the Development of China, in *Southeast Asian Chinese and China: The Politico-Economic Dimension*, ed. L. Suryadinata, Singapore: Times Academic Press, pp. 12–30.

———— & John Wong eds. (1999) *Hong Kong in China: The Challenges of Transition*, Singapore: Times Academic Press.

Wang Hui (2014) *China from Empire to Nation-State*, Cambridge: Harvard University Press.

Weber, Eugen (1976) *From Peasants to Frenchmen*, Stanford: Stanford University Press.

Wee, C. J. W.-L. (2008) *The Asian Modern: Culture, Capitalist Development, Singapore*, Hong Kong: Hong Kong University Press.

Wesley-Smith, Peter (1979) Diplomatic, Political and Legal Factors in Early Administration of the New Territories, paper presented at the Annual Meeting of the American Anthropological Association.

———— (1980) *Unequal Treaty, 1898–1997: China, Great Britain and Hong Kong's New Territories*, Hong Kong: Oxford University Press.

Williams, Raymond (1987) *Culture and Society, 1780–1950* [1958], London: Hogarth.

Wilson, Richard W. (1970) *The Political Socialization of Children in Taiwan*, Cambridge: MIT Press.

———— (1974) *The Moral State: A Study of the Political Socialization of Chinese and American Children*, New York: The Free Press.

Willis, Paul (1981) *Learning to Labour: How Working Class Kids Get Working Class Jobs* [1977], New York: Columbia University Press.

Wolf, Eric R. (1982) *Europe and the People Without History*, Berkeley: University of California Press.

———— (1988) Inventing Society, *American Ethnologist* 15(4): 752–61.

Wong, Michelangelo (1984) *1997 and All That: A Tremulous Look into the Future*, Hong Kong: Lincoln Green.

Wong, Peter (1992) *Weixian de shiqi sui* (A Dangerous 17 Years of Age), *Haowai* 193.

Wong Siu-lun (1999) Changing Hong Kong Identities, in *Hong Kong in China: The Challenges of Transition*, eds. Wang Gungwu & John Wong, Singapore: Times Academic Press, pp. 181–202.

Wrong, Dennis H. (1961) The Oversocialized Conception of Man in Modern Sociology, *American Sociological Review* 26(2): 183–193.

Wu, David Y. H. (1991) The Construction of Chinese and Non-Chinese Identities, *Daedalus* 120(2): 159–79.

Wu Kunru (1981) *Sanmin zhuyi zhexue de xianzai yu weilai* (The Present and Future of the Philosophy of The Three Principles), Taipei: National Taiwan University, Three Principles Institute.

Yamazumi Masami (1995) State Control and the Evolution of Ultra-nationalistic Textbooks, in *Japanese Schooling: Patterns of Socialization, Equality, and Political Control*, ed. J. J. Shields Jr., University Park: Pennsylvania State University Press, pp. 234–42.

Yan Yunxiang(1996a) *The Flow of Gifts: Reciprocity and Social Networks in a Chinese Village*, Stanford: Stanford University Press.

———— (1996b) The Culture of *Guanxi* in a North China Village, *China Journal* 35: 1–25.

Yang Guoshu, ed. (1988) *Zhongguoren de xinli* (The Psychology of the Chinese People), Taipei: Guiguan, pp. 75–104.

Yang Guoshu, et al. (1982) *Shehui ji xingwei kexue de zhongguohua* (The Sinicization of the Social and Behaviorial Sciences), Nankang: Institute of Ethnology, Academia Sinica, Taiwan.

———, eds. (1985) *Xiandaihua yu zhongguohua luncong* (Essays on Modernization and Sinicization), Taipei: Guiguan.

Yang Lien-sheng (1957) The Concept of *Pao* as the Basis for Social Relations in China, in *Chinese Thought and Institutions*, ed. J. K. Fairbanks, Chicago: University of Chicago Press, pp. 291–309.

Yang, Mayfair (1989) The Gift Economy and State Power in China, *Comparative Studies in Society and History* 31(1): 25–54.

——— (1994) *Gifts, Favors and Banquets: The Art of Social Relationships in China*, Ithaca: Cornell University Press.

Yang Qingkun (1925) *Jiangsu sheng nongye diaocha lu* (Agricultural Survey of Jiangsu), Department of Agriculture, Nantong University.

Yao Biyang (1995) *China's Secrets and Hong Kong's Future*, New York: Vintage Press.

Yao, Souchou (2007) *Singapore: The State and the Culture of Excess*, London: Routledge.

Yau Sai Man (1995) *Luelun haowai yuwen fengge de wenti* (On the Question of *Haowai*'s Language Writing Style: A General Commentary), *Haowai* 226.

Yeung, Henry W. C. & Kris Olds, eds. (2000) *Globalization of Chinese Business Firms*, London: Macmillan.

Yoneyama, Shoko (1999) *The Japanese High School: Silence and Resistance*, London: Routledge.

Yuan, Tongli (1961) *A Guide to Doctoral Dissertations by Chinese Students in America, 1905–1960*, Washington, DC.

——— (1963) *Doctoral Dissertations by Chinese students in Great Britain and Northern Ireland, 1916–1961*, Taipei.

——— (1964) *A Guide to Doctoral Dissertations by Chinese Students in Continental Europe, 1907–1962*, Washington, DC.

Zarrow, Peter (2012) *After Empire: The Conceptual Transformation of the Chinese State, 1885–1924*, Stanford: Stanford University Press.

Zhang Hao (1987) *Sanmin zhuyi de yuebian—yu zhengzhi zongjiao zou xiang gailiang zhuyi* (The Transition of the Three Principles—From Political Religion to Reformism), in *Sunwen sixiang de lilun yu shiji—cankao ziliao xuanji* (Sun Yat-sen's Thought in Theory and Practice—A Selection of Source Material), eds. Chen Yishen and Liu Arong, Taipei: Hungwen guan, pp. 180–99.

Zhang Longxi (1988) The Myth of the Other: China in the Eyes of the West, *Critical Inquiry* 15(1): 108–31.

Zhang Zhiming (1990) *Jiazhi lichang yu xueshu yanjiu—sanmin zhuyi dui shehui kexue yanjiu de gongxian* (Value Positions and Scholarly Research—The Contribution of the Three Principles with Regard to Social Scientific Research), in *Zhonghua minguo de fazhan jingyan* (The actuality of development in the

Republic of China), eds. Hung Quanhu, et al., Hsinchu: National Tsinghua University, General Education Department, pp. 1–14.

Zheng Rongzhou (1989) *Guomin zhongxue daode jiaocai de yishi xingtai zhi pipan yanjiu* (A Critical Study of Ideology in Middle School Morals Textbooks), MA thesis, Three Principles Institute, National Taiwan Normal University.

Zhu Ruiling (1988) *Zhongguoren de shehui hudong: Lun mianzi de wenti* (Social Interaction among Chinese: On the Problem of *Mianzi*), in *Zhongguoren de xinli* (The Psychology of the Chinese People), ed. Yang Guoshu, Taipei: Guiguan.

Index

www.ingramcontent.com/pod-product-compliance
Lightning Source LLC
Chambersburg PA
CBHW020338270326
41926CB00007B/236

* 9 7 8 1 4 3 8 4 6 4 7 2 5 *